Readings in

CAREER AND VOCATIONAL EDUCATION FOR THE HANDICAPPED

Special Learning Corporation

42 Boston Post Rd. Guilford, Connecticut 06437

Special Learning Corporation

Publisher's Message:

The Special Education Series is the first comprehensive series designed for special education courses of study. It is also the first series to offer such a wide variety of high quality books. In addition, the series will be expanded and up-dated each year. No other publications in the area of special education can equal this. We stress high quality content, a superb advisory and consulting group, and special features that help in understanding the course of study. In addition we believe we must also publish in very small enrollment areas in order to establish the credibility and strength of our series. We realize the enrollments in courses of study such as Autism, Visually Handicapped Education, or Diagnosis and Placement are not large. Nevertheless, we believe there is a need for course books in these areas and books that are kept up-to-date on an annual basis! Special Learning Corporation's goal is to publish the highest quality materials for the college and university courses of study. With your comments and support we will continue to do this.

John P. Quirk

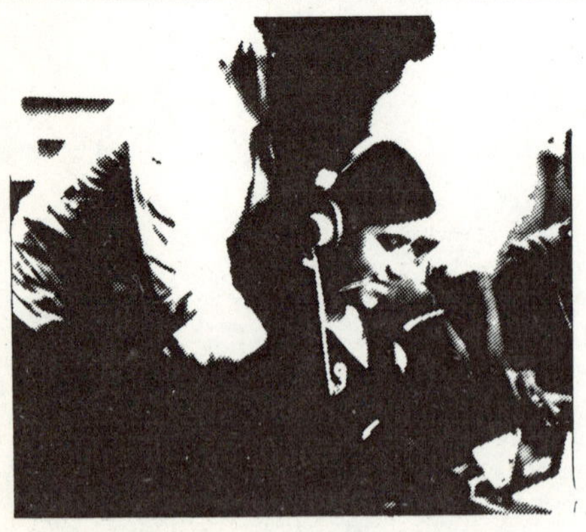

ISBN No. 0-89568-083-1

CONTENTS

3. Attitudes and Perceptions

4. The Handicapped: Choosing the Appropriate Career

GLOSSARY OF TERMS

Career Education The entire educational curriculum, coordinating all school, family and community components together to develop each individual's potential for economic, social and personal success.

Employability Processing a "marketable skill," one that enables a student to be attractive as an employee in a work setting appropriate to that student's potential.

Job Samples Mock work situations set up within the school to provide practice applicable to a job in the community.

Mainstreatming Process of placing exceptional children in a regular class by withdrawing them from a special class.

Mildly Handicapped Those handicapped students affected the least and most like the normal student. An example would be the Educable Mentally Retarded with an I.Q. of 50-70 and exhibiting some problems with adaptive behavior. This student would be able to become an independent self-sufficient member of society. Another example would be the student with a minimal learning disability.

Moderately Handicapped Those handicapped students affected in a large extent and usually unable to become a self-sufficient independent member of society. This student usually works in a sheltered workshop and needs some supervision and guidance in daily living. An example would be the Trainable Mentally Retarded individual with an I.Q. of 25-50

Normalization The opportunity of an individual to function in as normal a setting as possible, to realize his potential, and to maintain behaviors and characteristics which are as culturally normal as possible.

Severely handicapped Those handicapped students very strongly affected. These students should be planned for and worked with so that they can realize full potential and find purpose in life. The new P.L. 94-142 ensures public school responsibility for these students and their appropriate curriculum.

Sheltered workshops A work setting for those handicapped workers who are deemed unable to meet the demands of competitive employment after training.

Vocational Counseling Guidance and assistance for the student in choosing a vocational field, seeking, obtaining and maintaining employment.

Vocational Education That part of the curriculum concerned with the competencies involved in successful employment, and vocational choice.

Work Attitude Values and feelings toward the responsibilities and tasks involved in maintaining a job.

Work personality Outward actions and performances in dealing with punctuality, cleanliness, human relations, accuracy, rate, taking criticism and dependability on the job.

Work samples A simulated task or work activity for which there exists no industrial, business or other counterpart.

Work Study Program School curriculum set up so student can work part of the time in the school dealing with academics and job related subject matters, and part of the time in the community on the job.

PREFACE

The readings in this text have been compiled and organized to meet the needs of educators, students and administrators who are interested in improving education of the handicapped by the way of career and vocational education.

While career education is a relatively new concept, and vocational education a rather old one, many professionals in the field of education now recognize the relevance and utility of both terms.

With the passage of Public Law 94-142, The Education of All Handicapped Children Act, handicapped students must be provided with an appropriate educational program. It is felt that career and vocational education will provide not only an appropriate education for the handicapped, but the opportunity to realize full educational potential.

Providing a relevant curriculum for the handicapped under career and vocational education is by no means an easy task. Teacher training institutions must begin to recognize the need for preparing their students for career and vocational education. Public school systems must prepare for career and vocational education at the very earliest levels. Administrators must separate fact from fiction in examining relevant career and vocational education programs.

Career and vocational educations is by no means useful only to the handicapped. All students could benefit from this type of educational program. However, the purpose of this text is to improve the education and potential of the handicapped student. At the same time, it should be noted that educators and laymen alike, in all aspects of the world of work will gain insights and information about potential careers for the handicapped, and new aspects of education possible under career and vocational education.

INTRODUCTION: CAREER AND VOCATIONAL EDUCATION FOR THE HANDICAPPED DEFINED

For many years, vocational education has been a part of many shcool curriculums throughout the nation. However,the term vocational education has always meant many things to many people. For some educators, it meant a work-study program with shared time between school and community work placement. For others it meant theory and practice characterized by classwork and simulated work experience. For teahers of the handicapped it meant anything from sheltered workshops to community work-study programs depending on the severity of the handicap.

However, it is clear that no matter what aspect of vocational education was utilized, there was one common fact for all. Vocational education was only for the older student. Usually high school curriculums were the only places where vocational education was to be found.

It has become obvious that this presents many problems. First of all, it is very difficult for students, handicapped or not, to develop a proper work attitude so late in their educational lives. Furthermore, students were being asked to consider careers on a part time basis, or only when they were in vocational education class. Also, it has always been assumed in education that those students interested in vocational education were of lower educational quality than those interested in academic, or college bound curriculum. By the same token, little vocational concern was paid to the handicapped child because of apprehension, misinformation or neglect.

Vocational education is still with us. However, it may now be considered as a part of a much larger and more relevant approach ---career eucation.

Career education begins when a child first enters school. Career concerns begin with the first school work a child does. As a student's school career progresses, so does his vocational--occupational curriculum. Students examine their own potentials, interests, and abilities at a very early stage. Maturity includes career attitudes and vocational interests. Most of the school curriculum is affected by the future career responsibilities and opportunities of each student.

For the handicapped, career and vocational education seems to be a welcome change. The very severely handicapped can be helped to realize their potentials and find uses for their lives. The more mildly handicapped can be assisted in finding places in society as independent, useful citizens.

The following articles will help define career and vocational education for the handicapped, and serve as a starting point for the rest of the book.

MONOGRAPHS ON CAREER EDUCATION

CAREER EDUCATION AND
VOCATIONAL EDUCATION:
Similarities and Contrasts

by

Rupert N. Evans
Professor of Vocational and Technical Education
School of Education
University of Illinois, Urbana

INTRODUCTION

The easiest way to describe the relationship between career education and vocational education is to point out that all of the latter is part of the former. But this is only part of the story. Governmental support of vocational education began in this country in the early 1900's, long before career education had been named. At that time, a coordinated educational program to meet the career needs of all persons simply was not salable, though a number of capable people, such as John Dewey, tried. Part of the problem was that faculty psychology was dominant; there was little knowledge of personal development or career development, and little was known of the pernicious effects of segregation by race, sex, and socioeconomic status.

The result was that vocational education was instituted as a group of programs designed to prepare people for jobs below the professional level. These programs were philosophically and often physically separate from the remainder of the school. Students who desired to attend college were excluded summarily, on the not unreasonable assumption that schools would use their own resources for the college-bound, so Federal funds for their aid were not as necessary. Despite this limitation to lower level jobs, vocational education was an enormous step forward because it met the needs of many students who otherwise almost certainly would have dropped out of a school designed solely for those who intended to go on to baccalaureate degrees.

WHAT IS CAREER EDUCATION?

The term "career education" was first used by U.S. Commissioner of Education James Allen in 1970 (Bailey and Stadt, 1973, p. 268). It was described and popularized by Allen's successor, Sidney P. Marland, who undoubtedly deserves credit as the father of the movement.

Dr. Marland wisely refused to define career education precisely, leaving that to local and State initiative. If an official Federal definition had been proposed, it is likely that much effort would have been expended in attacking and defending it rather than in building career education programs. Instead, Marland suggested the need for:

"Career Education And Vocational Education: Similarities and Contrasts", Rupert N. Evans, *Monographs On Career Education* US Government Printing Office, Washington, D.C.

a. More emphasis on vocational education, as the core of career education, and less on the general curriculum,

b. Each person to exit from the high school prepared for either continuing education or productive work,

c. Education for and about work, using a variety of delivery systems (which he called models), and

d. Increasing the career options open to individuals.

The authority of Marland's position as well as the timeliness of his ideas encouraged many people to begin working on career education in all parts of the country. Almost every State and many local schools adopted a definition of career education, and many of them began programs. While the definitions and programs have differences, it is obvious that most of them were influenced by the Hoyt definition in *Career Education: What It Is and How To Do It*. Virtually every program includes the phases of awareness, exploration, and preparation, and almost every definition includes the following:

a. Career education is concerned with education for work, both paid and unpaid.

b. Awareness and exploration of self is as important as and must be related to awareness and exploration of the world of work.

c. A major goal is to increase individual career options, and to make work possible, meaningful and satisfying for everyone.

d. Because attitudes are formed early in life, career education should begin with the first year of school (or earlier, in the home), and because the nature of work changes, career education must continue throughout life.

e. The program must involve the entire community and all parts of the school program.

Almost every program began to try to develop "awareness" of the world of work in the elementary school, "exploration" in the junior high school, and "preparation" in the senior high school. (Unfortunately, some of them assumed that each of these three programs ended at the school level in which it was begun, instead of recognizing that each continues throughout life.) Few career education programs, in spite of their rhetoric about serving all people, made any provision for adults, either through educational assistance in maintaining career competence, or by recognizing that many adults need educational assistance to further career awareness, exploration, and preparation for changed careers. At the same time, vocational education continued a trend of concentrating more and more on school age youth and less and less on meeting adult needs.

Almost every program adopted some method of grouping activities in the world of work into some ten to fifteen "clusters" of similar jobs in order to ensure that no major portions of the world of work were omitted, and presumably in order to make learning more efficient by promoting the study of similar products at the same time (although just what this had to do with efficiency of learning about careers was not clear). Almost every system of clustering grouped together jobs ranging from unskilled to managerial and professional so that the student who studied "Construction," for example, would be exposed to a wide range of occupational levels and could learn the advantages and disadvantages of each. This appears to be sound, but most clusters suffer from overlap which, for example, leads to the study of clerical jobs in every cluster. A few programs use the clusters of "people," "data," "things," and at least one program (American College Testing Service) adds "ideas" to the previous three. This type of clustering is based on studies of actual jobs and careers rather than depending on "logical" grouping which may or may not be closely related to the ways in which people really think about themselves in relation to careers.

Although career education has used as few as three and as many as fifteen clusters to categorize the entire world of work, vocational education has used a larger number of clusters to represent the subprofessional occupations with which it is concerned. The recent trend in vocational education definitely is toward use of a smaller number of (and hence broader) clusters. This trend, however, is in sharp contrast to the situation which existed when Federal support for vocational education was initiated.

At the turn of the century, schools were employing nearly the ultimate in clustering. Faculty psychology was in vogue, and in accord with its dictates, the two basic groups of school programs trained the mind and the hand. The latter of these programs, manual training, purported to prepare students for any non-professional occupation. Unfortunately it did not produce the desired results, and Federally supported vocational education was substituted for it. These early vocational programs went to the opposite extreme, under the assumption that it was necessary to have separate educational programs for each job title. Thus there were separate programs for tool and cutter grinders, wheat farmers, and hundreds of other specialized job titles.

Because even the largest school could offer specialized programs for only a small proportion of the more than 20,000 job titles, there was a gradual movement toward grouping similar job titles and developing a vocational program for these groups of jobs. This led to broader programs such as machine shop and production agriculture. The grouping of job titles progressed slowly, however, because of fears that this was a return to the discredited manual training concept.

The most recent clustering system in vocational education was developed in Oregon by Dr. David Fretwell (Lee and Sartin, 1973, p. 190-205). Nineteen clusters were used, but one of these is a "miscellaneous" category which includes less than 5 percent of vocational education students. These clusters can be used in two ways: For data collection and for instruction. If used for instruction, a student receives a program designed to prepare him or her for employment in any job in the cluster. The majority of the clusters are used for instruction in most parts of the country, e.g., marketing, food service, and electricity-electronics. Other clusters, e.g., metals, construction, and health, are used for instruction in only a few States. Every State, however, can use these clusters for data collection. Each cluster can be subdivided into specialized programs if the local school feels that instruction covering the entire cluster would be so broad as to decrease its utility. The State can then add data from all of the specialized programs in a cluster for reporting enrollments, costs, etc. This clustering system almost certainly will increase the uniformity of vocational education programming and data reporting.

The degree of uniformity of program which has been achieved independently in career education across the country is remarkable, particularly when one considers that there was no one charged with career education leadership in the U.S. Office of Education until 1974. Occasionally one still hears remarks that career education will never amount to anything until it has a single definition upon which everyone agrees. This type of assertion implies that because there are slightly different definitions of secondary education in use that therefore secondary education is hampered significantly. Whether or not this is the case is not at all clear.

What is clear is that anyone who has the opportunity to read the career education literature or to visit a number of career education programs will find similar goals and activities under way throughout the nation. Misunderstanding of career education tend to come from those who have not read the literature or visited programs.

The rapidity of development of career education is particularly surprising because for the first 4 years of its life, career education received very little Federal money, and what it did receive was taken from monies appropriated for vocational education.

WHAT IS VOCATIONAL EDUCATION?

Vocational education began to receive Federal funds more than 50 years ago because of a feeling that the local and State controlled schools were placing almost their entire emphasis on preparing an elite group of students for college and little or no emphasis on preparing the majority of students for the kinds of work needed by society. Three types of programs were subsidized by the new legislation: Agriculture, home economics, and trades and industries. The first of these emphasized entrepreneurship, the second stressed nonpaid work in the home, and the third prepared people for employment in factories and repair shops.

The next half-century saw a number of gradual shifts in the types of programs which were supported:

a. More occupational fields were included.

b. There was more and more stress on employability and less on entrepreneurship.

c. Paid work was emphasized and nonpaid work (e.g., homemaking) deemphasized.

d. More emphasis was placed on programs in post-secondary schools for full-time students and less on programs designed for adults who were occasional students.

e. Part-time cooperative programs (school-supervised employment in business and industry) increased markedly.

The late 1960's and early 1970's produced a series of research results which changed vocational education significantly and laid the groundwork for career education:

a. Persons with no salable skills have greater difficulties in the labor market than those who have skills of almost any variety.

b. Because unskilled jobs are usually the easiest to automate, the average level of knowledge and skill required by jobs continues to increase.

c. Socioeconomic segregation has greater adverse educational effects than does even racial segregation.

d. The school curriculum in which a student is enrolled is related to the student's race, sex, socioeconomic status, and verbal ability. Measures of educational effectiveness of the various curriculums which do not control for these variables are very misleading.

e. Handicapped youth learn less when they are segregated than when they have both special assistance and exposure to regular classes. Segregation appears to have a greater negative effect on the learning of attitudes and cognitive skills than on the learning of manual skills, but vocational education involves all three types of learning.

f. We have been unable to develop effective methods of forecasting local employment needs for even a 10-year period, but students and their parents know what types of vocational education they want. If given a choice, they appear to choose wisely in the long run. A program which does not have acceptance from both students and parents will disappear because of low enrollment.

g. The student who drops out of school (physically or mentally) does so in large part because he or she sees school as being personally irrelevant.

h. The old notion of a career requiring continued promotion until a person reaches his level of incompetence with its accompanying frustration is beginning to be replaced by the concept that a career should lead to greater and greater personal satisfaction, even if this means a shift to a different career ladder or a step down the career ladder.

Not all of these research results have been incorporated in all vocational education programs, but enough people accept them to affect markedly the formation of new vocational education programs. The blend of new and continuing programs has increased until now about one-third of high school graduates and community college students have access to vocational education of some type. The proportion of students enrolling in college preparatory and college transfer curricula is static and general curriculums are contracting. Vocational education is growing in enrollment, so if one uses the criterion of consumer acceptance, it is succeeding. Many vocational educators believe that career education programs in the elementary and junior high schools will increase this acceptance of vocational education by students and parents. It would appear that this same assumption leads some nonvocational teachers to be wary of career education because they fear it will decrease emphasis on preparation for college. Many parents, especially those in minority groups, have similar fears. This is discussed further on p. 15.

VOCATIONAL EDUCATION AND THE "AWARENESS" AND "EXPLORATION" PHASES OF CAREER EDUCATION

Many vocational educators who have not had contact with career education programs in the elementary and junior high schools assume that career awareness and exploration are simple matters which can be handled by a course or two taught by vocational educators in high school. Several things are wrong with this attitude:

1. Attitudes are learned early in life, and attitudes toward work are difficult to change by the time a student has reached high school age.

2. A "course" (or even two courses) is not a very effective way of teaching people to become aware of or to explore the world of work. Thousands of students during the 1920's suffered through "occupations" courses

which consisted of the teacher reading long lists of job descriptions, pay scales, and job entry requirements. This type of course cannot substitute for observation, simulation, and discussion which are best spread over several years and are best presented in relationship to other types of school learnings.

3. The vocational educator is not necessarily the best person to teach career awareness and exploration. As a specialist in one part of career preparation, he or she is apt to seek recruits for that specialty and may have little patience with those who are not interested in or qualified for that specialty. And, because nonprofessional careers are emphasized in vocational education, the vocational educator may be suspect of not giving adequate attention to professional careers. As with academic teachers and guidance counselors, vocational educators need special training to do the best possible job of helping students to develop career awareness and to explore a wide variety of careers.

VOCATIONAL EDUCATION AND THE "PREPARATION" PHASE OF CAREER EDUCATION

Because vocational education constitutes an indispensible part of the preparation phase of career education, an understanding of this phase is necessary to an understanding of the relationship of vocational and career education. "Awareness" and "exploration" precede "preparation," the phase in which:

1. Students acquire career decision making skills, work seeking skills, and work evaluation skills;

2. They perfect skills in communication, computation, and human relations which are needed by everyone; and

3. They acquire additional salable skills which apply more to some types of work than to others.

The preparation phase of career education can be (and once was) conducted entirely on the job. However, there has been a continuing trend toward a combination of preparation in school with training on the job. This combination may be done *sequentially* (as is the case when a person goes to engineering school for 4 years, and follows this with 2 years of experience on the job), or *concurrently* (as in a part-time cooperative education program, in which the student engages in alternating periods of study and work under the supervision of the school). Both the sequential and the concurrent methods of instruction are usually accompanied by a certain amount of general education. (Most commonly, 50 percent of the school time in any one school year is spent in general education and 50 percent in specialized instruction).

The length of the in-school preparation phase varies considerably from one type of career to another. For convenience, careers can be divided into four categories of length of specialized preparation:

1. Professional—40 to 100 semester hours spread over 4 to 7 years of full-time schooling, usually in a university.

2. Technical—30 to 45 semester hours spread over 2 years of full-time schooling, usually in a community college.

3. Vocational, Skilled—20 to 35 semester hours in 1 year of full-time schooling, usually in a community college; or approximately the same amount of instruction (4 to 6 Carnegie Units) spread over 2 to 4 years of high school.

4. Vocational, Specialized—One day to 6 months of intensive instruction, usually offered to adults by high schools, proprietary schools (e.g., trade and business schools), community colleges, or universities. Specialized preparation is usually completed by persons who are already employed and hence does not provide additional entrants to the labor force.

Figure 1

Types of School-Based Career Preparation:

Estimated Percent Employable In and Percent Completing
Preparation for Each Level

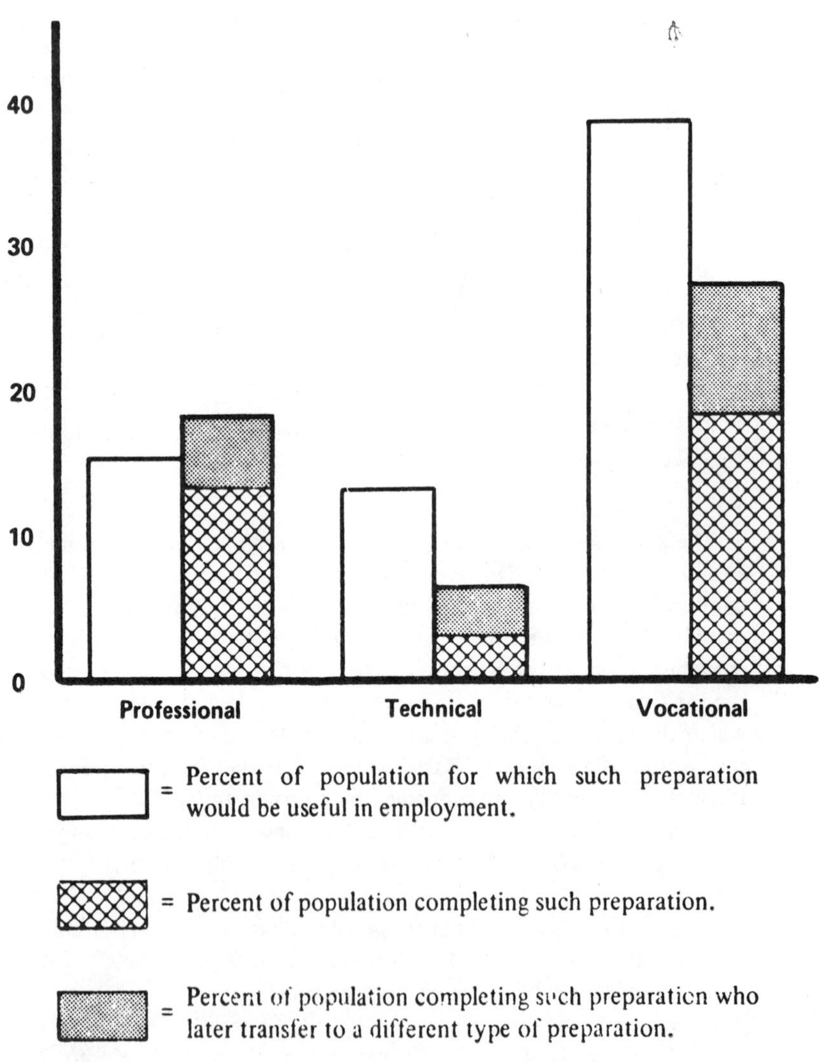

There are no in-school programs preparing people for job entry to approximately 20 percent of the careers in the labor market, and about 50 percent of new entrants to the labor force have not participated in career preparation programs of any type.

When one studies the data on the percentage of people employed in various types of occupations and the proportion of students in different types of occupational education programs, some interesting comparisons emerge (see Figure 1): 1) Professional preparation is useful for about 20 percent of the labor market and is completed by about 20 percent of students, 2) technical preparation is useful for about 15 percent of the labor market, but less than 10 percent of students complete it, and 3) vocational preparation is useful for about 40 percent of the labor market, but less than 30 percent of students complete it, and about one-third of its graduates go on to technical or professional preparation.

It is a common assumption that vocational education is synonymous with the career preparation phase of career education. This assumption is not quite accurate. Vocational education is concerned with preparation for the large numbers of vocational and technical careers which are nonprofessional and require less than a college degree for entrance, but which require more knowledge and skill than is possessed by the typical high school graduate from the general curriculum.

Career preparation includes (but vocational education usually omits):

1. Preparation for the professions and for similar careers requiring a baccalaureate for entry (about 20 percent of the labor force);

2. Preparation for nonpaid work such as homemaking (once a full-fledge part of vocational education, but now half-in, half-out due to evaluation specialists who convinced Congress that placement of vocational graduates in homemaking was equivalent to unemployment) and volunteer work. (Both of these major types of work are, of course, outside the paid labor force); and

3. Education which is needed for more effective involvement in all types of work, e.g., work-seeking skills, personal and work evaluation skills, and knowledge of how work is organized and carried out (preparation for all work inside and outside the labor force).

It is a common mistake to say that the vocational education curriculum prepares people for 80 percent of the jobs, while the college preparatory curriculum in the secondary school prepares people for only 20 percent of the jobs. It would be more accurate to say that at least 50 percent of high school students are not now prepared for work of any type, and that traditional programs of vocational education which are designed to prepare people for skilled occupations are unlikely to meet this need. Career education programs which emphasize preparation for nonpaid work and preparation which is useful for all types of work (2. and 3. above) offer real promise of meeting some of the needs of this 50 percent.

It might be assumed that there would be no conflict between vocational educators and other career educators with regard to career preparation programs in the high school and community college. This is not quite true, however. The greatest conflict appears to arise between career educators and the coordinators of part-time cooperative education (co-op) programs. Co-op coordinators arrange and supervise employment for students and provide an educational link between the half of the student's time spent at work and the half-time spent in school. Such programs rarely serve more than 10 percent of the school population, and in order to get participation which is this extensive, the co-op coordinators work night and day to find willing and able employers with whom they can work. A coordinator will do nearly anything to preserve a good "training station." But, along comes career education with blithe promises of providing work experience for everyone. Very often, the first reaction of the co-op coordinator is fear of the loss of training stations, and, more basically, a fear that unsupervised work experience will destroy cooperative education, which many people feel is the best method vocational education uses. The more knowledgeable coordinators cite statistics of 73 percent unemployment among unsupervised work experience students in Maryland during the early 1970's.

Other conflicts are certain to arise as high schools begin to expand their career education beyond what they have been doing in vocational education. These conflicts will not be resolved simply by castigating vocational educators as being resistant to change. They were, after all, in career education before it had that name, and they do know some things which have worked and some things that have not. The co-op coordinators, for example, can supply excellent suggestions on a variety of methods of working with the business and industrial community. And, perhaps they are right that unsupervised work experience programs are far from what they might be.

YOUTH CLUBS AS A MEANS OF CAREER PREPARATION AND EXPLORATION

Almost 2 million high school and post-secondary school vocational education students participate in five youth organizations. The oldest and largest of these organizations are the Future Farmers of America and the Future Homemakers of America. All five of the groups are organized to parallel the traditional vocational programs of agriculture, business, distributive education, homemaking, and trades and industries. The closest major parallel in the health occupations field is the Student Nurses Association, which is limited to post-secondary students of nursing. In each organization a vocational teacher is usually the club adult advisor.

These clubs hold local, regional, and national conferences, and most of them conduct competitive contests in a wide variety of activities and publish materials for student use. Their principal emphasis is on development of leadership skills, and the results are impressive. Their State and national officers are perhaps the best spokesman for vocational education in the Congress and before business and industry groups.

There are also youth organizations for high school youth who wish to explore one or more of several professions. Future Teachers of America, Junior Engineering Technical Society, and Junior Academy of Science are three large national groups. There are national or local counterparts in journalism, music, theater, and many other professions. The adult sponsor may be a local teacher or practitioner who has expertise in the field with which the club is concerned.

At first glance it might appear that vocational and preprofessional youth groups have similar goals, but this is not the case, in spite of the fact that their programs are remarkably alike. Vocational youth groups usually require that the student member be enrolled in the related vocational program. This, in turn, means that the student has made at least a nominal career choice and is in the preparation phase of career education. Consequently, the club program emphasizes proficiency in, rather than exploration of careers. In contrast, the students in preprofessional youth groups are encouraged to explore more widely (but only within the professions represented by the club charter), and there usually is an open-entry, open-exit membership policy which is unrelated to the student's major field of study.

The undisputed value of youth clubs in developing attitudes and leadership skills leads one to inquire why there are so few career education clubs, or at least prevocational clubs. Such groups could play a major role in developing career awareness and assisting with career exploration. Some industrial arts and home economics clubs play this role, but most seem to be avocational.

The youth groups with the most extensive career exploration programs usually are operated outside the schools. Explorers (formerly Explorer Scouts) have an extremely well-developed career exploration program which encompasses all types of careers. Somewhat less extensive exploration is offered by 4-H Clubs and by Junior Achievement.

JOB CONFORMITY VERSUS JOB REFORM AS GOALS OF EDUCATION

Traditionally, Americans have expected the educational system to prepare people to exist comfortably in the existing society. At the same time the influential critics of education have charged education with failure to revolutionize the society or even to change it markedly. Most educators would like to prepare people who can enjoy life as it is, but at the same time can perceive areas of life in which change is needed, and are willing and able to work for such change. Almost invariably, however, the principal emphasis is placed on conformity because society controls the schools, and society is more interested in educating conformists than it is in educating even a small number of revolutionaries.

All education has the dilemma of the need to prepare people both to exist comfortably in society and to change or even to revolutionize that society. The same dilemma exists in career education, but especially in its vocational education phase. A frequently stated objective of vocational education is to enable the graduate to succeed in a given line of work. Success is usually measured in terms of the employer's satisfaction with the graduate, and less frequently in terms of the worker's satisfaction with the job. Both of these evaluative measures encourage educational programs which stress learning to "get along with others," to "practice good human relations," and learning not to "rock the boat."

But at the same time there is societal dissatisfaction with job structure. Vocational education is seen as a means of promoting job enlargement, eliminating discrimination based on sex or race, changing the distribution of national income by finding jobs for the poor, and eliminating socioeconomic barriers to career mobility.

It should be clear that a vocational education program whose graduates enjoy their work and are experts at getting along and not rocking the boat is unlikely to produce many graduates who will push employers or fellow employees for costly improvements in job safety or major changes in job content, promotion patterns, or job assignments. Nor would the vocational education program which graduated large numbers of male homemakers or black electricians (at a time when there was substantial discrimination against such people in society) be likely to have a record of 100 percent placement of graduates in productive work, or to have a record of high job satisfaction on the part of its graduates.

A case in point is the limited role of females in vocational education. Although more females than males are enrolled in vocational programs, more than half of the females are being educated in only one area—home economics—and about one third are studying office practices. Part of this

1. INTRODUCTION

segregation is due to actions of educators and part of it is due to attitudes of potential enrollees. Vocational education is being pressured by recent Federal legislation to increase the mobility of both sexes across educational and employment barriers. It appears that social scientists and Congress are more concerned about non-sexist vocational education than are employers and employees whose major concern is for continuity in their present operations.

There is no known method of preparing a person simultaneously to conform to the expectations of the job market and to revolutionize the job market. Employers tend to emphasize the former and social scientists tend to emphasize the latter, while most vocational educators try to meet both objectives in part. This allows both employers and social scientists to charge that vocational education has failed.

**GOALS OF VOCATIONAL EDUCATION AND
CAREER PREPARATION**

Vocational education and the preparation phase of career education have precisely the same goals of:

1. Meeting the manpower needs of society;

2. Increasing individual options related to work; and

3. Conveying knowledge of the relevance of general education in work.

Because the goal of meeting the manpower needs of society was the initial goal of vocational education, it is sometimes believed by nonvocational educators to be its sole goal. Equally bad is the belief that career education has this as its sole goal.

Vocational education has been continually hampered in achieving its goal of increasing individual options by systems of evaluation which measure its effectiveness in terms of the percentage of graduates placed on jobs in the field for which they were "trained." This type of evaluation counts as a failure the realization by a student that the type of career for which he is being prepared is unlikely to be personally satisfying, and that a shift to a different type of career is therefore desirable. Most educators agree that far from being a failure, such realization represents a success.

Awareness of self inevitably will be enhanced by high quality vocational education. Exploration of the world of work is included in every vocational program, but sometimes the range of exploration allowed is not great. Evaluation of the vocational education phase of career education should include measurement of the effects of awareness and exploration as well as the results of preparation. The career education concept should make such a broadened evaluation more readily acceptable to labor economists and academicians who in the past have seen only one goal for vocational education.

The process of helping students to find work which is meaningful and satisfying is not aided by evaluation procedures which reward schools for restricting student placement to the small number of vocations for which the school has established specific training programs, or for restricting admission to students who are so highly qualified that they are placeable with or without training. The evaluation should be made, first, in terms of the proportion of former students who secured paid and unpaid work, and, second, in terms of the proportion who found their work satisfying and meaningful.

Even more difficult to understand is the type of evaluation which counts it as a failure of vocational education if a student continues his or her education rather than immediately going to work after graduation. In the early days of vocational education such an evaluation might have been justifiable to prevent school administrators from using Federal funds which had been earmarked for nonbaccalaureate jobs as a subsidy for college preparatory classes. But now such evaluation can only serve to limit student options.

PERSONS SERVED BY VOCATIONAL EDUCATION AND CAREER EDUCATION

Career education is designed to serve all of the people. In contrast, vocational education has tended to serve those high school students who are low in verbal ability *and* have low socioeconomic status (Evans and Galloway, 1973). In the post-secondary school it serves those who are low in verbal ability *or* are low in socioeconomic status (Evans and Jackson). Those who are low in both rarely attend post-secondary schools. Clearly, vocational education does not serve all.

The most obvious difference between career education and vocational education is in the minimum age of persons served. Career education may begin in early childhood, while vocational education usually begins about age 16. It seldom or never begins below age 14, and the average age of entry to vocational education has been increasing ever since its inception.

Vocational education is usually thought of as a program for males, but slightly more than half (55%) of its enrollment is female. Sex stereotypes in enrollment parallel those in the world of work, with business education, health occupations, and home economics having female students and teachers almost exclusively. Agriculture, trades, and industries are as solidly male.

Some spokesmen for minority groups see vocational education as a means of teaching which destroys opportunities for higher education for minority students, by providing another rationale for "tracking" students (segregating students who have dissimilar test scores, grades or goals; often used as an excuse for racial segregation). This may be true in certain communities, but in the nation as a whole minorities are neither over- nor under-represented in the vocational education student body. They are under-represented, however, in the teaching staff and in certain higher level technical education programs.

PROBLEMS IN THE RELATIONSHIP OF CAREER AND VOCATIONAL EDUCATION

1. Career education has had its greatest successes in the elementary school. It now appears that its introduction into junior high schools is well under way, but in high schools, there is little to be seen of career education except for vocational education. This can be explained in a variety of ways:

   a. Some persons feel that vocational education and the preparation phase of career education are synonymous, so if their high school has the former, they feel that the latter is accomplished.

   b. Parents want career education to be available in high school, but don't necessarily want their children to enroll in it, especially not in its career preparation phase.

c. The curriculum in high school is mandated by colleges and by accrediting associations.

d. High school teachers who accept career education goals feel that little can be done until awareness and exploration activities are well under way in the lower grades.

e. Some of the high school teachers who accept career education goals know that they have only a limited awareness of the vast range of career options existing in the world of work, and are uncomfortable with the thought that they will be involved in preparing students for careers with which they are unfamiliar.

f. Some persons who accept awareness and exploration of careers as legitimate school activities feel that preparation is the job of private trade schools or employers rather than of the schools.

The true reasons need to be identified and means found to cope with them. A career education program which is full blown only until it reaches the preparation stage cannot long survive if it then becomes a program only for those who are low in verbal ability and low in socioeconomic status.

2. Career education obtained its initial financing and leadership from vocational education. In the U.S. Office of Education it is difficult to identify more than a handful of people involved in career education who did not come from vocational education. In other parts of government, however, the reverse is true: It is hard to find more than a handful of people who understand what vocational education is or who see its vital role in career education.

The popularity of the career education concept with the Congress and parts of the Executive Branch is causing all sorts of people who don't understand either career education or vocational education to try to get in on the act. This would be fine except that they seem to be less interested in career education than in relabeling their pet projects (e.g., year-round school and modular scheduling) so that they can become eligible for career education funding.

One former official of the Department of Health, Education, and Welfare set career education back several years by trying to equate career education with all education. Two results were apparent: Career education began to be diluted, because it had diffuse goals and fears of educators were heightened because they saw this as a move by career educators to take over all of education. Education has several key goals, e.g., citizenship and health, which are important in their own right, and are only tangentially related to career education. Careers are important and deserve the attention of the school, but they are not and should not be the sole concern of the school. Every part of the school has something to contribute to career education, but every part of the school also has concerns outside of career education.

This mistake of stating that all of education is career education must not be repeated, and the only way to be sure to avoid it is to develop leadership, especially from the fields of career development, educational administration, learning resource management, special education and vocational education to work with subject matter specialists in building a complete program of career education. Internships in active career education programs along with graduate work in career education would make a useful and attractive package for leadership development. Leadership can no longer be allowed to rest solely with vocational educators, nor can it be turned over to persons who see it as a means to the end of furthering their noncareer education ambitions.

3. Career education is needed as much in postsecondary and adult education as in the common schools, and programs aimed at enhancing career awareness and exploration are needed as much as career preparation. Ideally, a career education program which extends from early childhood through adulthood would be planned by all agencies concerned. It is obvious, however, that it is easier to plan around a single K-12 school system than to develop plans which involve several K-12 school systems plus one or more postsecondary institutions, public or private. To overcome such obstacles to coordinated action, incentives should be provided to encourage joint planning which brings together educational institutions of various levels, Comprehensive Education and Training Act (CETA) agencies, and the various adult education agencies.

SUMMARY

This paper has examined some of the similarities and contrasts between vocational education and the remainder of career education with the goal of a better understanding of both. It has indicated ways in which the older, more specialized field of vocational education is an essential part of the newer, broader, concept of career education. The fact that these two programs must rely on each other will not prevent their having conflicting views, due in part to their different genesis, goals, and types of persons served.

Both educators and evaluators of education should recognize that career education is now faced with a dilemma which many vocational educators have been unwilling to recognize: That it is extremely difficult to prepare workers who are both conformists and change agents. How can one be both satisfied with one's job and eager to change its content? How can one learn to have good human relations and at the same time be pushing other humans to change age-old problems in the work place?

Career education has begun to be important enough to attract critics. One of the criticisms is that it is designed to produce docile workers for the military-industrial complex. It would appear, however, that even modest programs of career awareness, exploration, and preparation are likely to decrease docility by affording both blue-collar and white-collar workers new ways of looking at work as well as new opportunities for mobility. If this is true, one can expect soon to hear cries from other critics, that career education is producing people who expect too much from their work. Steering a course between these two groups of critics will be difficult, but it is better than using education to perpetuate the notion that work is necessarily bad and fit only for slaves. Career education and vocational education share the goal of making work possible, meaningful, and satisfying for everyone.

CAREER EDUCATION AND THE HANDICAPPED PERSON

by

Kenneth Hoyt, *Director*
Office of Career Education
Office of Education

Career Education represents a response to a call for educational reform. This call has arisen from a variety of sources, each of which has voiced dissatisfaction with American education as it currently exists. Such sources include students, parents, the business-labor-industry-professional community, and the general public. Special segments of the population, including the economically disadvantaged, minorities, the handicapped, and gifted persons have also expressed deep dissatisfaction with both the appropriateness and the adequacy cf educational opportunities that are made available to them. While their specific concerns vary, all seem to agree that American education is in need of major reform at all levels. Career Education is properly viewed as *one* of several possible responses that could be given to this call.

Career Education seeks to respond to this call for change through making education as preparation for work both a prominent and a permanent goal of our entire educational system. To accomplish this goal, career education seeks first to unite all segments of the formal educational system in this common effort. To this, we seek to add the collaborative efforts of both the business-labor-industry-professional community and the home and family structure in ways that enhance attainment of this goal for all persons through a broad range of community services and activities.

From the beginning, career education advocates have proclaimed that they seek to serve *all* persons of all ages in all kinds of educational settings. In practice, we have seen career education programs primarily limited to elementary and secondary school youth enrolled in regular public school programs. This situation cannot continue if the promises of career education are to be attained. In this article, the problem will be illustrated through considering implications of career education for handicapped persons.

Basic Definitions Essential for Understanding Career Education

Six basic words must be redefined in order to understand the concept of career education itself. These six words are: (1) "work"; (2) "career"; (3) "vocation"; (4) "occupation"; (5) "leisure"; and (6) "education."

"Work" is conscious effort aimed at producing benefits for oneself and/or for oneself and others. As such, it is unimportant whether such effort is paid or unpaid in nature. What is important is that it represent the basic need of all human beings to achieve—to accomplish—to *do* something productive that allows the individual to discover both who he/she is and why he/she is. With this definition, work is properly viewed as a human right—not as a societal obligation.

"Career Education For Special Populations, Career Education And The Handicapped Person", Kenneth Hoyt, *Monographs On Career Education* U.S. Government Printing Office, Washington 1976

"Career" is the totality of work one does in his or her lifetime. Thus, any person can have only one career. That career typically begins prior to entering formal schooling and continues well into the retirement years.

"Vocation" is one's primary work role at any given point in time. Vocations include paid employment, but they also extend to unpaid work roles. For example, we can speak of the "vocation" of the student, the full-time volunteer worker, or the full-time homemaker just as easily as we can speak about the "vocation" of the plumber, the physician, or the engineer.

"Occupation" is one's primary work role in the world of paid employment. Economic returns are always considered among the work values of persons engaged in occupations although these might not be considered at all by persons in certain vocations. The occupations of many persons will be synonomous with their vocations. One can never have an occupation without having a vocation although, of course, one can have a "vocation" without being engaged in an "occupation."

"Leisure" consists of activities, other than sleeping, in which one engages when not performing in his or her vocation. Thus, "leisure" holds possibilities for both "work" and for "play."

"Education" consists of all those activities and experiences through which one learns. As such, it is obviously a lifelong process and considerably broader in meaning than the term "schooling."

All that follows is based on an assumption that these six basic words are understood and their meanings agreed upon. Those who disagree with one or more of these definitions will necessarily find themselves disagreeing with much of the remainder of this presentation.

With the way in which these six terms are defined, "career education's" definition, in a generic sense, becomes simple and straightforward. *Career Education consists of all those activities and experiences through which one learns about work.* As such, it makes no restrictions in meaning whether one speaks about work of the homemaker, the musician, the lawyer, or the bricklayer. Some work will require advanced college degrees while other work may include no formal schooling of any kind. Some work will be in the form of primary work roles, paid or unpaid, while other work will be carried out as part of one's leisure time. To the extent that work is judged "successful," it does typically—and, in these times, increasingly—require some learned set of vocational skills.

Further Consideration of the Meaning of Work

The preceding definition of "career education" brings us back to further consideration of the meaning and implications of the four letter word "work." Work, as used here, is a concept available only to human beings in that it is restricted to conscious effort - to something that the individual thinks about and chooses to do. It is this quality of conscious choice that most clearly distinguishes the word "work" from the word "labor." That it, "labor," like "work," may very well result in production of benefits, but it does not carry with it the connotation of something that the individual consciously chooses to do. Instead, "labor" is more accurately regarded as forced, involuntary effort that lacks personal meaningfulness and significance for those who perform it.

1. INTRODUCTION

Why do people work? Answers given to this question can be grouped into three broad classifications of reasons - economic, sociological, and psychological. Work, in the world of paid employment, always includes economic reasons and, if maximally meaningful to the individual, carries sociological and psychological reasons as well. Economic reasons, of course, center around the needs most of us have to accumulate income so that we can purchase goods, products, or services produced through the work of others. Sociological reasons center around recognition that one's work contributes to the goals of our society in a positive way—that what one does has benefit for one's fellow human beings. Psychological reasons center around personal recognition of one's accomplishments— around the feeling of being *someone* through being able to say that one has accomplished *something.*

While most persons experience economic reasons for working and many, although not all, can readily observe the sociological significance of the work that they do, the single reason for working that can be said to apply to all persons is that which centers around the psychological dimension. Former President Lyndon Johnson perhaps expressed this need for work as clearly as anyone when, in a speech, he said

> To hunger for use and to go unused is the
> greatest hunger of all.

He was, of course, referring to the human need of all human beings to feel that someone needs them for something—that it does matter to someone that they exist—that, because they are alive, the world is, in some way and to some degree better off.

The concerns and scope of career education extend to all three of these basic reasons for working. It is this breadth of concern that enables career education to say that it is concerned with all persons of all ages in all settings from all levels of educational background. The basic premise of career education is that the need to work is a basic human need for all human beings. That is why we refer to work as a "human right" rather than as a "societal obligation."

Career Education and Handicapped Persons

In a recent paper, C. Samuel Barone, USOE Bureau of Education for the Handicapped, presented the following predictions regarding the approximately 2.5 million handicapped youth who will leave our school systems in the next four years:

525,000 - 21% - will be either fully employed or enrolled in college.

1,000,000 - 40% - will be *underemployed* and at the poverty level.

200,000 - 8% - will be in their home community and idle much of the time.

650,000 - 26% - will be unemployed and on welfare.

75,000 - 3% - will be totally dependent and institutionalized.*

Predications, such as these, raise very grave concerns for those dedicated to the career education movement. The prediction that one million of these handicapped youth will be *underemployed* is a very serious matter indeed. The concept of underemployment is one that pictures a person as possessing greater degrees of productive capability than the tasks he or she is asked to perform routinely require. Underemployment leads to boredom on the job and is seen by many as a major contributor to worker alienation in our society at the present time. To predict that this will be the fate of 2 out of every 5 handicapped youth leaving our school system in the next four years can only be regarded as a serious indictment of our educational system and of the larger society.

We have, for far too long, seemed to act as though a handicapped person should be both pleased with and grateful for any kind of work society provides. Unlike other persons, we seem to assume that, if a person is handicapped, boredom on a job is impossible. Worse, much of society has seemed to assume that, while most persons should seek work compatible with their interests and aptitudes, such consideration are not necessary when seeking to find employment for handicapped persons. If *any* job in the world of paid employment can be found for the handicapped person, we seem far too often to be personally relieved and surprised when the handicapped person is anything less than effusively grateful.

Similarly, we seem to assume that those handicapped persons who are not employed in the world of paid employment are not and cannot be working. This is, in the philosophy of career education, both false and wrong. We know that, for example, the fact that a person is unemployed and on welfare certainly does not mean, for many such persons, that they do not work. There is a very great deal of work being carried out in many welfare homes, the results of which are readily apparent to any who visit in such homes. Yet, because persons on welfare are not engaged in the world of paid employment, society seems to assume that they are not working. Even more tragic, some seem to assume that people on welfare do not want to work. If the human need to work pictured here has any validity at all, it certainly applies to persons on welfare just as to all other persons.

The 200,000 youth who are predicted to be in their home community and idle much of the time can certainly not be written off as persons with no interest in working or no personal needs to work. Something should be provided for such persons, whether it be paid or unpaid work. The field of the handicapped has, for years, be promiting the concept of the sheltered workshop for those who are unable to compete effectively in the world of paid employment. The prime rationale for the sheltered workshop must surely lie in recognition of the human need for work that is being discussed here. If this concept is valid for those in sheltered workshops, it is certainly also valid for those who are not.

Career education seeks to make work possible, meaningful, and satisfying for *all* individuals. To do so for handicapped persons demands, first of all, that we regard their right to choose from among the widest possible set of opportunities equally as important as for any other individual. We seem too often to be satisfied when we have found *something* that a handicapped person can do. We should be dissatisfied until and unless we have explored, to the fullest possible extent, the total array of work that might be possible for a given handicapped person. To stop prior to reaching this point is being less than fair to the handicapped person and to the larger society.

One further basic principle of the career education movement would seem to have some relevance for handicapped persons. This is the principle that holds that we should seek to emphasize the individual's successes, not his or her failures. In career education, a conscientious attempt is made to emphasize accomplishments—attainments—achievements—*doing*. This can best be carried out by refusing to emphasize failures and shortcomings. It would seem that this principle holds some positive potential for working with handicapped persons who, far too often, are made well aware of their limitations and, in the process, effectively limited in discovering their talents. We have, it would seem, been sometimes too much concerned about helping the handicapped realize and appreciate how much society is doing *for* them. In so doing, we run the risk of de-emphasizing, for many handicapped persons, how much each can do for himself or herself.

Handicapped persons are as deserving of whatever benefits career education has to offer as are any other individuals. To date, not many career education programs have made the kinds of special efforts necessary in order to make career education a reality for handicapped persons. It is hoped that these remarks may stimulate both those in career education and those working in the field of the handicapped to work together in order to correct this lack of attention. The need to work *is* a human need of all human beings. Handicapped persons *are* human beings.

TEACHING WORK ATTITUDES AT THE ELEMENTARY LEVEL

Joseph E. Justen III
Terry G. Cronis

Joseph E. Justen is Assistant Professor, Special Education, University of Missouri, Columbia.

Terry G. Cronis is Assistant Professor, Special Education, University of South Alabama, Mobile.

■ Studies of job failure in mentally retarded populations have consistently indicated that most retarded individuals lose their jobs, not because of inability to do the work but rather because of a failure to adjust to the social demands of the world of work (Gold, 1973; Kolstoe, 1961; Kolstoe & Frey, 1965). In addition, there is some evidence that retarded individuals are unrealistic in the establishment of their vocational goals (Knight, 1972). Introducing vocational and career education to the retarded child at the secondary level may well be too late. Job attitudes and work habits are formed early. By exposing young retarded children to the world of work and by fostering proper work attitudes and habits at an early age, a sound foundation can be established for later success on the job. Thus, curricula for the primary and intermediate level special class should contain experiences for each of these two areas.

THE WORLD OF WORK

While even preprimary level retarded children are generally aware that people work, retarded children are often unaware of the various occupations that exist in modern society. They are even less aware of the requirements needed to fulfill those jobs. If one were to ask a retarded child what he wished to be when he finished school, likely responses would be "an airplane pilot," "a race car driver," "a nurse," and so on. If the child were then asked what a person needs to know or do to become qualified for such work, the retarded child would probably not be able to answer. Thus, the purpose of career education for the young retarded child should be (a) to introduce them to typical occupations performed by average citizens as opposed to the highly idealized and publicized jobs to which they are typically exposed, (b) to acquaint them with the qualifications required and the duties and responsibilities expected in these occupations, and (c) to aid students in establishing effective vocational choices by comparing their interests and abilities with the requirements of the various jobs surveyed. The following activities were designed as an aid in accomplishing these goals.

Job of the Week

Before the mentally retarded can develop an interest in jobs within their capabilities, they must be introduced to these jobs. A simple means of providing exposure to a wide variety of occupations is to select a new job for discussion each week. A special section of the bulletin board can be set aside for pictures and other information illustrating this job. Each day a specific period of time, preferably 15 to 20 minutes, should be set aside for discussion of the "job of the week." On the first day of the school week the new job should be introduced to the class, the appropriate section of the bulletin board pointed out, and a discussion conducted on basic aspects of the particular job. On each of the following days a brief discussion should be devoted to a different aspect of the job of the week. Topics for discussion and presentation might include skills and abilities required on the job, tools and equipment required on the job, the role the job plays in the community, and the need for persons interested in performing the job.

Job Work sheets

Studies of memory in the mentally retarded have generally indicated that a retarded person's short term memory is defective (Robinson & Robinson, 1965). This leads to problems in the acquisition of new information. Once a retarded individual has thoroughly learned something, however, he is likely to remember it. Thus, if a retarded child is provided with but one brief exposure to a new occupation he will probably forget much of the important information concerning this job. However, if the child is given multiple exposures to the important aspects of the job, his recall will be greatly improved. An effective means of following up discussions of jobs available in the community is the job work sheet. These work sheets are essentially drill sheets prepared on standard ditto masters and duplicated for the class. At the lowest level these sheets might involve matching a picture of a worker with a job (fireman with crew putting out fire) or a tool with a worker or job. At a more complex

1. INTRODUCTION

level they might involve reading a brief question and selecting the correct answer.

Meet the Worker

A motivating way to introduce students to the world of work is through a modification of the television show *Meet the Press*. By periodically having representatives of various occupations discuss their jobs for the class (or for several classes together), students are afforded an opportunity to ask the experts. It is surprisingly easy to obtain workers from various fields for student interviews. Most companies are more than willing to release or supply persons to serve in this capacity. Whenever possible, a "meet the worker session" is an invaluable means of reinforcing the job of the week.

Job Analysis

If mentally retarded individuals are to develop realistic vocational choices, they must be made aware of the requirements of various jobs as well as their own strengths and weaknesses. One means of increasing pupil awareness in these areas is to have students perform job analyses on different occupations. In this activity the student is read a story, shown a film, or otherwise exposed to a specific job. After this presentation the teacher conducts a class lesson aimed at analyzing the attributes needed to fulfill the requirements of this job. Generally, this lesson would consist of a class discussion in which students explore questions such as: Does a person who works at this type of job need to be able to stand on his feet for long periods of time, lift heavy weights, distinguish between fine shades of colors? These discussions should be followed up with discussions of individual strengths and weaknesses as they relate to the job presented (e.g., Could Betty load cement bags on a truck?).

What's My Job

Assuming teachers have introduced a program to expose children to the world of work and the requirements of various occupations, a way to increase motivation and reinforce information previously learned is through the game "What's My Job?" This game is basically a modification of the television panel show *What's My Line?* To start the game the teacher thinks of a job and the students must ask questions which can be answered by a *yes* or *no* in order to gain clues about the job. When a student thinks he knows the job, he may raise his hand and guess. If he is correct he wins the game and may pick the next job. If incorrect he may not guess again, though he may continue to ask a *yes* or *no* type question and confer with others who are preparing to guess.

A Class Business

In addition to exposure to the various types of occupations available, it would also be advantageous for retarded individuals to be exposed to business operations. This exposure should not be aimed at producing future entrepreneurs; rather it should be cursory, designed primarily to enhance the retarded child's understanding of the factors involved in even the smallest business. A class business can be an excellent way to accomplish this end.

Such an operation should be constructed along lines similar to that of Junior Achievement. While the teacher or school will supply ample capital to initiate the business, students must return a portion of their income toward paying off the loan granted them for initial wares and toward the purchase of new materials. Class art projects, foodstuffs from the class kitchen, and car washes can be excellent starting places for a class business.

WORK HABITS AND ATTITUDES

Vocational education for the elementary age level mentally retarded child should emphasize the development of adequate work habits and good job attitudes rather than specific job skills or on-the-job training. This is not meant to suggest that these latter skills have no place in a curriculum for the elementary age retarded child. Early work experiences such as those in the school cafeteria or with the school janitor can provide the child with invaluable initial on-the-job training. Likewise, many of the skills subsumed under the heading of practical arts are actually skills which will be useful to the vocational training of the mentally retarded.

Sign In Sheets

By requiring students to sign in and out of the classroom, the teacher can reinforce one of the primary prerequisites to success on the job, that of being on time. The sign in sheet may be varied in complexity to suit the level of the class. At the lowest level it could consist of laminated cards bearing a photograph and the name of the child with a space for the child to write in his time of arrival (in grease pencil) copied from a digital clock. The higher level students could be expected to fill out a work sheet providing their name, the time, and so on. Whatever format is used, the activity should resemble punching a time clock on a job. To provide transfer, much discussion could be centered on who was earliest, who was latest, and who arrived at the same time. One novel method consisted of a teacher-made tape recording of the time, each minute repeated every 15 seconds before the new time was given. This tape was started 5 minutes before class and played for 10 minutes. Students had to write the time they heard on the tape, then put their paper in a time clock for validation.

Work Wheels

The ability to assume responsibility is essential for success on even the simplest jobs. Assigning students a certain job to perform each day is one method of developing responsibility not only in performing an assigned task but also in being aware of a responsibility that changes daily or weekly. A work chart or wheel may be constructed by the teacher and class. It may be a simple slot chart or a large

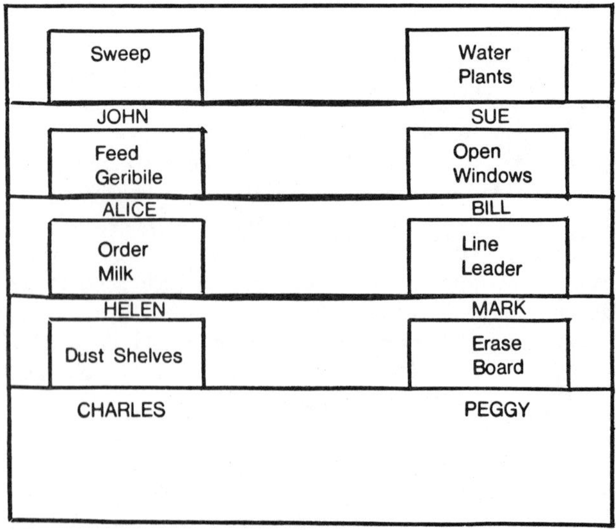

FIGURE 1
A SLOT CHART

wheel which matches a student to a job (see Figures 1 and 2). Nothing more than the name of a job is necessary because a reference book may contain an illustrated description of each job.

Tool License

The tool license is a simple means of providing status (reinforcement) for gaining skill with various equipment and tools. This procedure gives students a realistic view of job qualifications.

Such licenses may be limited in design only by the teacher's imagination and creativity. A wallet size card which depicts the tool, the bearer's name, and perhaps his picture can be obtained by each student who successfully demonstrates his skill by a series of training periods and competency checks. Such licenses may be given for scissors, ruler, paper cutter, claw hammer, stapler, staple gun, etc. No large classroom chart need be kept because part of the status of achieving the license is showing it on request when the teacher needs someone to use the particular tool or to help train another individual. A plain white card may indicate apprentice status and a colored card with picture and place for the bearer's signature may indicate journeyman status. A scissors license, for example, may require competency checks on safely carrying, passing, and holding scissors, as well as cutting along lines of varying difficulty marked on duplicated work sheets.

Task Sheets

One of the most important concepts for retarded individuals to internalize is the notion that a certain amount of work must be accomplished in a day's time. Various assignments may be listed, such as work sheets for math, spelling, and reading. Classroom tasks such as sweeping or opening the windows may also be put on the task sheet. Another item might be a particular "special" activity that will be included in the day's curriculum such as music, physical education, or art. A space may be provided for the student to check

or have the teacher check off each completed task. These sheets may be taped to the desk or hung at a work area, locker, or mailbox so that both student and teacher will have ready reference to the progress being made.

Job Evaluation

Quality is an important aspect of work and should be introduced early. Students are not always aware of the vast number of gradations between not doing a job and doing it well. Establishing a quality evaluation rather than a simple *done/not done* standard can be essential in developing pride and extending skill attainment. At first, such quality checks can be simple levels such as *not done, not OK, needs improvement, OK,* and *good.* Using general descriptors allows for variations of ability and for working up to one's ability level. Care should be taken to use an absolute standard at both ends of the scale, however. This provides needed reality which enables a mentally retarded child to assess his own ability level when called upon to do so.

Worker of the Week Award

A weekly award for a selected good worker (not necessarily the best) can be established as a means of reinforcing good work habits or production. Varying criteria such as most improvement or consistent high quality may be used. A plaque, certificate, or picture on the bulletin board may be used with whatever ceremony the teacher may wish to include. Using the principal to present the award can elevate the worker of the week award to a very high level of status.

Hopefully, the above ideas will provide special educators with at least a meager start towards providing for the vocational and career education needs of the young retarded child. With a little extra effort, classroom teachers can lay a solid foundation for the future vocational success of their pupils.

**FIGURE 2
A WHEEL CHART**

REFERENCES

Gold, M. W. Research on the vocational habilitation of the retarded: The present, the future. In N. R. Ellis (Ed.), *International Review of Research in Mental Retardation* (Vol. 6). New York: Academic Press, 1973.

Knight, O. B. Occupational aspirations of the educable mentally retarded. *Training School Bulletin,* 1972, *69,* 54-57.

Kolstoe, O. P. An examination of some characteristics which discriminate between employed and not-employed mentally retarded males. *American Journal of Mental Deficiency,* 1961, *66,* 472-482.

Kolstoe, O. P., & Frey, R. M. *A high school work-study program for mentally subnormal students.* Carbondale: Southern Illinois Press, 1965.

Robinson, H., & Robinson, N. *The mentally retarded child: A psychological approach.* New York: McGraw-Hill, 1965.

CAREER GUIDANCE AND THE DICTIONARY OF OCCUPATIONAL TITLES

MARY LOU McEVER

MARY LOU McEVER *is Assistant Professor, Department of Rehabilitation Counseling, College of Health Related Professions, University of Florida, Gainesville.*

An increasing number of young adults, labeled retarded in their childhood, are entering employment and assuming new identities as workers. Verification of employment success comes from public schools, sheltered workshops, institutions, and community based vocational rehabilitation programs which have vocational training for disabled persons. One would assume that the efforts of special educators, rehabilitation counselors, and other personnel who believe in the potential of children and adults with handicaps is being reinforced by the accumulating followup employment data, collected as evidence of the effectiveness of the training programs.

Accountability should not be the final objective of training programs however reassuring these accumulating numbers of job placements may be. An equally important objective in collecting followup data from training programs would seem to be how best to classify and use an abundance of employment information. Within these job lists, which emerge in the followup studies of training programs, is substantial information about characteristics of jobs and the workers who perform them. This valuable information will remain hidden if the data is not organized in a manageable form and used for evaluation, placement, and curriculum enrichment.

Purpose

The purpose of this article is to introduce a system of classification, the *Dictionary of Occupational Titles* (DOT), to those persons who may be unfamiliar with it, to encourage those familiar with it to look more closely at its varied uses, and finally to demonstrate this system's usefulness in both organizing placement information and transferring it to curriculum use.

General Description

DOT is a dictionary for defining meaning, clarifying concepts, understanding relationships, and serving as an authority for a language in vocational areas. The language of the DOT is that of employment, and the concepts are those used in conveying information about occupations. This employment language therefore provides for standardization of job information from the job itself for use by rehabilitation counselors, training facilities, schools, teachers, students, and workers.

The DOT was developed and published by the US Department of Labor in 1939, and since that time it has had periodic revisions through research and job analysis. The massive information on jobs is now distributed in three books or volumes, each with a distinct function for helping the reader understand the complexities of employment characteristics and relationships.

Coding System

The first distinguishing feature of the DOT (and the focus of this report) is its classification of jobs through the use of a code in the form of a six digit number. Each digit contains specific clues which are related to both job and worker characteristics. For example, the code for "rehabilitation counselor" is 045.108; that of a "teacher of handicapped children" is 094.228. The information contained in these numbers indicates that both jobs are professional in category (conveyed through the first digit, 0); that the counselor is in the division of "life sciences" (04) while the teacher is in the division of "education" (09); that the occupational group for the counselor is that for "occupations in psychology" (045) while the teacher's occupational group is "education of the handicapped" (094).

The last three digits in the code are also specific clues but relate to the worker rather than to industry variables. The numbers indicate how the worker functions in relationship to data, people, and things. Characteristics for the rehabilitation counselor, .108, indicate that he coordinates data (1), counsels with people (0), and has little relationship with things (8). The teacher's relationship to data, people, and things is expressed in the numbers .228, which indicate that he analyzes data (2), instructs people (2), and has little significant relationship with things (8). (The "things" relationship has been questioned by active special educators.)

Followup Data

The use of this coding system in presenting followup data for graduates from special classes is demonstrated in the following example. A rehabilitation counselor reports that five former students were placed in jobs during the month of July. These five jobs of the students and the DOT job classification for each are shown in Table 1.

Using the DOT classification of occupations, these particular jobs reported for July could be inserted with other placements already reported in numerical sequence by the first three digits. A quick glance at the accumulation of placement data would provide the teacher and counselor with information about the nature of occupations held by graduates

TABLE 1

DOT Classification of Occupations

Occupation	Code
Stock clerk (auto supply)	223.387
Cafeteria server	311.878
Nurse's aide	355.878
Carpenter's helper	860.887
Plumber's helper	862.884

should particular industrial topics be under study in curriculum.

Considering the function or skills of the workers in relationship to data, people, and things, the last three digits become important. The DOT reports the hierarchies of function in the following format:

- *Data* (4th digit)
  - 0 Synthesizing
  - 1 Coordinating

- 2 Analyzing
- 3 Compiling
- 4 Computing
- 5 Copying
- 6 Comparing
- 7/8 No significant relationship

- *People* (5th digit)
  - 0 Mentoring
  - 1 Negotiating
  - 2 Instructing
  - 3 Supervising
  - 4 Diverting
  - 5 Persuading
  - 6 Speaking-signaling
  - 7 Serving
  - 8 No significant relationship

- *Things* (6th digit)
  - 0 Setting up
  - 1 Precision working
  - 2 Operating-controlling
  - 3 Driving-operating
  - 4 Manipulating
  - 5 Tending
  - 6 Feeding-offbearing
  - 7 Handling
  - 8 No significant relationship

Jobs can now be sequenced by the last three digits to reveal the levels of worker relationship to data, people, and things. For example, the stock clerk compiles data, has little responsibility for people, and handles things in his work. For the five jobs in Table 1, sequencing the jobs by the last three digits would result in transposing the last two jobs—the plumber's helper and the carpenter's helper.

An intellectual relationship to these hierarchies was not intended through the job analyses which developed this classification system. Other occupations which have the same relationship to data, people, and things as, for example that of a plumber's helper (884) are butcher (316.884), artist (741.884), film cutter (976.884), engraver (979.884), and poultry farm laborer (412.884).

Other descriptive characteristics of workers including education, aptitudes, training needs, and physical demands can be found in Volume 2 of the DOT. The volume also assists in determining if the transfer of skills from one job to another is indicated. Sometimes jobs sounding quite different in name have similar characteristics; therefore, the job options for disabled people could be broadened through the use of this system.

Conclusion

Although counselors and educators can obtain valuable career guidance assistance with the use of the DOT, the work environ-

1. INTRODUCTION

ment itself and personality variables of individuals still hold much importance in the success of training and placement. Perceptive counselors know that a plumber's helper in a school system may have different work expectations than one who works in his father's business.

This brief introduction to the US Department of Labor's system of classification of employment data is offered to promote the use of this system as a starting point for organizing followup occupational information. When data is organized, it can be better used for the benefit of students who want adult identities as contributing workers.

Reference

US Department of Labor, *Dictionary of occupational titles* (3 vols.). Washington DC: US Government Printing Office, 1965, 1966, 1966.

CAREER EDUCATION NEEDS OF SECONDARY EDUCABLE STUDENTS

DONN BROLIN

Abstract: The major purpose of this study was to identify the needs of secondary level educable mentally retarded students and the competencies teachers must have to meet these needs. From the data received at a conference for state and national authorities, a field questionnaire was developed and sent to 30 randomly selected administrators and 251 secondary level teachers of the educable retarded in Wisconsin. The results showed that a greater emphasis is needed to prepare secondary teachers of the educable retarded with knowledge and skills in vocational rehabilitation and vocational education. The teachers indicated that increased involvement of other school and out-of-school personnel was needed to meet some of their students' primary needs, and that a prevocational coordinator position was especially needed. The study reflected needed changes in both regular and special education teacher preparation.

Donn Brolin *is Associate Professor of Education, Department of Counseling and Personnel Services, University of Missouri–Columbia. He was formerly the Initiator and Director of the Special Education Project at the University of Wisconsin–Stout, Menomonie, Wisconsin. The research reported herein was performed pursuant to a grant from the US Office of Education, Department of Health, Education, and Welfare. However, the opinions expressed herein do not necessarily reflect the position or policy of the US Office of Education, and no official endorsement by the US Office of Education should be inferred.*

Work-study programs, in which students spend part of the day or week acquiring work experience and skills in specific jobs in the community, have developed rapidly in many high school programs during the past decade. Nevertheless, special education teachers are still trained to teach primarily academic skills, and their classrooms place much emphasis on purely academic instruction and little emphasis on vocational evaluation, adjustment, training, placement techniques, and other important career education areas. Hammerlynck and Espeseth (1969) indicated that another problem is inadequate communication between the teacher and vocational rehabilitation workers. This results in a sporadic and inadequate continuity of services as students progress through work-study programs. Other problems are the limited time to develop and supervise work experiences, the lack of vocational education skills by the special education teacher, limited teacher communication with and use of other school disciplines, and insufficient knowledge of mental retardation by supporting personnel (e.g., sheltered workshop, employment service, social service, and rehabilitation workers).

Martin (1972) pointed out that the educational system is just beginning to view employment as an important subgoal, and he presented these disturbing statistics:

> Only 21 percent of handicapped children leaving school in the next 4 years will be fully employed or go on to college. Another 40 percent will be underemployed, and 26 percent will be unemployed. An additional 10 percent will require at least a partially sheltered setting and family, and 3 percent will probably be almost totally dependent [pp. 523-524].

Martin recommended redefining our basic instructional program and developing career edu-

1. INTRODUCTION

cation programs where work habits and skills related to future employment could be learned.

The primary purpose of this study was to identify the instructional needs of secondary level educable retarded students and the competencies teachers must have to meet these needs so that relevant teacher education changes can be initiated. A second purpose was to determine the extent to which other types of personnel should be involved in meeting student needs.

Method

A 2 day conference was held at the University of Wisconsin–Stout on November 12-13, 1970. The purpose of the conference was for national and state authorities and special education practitioners to provide their input on the needs of secondary educable students and the teacher competencies necessary to meet these needs. Before the conference the participants were asked to send to the project staff a list of what they believed to be the needs and competencies. During the conference the participants were asked to develop the lists further and rate all identified needs and competencies according to degree of importance. At the end of the conference all the participants were shown the group consensus on each item and then each individual participant was asked either to revise his opinion (if it differed from the consensus) or to specify his reason for remaining outside the consensus.

The conference participants identified and rated the importance of over 200 needs and competencies by using the above method (the Delphi technique). They were classified into one of four curriculum areas, i.e., academic, activities of daily living, psychosocial, or occupational. The project staff then used the statements and the ratings to refine and compile a revised and more condensed list of the 31 most highly rated competencies for the secondary level teachers of the educable. These competencies were included in a field questionnaire developed by the project staff. Conference participants were asked to react to the instrument prior to its use, and based on their suggestions, a number of modifications were made before the questionnaire was finalized.

The questionnaire was sent to all secondary (grades 10-12) special education teachers in Wisconsin ($N = 251$) and to 30 randomly selected administrators. Two followup mailings at 3 week intervals were conducted; total response was 73 percent ($N = 205$). The teachers varied considerably in age, education, teaching experience with educable students, and non-teaching work experience. There were 115 men teachers, 83 women, and 7 unidentified (respondents were not required to identify themselves). All but 4 percent were either certified or working toward certification in special education; 20 percent had a master's degree and 24 percent a bachelor's degree in special education.

The questionnaire consisted of two parts. Part I included a list of the four curriculum areas—psychosocial, activities of daily living (ADL), academic, and occupational. The re-

TABLE 1

Percent of Time Needed for the Four Curriculum Areas as Rated by Three Groups of Respondents

	Respondents' classroom teaching responsibility			
Curriculum area	*Major* *(N=149)*	*Minor* *(N=24)*	*None* *(N=25)*	*Total[1]* *(N=198)*
Occupational	28	32	34*	30
ADL	25	26	22*	24
Psychosocial	24	24	19*	23
Academic	23	18	25**	23
TOTAL	100	100	100	100

[1] Of the 205 respondents 7 failed to indicate the percentage of time they spent teaching educable students.
*$p < .05$
**$p < .01$

TABLE 2

Ranked Mean Priority of 31 Competencies

Rank	Mean	Curriculum area	Teacher competency
1	4.72	Occupational	Using appropriate work adjustment techniques
2	4.57	Occupational	Teaching job seeking skills
3	4.56	ADL	Preparing students to care for personal needs
4	4.54	Psychosocial	Teaching social behavior expression
6	4.52	Occupational	Finding appropriate job tryout sites
6	4.52	Occupational	Finding the student suitable employment
6	4.52	Occupational	Conducting a vocational evaluation program
8	4.49	Psychosocial	Developing the students' self confidence
9	4.42	Occupational	Providing vocational guidance
10	4.41	ADL	Teaching responsibilities to self and others
11	4.40	ADL	Developing the students' communication skills
12	4.38	ADL	Instructing in home management
13	4.36	Academic	Teaching adequate academic skills
14	4.29	Occupational	Using community agencies that assist in vocational adjustment
15	4.22	Occupational	Writing reports to agencies
16	4.19	Psychosocial	Providing opportunity for interaction with normal students
17	4.17	Psychosocial	Providing professional guidance in developing personal responsibility
18	4.05	Occupational	Coordinating postschool activities
19	4.03	Occupational	Developing the students' manual abilities
20	4.02	ADL	Instructing in uses of leisure time
21	4.01	ADL	Teaching home mechanics
22.5	4.00	ADL	Teaching civic responsibilities
22.5	4.00	ADL	Using transportation methods
24	3.98	Academic	Organizing academic instruction appropriately
25	3.95	Occupational	Providing specific job training
26	3.94	Psychosocial	Developing social, emotional, & intellectual functioning related to students' environment
27	3.93	ADL	Using community resources
28	3.92	Psychosocial	Helping parents meet student needs
29	3.87	Psychosocial	Providing for independent thinking
30	3.84	Academic	Providing ongoing evaluation of academic abilities
31	3.46	Psychosocial	Teaching aesthetic values

spondents were asked to indicate the percentage of curriculum emphasis that they believed should be given to instructing secondary educable students in each of the four areas.

Part II included the same four curriculum areas accompanied by a list of the teacher competencies needed to meet the student needs listed in Part I. The number of competency statements were 11 occupational, 9 ADL, 8 psychosocial, and 3 academic. The respondents were asked to rate (on a 5 point scale) how important they judged each of the 31 competencies to be for a secondary teacher of the educable to adequately meet students' needs and to indicate what personnel they thought ideally should be responsible for each competency and which ones in practice were doing it. Choices of personnel included a special education teacher, prevocational coordinator, other school personnel (counselor, psychologist, regular class teacher, social worker), or others outside of school (welfare, vocational rehabilita-tion agency, sheltered workshop). More than one person could be checked.

Results

Part I

Table 1 presents the percentage of emphasis that the respondents indicated should be devoted to each of the four curriculum areas of secondary educable programs. The respondents were categorized as those who spent the majority of their time in classroom teaching (> 50 percent), those who spent a minority of time (< 50 percent), and those who did no teaching (administrators). The ratings support the position that a high school curriculum for the educable retarded should contain as much or more emphasis in occupational skills and activities of daily living as in psychosocial and academic instruction. The ratings of the administrators indicated somewhat different expectations about curriculum emphasis than did the teachers' ratings.

1. INTRODUCTION

TABLE 3

Frequency of Competencies Categorized by Their Ranked Importance and Curriculum Area

	Curriculum area	
Ranking of importance	*Occupational*	*All other*
Most important (1-10)	6	4
Intermediate (11-20)	4	6
Least important (21-31)	1	10

NOTE: Overall chi square = 6.12; df = 2; $p < .05$

Part II

Teacher competencies ratings. The 31 teacher competencies resulting from the Stout conference were rated on a 5 point scale of importance. These ratings were 1 for not important, 2 for slightly important, 3 for moderately important, 4 for important, and 5 for very important. Table 2 presents, in rank order, the mean rating and curriculum area of each teacher competency.

Table 2 reveals that a large proportion of the occupational competencies were rated highly. To determine whether occupational competencies were rated significantly different from the other competencies, a chi square analysis was conducted (Table 3). The analysis was statistically significant at the .05 level of confidence indicating that significantly more occupational competencies were rated as most important than the other three types of competencies combined.

Ideal versus in practice ratings. Analysis of the respondents' indications of what personnel are and should be responsible for the 31 competencies is summarized in Table 4. For the 11 occupational competencies, the percent of respondents who indicated that in practice special education teachers are primarily responsible ranged from a low of 32 percent for coordinating postschool activities to 96 percent for teaching job seeking skills. The median percentage was 60 percent. This degree of competency responsibility did not differ significantly from their ratings of how they ideally should be responsible for these occupational competencies (56 percent). Significantly greater responsibility was endorsed for a prevocational coordinator for the occupational area competencies, i.e., ideally, 60 percent, and in practice, 30 percent. Similarly, the ideal and in practice percentages for out-of-school personnel were significantly different, 28 and 17 percent.

Further inspection of Table 4 reveals that, in contrast to the ratings of the occupational competencies, the respondents (special education teachers and administrators) rated the special education teacher as the one who should assume primary responsibility for the students' instruction in the ADL, psychosocial, and academic areas with some assistance from the other disciplines, particularly other school personnel. Although a prevocational coordinator

TABLE 4

Median Percent of Respondents' In Practice and Ideal Endorsement of Specific Competencies in Each Curriculum Area for Four Types of Personnel

		Curriculum areas			
Personnel type	*Endorsement*	*Occupational*	*ADL*	*Psychosocial*	*Academic*[1]
Special education	Ideally	56	81	81	87
teacher	In practice	60	88	90	86
Prevocational	Ideally	60*	17*	26*	33
coordinator	In practice	30	7	12	15
Other school	Ideally	39	54	55*	43
personnel	In practice	25	42	33	27
Out-of-school	Ideally	28*	33*	38*	14
personnel	In practice	17	17	19	17

NOTE: Median test computed on the arrays of percent endorsement of the specific competencies in a given curriculum area for the ideal and in practice categories.

[1] The 3 academic competencies were too few to be statistically analyzed by this procedure.
*$p < .05$

and out-of-school personnel were not frequently checked as providing these competencies, significantly more involvement was indicated. Other school personnel were also checked as needing significantly more involvement in the psychosocial area. The three academic competencies were too few to be statistically analyzed by this procedure

Discussion and Implications

The results indicate that secondary teachers of educable students should be prepared to provide considerable instruction in the occupational, ADL, and psychosocial areas as well as in strictly academic material. The study found that the importance of occupational curriculum competencies was rated significantly higher than the other three curriculum areas. Also, administrators rated the curriculum emphasis differently than the classroom teacher in the occupational area. However, the respondents (primarily teachers) believed that many of these competencies should not be the primary responsibility of the traditional special education teacher. Instead, they expressed the need for a prevocational coordinator for secondary programs, i.e., a special educator who is concerned both with educative and habilitative functions but gives greater attention to the latter (Younie & Clark, 1969; Clark, 1971). However, only 4 of the 205 respondents indicated that they could be considered prevocational coordinators.

It seems that administrators employing more than one special education teacher should consider a prevocational specialist. Otherwise, because of the discrepancies between ideal and in practice ratings for the prevocational coordinator, special education teachers have to assume much more responsibility for meeting the students' occupational development needs. However, many do not believe some of the occupational competencies are their main responsibility, particularly providing skill training, job tryouts, job placement, and postschool activities, and writing reports to agencies. Thus, despite its high rating of importance, the occupational area appears the most neglected of the four areas studied (Table 4).

The findings indicate that other school personnel should become more involved in meeting some of the primary needs of the educable student. Other school personnel are involved somewhat in helping with personal care instruction, home management, interaction with "normal" students, development of manual abilities, home mechanics, mobility training, vocational skills training, parental assistance, and evaluation of academic abilities. However, many respondents felt that more involvement is needed, particularly in the psychosocial development area (Table 4). Perhaps the new thrust toward career education will force this involvement.

Many respondents indicated that out-of-school personnel should be accepting more responsibility in a number of areas, e.g., postschool activities, leisure time training, and parental assistance. They indicated that presently there is too little involvement in the occupational, ADL, and psychosocial areas (Table 4). Thus, there is evidence of a need for community agencies to provide more direct services to special education programs.

This study has significant implications for both regular and special education teacher preparation. Probably few special education teacher preparation programs provide the opportunity for students to develop the majority of competencies found to be most important in this study. However, a clearly expressed need for a prevocational coordinator or a more vocationally oriented and prepared special educator was indicated. Therefore, future special education teachers must receive training in vocational rehabilitation and vocational education for the handicapped if they are adequately to perform vocational evaluation, work adjustment, and job placement and to prepare their students in the independent living skills areas. A few years ago Hammerlynck and Espeseth developed a master's degree training program for a dual specialist—a vocational rehabilitation counselor and teacher of the retarded. The Stout project has resulted in the promotion of a new undergraduate preparation model for secondary special education teachers of the educable retarded at that university combining these components and those of vocational education (Brolin & Thomas, 1972).

With the current emphasis on career education, this study supports those who strongly recommend redirecting curricula and teacher education so they really begin meeting students' needs. Coursework for regular class teachers focusing on the unique characteristics and needs of special education students and techniques of teaching them is highly recommended. More understanding and cooperation with community agencies is also an area needing improvement.

This study should be considered exploratory because of its limited generalizability, i.e., on Wisconsin teachers only. The absence of test-retest reliability and the small number of academic competencies may also be considered limitations (many of the ADL competencies were academic in nature). In several states there are undoubtedly many prevocational coordinators employed in the schools. It is hoped that many of them have the competencies found necessary in this study. However, the general positive reaction and interest throughout the country in the Stout project (Brolin & Thomas,

1. INTRODUCTION

1972) reflects the nationwide concern in improving our educational services to handicapped children and several related projects have been generated from this study. Further research of this nature is highly recommended.

Conclusion

Teachers of the secondary educable retarded are currently responsible for meeting most of the many needs of their students, and these students require and deserve a quality education which can be provided only by specially prepared teachers. Since educable students do not generally go on to other education, it is even more essential they they receive the career education they need at the secondary level. If the educators of special education personnel do not redirect their curricula more toward career education, there may be no market for their graduates in secondary programs. Today, there are many who advocate that other types of teachers can better meet these student needs. Thus, teacher education programs must prepare their student teachers more appropriately so that educable students may be better equipped to meet the stringent demands of today's society.

References

Brolin, D., & Thomas, B. *Preparing teachers of secondary level educable mentally retarded: A new model.* Final Report. University of Wisconsin–Stout, Menomonie, Wisconsin, August 1972.

Clark, G. M. Secondary pupil needs and teacher competencies. In D. Brolin & B. Thomas (Eds.), *Preparing teachers of secondary level educable mentally retarded: Proposal for a new model.* Project Report No. 1, University of Wisconsin–Stout, Menomonie, Wisconsin, April 1971, Pp. 41-50.

Hammerlynck, L. A., & Espeseth, V. K. Dual specialist: Vocational rehabilitation counselor and teacher of the mentally retarded. *Mental Retardation,* 1969, 7, 49-50.

Martin, E. W. Individualism and behaviorism as future trends in educating handicapped children. *Exceptional Children,* 1972, 38, 517-525.

Younie, W. J., & Clark, G. M. Personnel training needs for cooperative secondary school programs for mentally retarded youth. *Education and Training of the Mentally Retarded,* 1969, 4, 186-194.

VOCATIONAL TRAINING

Pre-vocational programs give students the opportunity to explore many different kinds of work possibilities and develop some skills while doing so. Since the skills themselves are not of primary importance at that stage, they are developed at a general level. By contrast, vocational programs provide for a narrowing of occupational interests and greater depth of skill development. The change of emphasis is not--and should not be--an abrupt one if services have been integrated to prepare students for vocational training. General work skills are cultivated first followed by skill training specific to a particular job or cluster of jobs.

Effective vocational programs for the handicapped require a graduated but flexible curriculum. The vocational portion of the overall program varies according to the extent of fiscal and other resources available, the educational environment and the nature and degree of handicaps involved. There is a wide variety of possibilities ranging from low-cost work-study programs to more sophisticated and more expensive skill training programs. Work-study opportunities will usually tend to be unskilled because of the reluctance of employers to train unskilled and handicapped workers. A variation of the work-study type of program is on-the-job training where the student usually receives more supervision either from the program staff or from the employer--sometimes through available vocational rehabilitation subsidies to employers. Higher level skill training offers a greater probability of the student's becoming more attractive to employers as a semi-skilled or skilled worker. Skill training also varies depending on the number and degree of technical complexity of the occupational options offered. The basic options can be made more sophisticated by combining them. The Roanoke County Occupational School in Salem, Virginia does this successfully by offering vocational skill training to tenth and eleventh grade students prior to full or part-time work experience in a work-study arrangement in twelfth grade.

<u>Low Cost Skill Training</u>

<u>Work Experience.</u> One of the least expensive formulas for providing vocational training among the examples given here is that represented by the cooperating portion of the Special Vocational Needs program in Bellevue, Nebraska, at the Vocational Center for moderately to severely, mentally or physically handicapped. The training offered is only slightly

1. INTRODUCTION

more advanced than the average pre-vocational preparation. At Bellevue,
the workshop experience is nevertheless aimed at the student's eventual
outside employment after an acceptable skill level has been achieved.
This example also illustrates how closely linked progress monitoring is
with skill development in a supervised work environment. The
Vocational Center, just outside Omaha, Nebraska, provides year-round,
workshop-centered experience. Students work in piece-rate contracts
and earn money for their production. All other training (academics,
grooming, survival and socialization skills) are as vocationally oriented
as possible. The training, generally, is not oriented to specific jobs
but to employment in general. The workshop environment is structured.
Students may be at the work tables assembling curlers or nagles, in the
boxing area (gluing plastic bags into boxes under a contract to Anderson
Box), doing janitorial work, or in the warehouse area where they load
and unload contract work (some using a forklift). They also have academic
instruction, counseling and field trips. Bells ring at the beginning and
end of the day, at breaks and lunch hours. Students must fill out a time-
card for each activity. There are four trainers, averaging seven clients
per trainer. The trainers teach work skills and supervise the production
area. There are also two related instruction teachers. Students are
given housekeeping duties, clerical assignments and warehousing duties
to provide additional work experience. The related instruction teachers
provide both individual and group instruction depending on needs and
interest. Individual instruction could last anywhere from 15 to 45 minutes.
While the work environment is highly structured, training and teaching is
performed in an individualistic, flexible manner. Each student is trained
according to his needs and the goals specified for him.

Precision teaching techniques are employed by both the trainers and teachers. Each student participates in from six to ten programs. Of these,
from three to five are for vocational training and related instruction. The
program goals and objectives are specified in behavior sheets. Essentially, each program represents a behavior, skill or piece of knowledge
to be acquired by the student. Programs are further specified in planning
sheets. Each program is broken down into an event, a movement cycle
(response of the student), the ratio of reinforcement to successful student
response or movement and the form of the favorable feedback (arranged
event). Movements or occurrences are recorded on a frequency record
sheet. Then, these frequencies are plotted on a daily behavior chart.
Targets are also plotted on the behavior chart. Slopes of the lines drawn
through data on the chart indicate the rate of progress of students. Standard rates of progress are used as comparisons to evaluate progress.

<u>Work-Study</u>. The Work-Study Experience Program in Russellville,
Arkansas is probably the purest form of the work-study type of program.
It is a small program serving approximately 15 students in a semi-rural
school district in northwest Arkansas. The program for most students
spans three years during which they receive one-half day of work experience in either an on- or off-campus work station, depending on their
abilities and the progress they demonstrate on the job. Work stations

off-campus are not fixed but depend on current employment opportunities. Many trainees go on in the same jobs on a full time basis upon graduation.

On-the-Job Training. The Cooperative Vocational Education program in Doylestown, Pennsylvania, has selected a more supervised, on-the-job training type of preparation, partly because of the nature of its students, all of whom are moderately to severely, mentally or physically handicapped. In this program, virtually all the specific skill training is done on the job by occupational training specialists who follow a five-step procedure.

1. Identifying a potential job: The director has a list of industrial areas of opportunity from which the training specialist may choose and visit the prospective employer. Presumably, they do the job search with the general skills of their student group or individuals in mind. There is no formal assessment and matching procedure of job to student and vice-versa.

2. Learning the job: By working on the job for approximately one week, the training specialist becomes familiar not only with the job but also with the work environment. He is now qualified to train the student on the job.

3. Fitting the student to the job: This step may precede Step 2 and differs in degree. The training specialist will often bring a work sample back to the class, if possible, to work with the student in the classroom to build confidence prior to actually trying it on the job. This approach obviously is not possible for jobs requiring substantial equipment or machinery.

4. On-the-job training: The training specialist works alongside the trainee on the job for approximately 2-3 weeks, gradually allowing the trainee to become more independent and self-reliant. In addition to the immediate task, the training specialist also trains the student in good work habits such as cleanliness and promptness.

5. Follow-up: Depending on how rapidly or slowly the trainee begins to function efficiently on the job, the training specialist will begin to appear less frequently, leaving the trainee alone for longer periods or take him off the job if it appears that he is not making sufficient progress. If the trainee is successful, the training specialist will continue to make follow-up calls with decreasing frequency until the trainee reaches the age of 21. These later calls often are not with the "employee" but with the employer. Once the trainee is acclimated, the training specialist tends to keep as low a profile as possible in the hope that the employee eventually will be accepted as no different from others.

Given the aptitude level of the students in the program, the skills in the initial job placement are repetitive. Examples are assembler of a part of fluorescent lights, armature winder, cosmetics packer and chipper/grinder. The jobs do show, however, some positive variance from the traditional positions for severely handicapped students of dishwasher,

1. INTRODUCTION

janitor's assistant and yard attendant. It is evident that the program has made successful attempts to introduce moderately to severely retarded individuals to tasks of higher levels of difficulty. The individualized, on-the-job training is probably the key to its success.

<u>Off-Campus Work Stations.</u> Similarly, close supervision in off-campus work stations in industrial locations is the approach of Aux Chandelles, a program that also serves moderately to severely handicapped students. The work station in industry is an intermediate placement between competitive placement and a sheltered workshop setting. It is comprised of a full time supervisor for approximately eight trainees engaged in a maintenance contract with a large department store. The contract is actually held by a local contract maintenance firm that in turn employs the trainees and supervisor. The contract was won in competitive bidding with other maintenance firms. The work station offers closer supervision, greater assistance and a longer start-up period for trainees than is possible in most competitive job situations. The results of the first work station have proved so satisfactory for the trainees, the employer and the department store that a second work station has been established in the local Sears store. That contract was also won in competitive bidding.

<u>Cooperative Programs.</u> Institutions often house students who are similarly handicapped to those in the target groups of the four programs just discussed. Certainly, given the resources, similar techniques could be used in an institutional environment to offer vocational preparation. The New York State School for the Deaf in Rome, New York, on the other hand, has successfully established a cooperative program with the local Board of Cooperative Educational Services facility that provides fairly high level skill instruction to its students in integrated, normal hearing classes. Students are transported to the program in their senior year each day for a half-day session of vocational training. Similar cooperative efforts between institutions and local vocational-technical schools or even community colleges for post-secondary students exist around the country.

<u>Higher Cost Skill Training</u>

Many programs offering specific skill training to handicapped students teach general skills in the beginning and move to more specific and difficult skills as the student demonstrates proficiency. The general course outline of one of the occupational areas of the Keefe School Special Needs program in Framingham, Massachusetts, illustrates the movement from general to specific skills for its students in a relatively high-cost program. The basic maintenance and groundskeeping course is divided into three major sections:

> <u>Section A: Preparing the Student for A Condition of General Work Readiness</u> lists the objectives (16) and suggested activities that the low capability trainable mentally retarded students in the training program should accomplish if they are to be pre-

pared to work anywhere. These activities should be a part of a total program, constantly reinforced and used where applicable.

The following are examples of specific educational objectives used in Section A:

A-1   The student will <u>understand the meaning of job responsibility,</u> especially as it applies to the performance of each job task.

A-2   The student will <u>understand the meaning of job satisfaction.</u>

A-3   The student will <u>understand the necessities for working</u> and the differences in life styles between people who work and those who do not work.

A-4   The student will <u>understand the importance of practicing responsible behavior</u> in appearance, cleanliness, punctuality and using a time clock.

<u>Section B: Introduction to Basic Maintenance and Groundskeeping as a Work Area</u> lists suggestions (14) for preparing the student to perform on the job in these specific areas. They include learning the job vocabulary, the appropriate clothing and other factors related to job preparation. In this section, worker qualities such as speed, tolerance and doing an acceptable job are also stressed as well as learning the meaning of responsibility.

<u>Section C: Specific Job Training in Basic Maintenance and Groundskeeping</u> lists the specific tasks (51) included in the program which the student might have to perform on the job in the areas of maintenance and groundskeeping.

Examples of tasks defined in Section C are:

C-1   The student will be able to <u>use a hand duster.</u>

C-2   The student will be able to <u>use a whisk broom</u> for cleaning draperies, slipcovers on furniture, furniture in general

C-3   The student will be able to <u>use a dustpan and counter brush</u> to pick up dust and other waste material.

C-4   The student will be able to use a <u>radiator brush</u> to dust in places that are too narrow for a <u>counter duster.</u>

This graduated progression of the student from less difficult to more difficult skill levels in a skill-training program is seen even more distinctly in the skills cluster approach of the Vocational Individual

1. INTRODUCTION

Assistance program in Eastlake, Ohio. The cluster concept is used in
each of the five vocational areas offered. They are arranged by ascending
levels of difficulty. Each student's progress is noted on a set of cards
and on a wall chart. For example, the curriculum in the custodial and
building and maintenance area has been divided into five clusters. The
first cluster concentrates on desired work and social behavior such as
personal cleanliness. The second cluster focuses on simple mopping
and cleaning. The third cluster progresses to more difficult cleaning
such as cleaning lavatories. The fourth cluster is more advanced. Students master waxing, stripping and minor plumbing. The fifth cluster
emphasizes independence on the job. As the student progresses through
the clusters, his performance is tracked on a set of cards. A slightly
different progress record is kept in the welding area. In this area, the
clusters focus on four types of welding. A progress record for each
student indicates the day the student began a particular step, the number
of days it took to finish the step, a grade for the final product and a running monthly average grade. Students must successfully complete one
task to advance to the next. If a student reaches a plateau, as determined
by the vocational teacher, the progress cards serve as a guide to the
tasks he can or cannot perform. This information is useful to the coun-
selor-evaluator if transfer to another area is being considered and to the
work-study coordinator for placement purposes.

The Keefe School Special Needs Program, although housed in a regular
vocational high school, and the Eastlake, Ohio Program both offer vocational preparation in classes attended only by handicapped students.
Several programs observed greatly augmented their resources for providing skill training by integrating students into primarily non-handicapped
vocational classes whenever possible. This approach is not possible, of
course, for all handicapped students. But it is desirable if for no other
reason than that more handicapped students can be served if fewer programs
and facilities must be established.

The Special Needs Program integrates handicapped students at the Calhoun
Area Vocational Center in Battle Creek, Michigan, to provide them with
specific skill training. Students requiring special assistance are referred
to the special needs team for remedial reading or math work or vocational
and personal counseling. A graduated skills cluster approach is used for
its integrated classes but supported by the special needs team. A research project developed ten individualized training packets for handicapped students. The packets are based on a modular approach and are
designed to build on success and to foster cooperation between vocational
and special education teachers (at the home school) in the program planning for and teaching of the handicapped. Once the student is placed in
an occupational cluster or subcluster program, teachers begin the actual
process of cooperative teaching. A series of instructional units is chosen
or developed for each student. Each instructional unit is based on entry-
level job tasks. Task sheets (instructional units) represent the basic tool
that teachers may use to plan, implement, and evaluate a cooperative
vocational education/special education program. Exhibit 5 in Appendix

C is a sample task sheet. The front side of the task sheet is composed of
four sections. The behavioral/task skills identify the specific mental
understandings or associations needed in the performance of the task as
well as the physical, manipulative activities associated with performing the
task. The instructional methods and materials portion is designed to
suggest specific teaching techniques, strategies and materials that have
been used effectively with handicapped students. The task-related competencies section identifies some specific learning readiness skills
associated with the task. The reverse side of the task sheet is designed
to help the special education teacher teach more effectively. The language
of the task and quantitative concepts provides a common ground for communication between the cooperating teacher and the vocational teachers. Suggestions and supportive instructional materials include a variety of suggested teaching activities--ideas, games or materials that may be used in
providing an effective and supportive link with vocational instruction.
Packets or "cluster guides" have been developed for ten occupational clusters: health occupations, food preparation, agriculture/national resources,
clothing and textile services, office and business occupations, distribution, construction, graphics and communications media, automotive and
power service and manufacturing.

The instructional units, modules, or clusters approach in an integrated
program is also used by Vocational Village in Portland, Oregon. Vocational Village uses an individualized instruction approach in which each
student works at his own pace toward achieving his objectives. This
approach is accomplished by means of a basic unit of instruction called
a job sheet. The job sheet is a description of a task the student must do.
It also details the specific activities encompassed in the task. Completing the activities listed in the job sheet requires from one to two hours.
Students work on the job sheet individually during the class period and the
teachers are able to provide individual attention to selected students at
this time. Job sheets are used exclusively in both the vocational and basic
education courses.

The Range of Occupational Opportunities

There is a wide range of occupational possibilities open to both mentally
and physically handicapped students. The Calhoun Area Vocational Center
offers 26 occupational areas for the students it serves. They include
normal, disadvantaged and handicapped. Students attend their home high
schools half a day for academic training and the Calhoun Center the other
half of the day for vocational training. Handicapped children are enrolled
in 20 of the 26 occupational areas.

In the period 1972-74, the handicapped children were enrolled as follows:
agricultural mechanics (2), air conditioning and refrigeration (1), auto
body repair (2), auto mechanics (9), building maintenance (15), carpentry
(5), child care (5), commercial art (2), cosmetology (1), drafting (1),
food service (15), graphic reproduction (1), institutional and domestic
service (18), landscaping, horticulture, and floriculture (4), marketing

and retailing (2), nurse's aide and male attendant (3), radio and TV repair
(2), secretarial and office practice (2), small engines repair (1) and
welding (5).

Depending on the capabilities of the handicapped group served, the possibilities are even wider than the above list indicates. The innovative
jewelry program at On-Campus Vocational Education in Los Angeles,
California, for deaf and orthopedically handicapped students was
developed by a special education teacher who had been operating a
jewelry-making business in her home. A class in jewelry-making was
begun, using the teacher's equipment and a buffer purchased with trading
stamps. After the program had operated for a year, the school district
purchased more jewelry-making equipment. Eight super 8 mm loop films
have been developed by the district to help train students in machine buf-
fing, flex shaft polishing, hand polishing, hand sawing, silver soldering,
wax processes, forging and setting stones. Most instruction is highly individualized, and special jigs and teaching techniques have been developed
to accommodate particular handicap conditions. Materials for projects
are generally paid for by the parents. The students produce rings, pen-
dants, tie clasps and other jewelry, many of which are sold to the public
for the price of the materials. According to the jewelry-making teacher,
skills taught in the class are similar to the skills required for many other
trades, including dental lab work, lock manufacturing, golf head casting,
aerospace and high technology assembly manufacture.

The Missoula Technical Center in Missoula, Montana serves a group of
handicapped students and adults integrated with regular vocational students.
More than 17 percent of the students have a handicap of some kind. They
include educable mentally retarded, emotionally disturbed, disabled,
crippled, visually handicapped, speech impaired, hard of hearing and other
health impaired. There are a number of multihandicapped students enrolled. The program is directed toward full time employment in a normal
work environment and has demonstrated the ability of some handicapped
students to perform skilled jobs if given the training and opportunity to
work. Handicapped students have received training in several advanced
vocational/occupational areas including aviation, business and office,
electromechanical, data processing, forestry, heavy equipment, small
engine repair, welding and road construction. The school uses a team
approach tailored to the individual. Students progress at their own rate
and handicapped students particularly are apt to try different programs
before they find a suitable one. This is encouraged as a valuable occupational experience. The coordinator of services to the handicapped and the
Center's staff use diversified methods of special help and educational
materials, including textbooks on cassettes, sound-on slide series and
close work arrangements with occupational therapists.

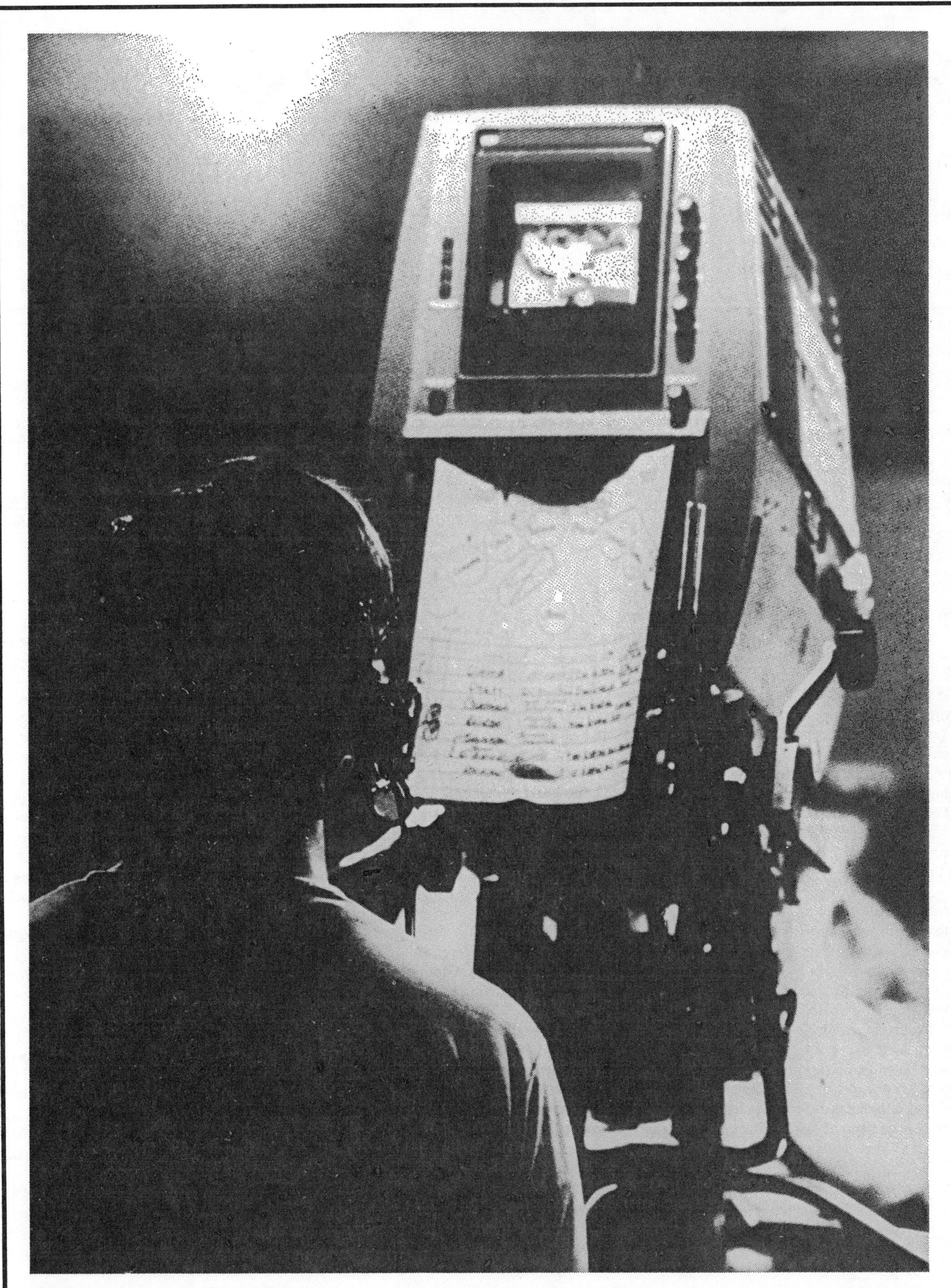

A Work Experience Program in Rural Areas

J. GARY HAYDEN

J. Gary Hayden is Special Education Regional Consultant in the East Metropolitan area of the Twin Cities, Minnesota.

Good work experience programs for handicapped youth are needed in rural areas. The components discussed in this program include planning work experience as part of a total career education program and developing a 2 year work experience program for the junior and senior years of high school. The program emphasizes working in the school during the first year to develop appropriate work habits and attitudes; completing a work evaluation between the first and second years to determine the student's occupational strengths; and working in a supervised, community based job during the second year to learn specific job skills.

■ Organizing meaningful work-study programs for handicapped youth living in rural areas presents a many faceted challenge. The limited number of students who qualify for the program, the limited number of professionals available to organize and operate the program, and the difficulty in locating appropriate community jobs head the list of problems to be overcome in meeting the challenge. Transportation, the bane of many good programs, creates additional stresses.

Solutions to the above problems can be found, however, and high quality work-study programs in rural areas can be organized. For such a program to be successful, the people involved must first commit themselves to the belief that career education for handicapped youth is vital.

COMPONENTS OF A WORK -STUDY PROGRAM

Most educators will nod their heads in agreement with the concept that career education is extremely important throughout every student's elementary and secondary school program. Difficulties may arise, however, when these same educators are asked to devote their energies to the difficult and time consuming task of actually implementing a good career education program.

Career education for all children must begin in the first years of school. At that level the child should begin to understand what work is, what his parents do, and that even classmates have school jobs such as picking up papers. The concept of career education grows and expands through high school to the point where career education becomes a major component of the student's education. Students graduating from any program, particularly a special education program, need to understand how to find and keep a job and how to get along with themselves and others. These goals are crucial in a career education program.

All high school students need to understand that work is important and is a legitimate use of time. Some students may not have a good parental example from which to learn the importance of work. Many students have to be taught that each person can be a productive, contributing member of society by working on a job. In addition, the high school program needs to schedule adequate school time to thoroughly survey the jobs available in the community and geographical area and to study what kinds of occupations are suitable for the students. Students also need to develop worthy uses of leisure time. They need to be counseled on their own aptitudes and interests.

The school guidance counselor and special education teacher both have a responsibility to work with the handicapped students in career education. The vocational rehabilitation counselor should also be part of the professional team providing services to the handicapped student. The culmination of this program is appropriate job training at the high school level.

These, then, are the important components of a work-study program for handicapped students. A work-study model incorporating these components has been developed and implemented in a rural Iowa county.

FIRST YEAR WORK EXPERIENCE

The actual work experience aspect of the Iowa career education program for handicapped youths began during the junior year of high school. Other school districts developing similar programs may want to start this work experience program earlier.

All students who were eligible to begin the work experience program were evaluated before the junior year of high school to determine the student's strengths and weaknesses and to find suitable school work stations for the child. The child's teacher, school psychologist, director of special education, vocational rehabilitation counselor, and regular school administrator were involved in this initial planning. The students were counseled in developing their own work plan. Each student's parents were scheduled for a conference during which they were informed of the work plan for their child. Parents' ideas about the school job, future jobs for their teenager, the school's plan, and ways these plans should be modified were discussed and used in planning.

During the junior year, each student was employed in the school, e.g., helping in the cafeteria, helping the janitor, washing towels, working in the bus barn, or helping the school librarian. The variety of jobs available in any program will depend on the job possibilities in the school and the imagination of those planning the employment.

A critical factor in the school work program is the student's supervision on the job. The only occasion a student's assignment had to be changed in the Iowa project resulted from lack of supervision and lack of enough work to keep the student busy. Only minimal problems occurred when the student's time was scheduled so that he was busy during the entire work period and when he knew he was being supervised.

Each student was scheduled to work 2 hours a day, with the school paying the student for his work. The student had to keep a time slip and turn it in to the school in order to be paid. In the Iowa project, the school requested a waiver from the Federal Wage and

Hour Division of the Department of Labor to pay below the minimum wage. It was felt that it would be better to begin the wage at a lower level so raises could be given to the student as he learned the job. In this way the improvement would be rewarded by higher wages.

The basic goal of the junior year work program was for each student to develop appropriate job habits and attitudes. It was hoped that the first year school employment would teach the student to get along with his supervisor, to be prompt, to be willing to listen and accept instruction, to follow directions, to work alone, to be neat and clean, and to accept criticism.

An evaluation form was completed at the end of the junior year (see Figure 1). This evaluation form should be discussed with the student to indicate how he is doing in the work program. It is also important to meet regularly with the student's job supervisor so that problems can be identified and solved as they arise. Initially, these discussions with the student and his supervisor should be held every 2 weeks. Later the meetings can be held monthly. In addition, the student's teacher can serve as a continual monitor, talking frequently to the student about his job.

The first year of work experience can be summarized as follows:
1. Evaluate the student to determine the best program for him.
2. Plan appropriate school employment for the first year.
3. Be sure the student is supervised on the job.
4. Emphasize appropriate job habits and attitudes rather than learning a particular occupation.
5. Continually monitor the progress of the student's program.

WORK EVALUATION

An important component of a total work experience program is work evaluation. This is a formal program assessing the student's occupational strengths and weaknesses and making appropriate recommendations on the types of occupations suitable for the student. Most work evaluation programs evaluate the areas of independent living skills, counsel on occupational preferences and personal growth, provide work samples to determine occupational skills in a number of vocational areas, and make student recommendations in the above areas.

The students attended the work evaluation center for 3 to 6 weeks in the spring or summer. Since the center was located 25 miles from the home school district, transportation was a major problem for this part of the program. Some students commuted every day and others stayed in a group living center during the work evaluation. This particular work evaluation center was administered by the Division of Vocational Rehabilitation, which also sponsored the group living facility.

At the work evaluation center, the student typically tries three or four different types of jobs so that the student's abilities and interests can be matched. Tests such as the General Aptitude Test Battery are administered to determine occupational strengths. Job recommendations are made based on all information available at the completion of the work evaluation program. These recommendations are used to plan the student's senior work experience.

SECOND YEAR WORK EXPERIENCE

The work program during the senior year of school was typically an out of school placement. Jobs held by the students included work in a nursing home, on an assembly line, in a manufacturing concern, as a service station attendant, as a janitor, and as a baker's assistant. The types of jobs available for any program will depend on the community itself.

1. INTRODUCTION

The basic goals of the senior year work experience include (a) learning a job skill that may be used after graduation, (b) learning to work independently on the job, and (c) continuing to develop positive personal habits and attitudes. The senior year work experience may be a training job that will terminate at the end of the school year, so that the work station can be used for another trainee the next year, or it may become a permanent job for the student who can gain the necessary job skills during his senior year. A combination of the two types of job stations can be used in a program, but there are many advantages for the student if he is able to continue in the same job after graduation. He will already know the job and the particular business, and this continuity can help the student adjust to the world of work after school. It presents the problem, however, of locating new training positions each year. Which method a school chooses will depend on the composition of the local area.

Four other points need to be made about the senior year work experience.

1. If a student is not working satisfactorily in his assigned job, the assignment should be changed to one where he can achieve success. A job station in which the student cannot function adequately is not a good work program and does not provide the student with the postschool skills he will need.
2. Some students are not ready for competitive employment during their senior year. For these students a more controlled work program in the school is preferable. Following the senior year those students who need further job training can get it through vocational rehabilitation programs or a work activity program in a sheltered setting.
3. Some students who perform adequately in a community job may still need further vocational training in a specialized field after high school graduation. This decision must be made on an individual basis.
4. All students in work programs need continual supervision. A regular schedule of supervision by the employer and by school personnel, including discussions with both the employer and employee, should be developed. The employer should use an evaluation form provided by the school (see Figure 2). This evaluation should emphasize work skills, industriousness, reliability, cooperation, appearance, and personality. This form differs from the form used during the first year of the work program by placing emphasis on work skills rather than job habits and attitudes.

ORGANIZATIONAL CONSIDERATIONS

Communication and Commitment

Communication is an extremely important aspect in any work experience program. Informal and formal discussions and conferences must be held to organize the work experience program. These conferences should include the superintendent of schools, principal, special education teacher, director of special education, school psychologist, school counselor, vocational rehabilitation counselor, and others who can assist in the program.

The career education program and work experience program should be discussed with community groups (e.g., Kiwanis, Lions, Chamber of Commerce, church groups, women's groups) to gain the groups' understanding and general support of the program. Many times these presentations will lead to specific contacts where an employer will offer a job station possibility.

Those planning such a program should also meet with potential employers at their convenience to fully explain the program. They should be sure the employer understands what the individual students can and cannot do, that daily on the job supervision is their responsibility as an employer, that special education personnel will offer regular consultation with the employer, and that the students must be paid for their work. The potential employer must also understand that no student will be continued in a job station where he cannot perform satisfactorily.

A great number of potential employer contacts must be made in order to find enough work stations. The program should be fully explained to all potential employers even though they may not have a job station to offer this year since they might have one next year.

FIGURE 1

WORK EXPERIENCE EVALUATION
First Year — School Job

NAME _______________________ DATE _______________

SUPERVISOR _______________________

Work factors	Excellent or always	Above average or usually	Average or occasionally	Below average or seldom	Poor or never
1. Gets along with employer, respects authority.					
2. Gets along with fellow workers.					
3. Is prompt on the job.					
4. Comes prepared to work.					
5. Is willing to listen and accept instruction.					
6. Remembers instructions, locations, etc.					
7. Follows directions or does what he is told.					
8. Works independently, can work alone.					
9. Observes safety rules and uses tools safely.					
10. Uses and cares for equipment properly.					
11. Does not waste time.					
12. Normally dresses properly.					
13. Is neat and clean.					
14. Shows pride in self.					
15. Accepts supervisory criticism.					
16. Can be trusted.					
17. Exercises control of emotions.					
18. Has pleasant facial expressions.					

COMMENTS:

FIGURE 2

WORK EXPERIENCE EVALUATION
Second Year — Community Job

NAME _______________________ DATE _______________

FIRM _______________________

SUPERVISOR _______________________

Work factors	Excellent or always	Above average or usually	Average or occasionally	Below average or seldom	Poor or never
Work Skills					
1 Is capable of doing work					
2 Has adequate work speed					
3 Has good safety habits					
4 Is thorough in work					
5 Corrects own mistakes					
6 Takes care of equipment					
7 Shows progress on job					
Industriousness					
1 Is a hard worker					
2 Works steadily					
3 Works unsupervised					
4 Shows initiative					
Reliability,					
1 Is punctual					
2 Has favorable attitude toward work					
3 Follows directions					
4 Assumes responsibility					
Cooperation,					
1. Works well with others					
2. Goes out of his way to help					
3. Sees things to be done					
4. Accepts instruction & criticism					
5. Asks for help when needed					
Appearance and Personality:					
1. Is cheerful					
2. Is polite					
3. Is well groomed					

COMMENTS

Some employers will initially say "No" to a job station but will later decide to participate when they understand the program better. Followup visits will be necessary after the potential employer has had time to think about it.

The Iowa program found it helpful for two persons to make these employer contacts. In this way two professionals, such as the director of special education and a vocational rehabilitation counselor, can work together to give a more complete description of the program. Organizing a work experience program requires considerable time and leg work. Numerous contacts and followup visits have to be made to develop the needed work stations.

The school and all employers must understand the financial commitment to the program. Students in the work programs, both in the school and in the community, must be paid. If needed, the school or business may apply for a minimum wage waiver. This will allow an increase in the child's wages which he can recognize as a reward for improved job performance. Employers should pay the student with their funds since the student is performing work for their business. The employer is more involved in and committed to the project if he pays the wages rather than letting the Division of Vocational Rehabilitation, the school, or a special fund assume that cost.

Parents must be kept informed and involved throughout the work program. Individual conferences should be held that fully explain the student's program. Parents should be encouraged to give ideas on potential occupations for their child.

It is helpful to form an advisory committee to make suggestions and recommendations regarding the total program and to serve as a public relations group. The committee can be composed of school personnel, special education personnel, employers, and parents. This gives the school a way of assisting community leaders and employers in promoting the program throughout the community.

Job Placement and Scheduling

Determining the best placement for a particular child can sometimes present a problem. Placement has to be based on the individual strengths of the student, but the community job placement does not have to be considered a lifelong placement. Present statistics indicate that most people change occupational fields three to five times during their lifetime. Numerous job changes are not uncommon regardless of the skills of the individual, and this applies to students in work experience programs as well. The job placement also does not need to be the one that will pay the most money to the student. More important for the student is that he can perform the job well, get along with fellow workers, and be happy in the job.

Transportation can create problems for the total work experience program. Many times transportation problems force the school to be creative in scheduling the work program. The school may have to work around a transportation schedule rather than fighting it, scheduling the work experience to fit the transportation schedule. The student's work experience should take precedence over school classes. The work program should be scheduled for the time it is most feasible and when the job needs to be done, rather than when it best fits into the school schedule.

The student should receive a high school diploma upon completion of the work experience program. A high school diploma signifies the completion of a prescribed course of studies. The work experience program meets this criteria. It signifies that the handicapped student has worked as hard to complete his program as other students have worked to complete theirs, with completion being based on what is appropriate for the individual student. The work experience program recognizes the need for individual programing for school students regardless of ability or handicap.

CONCLUDING COMMENTS

Establishing a good work experience program takes time and patience. Numerous contacts with school personnel, parents, students, and community employers must be made. Communication, job supervision, and continual planning are essential. Through these efforts, however, a meaningful work experience program can be developed which will greatly assist handicapped students in finding and succeeding in competitive employment after graduation.

RECOGNIZING THE NEED FOR CAREER AND VOCATIONAL EDUCATION FOR THE HANDICAPPED

At the present time, few educators are prepared for the new emphasis on career ad vocational education. On the college level, programs of teacher training in career and vocational education are either very new or nonexistent.

In implementing career and vocational education programs for the handicapped, school personnel are needed who recognize the potential of handicapped students and the great possibilities of career and vocational education programs.

If many parents, teachers, school administrators and community leaders are dissatisfied with the educational situation in this country, steps should be taken to change the present structure. Judging by the law suits being brought against many school systems to date, the courts may be forcing change upon the education structure.

Public Law 94-142 has forced attention on the potential of the handicapped and the need for individualized programs. A logical step in preparing the handicapped to realize full potential is a career education program, complete with competent school staff and support personnel.

If educators are to provide an appropriate and equal education for the handicapped, it would seem that a career education program would help ensure individualization, an environment without restriction, and the opportunity to realize one's potential.

If all handicapped children could acquire a "marketable skill," a skill that would enable each child to someday work to his highest possible ability, then the special educators of this country could finally acknowledge a relevant curriculum and successful product of special education--meaningful careers for the handicapped.

The following articles examine the need for trained personnel in career and vocational education for the handicapped. Also recognized is the responsibility to the handicapped that is carried by special educators, and how that responsibility relates to career and vocational education.

PERSONNEL PREPARATIONS FOR CAREER EDUCATION OF HANDICAPPED STUDENTS

BY

DONN E. BROLIN, DONALD J. MCKAY AND LYNDA L. WEST[1]

Two new movements have emerged in education in recent years to alter the career preparation and work role of American educators. The first movement, career education, is challenging educators to focus their curriculum and instruction on the centrality of life roles in society (Keller, 1972). Career education has emerged because several philosophical, economic, social and legislative issues have highlighted the lack of a comprehensive and satisfactory utilization of school, community and family resources to facilitate the career development needs of today's students.

The second movement is the right to an appropriate and equal education for *all* American children including "the handicapped". In the case of handicapped students, the emphasis on appropriate educational services and the emphasis on career education have created a need for American educators to acquire additional competencies in order to deal more effectively with these students so that a greater proportion will attain a satisfactory level of social, personal and vocational adjustment. Career education holds the promise for best meeting the pressing life needs of handicapped students.

A CONCEPTUALIZATION OF CAREER EDUCATION

Unlike many professional workers who conceive career education as preparation primarily for work, we believe it should consist of preparation for all aspects of successful community living. The term "Career"

---

[1]Dr. Brolin is Associate Professor, Dr. McKay is Assistant Professor and Ms. West is Research Associate, Department of Counseling and Personnel Services, University of Missouri-Columbia. They served as special editors for this issue of JCE.

"Personnel Preparations for Career Education of Handicapped Students," Donn E. Brolin, Donald J. McKay, Lynda L. West, Vol. 3, No. 3, Winter, 1977.

connotes many *settings* -- home, school, occupation, community; many
roles -- student, worker, consumer, citizen, family member; and many
events -- job entry, marriage, and retirement (Gysbers and Moore, 1973).
Thus, "Career" connotes one's role not just as a producer (or worker)
but as a learner, consumer, citizen, family member, and social-political
human being (Gordon, 1973). From this perspective career education is
a complete educational concept, focuses on all phases of life, is
education over the life span, is open and continuous, involves all education staff, is community-based education, and is accountable education
(Gysbers, 1975). It systematically coordinates all school, family and
community components together to facilitate each individual's potential
for economic, social and personal fulfillment. Career education, so
conceptualized, can be a vehicle educators are seeking to meet the
needs of handicapped and other students and serve as the means for
accommodating them into the ongoing educational processes.

We believe there are twenty-two career education competencies that
handicapped students must acquire before they leave the educational
program. These competencies can be classified under three curriculum
areas: daily living, personal-social and occupational skills (Brolin,
1974). Therefore, academic instruction should be directed toward
developing these skills (Table I).

If career education is to be implemented, several changes must be
initiated. There must be the active cooperation and involvement of
both school and non-school personnel (i.e., parents, business and industry workers, community agency representatives). The total curriculum
needs to be sequenced from elementary to post-secondary. Elementary and
secondary personnel must coordinate their efforts to provide sequentially
for the learning of each competency. Some handicapped students may
have to go beyond the traditional period of time allotted in a secondary program. Some students may need an appropriately designated post-
secondary program, thus fixing the responsibility on the educational
system to assure that students acquire essential competencies deemed
for community living and working.

TABLE I

CAREER EDUCATION COMPETENCIES*

____

CURRICULUM AREA AND COMPETENCY

____

DAILY LIVING SKILLS

1. Managing Family Finances
2. Selecting, Managing and Maintaining a Home
3. Caring for Personal Needs
4. Raising Children, Family Living
5. Buying and Preparing Food
6. Buying and Caring for Clothing
7. Engaging in Civic Activities
8. Utilizing Recreation and Leisure
9. Getting Around in the Community

PERSONAL-SOCIAL SKILLS

10. Achieving Self-Awareness
11. Acquiring Self-Confidence
12. Achieving Socially Responsible Behavior
13. Maintaining Good Interpersonal Skills
14. Achieving Independence
15. Achieving Problem-Solving Skills
16. Communicating Adequately with Others.

OCCUPATIONAL GUIDANCE & PREPARATION

17. **Knowing** & Exploring Occupational Possibilities
18. Selecting and Planning Occupational Choices
19. Exhibiting Appropriate Work Habits and Behaviors
20. Exhibiting Sufficient Physical & Manual Skills
21. Obtaining a Specific Occupational Skill
22. Seeking, Securing, and Maintaining Employment

____

INSTRUCTIONAL RESPONSIBILITIES FOR CAREER EDUCATION

Implementing effective career education requires appropriate re-directing of traditional teacher/counselor roles and greater involvement from parents, community agencies and industries by coordinating and integrating services to meet each student's career education needs. Special educators can be particularly helpful to other educators with inservice assistance, methods and materials consultation, modifying or developing materials and by sharing relevant information about the student. The special education teacher must provide specific classroom instruction for certain students when it is more appropriate than

____

*Brolin (1974)

being provided in regular classes or community services. Tutoring and
monitoring student progress are other services needed from special education personnel.

Most regular classroom teachers and counselors can assist many
handicapped students acquire several comptencies. If career education
goals are clearly delineated and assistance from special education
teachers is readily available, most handicapped students can be integrated ito a variety of regular classes and programs. A good inservice
program and career education plan will clearly identify these instructional responsibilities.

The family can contribute to the student's learning if they
receive the necessary guidance and support from school personnel. The
home is a fertile ground for teaching personal-social, daily living
and occupational skills. Parents can assist their children by providing specific hands-on responsibilities, developing career awareness,
teaching specific skills, and providing a secure psychological environment where self-confidence and independence can be adequately developed.
Family members should also be encouraged to visit the school and participate in class activities.

The family can contribute to the student's learning if they receive the necessary guidance and support from school personnel. The
home is a fertile ground for teaching personal-social, daily living and
occupational skills. Parents can assist their children by providing
specific hands-on responsibilities, developing career awareness,
teaching specific skills, and providing a secure psychological environment where self-confidence and independence can be adequately developed.
Family members should also be encouraged to visit the school and participate in class activities.

An effective and comprehensive school-community relationship will
greatly enhance the implementation of a meaningful career education
curriculum for handicapped and other students. Career education requires the effective use of community resources for students to adequately explore and be prepared for the real world.

PRESERVICE TRAINING

The two major modes of obtaining professional teacher training are via preservice and inservice education. Unfortunately, higher education has just begun to respond to the career education movement. Some special education teacher training programs have initiated one or two courses and a few others are beginning to emphasize career education. Recently, graduate training programs in vocational special needs have been instituted in some vocational education departments in response to the need that vocational educators be better trained to educate the handicapped and disadvantaged.

University faculty are beginning to receive training concerning handicapped students' needs through the Dean's Mainstreaming Grants with assistance from the Leadership Training Institute at the University of Minnesota and also through the Midwest Retool Consortium on Career Education for the Handicapped at the University of Kansas. Both of these projects, funded by the U. S. Office of Education's Bureau of Education for the Handicapped, are excellent attempts to get educators informed and inclined to initiate curricular changes. In addition, two national workshops for vocational educators, special educators and school counselor educators at the University of Illinois were conducted in 1976 to stimulate inservice and preservice models for career/vocational education at their universities. A similar workshop for other universities is being planned at The University of Kentucky.

University training programs need to change many of their current practices for career education to become a reality for handicapped students. They need to hire faculty who have the interest and expertise in career education. In addition, we suggest the following as changes needed in teacher and counselor training programs:

---Better orientation and selection procedures for admitting students in each department. Special education should admit not only those who wish to teach traditional academics to children but also those who would be interested and willing to work with all ages in career development activities such as vocational assessment, counseling, job seeking skills training and job placement. Vocational education and counseling departments should enlist students interested and willing to teach and counsel handicapped as well as regular students.

---Orientation of special education faculty to the career education concept and the changing roles of special educators. They must learn how to re-direct the training of future special education teachers for inservicing other personnel about handicapped students, assiting regular teachers in mainstreaming, providing instructional materials, consultation, working with parents, developing community resources, monitoring student progress and directing vocational preparation activities.

---Orientation of vocational education faculty to the importance
of their students being prepared to teach the handicapped within
a mainstreaming and career education context. They must re-direct
their curriculum so students learn about the nature of handicapped individuals, their learning characteristics, their vocational
·potential, methods of vocational assessment, instructional methods
and materials, and community resources. In this way, the necessary
positive attitudes to teach these students can be acquired.

---Orientation of counseling faculty about the career guidance and
counseling needs of handicapped and the school counselors role in
meeting these needs, particularly in the personal-social and
occupational guidance and preparation areas. Counseling departments must re-direct their curricula so that prospective counselors know more about the nature of handicapped students and
appropriate diagnostic, vocational and counseling techniques,
occupational information, training, resources and parent counseling needs and techniques.

Other departments in schools of education must provide opportunities for their students to learn basic career education concepts and
methodologies and how they can be applied to both handicapped and
non-handicapped students. This should include: how to relate one's
subject matter to its career implications for career awareness,
exploration , guidance, and skills development; how the home, community
and business establishments can be used for such learning; how to
assume a shared responsibility with other members of the school community in the students' career development; and how the school atmosphere can be democratically oriented to provide for the total career
education needed by handicapped students. A greater understanding of
the characteristics and vocational potential of handicapped persons
is vitally needed by all educators.

Most university training programs are not presently meeting the
needs of school systems which seek to employ personnel who can effectively meet the career education needs of handicapped students. If
these needs are to be met, then meaningful cooperative relationships
must be developed between special education and other university
departments. Philosophies must be changed and curricula redesigned
so that well-qualified personnel are prepared. Earlier exposure to
handicapped students, more field experiences in sheltered workshops,
institutions, work-study programs, and a focus on developing communication and interpersonal skills will assist future teachers and counselors to be more effective with all students.

INSERVICE TRAINING

Because of rapid changes transpiring within the society which directly influence the educational system, inservice education must be used to upgrade existing school staff's competencies. This need is supported by Yafeh (1972) who cautions that there is *no* preservice training today which will prepare educators for all the tasks they will encounter or provide professional knowhow required in today's work role.

Inservice education, to be successful, must provide a structure to initiate educational change effectively whenever such change is necessary. Change is a process, and, according to Miles, (1964) it is "willed rather than natural, planned rather than haphazard and specific rather than general". Effective educational change should consider using a management approach. This approach provides definite direction, clarity, and specific leadership by constantly advocating implementation of the desired innovation.

The inservice education philosophy goes directly to the "grass roots" level. As Mohr (1971) states, "change must begin at the teacher level" to be successful. Teachers must actively participate in the decisions which directly affect their occupational roles if permanent change is to occur. Inservice education, using this approach, is rapidly gaining in popularity as an education process designed to assist educators who must cope with changes and also improve their professional competencies.

Inservice education provides professional regeneration, i.e., conveys new knowledge or information, develops new educational skills, and fosters new positive attitudes that intensify personal commitment and involvement. Teacher preparation must be continuous, sequential and terminate only at the conclusion of the individual's educational career, since it is not possible to base educational preparation totally upon a preservice training model.

The main strength of inservice training comes from its recognition of the classroom teacher as someone of central importance. This feeling permeates the general structure of the program and provides additional direction in developing positive meaningful experience for teachers.

In the final analysis, the success of any educational delivery system is the result of efforts expended by classroom teachers. The role of inservice education is to eliminate identified deficiencies and acquire the additional teaching competencies necessary to upgrade these educators.

Several inservice education models are presently being developed to deal with the career needs of handicapped students. At the University of Missouri--Columbia, a staff inservice training model is being developed and fieldtested (Project PRICE) as an example of current efforts to create meaningful career education inservice training for school personnel. The foundation of the PRICE inservice model is focused on a competency-based curriculum which can be conducted by a school district's own personnel.

The following represent what we consider critical components of an effective inservice training delivery system: effective trainers, a viable workshop format and processes, development and implementation of a career education plan and appropriate evaluation procedures.

EFFECTIVE TRAINERS

The success of an inservice training program depends upon the individuals conducting the workshops. The most important characteristic to effective inservice is a well-organized team of leaders, i.e., a cadre of trainers. It is essential that these trainers be well-prepared for conducting successful workshops. They must be organized and able to divide responsibilities among themselves from session to session so there is a smooth transition throughout each workshop.

The inservice training team must be composed of educators of complementary talents for example, a counselor, regular and special education teachers and administrators representing participating schools. Using a team of local trainers, rather than outside consultants, provides dedicated leadership within the school district, better assuring that the goals of the inservice program will continue after the initial training has ended. The trainers must be personable, enthusiastic, and accepting individuals who can make effective presentations, answer participant questions and appropriately bring satisfactory closure to discussions. It is important for the trainers to make participants understand the importance of their involvement and the expected outcomes from the training. Participant involvement in decision-making and problem-solving helps develop a good team relationship. This team relationship is the structure which allows participants to work together in achieving workshop goals.

Trainers must keep participants informed of each workshop session's objectives while functioning as small group facilitators. They lead small group discussions, problem solving sessions, and keep the participants on task throughout the workshop. Some of the desirable human relations skills necessary for effective leadership are: a sense of humor, enthusiasm, confidence, ability to listen closely to every group member and provide the necessary feedback responses. It may be necessary for the trainer to clarify and summarize the group's concerns on certain topics so that a satisfactory group consensus can be realized. Some questions that a trainer should be concerned about are: Did I make the participants feel welcome? Was the atmosphere positive? Did I participate in all activities? Was I enthusiastic? Was I negative? Did all group members participate? Were any participants excluded? Did anyone dominate the group? Did anyone withdraw from the rest of the group?

The trainer's effect on the atmosphere of the workshop cannot be underestimated. If a trainer neglects to fulfill his or her responsibility or is negative about the philosophy of the program, participants will sense this and the workshops will fail miserably. Without the atmosphere of "acceptance", "working together for a common cause", "we're all in this together", and "cooperation", participants at inservice workshops will probably not follow through with the degree of commitment and dedication needed to effect significant change after the workshops.

VIABLE INSERVICE FORMAT AND PROCESSES

The success of any inservice program will be enhanced if the wealth of experience of the participants is utilized. Through discussions, much learning can take place for both trainers and participants. These discussion groups facilitate exchange of ideas, working through problems and possible solutions. Berelson and Steiner (1964, p. 353) support this approach by stating:

> Active discussion by a small group to determine goals, to
> choose methods of work, to reshape operations, or to
> solve other problems is more effective in changing group
> practices than in separate instruction of the individual
> members, external requests or the imposition of new
> practices by superior authority--more effective, that is,
> for bringing about better motivation and support of the
> change and better implementation and productivity of the
> new practice.

In our experience with suburban and urban school districts, active small group discussion is a particular strength of inservice programs. Through the exchange of information in small groups, dedication and commitment by participants can promote the cause and philosophy of the inservice program.

The format and structure of the inservice program must be designed to accomplish the major goals and objectives of the inservice program. The program can be structured in a variety of ways depending on what is the most feasible for each particular school district. It could be divided into a semester course which meets after school once a week for two-three hours. This flexible approach is accomplished by designing the program into specific training modules.

The next consideration is to select topics of relevance to the participants. This should be based on a Needs Assessment of the school's personnel, relative to career education for handicapped students. The present Project PRICE Inservice model of four days of inservice training includes the following:

1. The first workshop consists of: (1) overview of the inservice program; its goals and objectives and expected outcome; (2) group process techniques which will be used throughout the series; (3) nature of handicapping conditions; (4) career education; and (5) appropriate educational programming. The purpose of the first workshop is to lay the foundations for the inservice program by providing participants the opportunity to build a teamwork relationship, understand and discuss the issues, and to develop a positive attitude about helping handicapped students. It initiates an awareness of the problem and the possible solutions which depend upon individual teachers, parents, and community representatives.

2. The second workshop consists of: (1) classroom strategies for teaching handicapped students; (2) writing instructional units for teaching the identified Competencies; (3) instructional resources and materials

available for teaching the competencies; (4) teaching personal-social skills; and (5) teaching daily living and occupational skills. The purpose of this workshop is to emphasize the more specific how-to-do-it details for working with handicapped students. This workshop stresses student competency development and the importance of utilizing a variety of materials, resources, methods, and techniques so that *all* students might acquire these skills.

3. The third workshop includes: (1) a panel of community representatives to explain the role of their agency and the assistance it can provide teachers and students; (2) a panel discussion by parents of handicapped students; (3) establishing goals and objectives for a career education plan for each school; (4) identifying instructional roles and responsibilities of the participants for teaching handicapped students; and (5) assessment of students competency level. The purpose of this workshop is to begin the process of identifying how the participants will contribute in the career education of handicapped students. This is the beginning of an individual committment toward developing a comprehensive career education plan for each school.

4. The final workshop includes: (1) a review of data compiled and analyzed in the third workshop, i.e., goals and instructional responsibilities; (2) an identification of the resources and assistance the participants feel they will need in order to accomplish their career education goals; (3) program evaluation procedures to explain to the participants why and how to evaluate their career education activities; and (4) a plan of action following the workshops which will result in the final development and implementation of a career education program for handicapped students in each school. The purpose of this workshop is to bring together participants who will carry through with the plans they have formulated. It is the beginning of an ongoing process which a task force continues. The process will result in a career education plan for handicapped students that the district can put into action.

DEVELOPMENT OF A CAREER EDUCATION PLAN

The impact and significance of inservice training will be minimal unless something very definitive is accomplished by the participants and put into practice shortly thereafter. Effective inservice efforts permit workshop participants to assume a major role in determining how career education concepts can be infused into curriculum and their specific roles in the instructional processes.

Thus, besides developing more positive attitudes about handicapped persons and learning new information about handicaps, career education, instructional techniques, and resources and materials, the inservice model should allow a considerable period of time for developing a career education plan that each school can implement the next semester. To achieve this, the following are recommended:

--Organize a career education steering committee prior to conducting the inservice workshops. This committee should represent the K-12 continuum and a variety of disciplines.

-- Organize a special education task force to reflect the same general range of counselors, teachers, administrators and community representatives comprising the steering committee.

-- Identify specific goals in programming for handicapped students. These goals should be related to instruction, community involvement and administrative matters. They may be modified later by administrative and workshop participants.

-- Gain endorsement of the goals from the central steering committee and central administration to insure the commitment of the district leadership. These goals should reflect the perceived direction and goals of the district.

-- Design an inservice training program to meet the goals that have been agreed upon. Workshop details such as length, cost, materials needed, location, professional credit, time period, trainers, persons to be selected for training, substitutes, etc. need to be worked out and presented to the central steering committee and administration for approval.

-- Conduct a student competency assessment study to assist in determining curriculum modifications and emphasis needed for the new career education curriculum.

-- Conduct the inservice workshops for attitude and knowledge development. The task force and/or certain effective individuals should assume the role of workshop trainers. The career education plan should provide for considerable participant involvements and decision-making regarding curriculum changes.

-- Record and analyze input received from the workshops and develop further needed to develop the career education plan, e.g., examine programs, courses, services and facilities available or needed.

-- Prepare a career education plan for each school involved which includes: goals and objectives, instructional responsibilities, instructional action plan, staffing needs, course changes and additions, facilities needed, further inservice training needs, instructional resources and material needs, budget requirements, parent and community resources needs, evaluation plan.

-- Present plan to former workshop participants for their review, suggestions and ultimate approval. After modifications present to central steering committee, then to central administration and school board for approval.

-- Initiate action on preparatory components of the plan following
approval, e.g., ordering equipment and materials, preparing
facilities, establishing cooperative relationships, informing
parents, etc.

The development and implementation of an effective career education

plan for the handicapped is a complex, extensive task requiring extra

effort and the combined efforts of a great many people.

APPROPRIATE EVALUATION PROCEDURES

Innovative approaches, such as Project PRICE, which provide school

staff with new competencies as well as developing and implementing a

career education curriculum are concerned with designing an effective

evaluation/management system. This system's approach to program

appraisal assures than an improved career education program for

handicapped students becomes a reality. A systematic evaluation scheme

to analyze, assess, monitor and manage the staff development model is

vital to inservice program success. The evaluation component in essence,

determines whether the inservice training did indeed make a difference

for handicapped students, school staff, processes and school programs.

The formative-summative evaluation scheme advocated by Scriven

(1967) has gained wide acceptance for evaluating educational innovations

and can be used effectively for evaluating inservice programs. Forma-

tive (process) and summative (program) evaluation, according to Scriven,

should include judgements and not just descriptions of procedures and

outcome.

The formative and summative evaluation components can be further

delineated in a manner similar to the model advocat d by Glass (1972).

The formative component includes both *baseline* and transaction evaluative

information while the summative component is referred to as *outcome*

information. This approach clearly delineates specific criteria areas

for appraisal purposes. These categories are needed to systematically

assess large inservice programs if the design approaches any significant

magnitude.

Baseline information is gathered about all significant conditions

existing prior to implementing the inservice education program. These

data are used to establish a reference point which provides a basis

for making honest terminal judgements regarding improved school staff, program development, or program implementation. This method was used successfully in the PRICE staff development model, by developing several baseline assessment instruments (McKay, 1976).

Transaction information is derived from the succession of all activities comprising the inservice instruction and development/implementation plan. Assessments should be planned at various time intervals during the inservice program so additions and deletions can be made to maximize program outcome success. These data should emphasize the functional aspects of the inservice program, inservice organization, instructional strategies and implementation progress.

The outcome information is concerned with the terminal worth of the inservice program. Data gathered in this category will include such things as immediate and long-range effects, curriculum impact, student competency attainment, cost effectiveness, and program side effects evaluation. Program side effects include any phenomena which happened during the inservice program lifespan and were not included in the stated program goals and objectives. Outcome data provides the major rationale for allowing decisions to be made regarding the continuation, rejection or modification of the inservice format.

These three evaluation components; baseline, transaction and outcome, should provide the needed structure to analyze collecting data in such areas as: needs assessment, pretests to establish participant entry level competencies, pretests to establish entry level student competency, processes and teaching strategy alteration, terminal effects of the inservice program including participant and student performance, and school staff, parents, community and student satisfaction with the functioning career education program. A diverse approach in gathering input and assessment data from several sources provide a global methodology for evaluating an educational program. This is very much in line with and strongly recommended by formative-summative evaluation model designers.

CONCLUSION

If career education is to become fully implemented throughout this country, present and future school personnel must be trained more appropriately than they are now. Inservice and preservice models are being developed to meet this need and will soon be available. Institutions of higher learning must assume a leadership role in this endeavor and must work closely with local and state education agencies if career education is to become a reality for handicapped students. Handicapped students must have a more appropriate and humanistic education if they are to be successful in today's rapidly changing and complex society. Presently, the majority of handicapped citizens are either unemployed or underemployed. This problem will not exist if personnel preparation programs make the necessary changes so that school systems could provide a career education curriculum. Career education requires a truly mean meaningful interdisciplinary approach to educating students. Let us meet this challenge.

REFERENCES

Berelson, Bernard and Gary A. Steiner, *Human Behavior: an Inventory of Scientific Findings*. New York: Harcourt, Brace and World, Inc., 1964.

Brolin, Donn E, *Programming Retarded in Career Education*. Working Paper No. 1, University of Missouri-Columbia, September, 1974.

Glass, G. V., "The generations of evaluation models" in P.M. Taylor and D.M. Conley (ed.) *Readings in Curriculum evaluation*. Dubuque, Iowa: Wm. C. Brown and Co., 1972.

Gordon, E., Broadening the Concept of Career Education. In McClure, L. and C. Buan (eds) *Essays on Career Education*. Portland, Oregon: Northwest Regional Education Laboratory, 1973.

Gysbers, Norman, *Career Education*. In Donn E. Brolin (ed.) *Proceedings of Project PRICE Trainers' Workshop*. Working Paper No. 5, University of Missouri-Columbia, July 1975.

Gysbers, Norman and Earl J. Moore, Career Conscious Individual Model. *Life Career Development: a Model*. University of Missouri-Columbia, Spring, 1973.

Keller, Louise, J., *Career Education inservice guide*. Morristown, N.J.: General Learning Corporation, 1972.

McKay, Donald J., *Evaluation report for the second operational year of a fecerally funded project for preparing school personnel to accomodate EMR students in career education programs: Project PRICE*. University of Missouri-Columbia, June, 1976.

Miles, Mathen B. (ed.), *Innovation in education*. New York: Bureau of Publications, Teacher's College Columbia University, 1964.

Mohr, Paul, *Current research and development efforts in inservice training and curriculum planning*. Washington, D.C. U. S. Department of Health, Education and Welfare, Office of Education, 1971.

Scriven, Michael, "The methodology of evaluation" in R. Tyler (ed.) *Perspectives of curriculum evaluation*. Chicago: AERA Monograph Series on Education, #1, Rand McNally & Co., 1967.

Yafeh, Immuel, *A new look at continuing education (or inservice training) of educational workers*. Washington, D.C. U.S. Department of Health, Education and Welfare, U.S. Office of Education, 1972.

Career Education: A Survey of Teacher Preparation Institutions

PAMELA GILLET

Abstract: In order to assess the current status of teacher preparation in career education, questionnaires were sent to institutions of higher learning having a degree program in special education. The results of the survey showed that even with mandated legislation and the present emphasis at the federal level on career education for all children, the need for teacher preparation in the area of career education for the exceptional child is not being met. However, the majority of schools surveyed that did not have such a course offering felt that career education for the exceptional child was an advisable area to be covered. The responses to the questionnaire yielded content areas and objectives for proposed courses in career education for the exceptional child.

PAMELA GILLET is Assistant Director, Northwest Suburban Special Education Organization, Palatine, Illinois.

IF schools are to assume the responsibility for the education of exceptional children through the high school years, then teachers of exceptional children at all school levels need to be trained to provide career education for the exceptional child. Optimally, this training should occur at the colleges and universities where teachers receive their initial education or in-service training.

In an article entitled, "Career Education Needs of Secondary Educable Students," Donn Brolin (1973) presented the results of a survey which indicated that a greater emphasis was needed to equip teachers with skills for vocational preparation of exceptional children.

A Survey on Current Status

In order to assess the current status of teacher preparation in the area of career education, questionnaires were sent to 125 institutions of higher education that offered degree programs in special education. Followup procedures were initiated after 3 weeks. There were 95 respondents to the survey; 28 from private and 68 from public institutions (73% of the total institutions queried). From those institutions responding, course syllabi and bibliographies of suggested readings were obtained.

The results of this questionnaire showed that even with mandated legislation and the present emphasis at the federal level on career education for all children, the need for teacher preparation in the area of career education for the exceptional child is still not being met.

Extent of Course Offerings in Career Education

Only 3 of the private schools and 17 of the state schools responding did have a course offering in career education for exceptional children. Of those courses being offered, syllabi indicated that the primary emphasis was in mental retardation and/or the habilitative aspect of career education.

In half of the schools that offered these courses, students could graduate with a special education major without ever taking the course in career education. When a course in career education was required, it was placed solely in a sequence of courses involving an emphasis on mental retardation. Exception to this pattern occurred in only two special education departments—one required it of all special education majors enrolled in the high school sequence; the other required it only for rehabilitation counseling majors.

The majority of those schools surveyed that did not have such a course offering felt that career education for the exceptional child was an advisable area to be covered in the course sequence—mostly on an elective basis. Of all departments responding, 10 indicated that they definitely intended to offer such a course in the future; 29 had no plans for offering the course; and 48 were undetermined as to this action.

Content Areas for a Proposed Course

The responses to the questionnaire yielded areas of content and objectives for a proposed course in career education for the exceptional child. All respondents were asked to list some important areas of content for such a course. Fourteen did not make any suggestions, but the remainder suggested the following as important content areas:

1. Sequentially developed objectives, both academic and vocational, for a career education program for grades 1 through 12.
2. Stages of occupational development resulting in occupational choice.
3. Evaluation procedures and techniques for assessing job readiness and work performance on job stations.
4. Materials usable in a career education program for grades 1 through 12.
5. Components of a work-study program: job analysis, task analysis, job placement, types of jobs, kinds of work-study programs.
6. Personnel roles involved in a career education program.
7. Outside agency involvement in the career education program.

Objectives for a Proposed Course

The respondents were also asked to specify objectives for a course on career education for exceptional children. The 95 respondents contributed to the course objective suggestions that follow:

1. To enable the prospective teacher in developing a systematic approach to implement a career education program from early childhood through young adulthood, encompassing academic subject orientation, vocational content, and actual work experience.
2. To give the prospective teacher a general knowledge of the theories of career development.
3. To acquaint the prospective teacher with methodology, activities, and materials needed to conduct the academic, social-personal, and vocational components of a career education program from early childhood through young adulthood.
4. To assist the prospective teacher in developing a competency based checklist for the important curriculum areas that have relevance to vocational adjustment.
5. To assist the prospective teacher in becoming aware of the types of jobs in which these students are able to function and a knowledge of the job cluster to which they belong.
6. To assist the prospective teacher in identifying general as well as specific skills using task analysis for the purpose of instruction or job modification.
7. To assist the prospective teacher in developing the procedure for establishing, organizing, and maintaining a work-study program by using the employers of community businesses, outside agency services, and sheltered workshops.
8. To assist the prospective teacher in using the techniques of vocational and personal counseling to assist the student in understanding his or her potential and limitations so that the student can participate in the constructive planning of his or her vocational program.
9. To assist the prospective teacher in developing an awareness of the job role and duties of a work-study coordinator.
10. To assist the prospective teacher in developing techniques for assessing job readiness for work placement as well as work performance on the actual job.
11. To assist the prospective teacher in understanding the implications of the Vocational Rehabilitation Amendments and other state and federal laws pertaining to career education for the exceptional child.
12. To enable the prospective teacher to conduct a followup study of graduates of the career education program.

The respondents of those programs having the proposed course offering emphasized the preparation of the teacher for conducting work-study programs and relating the academic and social development phases of the special education curriculum to career orientation. Those colleges not having a course emphasized the need for a sequentially developed program from elementary through high school years.

The results of the study indicated that the majority of chairpersons believed career education was an important course offering for the preparation of special education teachers.

Proposed Courses in Career Education

From the survey, it appears to be necessary to assist teachers in developing skills to propose, implement, operate, and evaluate career education programs for exceptional children. The first course should present the basic principles to be considered when developing a career education program for exceptional children, which would cover the content areas and objectives reported in the results of this survey. The second course should use the practicum approach of having students design units of study for career education in their area of specialization, analyze a job into its component tasks, design a job training program, critique available commercial materials that could be used in a career education program, work with outside agencies and community employers, and counsel students in the area of occupational choice. In colleges that want to include this career component in teacher training but cannot offer an entire course on this, information pertaining to the career education concept should be specified as a definite part of existing methods and materials courses. Also, a 1 to 2 week summer workshop could be organized in special education departments to develop the concept of career programing for exceptional children. This workshop format would be a far more intensive approach than offering career programing as part of a methods course and yet cover the career education area without designing a new course.

With these results; the results of Brolin's prior study; the current emphasis of the US Department of Health, Education, and Welfare on career education for the regular child; and the existence of mandated legislation of Public Law 94-142 to educate exceptional children through the age of 21, career education for the exceptional child appears to be an important element to be included in teacher preparation programs thus allowing teachers to meet the occupational needs of *all* children.

Reference

Brolin, D. Career education needs of secondary educable students. *Exceptional Children*, 1973, *39*, 623.

PERSONNEL PREPARATIONS FOR VOCATIONAL PROGRAMMING OF SPECIAL NEEDS STUDENTS

BY
L. A. PHELPS AND G. M. CLARK[1]

INTRODUCTION

Preparing personnel to meet the vocational programming needs of handicapped and disadvantaged learners has begun to emerge as a significant priority in both the fields of vocational education and special education. The shifting of societal concerns, as reflected in favorable human rights litigation and new federal legislation has caused the educational community to re-examine the educational and employment potentials of persons who have unique educational needs. Within the past two years, the increased need for addressing these developments in the training of educational personnel has been acknowledged by the funding of three national conferences plus several regional and state-wide conferences to facilitate the development of effective personnel preparation programs.

Based, to some extent, on the authors' experiences in two of the three national conferences, this article outlines some general considerations and guidelines for those developing preservice and inservice programs which address the vocational programming needs of handicapped and disadvantaged students.

VOCATIONAL EDUCATION AND CAREER EDUCATION

Much of the discussion which follows can also be facilitated by noting a few similarities and contrasts between vocational education and career education. Hoyt (1975) broadly defines career education as: The totality of experiences through which one learns about

---

[1]Mr. Phelps is an intern with the Bureau of Education for the Handicapped, USOE; Dr. Clark is Professor of Speech Education, University of Kansas.

"Personnel Preparations for Vocational Programming of Special Needs Students," L.A. Phelps, G.M. Clark, *Journal of Career Education,* Vol. 3, No. 3, Winter 1977.

and prepares to engage in work as part of her or his way of living.
In an operational context, Hoyt foresees career education as a reform
movement in American education which should refocus a considerable
portion of the K-adult curriculum around experiences which will enable
individuals to engage in meaningful, productive, and satisfying work
throughout their life. Vocational-technical education, on the other
hand, is defined in the Education Amendment of 1976 as follows:

> Vocational education means organized educational programs
> which are directly related to the preparation of individuals
> for paid or unpaid employment, or for additional preparation
> for a career requiring other than a baccalaureate or advanced
> degree...

Vocational education has been offered exclusively at the secondary
and post-secondary level, and as such, is considered within the scope
and definition of career education. It represents a major segment
of the career exploration and preparation phases of career education
which tends to occur developmentally at the junior high, senior high,
and community college or technical institute levels. It should be
noted, however, that vocational-technical education has not encompassed some of the career cluster curricula such as the Fine Arts and
Humanities which are included in the broader context of career
education.

SPECIAL NEEDS STUDENTS

A clear and cogent analysis of the personnel preparation
needs for vocational programming is, to some extent, dependent upon
the definition and clarification of terminology which is fundamental
to the field. The term "handicapped student" is used here interchangeably with the term "special needs student" to identify those
students who encounter difficulty succeeding in the regular school
program becaue of the effects of a disability, disadvantagement, or
dysfunctional school placement. Because of the difficulties they
encounter in school, they can be considered to have educational needs
that demand significantly modified instruction and/or special services.
These students have also been labelled as "handicapped" or "disadvantaged." However, a number of authors (Jones, 1972; Lilly, 1970,
1971; Gallagher, 1972) have noted the importance of describing the

population to be served in terms of performance levels or observable
behaviors whenever possible, rather than by categories or labels such
as "mentally retarded." Functional descriptors are preferred because
of the inherent stigma associated with labels. The limited utility of
labels in planning daily instruction, the impact of labels on teacher
and parent expectations, and the tendency to apply labels or categories
without constitutional safeguards. The authors feel that identifying
and defining students by their functional abilities and their subsequently identifiable special educational needs is of crucial im-
importance. It challenges the educational system to more effectively
meet the needs of these students, instead of restricting educational
opportunities because their abilities and potentials are perceived as
limited.

PERSONNEL ROLES IN VOCATIONAL PROGRAMMING

Vocational programming at the secondary and post-secondary level
involves a number of professionals from different fields in the delivery of instruction and related services to special needs learners.
It is of primary importance that we recognize the existing roles of
vocational teachers, work experience coordinators, special class
teachers, and resource room teachers, and the manner in which professionals occupying these roles can effectively and efficiently
coordinate their expertise and efforts. Perhaps the most significant
problem confronting both preservice and inservice preparation programs
is teaching these professionals "how" to work together. As Evans
(1976) notes:

> Vocational education teachers with no special education
> background are teaching special needs students and special
> education teachers with no background in vocational educa-
> tion are trying to prepare these same types of students
> for employment. This situation exists in public schools
> because there are virtually no teacher education programs
> to prepare people with both types of skills.

To a large extent, the personnel roles for which training must be
provided are shaped by the state certification provisions. Generally,
however, it can be assumed that both specialists and regular vocational
educators will need various degrees of preparation relative to serving
special needs learners. At the junior high school or middle school

level where career exploration and prevocational experiences are provided, it is vitally important that industrial arts, home economics. general business, and other practical arts teachers be prepared to accommodate and teach the special student, as well as work closely with resource room consultants, specialists, and self-contained special class teachers.

Recently, there has been a loosening of the child labor laws which, in several states, has fostered the development of early work experience programs. Under the Work Experience and Career Exploration Program (WECEP) program, for instance, 14 and 15 year old potential drop-outs can work up to 23 hours per week and receive both pay and academic credit toward graduation. In the future it appears that more vocational and special education personnel employed at the early secondary level will also need competencies in planning both in-school and out-of-school early work observation and experience programs.

At the high school level where increased departmentalization of curricula has emerged, cooperation and communication between vocational and special education personnel has become increasingly difficult. However with the federal mandate to develop Individual Education Plans (PL 94-142) for each handicapped learner taking effect in September 1978, it is apparent that both regular and special educators, parents, and administrators will be required to collectively plan and implement individualized, prescriptive programs.

To insure that a broad range of occupational exploration and preparation options are open to special needs learners, vocational educators in all of the traditional fields (agriculture, business and office, distributive, health, home economics, and industrial education) must be prepared to serve the special needs learner. A recent General Accounting Office (1976) report reveals that in 78% of the school districts sampled nationally, vocational educators were insufficiently trained in special education skills. Only two percent (2%) of the school districts reported that nearly all of their vocational staff (81%--100%) were sufficiently trained.

With the advent of career education, an increasing emphasis is being placed on experienced-based learning activities at the late secondary level. For example, the nationally developed Experienced

Based Career Education program provides community based experiences in careers related to both academic and vocational education programming. The WECEP program extends similar experiential options into the junior high/middle school. Here again, this trend strongly suggests that vocational and special educators will need competencies related to development of work stations and coordination of work-school experiences, in addition to the vitally important instructional, assessment, and counseling skills.

At both the secondary and post-secondary level, the current trend emphasizes "special needs programs" which often provide special or separate programs and/or services (Olympus Research Corporation, 1975). This trend has been established, to a significant degree, by a large percentage of State Departments of Education choosing to spend their federal vocational education funds for the handicapped and disadvantaged on a local project or program basis. For administrative and accountability purposes it is much more expedient to channel the funds to teachers' salaries, equipment, supplies, and materials designated to be serving special needs students only. A recent assessment study of 25 states revealed that 22 states were spending their federal funds in this manner (Olympus Research Corporation, 1975). This pattern, along with new provisions in recently passed federal legislation for both vocational and special education, points to the need for training administrative or program management personnel. If the current trend of separate programming continues to any extent (which it probably will), there remains a significant need to provide inservice training to the directors or heads of these programs. This training should focus on both their administrative and direct service functions. Krantz and Weatherman (1976) examined the competencies needed by special needs coordinators at the post-secondary level in Minnesota and found the following to be the most essential:

--Evaluate the performance of special needs staff members

--Maintain a record system consistent with state regulations and format

--Provide and/or secure inservice training for regular and special needs staff

--Assist vocational instructors to modify their programs

--Use styles of leadership appropriate to different situations

--Design and implement a program evaluation process

--Design and implement a learner identification system

--Carry out effective public relations

--Provide vocational guidance and counseling to special
needs students

As the trend toward placement of special needs students in regular programs emerges concurrently, building principals and directors of vocational education and special education programs will also need additional training to enable them to carry out some of these functions effectively.

PERSONNEL TRAINING NEEDS

Although a substantial demand exists to train personnel in the types of professional roles previously described, the field is just now beginning to respond by developing inservice and preservice preparation programs. Preparation programs at both levels have been few in number because, in part, the specific skills needed by personnel involved in vocational programming for special needs learners have not been analyzed extensively except in a few isolated studies. These have focused on a single vocational program area, e.g., industrial education (Kruppa, Fritz, and Thrower, 1973), or single professional roles, e.g., special education teachers and work experience coordinators (Habilitation Personnel Training Project, 1976). The identification and careful analysis of tasks or competencies performed by personnel is obviously fundamental to the process of developing personnel preparation programs.

A brief review of the literature on personnel preparation in this field notes that there have been less than 10 competency studies focusing on the roles of vocational special needs personnel. At the first National Teacher Education Workshop for special and vocational education teacher educators held at the University of Illinois in January 1976, a composite list of tasks performed by special needs personnel was reviewed and evaluated by the 54 selected participants. The composite list of 49 tasks was drawn from existing competency and task lists that had been generated and validated from six previous studies. The participants who rated the tasks were teacher trainers from the fields of vocational education, special education, and counseling. There were also nine representatives of state departments of education. The vast majority of the participants had been at least somewhat involved with designing and/or implementing training programs in the vocational special needs area.

The list of 49 tasks was divided into four categories -- assessing needs, planning, implementation, and evaluation -- representing the four major functions associated with the delivery of instructional programs and/or supportive services. The participants were asked to review the list of tasks individually and assume that they were a person involved in vocational programming for special needs students in a local program. The participants were asked specifically not to assume a role responsibility for the tasks, but simply to rate the criticality of successful performance of the task to the overall effectiveness of a local program irrespective of who (by role) typically performs the task.

The two tasks which were clearly rated above all others dealt with providing direct instructional service. Utilizing appropriate instructional techniques and providing reinforcement appeared to be clearly more critical than all other tasks listed. Four other tasks related to direct instruction were rated among the top nine tasks. The included: appropriate sequencing of instruction, coordinating vocational with academic instruction, and developing, selecting, or modifying learning materials. Developing student performance goals and objectives was ranked 10th among the top 12 tasks.

Assessment and counseling skills appeared to be important also. Evaluating instruction, assessing a student's occupational interests, and providing career counseling were ranked among the six most critical tasks.

It should be noted that this data suggests some tentative, general direction for teacher training programs. It is limited in its utility for detailed planning of such programs, however. First, the sample (N=54) was exceptionally small and limited to teacher educators and a few state department of education personnel. Cross-validation with the Kent State University study (Albright, Nichols & Pinchak, 1975) which used responses from teachers in the field would be a first step in validating the University of Illinois workshop data.

Numerous other considerations need to be made in planning a competency based personnel preparation program. The state certifica-

tion licences and other role-defining mandates need to be considered
in light of the tasks generally performed in the identified roles.
The relative amount of time spent performing a given task in comparison to other tasks is also important information to obtain. In
providing inservice programs, determining the extent to which personnel can already adequately perform the tasks or competencies is a
major concern. Finally, the ultimate validity of a competency or
task list has to be judged in terms of whether or not the stated
competencies or tasks result in effective learning and improved
performance for special needs students. Empirical evidence which
would provide such data is still not available for most competency-
based teacher education programs (Rosenshine, 1974). Even then, a
sizable number of researchers argue that such evidence, when collected,
will be highly suspect for a variety of sampling and measurement
reasons.

PROGRAM DEVELOPMENT GUIDELINES

Planning a personnel preparation program is an increasingly
difficult task. In times of decreasing enrollments and limited funds
for staff and training activities, it becomes imperative that both
inservice and preservice teacher education programs be addressed to
significant needs, maximally efficient, and cost-effective.

The experiences of initiators of personnel preparation programs
in this field suggest that there are at least seven areas of concern
which should be addressed during program planning and development:
need identification, program design, program content and methods,
practicum experiences, certification, evaluation and staff selection
and development. These seven areas of concern touch upon effective
utilization of resources, as well as a number of additional concerns
which are both common and unique to preservice or inservice program
development.

NEED IDENTIFICATION

Prior to the development of a training program, it is imperative
that the nature and extent of training needed be determined. Collecting
and compiling the following information is important for justification
and planning:

---Types and numbers of special needs learners needing vocational programming in the district, region, or state

---Types and numbers of special needs learners currently receiving such services or programming locally, regionally, or statewide

---Adequacy of the services and programming being provided

---Personnel roles for which training is needed, such as: resource room teacher, regular vocational teacher, special needs vocational teacher, secondary special class teacher, work/study experience coordinator, vocational adjustment counselor, rehabilitation counselor, administrators

---Specific training needs of the audience to be trained, (e.g., assisting special needs learners to develop career plans)

PROGRAM DESIGN

Once the nature and extent of the training need is established, such consideration can be given to designing the training program, as:

---Use of an advisory committee to assist in program planning, which should include: business/industries/labor representatives, parents of special needs learners, trainee representatives (undergraduate, graduate, preservice, and inservice), administrative personnel (deans, department chairpersons, area chairpersons, etc.), instructional personnel (vocational education and special education), supportive service agency personnel (vocational rehabilitation, adult education, C.E.T.A., etc.)

---Full and appropriate utilization of available resources in the training program, such as: local community and governmental agency resources which may include: Goodwill Industries, Vocational Rehabilitation, Labor unions, faculty/staff expertise from other departments or nearby training institutions or agencies.

---Development of a formal plan for coordination of the training program between the appropriate departments (e.g., special education, vocational education, counselor education, etc.). Such a plan should specify all coordinated activities such as joint staff meetings, team teaching of courses or workshops, and joint supervision of practicum experiences. For examples of plans developed at the January 1976 University of Illinois National Workshop, refer to Phelps, Evans, Abbas, and Frison (1976).

PROGRAM CONTENT AND METHODS

Identification of training program content and methods is based somewhat on the previous two areas of concern. However, there are several specific considerations which should be undertaken by training program developers:

---Developing an appropriate balance of content focusing on understanding the world of work, career exploration and preparation programming, and the educational needs of special students.

---Providing trainees with a variety of learning experiences ranging from academic activities to demonstration of attained competencies with special needs learners.

---Identifying training program content which reflects sequential, articulated vocational programming to include: self awareness, career awareness, career exploration and orientation, career preparation, career retraining.

---Identifying training program content which reflects the identified personnel needs, and is also comprehensive in nature. A sampling of possible content topics may be: assessment/diagnostic services and processes, career counseling, job placement, legal aspects of occupational training and work experience (liability, workmen's compensation, wage and hour regulations, etc.), individual educational plans, parent involvement, due process procedures, community resource analysis and utilization, program placement, modification of instructional materials.

PRACTICUM EXPERIENCES

The opportunity to practice and refine obtained competencies in realistic settings is a critical component of any personnel training activity. For both preservice and inservice programs, the following two considerations are important for practicum experiences:

---Providing quality, sequential, and supervised practicum experiences.

---Utilizing a variety of appropriate practum sites related to vocational programming: local education agencies, area vocational centers, vocational evaluation centers, residential vocational schools, community junior colleges, sheltered workshops, state schools for the handicapped, rehabilitation agencies

CERTIFICATION

Credentialing of graduates of training programs has traditionally been a major outcome of preservice programs and some extended inservice or graduate level programs. To date only three states (Wisconsin, New Jersey, and Nebraska) have installed certification options which are specifically focused on vocational programming for special needs learners. The following suggestions are offered relative to certification:

---Involve personnel from the state or local teacher certification agency in planning and reviewing the program.

---Provide the teacher certification agency with data which justifies the need for unique or dual certification options.

---Consider unique certification or endorsement options at the secondary level such as: vocational adjustment counselor, special vocational needs teacher, prevocational work coordinator, special needs endorsement.

---Consider dual or multiple certification options such as: special education certification for vocational teachers, vocational education certification for special education teachers.

EVALUATION

Several concerns come to the forefront in designing the evaluation
component of a preparation program. With the increased emphasis on
accountability and the need to operate cost-effective training programs, the need for external as well as internal evaluation mechanisms
is substantial. Some general guidelines for program evaluation includes:

- ---Plan for systematic and continuous evaluation activities
  which collect and utilize relevant data and information from
  all appropriate constituencies: trainees, teacher trainers,
  practicum supervisors, advisory committee members, students
  or clients of the trainees.

- ---Assess and document the competencies attained by all trainees.

- ---Through follow up studies assess the contributions the
  trainees make toward providing for and/or improving the
  vocational adjustment of special needs learners.

STAFF SELECTION AND DEVELOPMENT

The final area of concern focuses on the personnel involved
in providing the training program. Major concerns include:

- ---Whenever appropriate and feasible, use personnel from different
  disciplines to demonstrate the concept of cooperative teaching.

- ---Carefully assess the experience and expertise of the training
  staff in the level and areas in which training is to be provided: preservice training, inservice training, vocational
  programming, special education (secondary), supportive
  services.

- ---Provide options and experiences which will enable the staff to
  expand and/or update their knowledge and skill.

CONCLUSION

These guidelines are, of course, easier to propose than to accomplish. They are considerations, however, which should be addressed to
provide minimally needed planning for preparing personnel to work in the
preparation phase of a career education program for special needs
students. It is hoped that they will provide some assistance to new
and developing teacher education programs.

REFERENCES

Albright, L., C. Nichols, & J. Pinchak, *Identification of Professional
Competencies Necessary for Teachers of Disadvantaged and Handi-
capped youth. Final Supplemental Document -- EPDA Project 74122,*
Kent State University, Kent, Ohio, 1975.

Education Amendments of 1976. PL 94-142. Washington, D.C.: U.S. Government Printing Office, 1976.

Education for All Handicapped Children Act of 1975. PL 94-142. Washington D.C.: U.S. Government Printing Office, 1975.

Evans, R. N., Everybody talks about it, in Phelps, L.A., et. al, *Vocational Education for the Special Needs Students: Competencies and Models for Personnel Preparation.* Urbana: Bureau of Educational Research, University of Illinois, 1976.

Gallagher, J. J., The special education contract for mildly handicapped children, *Exceptional Children,* 38, 1972, pp. 527-536.

General Accounting Office. Training educators for the handicapped: a need to redirect federal programs. Washington, D.C.: U.S. General Accounting Office, 1976.

Habilitation Personnel Training Project, *Special Project: Optimizing Habilitation Services in the Public Schools.* Department of Special Education, University of Kansas, Lawrence, Kansas, 1976.

Jones, R.L., Labels and stigma in special education. *Exceptional Children,* 38, 1972, pp. 553-564.

Lilly, M. S., Special education: a teapot in a tempest. *Exceptional Children,* 37, 1970, pp. 43-49.

Olympus Research Corporation. *An Assessment of Vocational Education Programs for the Handicapped under Part B of the 1968 Amendments to the Vocational Education Act: Executive Summary.* Salt Lake City, Utah: Olympus Research Corporation, 1975.

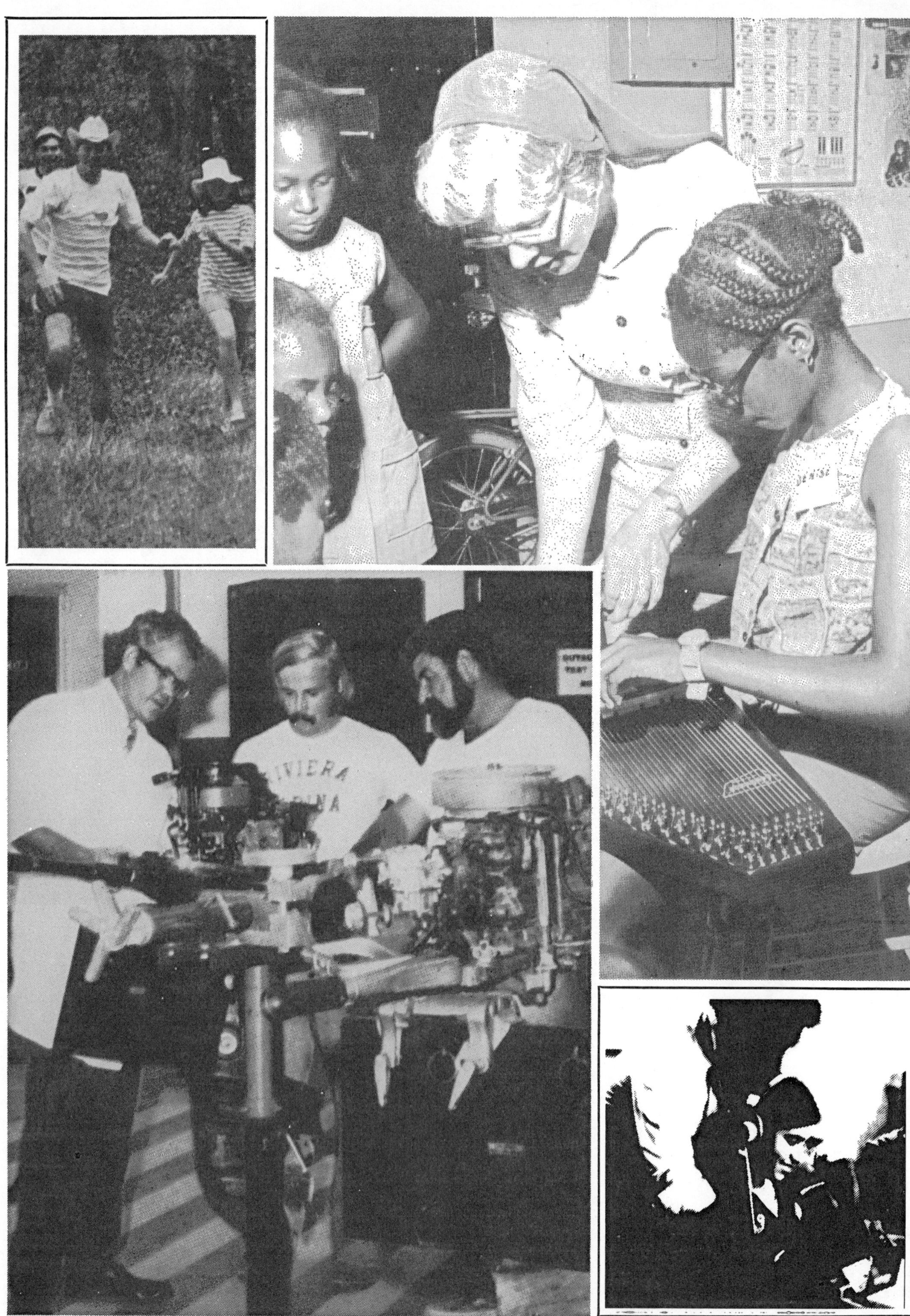

VOCATIONAL EVALUATION: SPECIAL EDUCATION's RESPONSIBILITY

Abstract: Many educable mentally retarded persons continue to lead a marginal life after school despite higher potentials. Schools can and should provide more relevant vocationally oriented programs to help eliminate the barriers formerly encountered by the mentally retarded after they leave school. Initiating vocational evaluation programs in the school is recommended and the components of the process are described. A model for operating a vocational evaluation and placement program is suggested.

DONN BROLIN *is Associate Professor, Department of Counseling and Personnel Services, University of Missouri—Columbia. He was formerly Director, Special Education Project, University of Wisconsin—Stout, Menomonie.* This article is based on a speech given at the Special Study Institute on Vocational Evaluation and Curriculum Modification, Department of Public Instruction, Des Moines, Iowa, February 1, 1972.

The majority of persons who are labeled as educable mentally retarded could achieve higher levels of personal, social, and vocational functioning if they had better educational and vocational opportunities. Too many retarded persons are not learning to live and work successfully in our society.

One reason is a lack of public understanding about the ability of the educable mentally retarded. Most of these students are not significantly brain damaged or otherwise medically disabled and have many positive abilities that can be converted to vocational assets. However, there is still a tendency to place the mentally retarded in routine, repetitive, simple, and low paying jobs even though many could perform successfully in more highly skilled and highly paid occupations (Kokaska, 1971; Oswald, 1968).

Another reason is the lack of appropriate educational and vocational programs in the secondary schools. Many professionals believe that too much emphasis is placed on academic instruction and too little on the development of socio-occupational competence (Goldstein, 1969). This criticism is being leveled against special education in secondary schools even though there has been a greater emphasis on vocational pro-graming in the secondary schools in the last decade. Work experience has been incorporated into the high school curriculum, often with the cooperation of the state rehabilitation agency, employment service, and sheltered workshops. These work study programs have had the benefit of getting the agencies involved in the vocational problems of the educable retarded students before graduation, but yet they have not worked as efficiently as was hoped.

Communication problems, in many cases, have existed between the secondary school and the rehabilitation agency, resulting in sporadic services and inadequate continuity of service (Hammerlynck & Espeseth, 1969). The same has been true of the relationship between the school and the employment service. In a recent study, Colorado State Employment Service counselors indicated that they did not feel it was their responsibility to find employment for the mentally retarded and were not knowledgeable about mental retardation; moreover, 38 percent of the counselors surveyed said that they often did not have any working relationship with special classroom programs for these students (Smith, 1970).

Sheltered workshops have provided vocational evaluation, training, and placement services for many of these students, thereby relieving participating schools of vocational responsibilities. But again the help provided by the workshops often has not met the needs of the students. Often workshop personnel are not well trained in mental retardation and are neither aware of the student's background nor are able to observe his functioning over a long period of time. Consequently, the students have not been able to receive the individual and specialized assistance they need. In addition, the performance of many educable retarded students has been lower than their actual potential because they have not yet reached a certain level of vocational maturity, motivation, and experience.

Giving the responsibility for vocational evaluation and training of these students to rehabilitation agencies, employment services, and sheltered workshops will not totally solve the problems. These agencies have many types of vocationally handicapped clients to serve and cannot be expected to train their already overloaded staff to deal effectively with all the vocational problems of the educable retarded student. Some secondary schools have provided vocational evaluation for their students, but this usually has not been done in any systematic way.

Up to this point the extent and quality of vocational programing for these students has depended primarily upon the individual teacher's inclination, ingenuity, training, vocational experience, and the like. Some teachers have developed good vocational programs; others have not, placing students in jobs with the hope that some vocational skills and interests will develop. Schools can and should be providing better programs to help eliminate the educational and vocational barriers that the retarded student encounters.

The secondary school program must assume a larger responsibility for the vocational development of its educable retarded students by initiating a vocational evaluation program as an integral part of its curriculum. This is consistent with the recent statement by US Commissioner of Education, Sidney P. Marland (1972) who listed career education for the handicapped as one of the nation's primary educational needs.

The Vocational Evaluation Procedure

Vocational evaluation, according to Gellman (1968), is concerned with the prognosis of whether a person can work, what kind, and what types of training are needed. Although there are varying opinions on how to do this, it is my opinion that vocational evaluation should consist of the following components: clinical assessment, work evaluation, work adjustment, and on-the-job tryout.

Clincial Assessment

There are four types of clinical assessment: medical, social, educational, and psychological.

Medical Assessment. This assessment involves evaluating the individual's physical capacity, general health, brain damage, vision, hearing, speech, perceptual motor functioning, coordination, dexterity, and any suspected or evident anomalies pre-

cluding optimal health and physical functioning. In addition to pointing out limitations to vocational functioning, a medical assessment should indicate whether treatment can modify or remedy some or all of the limitations and this information should be used for vocational planning.

Social Assessment. This assessment involves evaluating the educable retarded student's family relationship, social skills, interpersonal relationships, care of his personal needs, and ability to use leisure time. For example, it has been found that the parents have a significant influence on the student's eventual vocational outcome (Brolin, 1969). Moreover, lack of appropriate social skills, rather than inability to do the job, is the major reason for loss of employment.

Educational Assessment. This assessment involves evaluating the student's academic ability for job placement. Many jobs do not require a high academic level but a certain academic level is needed for care for one's everyday affairs. Proper educational assessment could assist in preventing a mildly retarded student from being placed in an unchallenging position and in becoming underemployed.

Psychological Assessment. This assessment at its best involves evaluating the educable retarded student's verbal skills, performance skills, special interests and knowledge, and the like. In the past, psychological assessment has focused on IQ scores despite their insignificance in determining the individual's vocational potential. The psychologist can be of real help in assessing the individual's skills and in pinpointing intellectual and personality strengths and weaknesses for eventual vocational programing.

Work Evaluation. The second component, work evaluation, in the vocational evaluation procedure consists of: intake and other counseling interviews; interest, dexterity, and other standarized vocational tests; work and job samples; and situational assessment. *Interviews.* These are extremely important in the work evaluation process, for they can provide essential information on the interests, needs, knowledge, and personality of the student.

Standardized Testing. This testing should be used with caution. The tests are often inappropriate for educable mentally retarded students because of the verbal ability required and/or the norm groups used. While there have been attempts to develop less verbal measures, such as *Standardization of the Vocational Interest Sophistication Assessment* (VISA), (Parnicky, Kahn, & Burdett, 1968), *The Geist Picture Interest Inventory*, (Geist, 1959), and the new *Reading-Free Vocational Interest Inventory*, the validity of all these measures is questionable and any interest test should be used with care. The *Purdue Pegboard* (Tobias & Gorelick, 1960), is perhaps the best fine finger dexterity test to use. The *General Aptitude Test Battery* (GATB), (US Department of Labor, 1966), should be used with caution despite a recent study in Minnesota (Lofquist, Dawis, & Weiss, 1970) concluding that it si appropriate.

Work and Job Samples. These are becoming increasingly important components of the work evaluation process and range from simple to complex operations. Work samples are simulated tasks or activities but do not actually replicate a specific job whereas a job sample is a model or replication of an actual job or part of a job that exists in industry. Both are set up like a testing procedure where there are definite instructions, standards, time and/or units performed requirements, and hopefully norms on which to compare the individual's performance with other groups. They do not consist merely of giving individuals work and seeing how they do on it.

Unlike standardized tests, however, work and job samples have these advantages: (a) they are more like jobs than tests are; (b) they are more motivating, less anxiety producing, and more appropriate than tests for persons with cultural and language difficulties; (c) they may sample actual operations of a job, and (d) they provide better evidence for the prospective employer of the types of abilities the client has.

The disadvantages most frequently cited of work and job samples are: (a) many clients may not take work samples related to jobs that they do not like; (b) it is difficult to develop enough representative job samples to cover all the major occupations; (c) they are expensive and time consuming to develop; and (d) there is still much subjective evaluation in the use of work and job samples. *The Dictionary of Occupational Titles* (DOT), (US Department of Labor, 1965), is valuable in conducting job analyses which is a first step in developing work and job samples.

Situational Assessment. This assessment is the typical technique used by sheltered workshops and is oriented toward simulating actual working conditions. Instead of focusing on specific work skills, as in the work or job sample, the situational assessment forcuses on general work habits and behaviors. The client usually works on subcontracted, production assembly work that is fairly simple. Clients are systematically observed and rated on their work personality and their behaviors are compared to behaviors deemed necessary to secure employment.

Work Adjustment

The third component work adjustment, of the vocational evaluation procedure is particularly helpful for the educable retarded student who is inexperienced and unmotivated. The work adjustment program is planned individually for each student and concentrates on his particular deficiencies that have been delineated in the work evaluation period. The work adjustment program helps the student develop adequate physical tolerances, change work behaviors, and acquire new vocational related information and experiences.

There are several different kinds of work adjustment techniques. One is a simulated work experience setting that provides work activities and that emphasizes productivity. Another is individual and group counseling. A third, and perhaps the most effective with many retarded individuals, is behavior modification in which operant conditioning focuses on reinforcement to control and shape behavior. The goal in the behavior modification approach is to alter the client's work environment so that appropriate behaviors are learned and maintained and inappropriate behaviors extinguished. After a period of work adjustment, a more realistic assessment of the educable retarded student's vocational strengths, weaknesses, and potentials can be made.

On-the-Job Tryouts

The final component of the vocational evaluation process, on-the-job tryouts, provides perhaps the only realistic assessment of the client's abilities. On-the-job tryouts should be separate from work evaluation because the former gives the student the opportunity to perform an actual job under the supervision of industrial and business personnel. Prerequisite to a relevant decision about the job tryout is the conducting of a job analysis, focusing on a description of the work to be performed and on the required characteristics of the worker.

Job analysis takes into consideration what the worker does, how he does it, why he does it, and the skill involved in doing it. When the student is engaged in the on-the-job tryout, the job analyst can observe him at the place of work and give whatever training and instruction is needed before making a final judgement as to the student's potential for that type of work. Neff (1970) has stated that perhaps "the site of the vocational evaluator ought to be in the work place itself [p. 29]." If the vocational evaluator has done his job, the student should be ready for the on-the-job experience and should do well. The on-the-job tryout should reflect the actual vocational capacities of the student, provided that the evaluation and adjustment that preceded it was adequate.

The above comprises the vocational evaluation process. It appears that special education teachers must have the competencies of a social worker, psychologist, counselor, evaluator, and placement specialist if vocational evaluation is their responsibility. This may well be true, but someone has to conduct and coordinate the vocational evaluation and it is going to have to be the teacher if the students are to be served adequately. Other resources should be utilized if they are available and appropriate.

A Vocational Evaluation Model

To make sense out of the mass of vocational evaluation data collected on students, there must be some systematic framework or model from which the teacher can operate so appropriate evaluation, adjustment, and placement techniques can be employed. One that could be useful is the *Minnesota Theory of Work Adjustment* (Dawis, 1967). This theory is concerned with placing the individual on an appropriate job and is based on the assumption that work adjustment depends on the correspondence between the individual's work personality and the work environment.

The individual's work personality is made up of his abilities and needs, and the work environment consists of the abilities required for satisfactory work performance and the needs that can be satisfied by the job reinforcer system. This can be depicted as seen in Figure 1.

When the individual's abilities correspond to the abilities required to do the job, there is *satisfactoriness*. When the individual's needs correspond to the job reinforcer system, there is satisfaction, that is, the individual is happy with what he is doing. There are well designed followup questionnaires to assess these two areas. If there is both satisfactoriness (the individual can do the job) and satisfaction (the individual is happy about his job), there is work adjustment and job stability (Dawis, 1967).

To measure the various components in the model, the following can be used:

- *Abilities* These can be measured by work samples, situational assessment, on-the-job tryouts, GATB, *Purdue Pegboard*, and other vocational aptitude tests and clinical assessments.

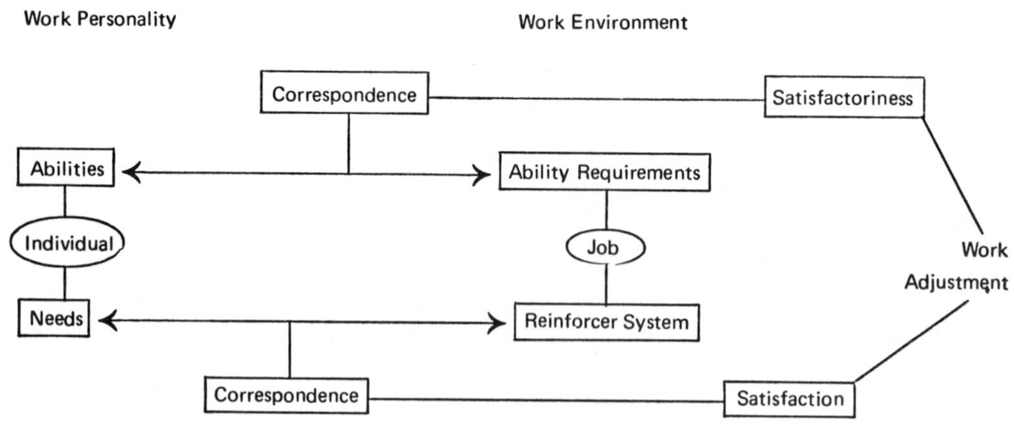

FIGURE 1. Minnesota Theory of
Work Adjustment

- *Ability Requirements.* These can be measured by the DOT, job analysis, *Guide to Jobs for the Mentally Retarded*, (Peterson & Jones, 1964) and *Occupational Adjustment Patterns*. (US Department of Labor, 1962).
- *Needs.* These can be measured by the *Minnesota Importance Questionnaire* (MIQ) (Lofquist, Dawis & Weiss, 1970), interest inventories, personality measures, expressed needs, and past history.
- *Reinforcer System.* These can be measured by the DOT, job analysis, and *Occuaptional Reinforcer Patterns* (ORPs), (Borgen, Weiss, Tinsley, Dawis, & Lofquist, 1968).

The *Minnesota Theory of Work Adjustment* provides a systematic framework for operating a vocational evaluation and placement program. It is a way to obtain information about work personalities, abilities, needs, and work environments to find the correspondence between all these factors that will lead to successful work adjustment.

A successful and effective vocational evaluation program can be designed within the school structure and be complemented by an appropriate community job site experience. By using the techniques described above, the secondary special education teacher will be able to enhance the opportunities for our mentally retarded citizens and truly provide a career education.

References

Borgen, F., Weiss, D., Tinsley, H. Dawis, R., & Lofquist, L. The measurement of Occupational Reinforcer Patterns. *Minnesota Studies in Vocational Rehabilitation.* 1968.

Brolin, D. E. The implementation of recommendations from an evaluation center for the mentally retarded and an analysis of variables related to client outcome. Unpublished doctoral dissertation, University of Wisconsin, 1969.

Dawis, R. The Minnesota studies in vocational rehabilitation. *Rehabilitation Counseling Bulletin,* 1967, 11, 1-10.

Geist, H. *Geist Picture Interest Inventory.* Berkeley: Southern Universities Press, 1959.

Gellman, W. The principles of vational evaluation. *Rehabilitation Literature,* 1968, 29, 98-102.

Goldstein, H. Construction of a social learning curriculum. *Focus on Exceptional Children,* 1969, 1, 1-10.

Hammerlynck, L. A., & Espeseth, V. K. Dual specialist: Vocational rehabilitation counselor and teacher of the mentally retarded. *Mental Retardation,* 1969, 7, 49-50.

Kokaska, C. The need for economic security for the mentally retarded. In Brolin, D., & Thomas, B. (Eds.), *Preparing teachers of secondary level educable mentally retarded: Proposal for a new model.* Menomonie, Wisconsin: Stout State University, 1971. Pp. 18-21.

Lofquist, L., Dawis, R., & Weiss, D. *Assessing the work personalities of mentally retarded adults.* Minnespolis: University of Minnesota, 1970.

Marland, S. Career education 300 days later. *American Vocational Journal,* 1972, 47, (2), 14-17.

Neff, W. Vocational Assessment - theory and models. *Journal of Rehabilitation,* 1970 36(1), 27-29.

Oswald, H. *A national follow-up study of mental retardates employed by the federal government.* Grant RD-2425-6, Washington, D.C.: Department of Vocational Rehabilitation, 1968.

Parnicky, J., Kahn, H. & Burdett, A. *Standardization of the Vocational Interest and Sophistication Assessment (VISA): A reading free test for retardates.* Bordentown, N.J.: Johnstone Training and Research Center, 1968.

Peterson, R., & Jones, E. *Guide to jobs for the mentally retarded.* Pittsburgh: American Institute for Research, 1964.

Smith, G. The mentally retarded: Is the public employment service prepared to serve them? *Mental Retardation,* 1970, 8, 26-29.

Tobias, J. & Gorelick, J. The effectiveness of the *Purdue Pegboard* in evaluating the work potential of retarded adults. *Training School Bulletin,* 1960, 57, 94-104.

US Department of Labor. *Dictionary of occupational titles.* (3rd ed.) 1965.

US Department of Labor, United States Employment Service. *General Aptitude Test Battery.* Washington: USGPO, 1966.

US Department of Labor, *Guide to the use of the General Aptitude Test Battery.* Section II: Norms; Occupational Aptitude Pattern Structure, 1962.

A Survey of the Present Status of Vocational Training in State Institutions for the MR

James B. Richardson

Author: JAMES B. RICHARDSON, M.S., Team Leader, Broome Developmental Service's Delaware Regional Center in Walton, New York and doctoral candidate in Special Education, Administration, Teachers College, Columbia University.

ABSTRACT. Questionnaires were sent to 203 state supported institutions for the mentally retarded in the United States for the purpose of gathering current information on institutional vocational training programs. One hundred forty-six replies were received giving information on the number of residents involved in such programs, areas used for training, institutional workshops, payment programs, persons responsible, and length of working days. The results were compared with a similar study carried out in 1957.

Review of the Literature

REFERENCE HAS OFTEN BEEN MADE to the conflict between the responsibility for resident training and the work needs of the institution. Windle (1962) questioned to what extent the ulterior motives of institutional employment were at the expense of therapeutic values. Others have stressed that while exploitation of residents is incompatible with institutional goals and philosophies, it is made necessary because of the realities of budget limitations, staff shortages and work pressures (Cohen, Zigler, Lipman, Adams, Morelli, 1961; Nagler & Kirkland, 1961; Rusalem, Peterson & McCraney, 1967).

Although many have criticized work training programs because of the emphasis on production, others have recommended such programs as providing realistic training (Belinson, Bensberg, & Erdman, 1963), especially if combined with extra-institutional experiences (Cohen, 1962). Furthermore, Rosen, Diggory, and Werlinsky (1966) reported that in the area of work, retarded persons with institutional backgrounds set higher goals, predicted higher performance, and produced more than retardates with non-sheltered community experiences.

A number of drawbacks to strictly institutional experiences have, nevertheless, been cited: (a) little or no opportunity to earn money, (b) no possibility of being fired, (c) no use of public resources or facilities on an individual basis, and (d) unrealistically low expectations on the part of supervising employees (Cohen, 1962; Rusalem, Peterson, & McCraney, 1967).

Other related studies have reported that monetary rewards for institutionalized workers provide the greatest work incentive (Rosen, Halenda, Nowakiwska, & Floor, 1970) and result in increased performance (Huddle, 1967; Hunt & Zimmerman, 1969; Dettenheim, 1969). Related studies have reported on other types of reinforcement such as status producing titles—Student Worker, Institutional Aide, etc. (Steiner, Baker, & Ward, 1965); titles combined with payment (Kott, 1963); playback of video recordings of work performance (DeRoo & Harralson, 1971); and formal operant conditioning methods (Roberts & Perry, 1970).

---

¹ This study was completed under the guidance of Dr. I. Ignacy Goldberg, Teachers College, Columbia University, and represents partial completion of the requirements for the Ed.D. degree.

A recent survey of the status of institutional vocational training programs was conducted by Goldberg in 1957, at which time he sent a questionnaire to 93 institutions for the mentally retarded. He received responses from 60 institutions (65%), with eight of the respondents indicating that the questionnaire was not applicable to them. The total population of the institutions represented was approximately 89,900 residents of both sexes.

The Study

With Goldberg's survey as a model, a questionnaire was sent to 203 institutions for the mentally retarded as listed with the National Association of Superintendents of Public Residential Facilities for the Mentally Retarded. Replies were received from 154 institutions (76%) with 19 indicating that the questionnaire was not applicable (usually because they served only profoundly retarded individuals). The responding institutions were responsible for the care of approximately 150,000 mentally retarded residents.

The 135 institutions for whom the questionnaire was applicable reported 32,178 residents were involved in some form of vocational training (approximately 21% of the institutions' populations). One hundred thirty of the 135 institutions reported that various working areas of the institution (kitchens, laundry, child care, etc.) were used as training areas for those in vocational training.

The questionnaire then tried to determine to what extent the work areas were used for training. The findings are reported in Table I.

When the percentages in Table 1 were applied to the number in vocational training in each institution, it was found that of the 32,178 receiving vocational training, approximately 20,700 received such training through "employment" in actual working areas. This figure represents approximately 14% of the total population of all reporting institutions and about 64% of all those in vocational training. In 1957, Goldberg reported that 24,600 were "employed" in the 52 responding institutions (27% of the total institutional populations). It may be safe to assume that this figure represents close to 100% of those in vocational training since the Goldberg survey made no mention of any alternative programs.

TABLE 1

EXTENT TO WHICH WORKING AREAS OF 135 INSTITUTIONS ARE USED FOR VOCATIONAL TRAINING

Trainees Assigned to Institution Work Areas (Per Cent)	Number of Institutions
0	5
1-24	28
25-49	16
50-74	34
75-99	39
100	13

Question 4 asked the institution to indicate what other types of training areas were used if less than 100% of vocational training was conducted in institution work areas. The respondents were given four choices: (a) institutional sheltered workshops, (b) community based workshops, (c) regular jobs in the community, and (d) other (they were asked to be specific). One hundred twenty-two institutions reported having a total of 281 such alternate training programs (most of the reporting institutions had more than one type of program). These 281 training areas involved approximately 11,478 residents, or about 36% of those in vocational training. The findings are summarized in Table 2 and show that the most common alternative program reported was the institutional sheltered workshop followed closely by community jobs. The "other" programs consisted of pre-vocational, formal evaluation programs, halfway houses and part-time day work.

In 1957, Goldberg asked for an indication of job areas in which residents were trained or employed. The most frequently mentioned at that time were various aspects of farm work followed by laundry, hospital, beauty shop, and barber shop. There was no mention in the findings he reported of any use of workshops, jobs in the community or other areas of training.

Question 5 asked the 87 institutions with workshops to indicate which item best described 50% of their activities: sub-contracts, institutional tasks (i.e., stuffing envelopes), workshop created projects, or other. Sixty-eight reported one such item in the following order of frequency: sub-contracts—46 institutions; workshop created projects—16 institutions; other—4 institutions; and institutional work, 2 institutions.

The questionnaire then sought to determine how many workshop-type programs were formalized enough to have certification under existing regulations governing workshop operation. Forty-four of the 87 workshops were certified. Of those uncertified workshops, 33 indicated that the workers received pay for their work. Some reported using tokens, either alone or in combination with money. The rest, however, were fairly equally divided between straight salary or allowance per week or month, piecework payment, or the sharing of income from projects. The amounts received ranged from such sums as five cents an hour or $1.50 per week to one report of $1.80 per hour.

In the following order of frequency are the primary sources of funds for the payment of workers in uncertified workshops: sub-contracts; state or institution appropriated funds; income from items sold; a combination of sources; or federal grants.

Question 8 was worded as follows:

In the past, institutions for the mentally retarded have reported some conflicts existing between the training of their residents and the institution's need for getting work done with a shortage of personnel. Do you feel that such a problem exists to any extent at your institution? Please elaborate.

Sixty-nine of the 135 institutions (approximately 51%) felt that it was a problem to some extent; 64 said "no" and two did not respond. In Goldberg's 1957 survey, 57% of those responding indicated that it was a problem.

TABLE 2

VOCATIONAL TRAINING SETTINGS OTHER THAN REGULAR WORK AREAS IN 122 INSTITUTIONS

Type of Program	Number Reported
Institutional Sheltered Workshop	87
Community Based Sheltered Workshop	60
Regular Jobs in the Community	82
Other	52

The comments received were similar to those reported in Goldberg's study, namely a shortage of personnel, inadequate budget, and confusion on the part of employees concerning the dual responsibility of doing their jobs and training residents. Another aspect of the problem, not as significant in 1957, concerned the lack of capable workers as a result of changing populations.

Among the responses, however, were a significant number of more positive replies indicating some solutions to the problem usually through careful planning or strong regulations.

Question 10 asked:

Of the residents involved in some sort of work program (other than a workshop), what per cent receive remuneration of some kind?

A summary of the responses is shown in Table 3. More than half (71) reported that all of their workers received remuneration of some kind. Approximately 90% (120) reported remuneration going to some percentage of their workers. In 1957, only 31% reported remunerating resident workers.

Applying current survey figures to the number employed in work areas of each institution, approximately 15,500 of the 20,700 employed retardates (about 75%) were found to receive remuneration of some kind.

TABLE 3

EXTENT TO WHICH INSTITUTIONAL RESIDENTS ASSIGNED TO REGULAR WORK AREAS RECEIVE SOME FORM OF REMUNERATION

Per Cent of Residents Remunerated	Institutions (Number)
0	13
1-24	13
25-49	4
50-74	10
75-99	15
100	71

2. RECOGNIZING

Question 11 asked what form the remuneration takes. Eighty-three institutions reported using cash; 32 using checks; 21 using some form of voucher; 9 rewarding with candy or treats; and 30 using various other forms of payment (many institutions used several different forms). Some "other" forms of payment were tokens, tobacco, activities, point systems, canteen cards, and money deposited in residents' accounts.

Goldberg's study merely indicated examples of existing payment systems and they corresponded closely with those reported in this study.

Question 12 asked for the percentage of those receiving money as opposed to treats or special privileges. The findings are reported in Table 4. When these findings are applied to the number employed in work areas of each institution, approximately 14,300 residents (about 69%) were found to receive monetary payment.

Question 13 asked how often and how much workers were paid. The most frequent arrangement was for weekly payment followed by monthly and then biweekly. Of the 112 replies to this question, however, 2 paid workers bi-monthly, one quarterly, and 2 on a yearly basis. Of the institutions responding, some paid as little as five or ten cents a week (one indicated a maximum of one to two dollars per year) while others went up to minimum wages. One facility reported that there was no limit. Another stated that the state did not permit residents to be paid more than five dollars per month. The majority of the institutions having pay programs (approximately 71%) reported paying a maximum figure which fell below ten dollars per week.

Questions 14 and 15 dealt with who was responsible for making and supervising vocational training assignments. Education and Training Departments were responsible for vocational training in 41% of the responding institutions. A wide variety of other departments were listed, however, ranging from Vocational Rehabilitation, Industrial Therapy, Program Development and Work Activity, to Nursing, Business Office, and Maintenance. While Goldberg's survey did not indicate the most frequently utilized department, his responses were similar to those in this survey.

TABLE 4

EXTENT TO WHICH INSTITUTIONAL RESIDENTS ASSIGNED TO REGULAR WORK AREAS RECEIVE MONETARY REMUNERATION

Per Cent of Residents Receiving Monetary Remuneration	Institutions (Number)
0	17
1-24	21
25-49	7
50-74	9
75-99	15
100	65

Fifty-nine per cent of the institutions reported having from 1 to 3 persons responsible for such assignments. Another 16% showed 4 to 6 people responsible. The remaining 22% (3% did not reply) reported 7 or more people as responsible. It is important, however, to compare the number of people responsible with the number of residents in vocational training. As shown in Table 5, institutions reporting 1 to 3 responsible people ranged in program size from 100 to almost 900 trainees. There seemed to be no clear relationship between the size of the program and the number of people responsible for workers.

Question 16 revealed that 70% of the responding institutions had maximum work days of 6 to 8 hours. In only 2 instances were working days signficantly longer.

In the final question, only 10% of the institutions reported conducting follow-up studies on residents who had returned to the community (as compared with 30% reported by Goldberg in 1957).

TABLE 5

SIZE OF VOCATIONAL TRAINING PROGRAM COMPARED WITH NUMBER OF PEOPLE RESPONSIBLE IN 122 RESPONDING INSTITUTIONS

Number in Vocational Training	Number Responsible										
	1	2	3	4	5	6	7	8	9	10+	Team
0-99	11	7	8	4	2		2			2	1
100-199	5	8	3	2		3		2	1	5	1
200-299	6	2	2	1	1	3				2	1
300-399	2	5	3	2							1
400-499	1	1	2		2	1				2	
500-599	1	3	3				1			1	
600-699	1		1							2	
700-799	2	2		1			1		1	2	
800-899		1									

Discussion

Institutions for the mentally retarded are changing rapidly in size, role, and population make-up. Even this survey dealing strictly with vocational training has shown evidence of such change. One very significant effect has been that training has begun to take a different form due to changing populations. The number of residents trained in actual working areas of institutions has dropped by about 20% and now represents only 64% of training as opposed to an estimated 100% in 1957.

Another result has been a reported reduction in the training-production conflict. Institutions are simply losing the capable workers who were relied on to keep things running. This latter change can also be explained by society's growing concern for individual rights. The JCAH Standards state that such programs should "ensure the optimal development or restoration of each resident physically, psychologically, socially and vocationally." That would seem unlikely when the main emphasis is on keeping the institution running. Consequently, many respondents reported careful planning and orientation of employees to eliminate the training-production conflict.

Resident pay has also become an issue of importance. While only 31% of workers received payment of any kind in 1957, 90% currently receive payment and 69% receive money. Nevertheless, only 20% of those employed full time in actual work areas earn more than ten dollars per week. Thus, although institutional work is being done, most workers are not being paid at a rate based on minimum wages. While this situation will improve as a result of the court's decision in *Souder v. Brennan*, the area of resident pay will nevertheless need monitoring to assure that previously "employed" institutional residents are not now merely allowed to sit and vegetate.

A primary concern for the future, however, must be the planning of vocational training programs to meet the needs of changing institutional populations. The increase in institution sheltered workshops and work activity centers represent the beginnings of such planning, but more must follow. Two-thirds of institutional vocational training is currently being carried out through the use of regular work areas of institutions. With the increase in severely and profoundly retarded residents, this plan will become less feasible. If vocational training is to play a part in the training of these residents, planning must begin now.

QUOTE WITHOUT COMMENT

There is a destiny that makes us brothers.
None goes his way alone.
All that we send into the lives of others
Comes back into our own.
—Edwin Markham

References

Belinson, L. I., Bensberg, G. J., & Erdman, R. L. Manual of standards for state residential institutional for the mentally retarded. *American Journal of Mental Deficiency*, 1963, 68(2).

Cohen, J. S., Zigler, R., Lipman, R., Adams, F., & Morelli, D. The development of a job instructor training program for institutional service workers. *American Journal of Mental Deficiency*, 1961, 66(3), 381-386.

Cohen, J. S. Community day work in an institutional vocational training program. *American Journal of Mental Deficiency*, 1962, 66(4), 574-579.

DeRoo, W. M. & Harralson, H. L. Increasing workshop production through self-visualization on videotape. *Mental Retardation*, 1971, 9(4), 22-25.

Dettenhiem, E. N. The monetary system. *Mental Retardation*, 1969, 7(1), 54-56.

Goldberg, I. I. A survey of the present status of vocational rehabilitation of the mentally retarded residents in state supported institutions. *American Journal of Mental Deficiency*, 1957, 61(6), 698-705.

Huddle, D. D. Work performance of trainable adults as influenced by competition cooperation, and monetary reward. *American Journal of Mental Deficiency*, 1967, 72(2), 198-211.

Hunt, J. G. & Zimmerman, J. Stimulating productivity in a simulated sheltered workshop setting. *American Journal of Mental Deficiency*, 1969, 74(1), 43-49.

Kott, M. G. Wage programs for mentally retarded residents of public institutions. *Mental Retardation*, 1963, 1(3), 161-163.

Nagler, B. & Kirkland, M. Institutional work programs—Boon or bane. *American Journal of Mental Deficiency*, 1961, 66(3), 375-380.

Roberts, C. L. & Perry, R. M. A total token economy. *Mental Retardation*, 1970, 8(1), 15-18.

Rosen, M., Diggory, J. C., & Werlinsky, B. E. Goal setting and expectancy of success in institutionalized and non-institutionalized mental subnormals. *American Journal of Mental Deficiency*, 1966, 71(2), 249-255.

Rosen, M., Halenda, R., Nowakiwski, M., & Floor, L. Employment satisfaction of previously institutionalized mentally subnormal workers. *Mental Retardation*, 1970, 8(3), 35-40.

Rusalem, H., Peterson, N., & McCraney, H. The role of the state rehabilitation counselor in institutional programming. *Mental Retardation*, 1967, 5(2), 15-19.

Steiner, K., Baker, A., & Ward, V. Resident training program: Housekeeping and elementary nursing procedures. *Mental Retardation*, 1965, 3(2), 24-25.

Windle, C. The literature: Institutional experiences. Prognosis of mental subnormals, Chapter VII. *American Journal of Mental Deficiency*, 1962, 66(5).

Souder v. Brennan. Civil Action No. 482-73 (United States District Court, District of Columbia).

Acknowledgments

The author wishes to thank Mr. Frank R. Giliverty, Superintendent of the Southbury Training School, Southbury, Connecticut, for his assistance in preparing the questionnaire.

ATTITUDES AND PERCEPTIONS

Many educators have faced a phenomenon referred to as "the self fulfilling prophecy." In simple terms this means that people will show you what you expect from them. Many studies show that low expectations foster low performance while the opposite is also true.

In special education, an educator must be aware of "the self fulfilling prophecy" and work toward negating its effects. Expectations for the handicapped should be realistic and attainable without being too easily reached. In the classroom the curriculum should reflect these realistic expectations.

However, in the world of work, "the self fulfilling prophecy" is even more difficult to deal with. Many employers and workers in the community have unrealistic conceptions of handicapped students and workers. Rumor and mythology do more to hurt the chances for success of the handicapped than any other single factor.

Career and vocational education are most important to the handicapped job seeker because preparation and confidence can lead to job attainment. If community employers are given information about job related curricula in the school systems, they may be more willing to hire the handicapped citizens.

If it is true that the handicapped are hindered by poor attitudes and mistaken perceptions in the community; and strong evidence supports that fact, then the handicapped female has an even more difficult task. Not only is she encumbered by low expectations and misinformation, but also sex stereotyping and generalization. In many cases, the male handicapped is given the chance to succeed in industry while the female handicapped is expected to take a secondary role. It seems that our world is changing and improving for the female, but ever so slowly in special education.

The following articles reflect the above points and will hopefully make educator and layman aware of the existent problems.

THE INFLUENCE OF ACADEMIC INFORMATION ON TEACHERS' JUDGMENTS OF VOCATIONAL POTENTIAL

SANDRA ALPER
PAUL M. RETISH

Work study programs have typically emphasized placing retarded persons in unskilled jobs (Gold, 1973; Kokaska, 1971). This practice continues despite much evidence that retarded persons can successfully be trained as skilled laborers (Gold, 1972, 1973, 1974; Oswald, 1968).

One often cited factor contributing to the underemployment of retarded workers is the use of standardized intelligence and achievement tests, with low predictive validity for vocational success, as devices for vocational evaluation (Blackman & Silperstein, 1968; Gold, 1973; Sarason, 1959). Morley (1972) raised the possibility that secondary special education personnel may be unduly influenced by IQ and achievement scores when making vocational decisions about their students.

The primary purpose of the present investigation was to determine to what extent academic information influences teachers' judgments of vocational potential of retarded persons. Level of job difficulty and teacher attitude toward the import of academic skills for job success were also evaluated.

Procedure

Subjects (n = 86) were all work-study teachers, grades 9 through 12, in the state of Iowa.

Three self administered questionnaires were designed for this study. Questionnaire 1 contained descriptions of 10 jobs, 5 unskilled jobs and 5 skilled jobs (see Peterson & Jones, 1964). These job descriptions were followed by a list of 6 academic skills and 20 vocational skills. The vocational skills had been determined to be necessary for employability in each of the 10 jobs (Peterson & Jones, 1964). The academic skills included functional skills incorporated into most secondary work-study programs (Iowa Department of Public Instruction, 1976).

Subjects were instructed to rate the import of each skill for the success of a retarded worker in each of the 10 jobs using a 5 point Likert scale. Three groups of subjects were thus created based on their mean ratings of the import of the academic skills. Also included in questionnaire 1 was a fictitious psychological report of a retarded individual of an employable age with no specific academic or vocational information included.

Questionnaire 2 contained two fictitious psychological reports of retarded individuals. One individual was described as having a Full Scale WISC-R IQ of 52 with corresponding WRAT scores, and the other individual was described as having an IQ of 70 with compatible WRAT scores. Both descriptions contained identical vocational skill information. Questionnaire 3 included a similar psychological report of a retarded person with only the vocational skills provided.

Subjects were instructed to read each of the four descriptions and rate the likelihood of each individual's successful employment in each of the 10 jobs using the 5 point Likert scale. Ten subjects were randomly selected to pretest the questionnaires. Of the remaining subjects, 58 (76.3%) returned three complete questionnaires.

Results and Discussion

A 4 × 2 × 3 (type of information × level of job difficulty × teacher attitude) ANOVA with repeated measures on the first two factors, Type VI design (Lindquist, 1953), was applied to the data. Results are presented in Table 1.

A significant main effect for type of information was obtained, $F (3, 165) = 24.773$, $p < .05$. A dependent t statistic employing the $error_1$ (w) term was used to test for differences between all possible pairs of means. Judgments of the vocational potential of a retarded person described as having an IQ of 52 with specific vocational skills (i.e., low academic plus vocational information condition) were significantly lower than similar judgments based on the high academic (IQ = 70) plus vocational information, vocational information only, or no information conditions.

The main effect for level of job difficulty attained statistical significance, $F (1, 55) =$

TABLE 1
Analysis of Variance Summary Table

Source	df	MS	F
Between subjects	57	1.3303	
Teacher attitude toward academic skills (C)	2	6.2608	5.4393*
error$_b$	55	1.1510	
Within subjects	406	0.4695	
Type of information (A)	3	13.4550	24.7733*
Level of job difficulty (B)	1	15.2431	50.2347*
A x B	3	0.7750	8.2004*
A x C	6	1.5909	2.9291*
B x C	2	0.2908	0.9582
A x B x C	6	0.1069	1.1321
error (w)	385	0.3166	
error$_1$ (w)	165	0.5431	
error$_2$ (w)	55	0.3034	
error$_3$ (w)	165	0.0945	
Total	463		

*$p < .05$.

50.235, $p < .05$. Teachers' judgments of vocational potential for the five skilled jobs were significantly lower than for the five unskilled jobs. The main effect for teacher attitude toward academic skills was also significant, $F(2, 55) = 5.439$, $p < .05$. Teachers who rated academic skills as important for job success judged vocational potential to be significantly lower than teachers who did not rate academic skills as important for job success.

The interaction between type of information and level of job difficulty obtained significance, $F(3, 165) = 8.200$, $p < .05$. A Scheffé (1959) test revealed one significant comparison. Judgments of vocational potential for skilled jobs were significantly lower than for unskilled jobs under the low academic (IQ = 52) plus vocational information condition than under the no information condition.

The interaction between type of information and teacher attitude toward academic skills was also significant, $F(6, 165) = 2.929$, $p < .05$. A Scheffé test indicated no significant difference, however, between judgments of vocational potential made by teachers who rated academic skills as important for job success and those who did not under the low academic plus vocational information and vocational information only conditions as had been predicted. It was felt that further comparisons would yield no additional relevant information.

These results tend to support Morley's (1972) contention that teachers may be influenced by academic information when making vocational decisions about their students. In addition, knowledge of IQ and academic achievement may cause teachers to underestimate or overlook more relevant vocational skill information.

References

Blackman, L. S., & Silperstein, G. Job analysis and the vocational evaluation of the mentally retarded. *Rehabilitation Literature*, 1968, *29*, 103-105.

Gold, M. W. Stimulus factors in skill training of the retarded on a complex assembly task: Acquisition, transfer, and attention. *American Journal of Mental Deficiency*, 1972, *76*, 517-526.

Gold, M. W. Research on the vocational habilitation of the retarded: The present, the future. In N.R. Ellis (Ed.), *International review of research in mental retardation* (Vol. 6). New York: Academic Press, 1973.

Gold, M. W. Redundant cue removal in skill training for the mildly and moderately retarded. *Education and Training of the Mentally Retarded*, 1974, *9*, 5-8.

Iowa Department of Public Instruction, Des Moines, Iowa. Personal correspondence, 1976.

Kokaska, C. J. The need for economic security for the mentally retarded. In D. E. Brolin & B. Thomas (Eds.), *Preparing teachers of secondary level educable mentally retarded: Proposal for a new model*. Menomonie WI: Stout State University, 1971.

Lindquist, E. F. *Design and analysis of experiments in education*. Boston: Houghton Mifflin, 1953.

Morley, R. E. Adult needs of the educable mentally retarded. *Vocational evaluation and curriculum modification*. Des Moines IA: Iowa Department of Public Instruction, 1972.

Oswald, H. *A national follow-up study of mentally retarded workers employed by the federal government* (Grant RD-2425-6.). Washington DC: Dept. of Vocational Rehabilitation, 1968.

Peterson, R. O., & Jones, E. M. *Guide to jobs for the mentally retarded*. Pittsburgh: American Institutes for Research, 1964.

Sarason, S. *Psychological problems in mental deficiency (2nd ed.)*. New York: Harper, 1959.

Scheffé, H. *The analysis of variance*. New York: Wiley, 1959.

SEX ROLE STEREOTYPING IN SPECIAL EDUCATION: A LOOK AT SECONDARY WORK STUDY PROGRAMS

PATRICIA THOMAS CEGELKA

PATRICIA THOMAS CEGELKA *is Assistant Professor, University of Kentucky, Lexington, Kentucky*

Abstract: An examination of special education practices relative to secondary work study programs for the mentally retarded reveals sex biases in favor of the male enrollees. These biases are apparent in program admission, program offerings, and program evaluation. Both ethical and legal considerations dictate that those practices which serve to doubly handicap individuals labeled both retarded and female be eradicated. Suggestions are made for assessing and restructuring secondary work study programs in order to provide equal quality of participation for all.

Commenting on the high placement ratio of boys to girls in classrooms for the educable mentally retarded (EMR), Mercer (1973) observed that girls must be slower than boys in order to be labeled and placed in special classes. She suggested that society is more tolerant of lower levels of intellectual ability in females. An analysis of special education curriculum reveals that sex role stereotyping is prevalent in all aspects of special education programing (Gillespie and Fink, 1974). The purpose of this article is to extend Gillespie and Fink's analysis by examining the literature on secondary work study programs and the subsequent adult adjustment patterns of those served. The focus is on the extent to which these programs may have provided differential training opportunities for the sexes, resulting in differentiated patterns of adult adjustment.

Effectiveness of Work Study Programs for EMR

Over the past century considerable progress has been made in the area of secondary vocational preparation programs for the retarded. Early efforts were, of course, centered exclusively in institutional settings. An institution in Kentucky took the lead by developing what was considered a mature vocational training program, with academic learning being confined to the mornings, the afternoons devoted to trade training (Doll, 1967). Stewart's report in 1882 of this program stated that:

> Those unable to master whole trades were trained in specific operations. Many were able to live without outside aid and the best girls were discharged to work for wages in families. (p. 237)

During the first few decades of the century, institutional colonies developed specifically for the rehabilitation of the mentally retarded; trade extension classes were begun and vocational education/special education liaisons budded. During the 1950's, monies from the Office of Vocational Rehabilitation (OVR) stimulated the development of model demonstration projects, resulting in the proliferation of secondary level work study programs for the mentally retarded.

An impetus to the expansion of vocational training programs for the mentally retarded, as well as a consequence of that expansion, has been the plethora of studies on adult adjustment patterns of the mentally handicapped. Some of the early studies (Baller, 1936; Muensch, 1944; Fairbanks, 1933; Hegge, 1944) suggested that even without special education programs, retarded individuals tended to make adequate adult adjustments. With employment ranging anywhere from 33% during the Depression to 89% during the war years, the retarded were found to be employed in all categories listed by the Dictionary of Occupational Titles. Boys were most frequently employed in labor occupations and girls in domestic service occupations. The marriage rates tended to be somewhat lower than for the average population, with divorce rates somewhat higher, particularly for girls. Run-ins with the law were somewhat greater for males, while there was a higher incidence of promiscuity among the girls than found in the general population.

Environmental intervention such as that reported by Skeels and Skodak, 1966 and specific training programs (Abel, 1940) indicated that the adult adjustment patterns of mentally retarded could be enhanced. More recent studies have attempted to determine the extent to which special class training and specific vocational training were affecting adult adjustment of EMRs. Acceptably high success rates have been reported for former special class students. Porter and Milazzo (1958) found that 75% of those in special classes were employed, compared with 17% of the nonspecial class group. Phelps (1956) found that 68% of his sample were employed, with an additional 11% listed in the categories of housewife, armed services, and unemployed. Dinger's (1961) followup reported an 83% success rate for his retarded sample.

A 1971 report of students who participated in the Kansas Work Study Project addressed the question of the efficacy of the OVR sponsored secondary programs (Chaffin, Spellman, Ragen & Davison, 1971). It concluded that cooperative work study programs of this nature were achieving at least limited success insofar as the project students were earning significantly more than a comparison group of nonproject students ($90 per week compared with $63 per week). However, while 83% of the experimental students were employed, 75% of the nonproject students were also employed, which corresponds to the rates reported in prework study followups. This lead to the conclusion that the goal of work study programs should not be to make students employable (which, apparently, they already are) but to enhance this employability.

Sex Role Stereotyping in the Curriculum

A careful analysis of followup studies of former special education pupils has led the author to conclude that although secondary programs may have enhanced the employability of their male clients, these programs have made no discernible impact on the employability of females. This is true in terms of percentage of employment, type of employment, and comparative female-male earnings. It does not appear that either the philosophy or the curriculum for training mentally handicapped females has altered much in the last hundred years.

The focus of vocational preparation training efforts for the mentally retarded continues to be on the male portion of the population. A sampling of the literature turned up reports of 10 model projects designed exclusively for boys and one such project for girls. Those projects serving both males and females reported sex ratios of from 2:1 to 4:1, boys to girls. The curricula of these programs are reflective of differential expectations for the sexes. For instance, the Illinois Curriculum Guide developed by Goldstein and Seigle (1958) suggested in the unit on Occupational Adequacy that girls engage in sewing and boys in woodworking. Dinger (1961) recommended units of instruction for boys which included home repairs—carpentry, plumbing, electrical and masonry. The girls' units in home economics involved grooming, child care, sewing, and cooking. Syden (1963), in recommending guidelines for cooperative work study programs, stated that:

> Each student should be given an opportunity to work in a school shop or home economics room. Boys should be assigned to one semester of general shop and one semester to specific shop class, such as metal, printing, and possibly, machine shop. Girls should be given the opportunity to participate in cooking, sewing, ceramics and typing classes. (p. 91)

It would appear that both the classroom training and the work placement components of the secondary programs have provided boys with sets of skills which are potentially transferable to higher levels of occupational attainment than the skill areas in which girls are trained. Kokaska (1964), in discussing a work study program in Phoenix, admitted that sex was a handicapping variable in finding job training samples for girls. Faced with this same problem, the Kansas Work Study Project developed a Domestic Work-Sample (Spellman, Chaffin, & Nelson, 1970) for girls, in which female students were placed in private homes to learn housecleaning skills in preparation for possible permanent job placements as cleaning ladies.

The extent to which these school experiences have resulted in differential adult occupational patterns for the sexes is impossible to assess precisely. Frequently, the reports list jobs held by the retarded (and possibly a comparison group of normals) but do not specify which jobs were held by boys and which by girls. Further, because wages are usually reported as a general mean or median for the total retarded sample, the wages of males and females cannot be compared. Thirdly, the reporting of gross percentage data of successful and unsuccessful subjects does not allow comparisons by sex. A final complicating factor, and a telling index of differential expectations, is the variance in criteria of success applied to males and females. A much more stringent criterion of success is applied to boys—they must be employed and economically self supporting. For a girl, being categorized as "successful" may mean any one of a variety of things:

1. She is fully employed and self-supporting;
2. She is a housewife and supported by her husband;
3. She may be married and also working outside the home; or
4. She is a *homemaker* or a *housekeeper*, neither label implying marriage. In other words, a woman meets success criteria if she helps around the house—her own, her parents', or others'.

Those reports where sufficient data are presented to determine the level or type of employment support the contention that there has been little alteration in the adult adjustment patterns of females, at least over the past 40 years. Fairbanks (1933) reported that 40% of her adult female sample were employed in domestic services (including marriage). Charles (1953) categorized 50% of his females as housekeepers (marriage not implied). Bobroff (1960) reported that 59% were employed as homemakers (again, marriage not implied). Chaffin's (1971) study found 50% of the females from the experimental work study population either in domestic service or married. Interestingly, 50% of the nonwork study females were similarly "employed."

Not only is the literature fairly consistent in reporting the category of jobs held by retarded women, it is also fairly consistent in reporting the relative earnings of retarded males and females. Phelps (1956) found the pay earned by retarded females to be 58% that of the retarded males. Although the avowed purpose of this study was to analyze the individual characteristics of those earning more and less than the median wage, females were excluded from the analysis because of their low salaries. Bobroff (1960) reported that earnings for the retarded females in his sample were 66% those of the retarded males. Peterson and Smith's (1960) study particularly dramatized the differential earnings picture. Figure 1 presents a comparison of the weekly earnings of the retarded and normal sample.

The retarded males and the normal females earned approximately 62% of what the normal males did. This suggests that being a female of average intelligence is an economic disability equal to being a male who is mentally handicapped. The retarded female earnings were approximately 35% of those of the former two groups, highlighting the double disability of being both retarded and female.

Conclusions

There are basically four conclusions that can be reached from this survey of the relationship of special education work study programs to mentally handicapped females. These are:

	Male	Female	Comparative earnings-male/female
Nonretarded	89.30	55.00	62%
Retarded	54.85	19.25	35%
Comparative earnings-nonretarded/retarded	62%	35%	

FIGURE 1. Comparative median weekly wages of retarded and nonretarded subjects.

1. Fewer girls than boys are found in special vocational preparation programs. Mercer's observations that girls, particularly Anglo girls, are less apt to be labeled as retarded and placed in special classes than boys with similar intelligence quotients, suggests that sex per se may be a determining variable in placement.

2. Once in, girls are not provided with equal vocational training opportunities. They are trained for jobs of low or no financial remuneration. The jobs for which they are trained frequently are not covered by minimum wage laws and often promise less stability than the occupations for which

males are trained.

3. The field expects lower levels of adjustment from females. Girls are expected to be more dependent, as reflected by the differential criteria for success. In order to be counted as successful, a male generally must be fully employed and economically self sufficient while a female need not be employed, economically self sufficient or married. The emphasis on training girls primarily for marriage has serious implications. Given national divorce rate estimations of from 25 to 40%, it appears that girls should be trained for more stable employment futures. Further, it is probable that a large number of married females will have to contribute to the family income through employment outside the home. Special education programs have been negligent in preparing girls for such employment other than in low paying jobs.

4. By using nonspecific success criteria (housewife, homemaker, etc.) for girls, the field has been able to report higher success rates than would otherwise be possible. For instance, Dinger (1961) optimistically reported an overall success rate of 83% for his group of former special class pupils. The revised percentage of 60% employed for pay, with the remainder being either housewives or still in school, is comparable to that of studies reporting the adult adjustment of nonspecial education mentally retarded.

It is more difficult for girls than boys to get into special education classes for the mentally handicapped. Once in, lesser training is provided for them and lower levels of adult adjustment are expected of them. Their ability to meet these lower success criteria is then interpreted as justification for the special education programs.

Recommendations

The history of education reveals that in primitive cultures girls were taught to cook, to make clothes, to care for children and to perform similar domestic tasks (Atkinson & Maleska, 1962). In 1882, the first mature vocational training program for the mentally handicapped sent "the best girls to work for wages in families" (Stewart, 1882). In the 1960's, Domestic Work Samples (Spellman, Chaffin, & Nelson, 1970) were developed for training girls enrolled in a model work study program. The fact that special education curricula continue to emphasize domestic skills for girls suggests that little has been done in the last century to enhance their employability. Both ethical and legal considerations dictate that those practices which serve to dou-

bly handicap individuals labeled both retarded and female must be eradicated. Various components of program admission, curriculum, and evaluation should be examined for evidence of discriminatory practices. The following considerations might serve as a framework for assessing and restructuring secondary work study programs for the EMR:

- Admission to special education programs. Assuming that secondary work study programs are educationally defensible in that they render a unique and positive training function, educationally relevant criteria for admission to these programs must be developed and applied equally to the sexes. Retarded females should be afforded the same opportunities for participation as retarded boys.

- Biases of curriculum and training opportunities. Responsible special education personnel should examine the curricula (instructional units and materials, course offerings, and general program emphases) of individual secondary programs for sex biases, particularly where such biases predict differential patterns of adult adjustment. Equality of opportunities, in terms of the salary potential, job stability, training and placement aspects of work study programs. While federal equal rights legislation and the women's liberation movement have made obtaining quality job placements for females a somewhat less difficult task than it once was, nonetheless, it will continue to require an extra measure of diligence and ardor on the part of the work study coordinators to ensure equality of training opportunities.

- Program evaluation. Efforts at evaluating the successfulness of secondary school programs must focus on the vocational and adult adjustment patterns of all participants, using a single set of criteria for both sexes. Adult independence or success status must be defined, with particular emphasis on the parameters, quantitative and qualitative, of the nonsalaried occupation of homemaking. If such evaluation efforts should demonstrate differential adjustment patterns for the sexes, these data must be analyzed to determine the responsible components and remedial steps that should be initiated in the training programs.

Not only must both females and males be provided with equal opportunity for participation in work study programs, but they must be afforded an equal quality of participation as well. Only then can special education begin to obtain its goal of maximizing the potential of all eligible participants.

3. ATTITUDES

References

Abel, T.M. A study of a group of subnormal girls successfully adjusted in industry and the community. *American Journal of Mental Deficiency*, 1940, *43*, 66–72.

Atkinson, C. & Maleska, E.T. *The Story of Education*. New York: Chilton, 1962.

Baller, W.R. A study of the present social status of a group of adults who, when they were in elementary school, were classified as mentally deficient. *Genetic Psychological Monographs*, 1936, *18*, 165–244.

Bobroff, A. Economic adjustment of 121 adults, formerly students in classes for the mentally retardates. *Exceptional Children*, 1960, *26*, 404–408.

Boly, L.F. & Cassell, J.T. An exploratory on-the-job training program for the institutionalized mentally retarded. *American Journal of Mental Deficiency*, 1956, *61*, 105–112.

Burchill, G.W. *Work-study programs for alienated youth: A casebook*. Chicago: Science Research Associates, 1962.

Charles, D.C. Ability and accomplishment of persons earlier judged mentally deficient. *Genetic Psychological Monographs*, 1953, *47*, 3–71.

Chaffin, J.D., Smith, J.O., & Haring, N.G. *Summary: selected demonstration for the vocational training of mentally retarded youth in public high schools*. Kansas City KA: University of Kansas Medical Center (RD Project 1548, Final Report, Vocational Rehabilitation Administration, United States Department of Health, Education, and Welfare, Division of Research Grants and Demonstrations, Washington DC), September, 1967.

Chaffin, J.D., Spellman, C.R., Ragen, C.E. & Davison, R. Two follow-up studies of former educable mentally retarded students from the Kansas Work Study Project. *Exceptional Children*, 1971, *37*, 733–738.

Dinger, J.C. Post-school adjustment of former educable retarded pupils. *Exceptional Children*, 1961, *66*, 353–360.

Doll, E.E. Trends and problems in the education of the mentally retarded: 1800–1940. *American Journal of Mental Deficiency*, 1967, *72*, 175–183.

Eskridge, C.S. & Partridge, D.L. Vocational rehabilitation for exceptional children through special education. *Exceptional Children*, 1963, *29*, 452–458.

Fairbanks, R.F. The sub-normal child—seventeen years later. *Mental Hygiene*, 1933, *17*, 177–208.

Gillespie, P.H. & Fink, A.H. The influence of sexism on the education of handicapped children. *Exceptional Children*, 1974, *41*, 155–162.

Goldstein, H. & Seigle, D.M. *The Illinois plan for special education of exceptional children: A curriculum guide for teachers of the educable mentally handicapped*. Danville IL: The Interstate Printers and Publishers, 1958.

Hegge, T.G. The occupational status of higher grade mental defectives in the armed forces. *American Journal of Mental Deficiency*, 1944, *49*, 86–98.

Kokaska, C. In-school work experience: A tool for community adjustment. *Mental Retardation*, 1964, *2*, 365–367.

Kolstoe, Oliver P. The employment evaluation and training program. *American Journal of Mental Deficiency*, 1960, *65*, 17–31.

Mercer, J.R. *Labelling the Mentally Retarded*. Berkeley: University of California Press, 1973.

Muensch, G.A. A follow-up of mental defectives after eighteen years. *Journal of Abnormal and Social Psychology*, 1944, *39*, 407–418.

Peck, J.R. The Marbridge Plan: A Texas experiment in habilitation for mentally retarded youth. *Exceptional Children*, 1958, *24*, 346–350.

Peterson, L. & Smith, L.L. A comparison of the post-school adjustment of educable mentally retarded adults with that of adults of normal intelligence. *Exceptional Children*, 1960, *26*, 404–408.

Phelps, H.R. Postschool adjustment of mentally retarded children in selected Ohio cities. *Exceptional Children*, 1956, *23*, 58–62.

Porter, R.B. & Milazzo, T.C. A comparison of mentally retarded adults who attended a special class with those who attended regular school classes. *Exceptional Children*, 1958, *24*, 410–418.

Skeels, H.M. & Skodak, M. Adult status of individuals who experienced early intervention. Paper presented at the 90th Annual Meeting of the American Association on Mental Deficiency, May 12, 1966.

Spellman, C.R., Chaffin, J.D., & Nelson, C.M. Domestic work-training of adolescent mentally retarded girls. *TEACHING Exceptional Children*, 1970, *2*, 67–72.

Stewart, J.Q.A. The industrial department of the Kentucky Institution for the Education and Training of Feeble-Minded Children. *Proc. American Association on Mental Deficiency*, 1881–1882, 236–239.

Syden, M. Guidelines for a cooperative work- study program for the educable mentally retarded. *Mental Retardation*, 1963, *1*, 91–94.

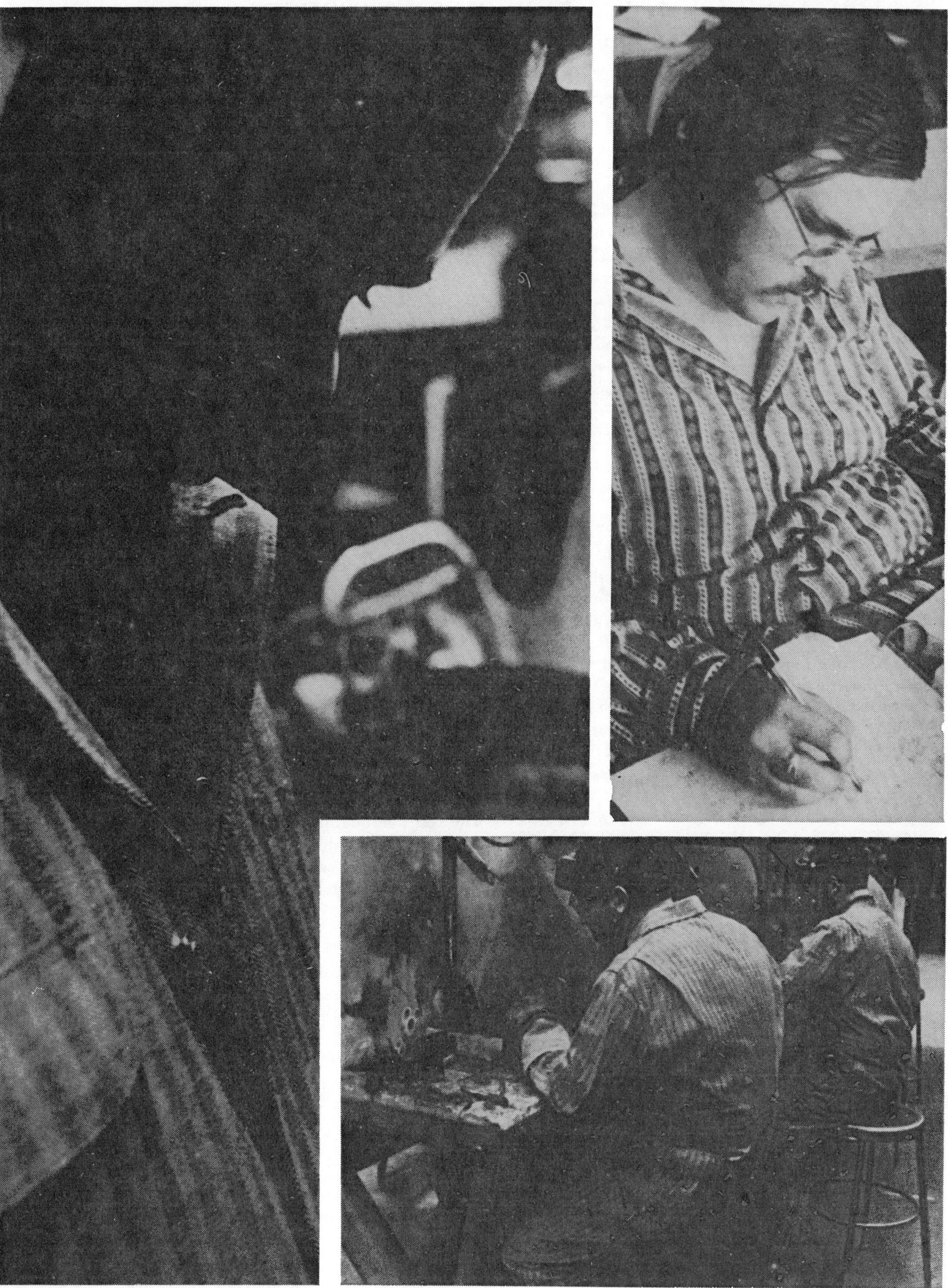

Student, Counselor, and Employer Perceptions of Employability of Severely Retarded

E. KEITH BYRD, Ph.D., P. DIANNE BYRD, M.S., and WILLIAM G. EMENER, Ph.D.

Dr. Byrd, assistant professor in rehabilitation counseling, Counselor Education Department, Auburn University, Auburn, Ala., was formerly with Florida State University, College of Education, Area of Professional and Clinical Programs. Mrs. Byrd earned her M.S. degree in rehabilitation counseling in 1975 at Florida State University and worked as a vocational evaluator for Goodwill Industries, Columbus, Ga. Dr. Emener is coordinator of rehabilitation counseling at Florida State University.

THE 1973 Rehabilitation Act *(P.L. 93-112, 93rd Congress, H.R. 8070, Sept. 26, 1973)* as amended and the regulations published in the Dec. 5, 1974, issue of the *Federal Register*[3] to implement the Act defined severely handicapped as those who have physical or mental disability that seriously limits their functional capacities, including mobility, communication, self-care, self-direction, work tolerance, and work skills. An expectation is that multiple rehabilitation services will be required over an extended period of time. Severe disabilities are listed, and it is suggested that those persons served by vocational rehabilitation will have multiple disabilities. State vocational rehabilitation agencies have been incorporating these mandates into a selection process, a service delivery system, and recording procedure.

Specific disability categories have been listed in order to expedite the selection process. Priority of the severely disabled creates a situation where fewer people with nonsevere disabilities may be eligible for service.

One of the critical issues arising from the 1973 Act and identified by The First Institute on Rehabilitation Issues[1] is job development and employment, a challenge for vocational rehabilitation agencies. A number of implications implicit in this issue were listed at the 1974 Institute:

1) Congress and state legislatures must be made aware of the cost of preparing those severely handicapped for the labor market,
2) proposed legislation could make it unlawful to discriminate in employment against persons who are physically handicapped,
3) affirmative action is a requirement regarding employment of the severely handicapped,
4) vocational rehabilitation must be concerned with transportation and architectural barriers, and
5) special informational resources and expertise in placement of severely handicapped must be developed.

Emphasis on severe disabilities will necessitate planning for special needs of this population, especially as it relates to readiness for employment on the part of the client and perhaps more importantly on the part of the employer. Projects with Industry, reported by Housman and Smith,[2] of The Human Resources Center, Albertson, L.I., N.Y., exemplifies the efforts to place and follow up clients in industry and other settings.

An important variable in employment of the severely disabled is the perceptions of severity for a specific disability held by various persons who have an impact on the rehabilitation process of the client. The employer's perception of severity obviously has a direct effect on the placement and successful employment of the severely disabled client. The counselor's perception, too, has a direct effect as a function of placement efforts required by the professional and the services delivery system. Perceptions of students of vocational rehabilitation are relevant to future effects on severely handicapped clients served. The research question asked in this study was: How are the severely disabled perceived by employers, counselors, and students in vocational rehabilitation regarding employability?

Instrumentation

Twenty severe disabilities were alphabetically listed and each subject was asked to respond anonymously to the question: How would you feel about hiring a person with any of the following disabilities? A five-point Likert Scale was applied to each disability with the following values: *1)* very likely to hire, *2)* likely to hire, *3)* undecided, *4)* unlikely to hire, and *5)* very unlikely to hire.

Four of the disabilities were judged to be least familiar to the respondents; respective definitions were afforded each subject for cerebral palsy, muscular dystrophy, multiple sclerosis, and paraplegia.

"Student Counselor and Employer Perception of Employability of Severely Retarded", E. Keith Byrd, Ph.D. Dianne Byrd, M.S., and William G. Emener, Ph.D. *Rehabilitation Literature*, Vol. 38, No. 2, February 1977, Pg. 42-44, © 1976 by the National Easter Seal Society for Crippled Children and Adults, 2023 W. Ogden Avenue, Chicago, Ill, 60612

Sample

Employers, counselors, and students in the Tallahassee, Fla., area were selected for the sample. Twenty-five employers were selected from the telephone book in such a fashion that no single industry was represented twice and a record was kept of the number of employees in an effort to approximate a reasonable cross-section in sizes of business. Size of

About the Study . . .

CONCERN for rehabilitation of the severely disabled, and placement of this client population, prompted the present study reflecting differences in perceptions by employers, counselors, and students. Severe disabilities were listed and the three samples were asked how they perceived the employability of persons within each of the disabilities. Disabilities were listed in order by mean score for all three samples and paired comparisons of the samples were made between employers-students, employers-counselors, and counselors-students. Perceptions of employers and counselors were relatively close. Students' perceptions differed from those of employers.

employer's business ranged from having 3 to 2,200 employees. Fourteen Department of Vocational Rehabilitation (DVR) counselors responded to the questionnaire. Twenty-five graduate and undergraduate majors in rehabilitation services at Florida State University also responded to the questionnaire. Employer's perceptions were solicited by telephone in order to assume a reasonable return rate. Counselors received the questionnaire by office mail and students responded to the questionnaire in class.

Statistical Analysis

Likert scores were tallied for each disability in each of the samples and a mean score calculated. Disabilities were rank-ordered according to degree of severity by mean score in each example. The Mann-Whitney U statistic was used to test for significant differences in perception of disability severity among three paired samples; employers-students, employers-counselors, and counselors-students.

Results and Discussion

Table 1 lists the disabilities in order of severity by samples with mean scores for each. Table 2 records z scores and alpha levels for each pair of samples. *(Tables are on next page.)*

It is interesting to note differences in rank ordering among the three samples from a visual scan of Table 1. Alcoholism was considered the most severe disability by employers but was ranked fourth by counselors and twelfth by students. Blindness was ranked second by employers and first by counselors, but fifth by students, perhaps due to the large number of blind students and their resulting familiarity on the Florida State University campus. Mental retardation was

TABLE 1.— *Disabilities in Order of Severity by Employers, Counselors, and Students with Mean Scores*

Disability	Employers		Counselors		Students	
	Rank	X	Rank	X	Rank	X
Alcoholism	1	4.08	4	4.43	12	2.4
Blindness	2	3.84	1	4.79	5	3.4
Cerebral Palsy	3	3.72	2	4.71	2	3.68
Muscular Dystrophy	4	3.68	6	4.29	1	4.0
Multiple Sclerosis	5	3.64	6	4.29	4	3.48
Paraplegia	6	3.60	3	4.64	7	2.96
Mental Illness	7	3.36	5	4.36	5	3.4
Mental Retardation	7	3.36	8	3.79	3	3.56
Social Disorder	8	3.28	12	3.07	8	2.72
Deafness	9	3.24	9	3.71	6	3.28
Epilepsy	10	3.00	8	3.79	8	2.72
Drug Abuse	11	2.96	13	3.0	11	2.48
Amputation-Upper	12	2.84	16	2.07	11	2.48
Stroke	13	2.76	7	4.07	6	3.28
Amputation-Lower	14	2.68	18	1.71	15	1.96
Arthritis	15	2.64	14	2.86	9	2.64
Heart Disease	16	2.48	11	3.29	10	2.6
Kidney Disorders	17	2.20	10	3.5	14	2.12
Cosmetic Disability	18	1.96	15	2.14	13	2.16
Diabetes	19	1.92	17	1.79	16	1.84

ranked seventh by employers, eighth by counselors, and third by students suggesting less awareness by students of the employability of the mentally retarded. Amputation (both upper and lower limbs) was considered to be less severe by counselors. These and other comparisons suggest many questions regarding differences in perceptions of disability severity among employers, counselors, and students.

Application of the Mann-Whitney U statistic to the three paired samples yields interesting results. Selection of alpha=.01 for significant differences in the samples suggests interesting comparisons among the three paired samples. Employers and students yielded a z score of 3.63 and alpha level equal to .00016, while the other two paired comparisons yielded alpha levels greater than .01 with employers and counselors yielding z=−1.77 and alpha=.038, and counselors and students yielding z=−1.230 and alpha=.109. Selection of alpha=.05 yields two pairs of samples with significant differences. They are employers-students and employers-counselors.

Employers' perceptions of disability severity as it relates to employability provide criteria from which counselors and students can be compared. Counselors' perceptions being closer to employer perceptions than student perceptions may be a function of frequent contacts by counselors with employers dur-

TABLE 2.— *Z Scores and Alpha Levels in Paired Samples of Employers, Counselors, and Students*

Employers-students 2		Employers-Counselors 2		Counselors-students 2	
z score	alpha level	z score	alpha level	z score	alpha level
3.63	.00016	−1.77	.038	−1.230	.109

ing placement activity and awareness of limitations on employment potential placed on the severely disabled by various work settings and job requirements. Differences in employer and student perceptions may be due to employers' hard-line position on job requirements and students' openness to disability and employability as a function of the educational process in which either sample operates. Students' openness may be a function of their sensitivity to individual differences and the need for openness to assets rather than limitations of a specific disability.

RESULTS seem to reflect differences in student and employer populations. Perhaps the critical question is: How close should the populations be? Should students be taught all of the realities of placement? Is it desirable for students to remain relatively naive of these realities and to become aware of them as professionals after their formal education? Should there be reasonable concern for the relative closeness in perceptions of employers and counselors? Do counselors need some continuing education as to client potential and the need for removing psychological barriers to employment of the severely handicapped?

List of References

1. Arkansas Rehabilitation Research and Training Center. *Report from the Study Group on Critical Issues Involved in Rehabilitation of the Severely Handicapped;* John Fenoglio, chairman; First Institute on Rehabilitation Issues, held Apr. 15-17, 1974, in Denver, Colo. Hot Springs, Ark.: The Center, 1975 (?).

2. Housman, Roberta, and Smith, Dania. Placement for Persons with Severe Physical Disabilities. *Rehab. Counseling Bul.* June, 1975. 18:4:245-252.

3. U.S. Department of Health, Education, and Welfare, Social and Rehabilitation Service. Vocational Rehabilitation Programs; Implementation Provisions. *Federal Register.* Dec. 5, 1974. 39:235:42470-42507.

SURVEY OF COMMUNITY EMPLOYER ATTITUDES TOWARD HIRING THE HANDICAPPED

David M. Stewart

In September 1974, Baltimore Goodwill Industries, Inc. initiated a survey of attitudes of Baltimore Community Employers toward hiring the handicapped. Goals were to expand and develop new avenues and opportunities for employment of the handicapped within the Baltimore Community; to use the data gathered from employers as an evaluation tool of success of our programs and services; and to determine the need for upgrading of training programs or the development of new programs that would better meet the needs of Community employers and to better prepare those whom we serve for the employment situation.

A total of 200 community employers were interviewed from the following 10 occupational areas:

- Clerical
- Custodial
- Food Service
- Hospitals/Nursing Homes
- Laundry/Dry Cleaning
- Radio & T.V. Repair
- Sales
- Service Stations
- Shoe Repairing
- Upholstery

Interviews were conducted at the employment site with the person responsible for employment practices within each company. A standardized survey form was developed and used for each interview.

TABLE 1

DATA SUMMARY

Occupational Areas	Positive Responses	Previous Experience in Employment of Handicapped	Annual Openings (Nationally)[1]
Clerical	13	9	123,280
Custodial	15	12	136,000
Food Service	20	12	86,000
Hospitals/ Nursing Homes	20	18	100,000
Laundry/Dry Cleaning	12	11	22,200
Radio & T.V. Repair	12	5	4,400
Sales	14	6	190,000
Service Stations	14	8	15,400
Shoe Repairing	4	6	900
Upholstery	12	10	1,400

[1] *Occupational Outlook Handbook*, 1974-75 Edition. U.S. Department of Labor, Bureau of Labor Statistics 1974.

3. ATTITUDES

In determining whether an employer had a negative or a positive attitude toward hiring the handicapped, the following assignments were used:

For a positive attitude —

a. the employer said that he would employ a qualified handicapped person.

b. if it was feasible at present or in the future for the employer to hire additional personnel.

c. if the employer expressed an interest in learning more about Goodwill, visiting Goodwill, or in becoming a cooperative O.J.T. employer.

For a negative attitude—

a. the employer actually stated that he would not hire a handicapped person.

b. the employer made prejudicial statements about handicapped people.

c. the employer did not feel that he could hire any additional personnel at present or in the future due to either space limitations or lack of business.

Conclusions

Based upon the results and the data collected in the 200 interviews, the following conclusions (which may be valid for Metropolitan Baltimore only) were drawn:

1. Viable training areas for handicapped people which present favorable employment climates are Clerical, Food Services, Custodial, Service Stations, and Upholstery.

2. There seems to be an employer reluctance to employ the handicapped in the occupational areas ot Sales and Laundry/Dry Cleaning (which seems to be on the decline in Baltimore). A large scale employer educational program would be needed in order to broaden employment opportunities for the handicapped in these areas.

3. Businessmen are looking for employees that have good work habits and are job ready. In many of the industries surveyed employers said that they are more interested in finding positive work attitudes and motivation to work among potential employees and they would rate these criteria higher than the need to possess technical skills.

Rehabilitation agencies serving the handicapped should provide those kinds of programs which will assist clients in becoming job ready. If we are involved in Vocational Training we should be offering skill training programs in those areas which present the most favorable opportunities for employment.

Author: DAVID M. STEWART, Director, Cumberland Goodwill Industries, Cumberland, MD 21502.

A JOB PLACEMENT PROCEDURE FOR THE MENTALLY RETARDED

Abstract: The authors focus upon techniques to use with prospective employers. These include qualifying the employer, developing initial contacts, and obtaining the interview. They also provide suggestions relative to a basic approach to the interview, the presentation, and overcoming objections.

GARY R. SIGLER *is a graduate student in Special Education, California State College, Long Beach.*

CHARLES J. KOKASKA *is Advisor, Special Education Programs, California State College, Long Beach.*

An examination of the literature related to job placement of the retarded led the authors to observe the predominance of the "do me a favor" approach for securing positions. Placing the retarded is not unlike other sales situations. For example, there is a demand (employers seek competent labor), a product (the retarded are efficient workers), and a solution (the placement of the retarded at the employer's business). What is lacking is a simple but effective marketing method which incorporates the businessman's own techniques in presenting the retarded to management personnel. In this article the authors will examine elements which comprise the design of a marketing plan from a placement point of view.

Why Hire the Retarded?

A solicitor of placement (vocational counselor, work study coordinator, or teacher) should be well equipped to show benefits and advantages of hiring the retarded. Within the past 10 years an increased amount of positive information about work histories and capabilities of the retarded has appeared in the literature. A few of these items of information are provided below to show placement personnel that they have a "marketable" item and need not provide excuses for it. The references also provide some basic themes which placement personnel can utilize in their interviews with prospective employers.

The retarded worker can do a variety of tasks. The following is a report of job areas for retarded workers taken from one study (President's Committee on Employment of the Handicapped, 1963): Service, 30.0 percent; Unskilled, 21.2 percent; Semiskilled, 19.3 percent; Clerical, 12.0 percent; Family workers, 6.2 percent; Agriculture, 55.9 percent; and Skilled, 5.4 percent.

The retarded are conscientious workers. A manufacturing company executive (Sleith, 1966) stated that: "Generally speaking, it takes no longer to train a retarded worker for a routine task than it does a person of normal intelligence." He continued, "One thing we've noticed about the retarded is the unusual personal pride they take in their work."

The retarded can do the job. A national

publication stated that "Employers still have trouble finding anyone who will deign to take a position considered boring or menial. . . . Some restaurateurs are hiring the mentally retarded because they are the only people willing to try— and even take some pride in—mopping floors and washing dishes [*Time*, 1970]."

Obviously, additional examples based upon the individual's experience with local employment of the retarded increases the persuasive qualities of the presentation. The essential item that must be continually emphasized is that the employer should hire the retarded because it will *increase efficiency* within his business.

Qualification of Prospective Employers

Prior to the initial contact with prospective employers, the placement person should investigate his prospect. He should become familiar with the employer's type of business, classification of employee's skill levels, number of employees, and any other data pertaining to the employment situation. Based on this information, he can judge whether a particular prospect can fill the needs of the special worker. If there is reasonable doubt, he can elect to search for another prospect and repeat the same process.

This screening procedure, prior to establishing contact with employers, saves time, money, and effort, but more importantly, it increases the number of successful placements as a result of the actual appointment. It also allows the individual to maintain a positive and productive attitude toward job placement by decreasing the amount of wasted effort.

Initial Contacts

The manner in which the first contact with the employer is made, and what is said or done at that contact, can make the difference between a successful or an unsuccessful close (conclusion). There are a variety of ways to make the first contact:

1. Mail. This approach can be divided into three categories:

    a. The pre-approach letter is sent to a prospect as an introduction and a statement of the intent of the sender. Generally a followup phone call for an appointment is made by the sender. The letter can have a favorable effect in that it announces ahead of time that a placement person will be calling on the prospective employer. It has a disadvantage of giving the prospect an opportunity to establish a defense or, worse yet, warn his secretary that he does not want to see the caller. In these cases the sender receives an automatic "no" or cannot obtain the opportunity to speak with the prospect. Occasionally the introductory letter can be coupled with a referral from a business or service club associate of the prospect, thereby indirectly obligating the prospect to at least speak with the sender.

    b. The business reply letter introduces the sender, states the business, and requests the prospect to respond either by phone or return card. It is the opinion of the authors that business reply letters are of little value for the dollars and time invested. The reply has the advantage that if it is returned, the prospect is interested, and the percentage of placements is generally high.

    c. The information letter provides the prospect with data about the business of the sender and does not include a followup or response. The information letter has little to recommend it since no measure of effectiveness can be obtained and placement cannot be traced directly to this type of contact.

2. Telephone solicitation. This method is often coupled with the preapproach letter or may be used with the referral, i.e., "Mr. Businessman, your associate Mr. Service Club suggested that I contact you." The caller may use this first contact only to introduce himself, describe his purpose, and then ask for an appointment. In another approach, the caller has no referral or pre-approach but, rather, calls "cold" and attempts to secure an appointment. In all cases, placement personnel should qualify prospective employers prior to contact.

3. Personal calls. This can be a very ef-

fective method of initial contact. It is very difficult to tell someone that you will not talk with him when you are looking him in the eye. Generally the personal call is made without prior notification, or it could be preceded by an introductory letter. The most effective use of this method may be when the placement person has a few minutes prior to an appointment, or between appointments, and uses the personal call to fill that time spot.

4. Referrals. By far the most effective method of obtaining prospects and securing appointments is the referral. To use the name of an associate of the prospect on the first contact has the effect of obligating the prospect to grant an appointment. Referrals can come from anyone with whom the prospect is in contact; for example, city mayor, service club member, business associate, and family. The referral can be used in conjunction with letters, personal calls or phone contacts. As added insurance the authors suggest that the special educator have the referral inform the prospect of the forthcoming contact and then use a phone call to secure an appointment.

Obtaining the Appointment

The logical first goal for the steps discussed thus far is to secure an appointment with the prospective employer. Placement personnel should never lose sight of this objective. It is critical that they move directly toward the appointment with the very first contact.

If the solicitor chooses contact by mail the letter must request a specific time for a meeting, or tell the prospect that he will be in his office at a specific date and time, or urge a specific response from the prospect. If the mail piece fails to do so, he has wasted time and money.

When the solicitor makes a "cold call" via telephone or a followup call to a letter, the approach should be simple.

> Mr. Businessman, my name is Mr. Teacher with Education High School. We, here at Education High, have programs which are tailored to the needs of businessmen like yourself. I would like to see you for thirty minutes, either Thursday at 2:00 p.m., or Monday at 4:00 p.m., to explain how we can be of benefit to you. Which time would be best?

Note that the solicitor was brief and to the point. He introduced himself, stated his purpose, and asked for an appointment to describe the benefits for the businessman. The solicitor did not speak around the point or ask the businessman when he would be available but, rather, stated clearly his needs and gave a choice of two specific times for the appointment. The businessman could not then be in a position to say simply "no" but must either accept one of the times or counter with a more appropriate time for the appointment. If the solicitor used a referral, such as, "Mr. Businessman, my name is Mr. Teacher with Education High School, and Mr. City asked that I contact you . . ." then the businessman is even more obligated to the appointment.

Much the same approach is used in the personal "cold call" where the solicitor stops in unannounced. The purpose here is to see the prospect face to face and set a time for an in depth appointment. It is possible to move into a presentation upon the initial contact, but generally one can present a more complete presentation and have the prospect's undivided attention by establishing another time. Again, the purpose is the appointment!

> Mr. Businessman, my name is Mr. Teacher from Education High School. Mr. City has told me so much about you and your business, I wanted to stop in to meet you personally. At Education High we have special programs for training workers in your area of manufacturing, and Mr. City knew you would be interested. I can stop in Tuesday at 2:00 p.m. or Wednesday at 9:00 a.m., to tell you the benefits. Which would be preferable for you?

The Appointment

It is crucial that the placement coordinator be well prepared and rehearsed in his presentation. Business appointments are not unlike classroom presentations, i.e., you have a specific amount of time to "bring home" a specific response or conclusion.

3. ATTITUDES

The use of visual aids can be most helpful. Charts and short phrases on flip pads or felt boards can emphasize the important points and summarize the material presented to the businessman. As in teaching, these aids also make it possible to review quickly and provide continuity to the presentation.

The objective of the presentation must be kept in mind. If one aspires to obtain the behavioral objective (the businessman will say "yes"), then one must control the appointment and guide him to the needed and desired response. The following points may assist in obtaining the objectives:

1. Keep the presentations short and simple. Don't overload the prospect with needless statistics and examples.
2. Speak in terms the businessman can understand. One misplaced term taken from the educational or psychological field can endanger the final goal of placement.
3. Sell the benefits. Tell the businessman why he will be better off to hire the mentally retarded. We have the evidence that the retarded are competent workers. Use this material.
4. Use small questions with obvious answers to condition the desired response. To say it another way, get the prospect used to saying "yes." "It's a nice day, isn't it Mr. Businessman? You use several machine operators in your shop, don't you Mr. Businessman?"
5. Use trial closes. A trial close can be compared with a city street. The beginning of the street is the start of the presentation, and the end of the street the conclusion. Along the way there are several stop signs, each representing a crossroad or, for our purposes, the termination of one point of the presentation. At each point try to obtain a desired response. "Mr. Businessman, you do agree that our students are as reliable as your current workers?" If the response is positive, then move directly to, "When can John Student begin?" If the response is uncertain, assume the positive, move to the next point. If the response is negative, stop, move back to where you first lost the prospect's agreement, and start again. *This is imperative.* Do not pass over a negative response.

    If you do, the prospect may at the end of the presentation use that one negative response to turn you down; however, if you obtain agreement to each point along the way, you will have an automatic close at the end of the presentation. After all, if the businessman has said, "yes" to every point in the presentation, he would look rather foolish to say "no" at the conclusion.
6. Avoid sidetracking. If you are asked a question which is not directly appropriate, avoid it. Don't ignore it; just answer the question with your next statement: Mr. Special Educator, how do you understand those kids?" "Mr. Businessman, you would not believe how easy it can be. Why, our students have proven themselves to be very dependable...." In almost every case the question will be lost and you can continue and maintain control of the interview.

Overcoming Objections

The various kinds of employer questions and objections have been discussed in the literature. They may include specific references to the lack of abilities or more global reflections of cultural stereotypes. Our concern at this juncture is with some basic techniques which may help overcome these objections:

1. Anticipate possible objections. They will vary according to the type of industry, level of employment, and the particular idiosyncrasies of the employer; however, through trial and error, the placement individual can estimate their occurrence and most certainly should be prepared to counter them.
2. Most objections are misunderstandings or misconceptions. When this is the case, the best approach is to meet the objection with honest and firm answers. Don't guess or be less than positive with the answers.
3. At times, placement personnel will encounter objections that are valid; for example, "Your students aren't as smart as average students, are they?" In this instance, the special educator can present evidence that emphasizes the retarded student's skill to perform the desired tasks, rather than his lack of comparative intellectual ability. Once again, the focus should be upon the *benefits* of employing this particular worker.

Discussion

The authors have attempted to present

procedures and suggestions which can be utilized in the work placement of the retarded. However, it has been our experience that there is no final or complete technique for convincing employers to hire the retarded. Each placement individual must continue to develop his own unique style for presenting the graduates of his training program. Our interest was to present basic considerations to those who are involved in the beginning stages of training programs or seek to refine current procedures.

Program planners should remember that these procedures cannot substitute for the quality of skill which is required of the trainee. There undoubtedly have been trainees who were highly capable and were not placed or misplaced on jobs due to the lack of a developed presentation. However, we seriously doubt whether those trainees who do not possess the work abilities can continue with an employer, no matter how sophisticated the placement operation may be. Placement is a logical extension of the work training program, but is of questionable value when adequate preparation is nonexistent.

Finally, placement personnel should continue to concentrate on "selling the benefits" of the retarded worker. We have mentioned this point throughout the article because it is our conviction that in too many instances we have taken a defensive position relative to our trainees. We must continue to expand and elevate the possible training and employment sites while also emphasizing the positive personal qualities that our trainees bring to a particular job. It is a potent consideration which must be vigorously included in the continuum of training which extends from the elementary school through the adult years.

References

America the inefficient. *Time*, March 23, 1970, 72-80.

Sleith, W. What a mentally retarded worker can do. *Supervisory Management Magazine*, January, 1966. (Reprinted by The President's Committee on Employment of the Handicapped.)

The President's Committee on Employment of the Handicapped. *Guide to job placement of the mentally retarded.* Washington, D. C.; USGPO, 1963.

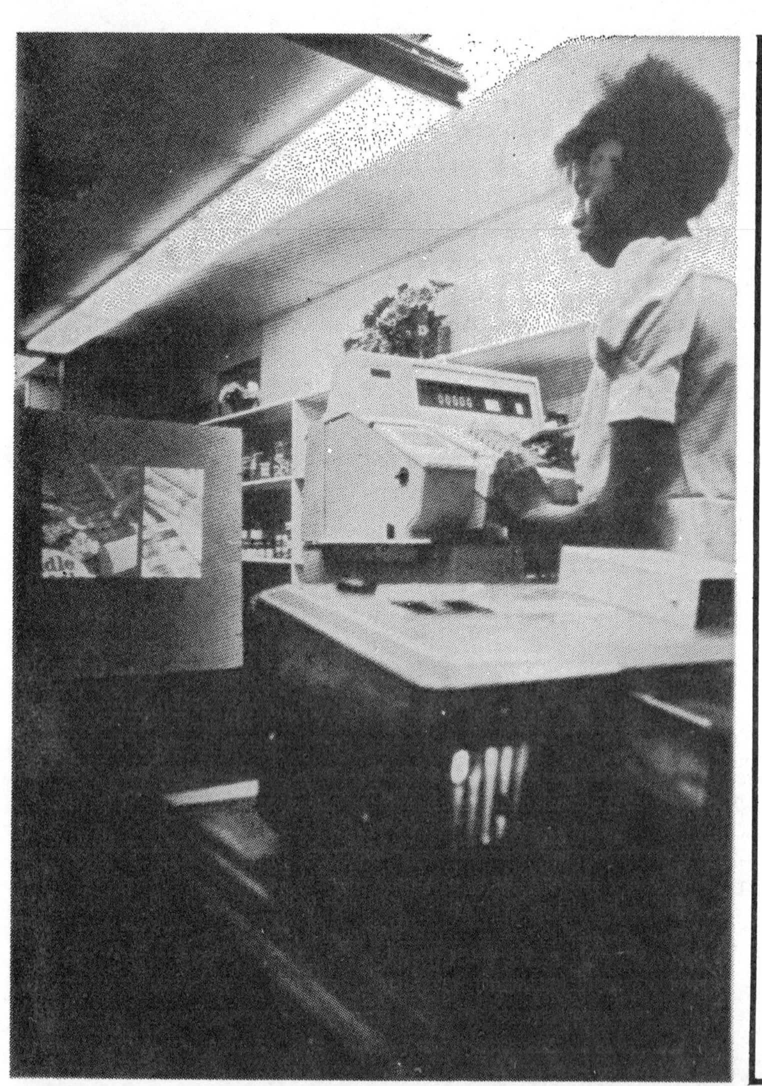

THE HANDICAPPED: CHOOSING THE APPROPRIATE CAREER

For those handicapped individuals who attain proper occupational preparation through an efficient career education curriculum, problems have not disappeared.

One question that must be answered is, "have I chosen a realistic and attainable career or vocation?"

Making the proper decision in this area is the responsibility of the school staff including the teacher, the guidance counselor, the vocational counselor and other support personnel as well as the student himself.

Inventories, checklists and assessment techniques are very important tools in choosing the appropriate career for the handicapped.

The special needs of the handicapped, the interests of the handicapped and the availability of employment are all realistic concerns of the special educator.

Documentation of work experience and expertise can be gained from the previously mentioned assessments and checklists, and this may be a favorable factor in securing employument for the handicapped.

The following articles give a sample of various tools used in assisting the handicapped in choosing appropriate careers. This is by no means an exact science. Special education teachers, various counselors and prospective employers can all add greatly to the process. Cooperation from the handicapped student himself can also aid in making the vocational choice meaningful and relevant.

VOCATIONAL CHOICES: AN INVENTORY APPROACH

Abstract: A representative sample of educable mentally retarded males and females in public secondary day schools and state residential institutions participated in standardizing the Reading-Free Vocational Interest Inventory, a recently devised nonreading method to measure vocational likes and dislikes. Separate norms tables were prepared for males and females to convert raw scores on each interest scale to standard scores and equivalent percentile ranks. Test-retest reliability on subsamples were highly satisfactory. Validity coefficients obtained with concurrent testing were encouraging with many values significant at high levels of confidence. Predictive validity is yet to be established as well as needed research with populations other than the mentally retarded.

RALPH L. BECKER

RALPH L. BECKER *is Research Psychologist, Ohio Department of Mental Health and Mental Retardation, Division of Mental Retardation and Developmental Disabilities, Columbus, Ohio.* The research reported herein was performed pursuant to a grant from the US office of Education, Department of Health, Education, and Welfare, Project No. 452227, Grant No. OEG-0-8-080188-4421 (607). (Because of the recent submission of the Reading–Free Vocational Interest Inventory to test publishers, the author is unable, at this point in time, to give interested educators a date for marketing of the Inventory. Other inquiries may be directed in care of the author at the Columbus State Institute, 1601 West Broad Street, Columbus, Ohio 43223.)

Interests have been the object of much attention from vocational and counseling personnel during the past generation. At least two scholarly books (Strong, 1943; Darley & Hagenah, 1955), a collection of eight significant monographs (Super, 1940; Darley, 1941; Carter, 1944; Barnett, 1952; Brogden, 1952; Guilford, 1954; Strong, 1955; Layton, 1960), and a number of published reviews in the journals (Berdie, 1944; Super, 1945, 1954; Roe, 1957), all dealing with the nature and role of interest are the result.

Implicit in these and other vocational studies by research personnel is the definite positive relation between inventoried interests and job satisfaction. The results indicate that the person who enters an occupation consistent with his interests is more likely to be a satisfied worker than the person who does not. Moreover, in assessing a person's interest the accumulated evidence shows that expressed interests have somewhat less permanence than inventoried interests—inventoried interests, on the other hand, are more stable and provide useful data for prediction (DiMichael & Dabelstein, 1947; Nunnally, 1959; Cronbach, 1960; Craven, 1961).

The review of relevant literature in the field of vocational measurement over the past 30 years clearly indicates: (a) the interest dimension may be critical to job satisfaction and adjustment; and (b) inventoried assessment of a person's vocational likes and dislikes are more permanent and stable than expressed interest. These findings by researchers were obtained from studies dealing with high school, post high school, and college students of normal intelligence aiming at the middle through the upper range of the occupational hierarchy. Attempts to measure vocational preference in the educable mentally retarded using the inventory method has generally not proven fruitful. This has been largely a matter of the inappropriateness of inventories requiring a level of reading comprehension beyond that achieved by a large proportion of mentally retarded persons; or unrealistic occupations for which the mentally retarded could not genuinely aspire.

In view of the value of the interest dimension as a positive component of job satisfaction and adjustment, the present project was undertaken to prepare an inventory that would: (a) assess the vocational choice of educable mentally retarded subjects in occupations in which they are proficient and productive; (b) have acceptable reliability for retarded persons in different types of training facilities; and (c) have acceptable correlates of validity.

Method

Based on the results of a pilot study (Becker, 1967; Becker & Ferguson, 1969), an extensive review of vocational literature dealing with the mentally retarded was made. Jobs demonstrating productive and proficient performance were analyzed for possible sorting of similar job tasks (i.e., sweeping, mopping, and dusting; serving, waiting tables, and preparing salads) into clusters that would be independent and mutually exclusive categories of known task activities performed by mentally retarded workers. The success of the sorting process and confirmed by extensive item analyses (Becker, 1971), resulted in 11 male clusters and 8 female clusters and they were as follows:

Males. Automotive, Building Trades, Clerical, Animal Care, Food Service, Patient Care, Horticulture, Janitorial, Personal Service, Laundry Service, and Materials Handling.

Females. Laundry Service, Light Industrial, Clerical, Personal Service, Food Service, Patient Care, Horticulture, and Housekeeping.

Clusters consisted of 15 pictorial items each with all illustrations depicting different occupational activities as reported in the literature. For males, 165 activities were illustrated and for females an additional 120 illustrations were prepared. All illustrations consisted of clean, bold, line drawings, and free of fine detail and figure–ground problems of perception. In addition,

pertinent occupational hardware and environment were included in the illustrations (see Figure 1).

For purposes of administering the inventory, pictorial items were grouped by

FIGURE 1. Sample of pictorial items presented in triad form by sex.

threes (triad) for a total of 55 triads in the male inventory and 40 triads in the female inventory. For each of the male and female forms, pages were bound into 8½″ by 11″ test booklets including a cover page of instructions and the purpose of the inventory. Examinees were administered the inventory for self estimates using a forced-choice technique, that is, given three alternative choices, subjects are instructed to select one item on a "like best" basis though all three may seem equally attractive or unattractive to them. Selections may be made directly in the test booklet by making a circle on the desired drawing, or scoring an answer sheet form that identifies each item in each triad. Items are keyed to arrive at raw score totals in each interest cluster. Depending on the agency type, public day school, or residential institution examinees' raw scores were converted to normalized standard scores (T score) and percentile ranks using the appropriate agency norm.

To record a subject's performance on the interest scales, an individual profile sheet was prepared for permanent keeping in the subject's school folder. A feature of the profile sheet is a percentile graph whereby a subject's rank in each of the interest scales is plotted for a visual chart of high and low interests.

To meet the demands of representative sampling in preparing the norms, a sample of 6,400 educable mentally retarded subjects from all geographical regions of the United States and from urban, rural, and inner city divisions were included. The strategy was contingent upon obtaining similar proportions of the regional distribution of the standardization sample with regional distribution of actual enrollment in public secondary day schools for the school year 1969-70. A discussion of the comparison study and efforts to obtain regional and institutional proportions were reported in a previous investigation (Becker, 1971).

Findings

Inventory Reliability

The reliability of the inventory was reported for four educable mentally retarded groups: public day school and institutionalized males, and public day school and institutionalized females. Subsamples from the standardization study were administered the inventory and retested after a 2 week interval. The Pearson product-moment method was used to compute the correlations.

Table 1 presents reliability coefficients for each interest scale (cluster) by agency type for subsamples of males. Table 2 presents reliability coefficients on sub-samples of females.

TABLE 1

Test-Retest Correlations of the Interest Scales for a Subsample of Males: Public Day Schools Grades 9-12, and Ungraded Institutions

| | Test-retest reliability* | |
| | Public day schools | Institutions |
Interest scales	(N=143)	(N=50)
Automotive	.91	.94
Building-trades	.86	.89
Clerical	.79	.80
Animal care	.89	.94
Food service	.83	.88
Patient care	.87	.89
Horticulture	.84	.89
Janitorial	.86	.85
Personal service	.88	.83
Laundry service	.75	.74
Materials handling	.73	.82

*Interval of 2 weeks.

TABLE 2

Test-Retest Correlations of the Interest Scales for a Subsample of Females: Public Day Schools Grades 9-12, and Ungraded Institutions

| | Test-retest reliability* | |
| | Public day schools | Institutions |
Interest scales	(N=90)	(N=45)
Laundry service	.72	.89
Light industrial	.73	.87
Clerical	.68	.85
Personal service	.80	.78
Food service	.78	.65
Patient care	.85	.88
Horticulture	.87	.89
Housekeeping	.86	.85

*Interval of 2 weeks.

Correlations were mainly in the 70's and 80's for subsamples of males and at high levels of statistical significance. Coefficients ranged from .73 to .91 in public day schools, and .74 to .94 in residential institutions. Correlations of institutionalized males were generally higher than their counterparts in public schools, indicating greater reliability of the scores. Since the institution sample averaged 2 years, 5 months older (mean CA, 19-10), the higher reliabilities could be explained, as experience has shown, by the more mature group being the more stable and thus illustrating the expected higher correlations. Group mean IQ's were not significantly different with the larger value observed in the public school sample (public school IQ, 69; institution IQ, 62).

Correlations in Table 2 for subsamples of females were mainly in the 70's and 80's and at high levels of statistical significance. Coefficients range from .68 to .87 in public day schools, and .65 to .89 in residential facilities. Institutionalized females obtained generally higher test-retest coefficients indicating greater reliability of the scores for the more mature group of girls (mean institution CA, 20-0; mean public school CA, 17-4). Group mean IQ's were not significantly different with the larger value observed in the public school sample (public school IQ, 68; institution IQ, 62).

Inventory Validity

Validity of the inventory was obtained with concurrent testing using the research instrument and a standardized vocational preference inventory. The *Geist Picture Interest Inventory* (GPII) was selected since it contains male and female forms (Geist, 1964) and may be administered as a group test. A random sample of subjects who were involved in the collection of test-retest data on reliability, were also administered the GPII at the initial testing for correlates on concurrent validity. Correlations were computed between the raw scores of the research instrument, the *Reading-Free Vocational Interest Inventory* (R-FVII), and raw scores of the GPII. Coefficients of correlation were computed when the interest scales, by inspection, appeared to be positively related. To interpret the relationship between the two instruments, a brief description of each of the selected inventory scales is worthwhile.

R-FVII

Automotive. Enjoys servicing and repairing all types of vehicles.

Building Trades. Enjoys using small and large hand tools or heavy equipment in construction work.

Clerical. Enjoys general office work; delivers mail or messages.

Animal Care. Enjoys tending domestic animals and pets.

Food Service. Enjoys preparing or serving food to guests and patrons.

Patient Care. Enjoys assisting patients in hospitals or clinics.

Horticulture. Enjoys greenhouse, gardening, and dirt farming activities.

Janitorial (Housekeeping-Females). Enjoys performing light maintenance and housekeeping services.

Personal Service. Enjoys providing a wide variety of services to guests or patrons.

Materials Handling. Enjoys general warehouse and delivery work.

Light Industrial. Enjoys using small hand tools in assembly or factory-type work.

GPII

Persuasive. Enjoys dealing with people, selling and promotion work.

Clerical. Enjoys keeping records, accounts, correspondence, and office work.

Mechanical. Enjoys exercise of manual skills; working with tools or machines.

Scientific. Enjoys field and laboratory sciences dealing with things and people.

Outdoor. Enjoys a variety of outdoor or open-air activities.

Literary. Enjoys reading; may enjoy writing.

Computational. Enjoys numerical activities; computing, counting, figuring, or keeping numerical records.

Social Service. Enjoys helping others; assists the sick, destitute, or unfortunate.

Personal Service. Enjoys providing services to people.

Table 3 presents correlations between selected scales of the GPII and R-FVII for samples of educable mentally retarded males in public day schools (mean CA, 17-7; mean IQ, 68) and state institutions (mean CA, 19-6; mean IQ 61). Inspection of the 30 coefficients shows the Materials Handling versus Computational scales to be the only relationship that is not statistically significant in either agency sample. All other correlations show at least one agency in each relationship at the .05 or .01 levels of confidence and beyond.

Differences in the magnitude of the coefficients between agencies on the same paired scales may suggest group differences in the educational and vocational training, work experience, and background of the sampled subjects, as well as differences in the way pictorial items are perceived on the two inventories. In general, correlations are very satisfying with many significant at the .01 level and beyond and with few low positive values. Most coefficients are in the 30's and 40's and although modest, reach levels of statistical confidence.

Table 4 presents correlations between selected scales of the GPII and R-FVII for public day school (mean CA, 17-6; mean IQ, 67) and institutionalized (mean CA, 19-8; mean IQ, 62) educable mentally retarded females. Inspection of the 30 coefficients shows three pairs of relationships not statistically significant in either agency sample. These are the Clerical versus Clerical, Horticulture versus Outdoor, and Personal Service versus Personal Service scales. All other correlations show at least one agency in each relationship at the .05 or .01 levels of confidence and beyond.

Differences in the magnitude of the coefficients between agencies on the same paired scales suggests there may be real group differences between the two samples for such characteristics as educational and vocational background, training, and work experience, and in the perception of a wide range of pictorial items having occupational significance. Correlations are generally satisfying with many significant at the .01 level and beyond. Most coefficients are in the 30's and 40's and reach levels of statistical confidence. In most cases, a low positive value in one agency sample is balanced by a high positive value in the second agency for the same relationship.

Job Trainee Profiles

In the process of collecting standardization data in local public day schools and state institutions in Ohio, work-study coordinators suggested that the project staff examiner obtain verbal data on subjects' vocational likes and a comparison be made

TABLE 3

**Product-Moment Correlations Between Scales of the GPII
and Reading-Free Vocational Interest Inventory
(R-FVII) for Samples of Males**

| | | Correlations | |
| | | Public day schools (N=38) | Institutions (N=38) |
R-FVII scales	GPII scales		
Automotive	Mechanical	.36*	.29
Building trades	Mechanical	.71**	.53**.
Clerical	Clerical	.35*	.35*
Clerical	Literary	.21	.50**
Clerical	Computational	.40*	.39*
Clerical	Persuasive	.22	.35*
Animal care	Outdoor	.28	.46**
Food service	Persuasive	.49**	.17
Patient care	Social service	.55**	.37*
Patient care	Scientific	.47**	.35*
Horticulture	Mechanical	.35*	.28
Horticulture	Outdoor	.50**	.47**
Janitorial	Mechanical	.17	.37*
Personal service	Social service	.26	.46**
Materials handling	Computational	.16	.16

*Significant at the .05 level.
**Significant at the .01 level.

TABLE 4

**Product-Moment Correlations Between Scales of the GPII
and Reading-Free Vocational Interest Inventory
(R-FVII) for Samples of Females**

| | | Correlations | |
| | | Public day schools (N=38) | Institutions (N=40) |
R-FVII scales	GPII scales		
Light industrial	Mechanical	.39*	.32*
Clerical	Clerical	.29	.25
Clerical	Literary	.48**	.09
Clerical	Computational	.42**	.12
Clerical	Persuasive	.40*	.26
Personal service	Personal service	.14	.19
Personal service	Social service	.26	.46**
Food service	Personal service	.42**	.38*
Food service	Persuasive	.06	.37*
Food service	Clerical	.41**	.46**
Patient care	Scientific	.78**	.59**
Patient care	Social service	.67**	.75**
Horticulture	Outdoor	.12	.18
Horticulture	Mechanical	.39*	.10
Housekeeping	Mechanical	.48**	.29

*Significant at the .05 level.
**Significant at the .01 level.

between expressed and inventoried results.

Within the limits of a working schedule, a total of 10 subjects were interviewed by the same project examiner for their vocational likes. Each subject was asked to name three kinds of jobs or types-of-work that he liked to do. They were cautioned to name as first, the work or job they liked best; to name as second, the work or job they liked next best; and to name as third, the job they liked to do but not as much as their first and second choices.

Of the 10 subjects for whom both interviews and inventory scores were obtained, data on four cases is presented as generally typical of the findings for the two kinds of information. Figures 2 and 3 present profiles of 2 males and 2 females, respectively, with a male and female, each, from work-study and vocational training programs in public secondary day schools and residential state institutions.

Subject 1. John is a 23 year old resident at a state institution for the mentally retarded. His IQ is 58 and he has attended the academic, prevocational and vocational training programs at the institution. For the last 3 years he has been the full time mail boy at this facility. John expressed his preference for a variety of job tasks including:

First: "Hospital work, mostly."

Second: "Mail boy."

Third: "Work in a theatre and shine a flashlight to show people where to sit; and help people in a motel and carry packages."

John was insistent in adding that he wants "no kitchen work and no maintenance work like fixing lights." (Note John's performance on the BTr and FS scales in Figure 2.)

Figure 2 presents John's inventoried profile on the 11 vocational interest scales. Inspection of his profile reveals a cluster of three interest areas with percentile ranks (PRs) of 95 and 98. The Personal Service (PSv) area ranks as his first choice (PR 98), with Patient Care (PCr, PR 95) and Clerical (Cl, PR 95) tied for second, for three areas of highest measured interest. The Laundry Service scale (Ly, PR 70) might be an alternative position for job entry if highest interest areas were closed out in the institution.

There is substantial agreement between John's stated interests and his measured interests. Though he expresses preference to work in a hospital, his measured interest shows a first choice in the Personal Service category with Patient Care in a very strong

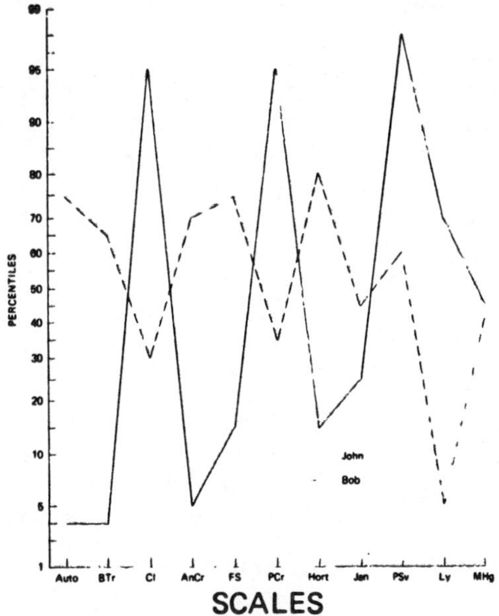

FIGURE 2. Job trainee profiles of male institutional and public day school workers.

second position. As a working mail boy, the Clerical scale in a second position tends to confirm John's positive feelings about his job when confronted with many other vocational activities. John's interest in working in a theatre or motel to assist patrons and guests as his third verbal choice, was his first measured choice in the Personal Service category.

Subject 2. Bob is an 18 year old special education student enrolled in the 11th grade at a public high school. His IQ is 75 and he has attended special classes for the educable retarded since the fourth grade. He is presently participating in the work-study curriculum for juniors. Bob indicated the following are the work activities he would like most to do:

First: "Remove trees and tree stumps."

Second: "Probably work on cars and repair them."

Third: "Get a job doing carpentry work—I like to work outside."

Figure 2 presents Bob's inventoried profile on the 11 vocational interest scales. Inspection of Bob's performance indicates that most scales are moderately above and below the median (PR 50). The Horticulture scale (Hort, PR 80) and Bob's verbal first choice along with the Automotive (Auto, PR 75) and Food Service (FS, PR 75) scales, are three areas of highest measured interest. Bob's verbal desire to "work on cars" appears to be borne out by his preference for automotive activities when faced with many alternative choices. The expressed interest in carpentry was only moderately borne out by measurement as indicated by the Building Trades scale (BTr, PR 65). Although the expected relationship did not occur, the fact that the Food Service scale did emerge as an interest area does identify a potential work field for exploration leading to job entry.

Subject 3. Judith is a 21 year old resident at a state institution for the mentally retarded. She was admitted at the age of 14 and has since attended programs in education and vocational training within the facility. On a recent intelligence test she earned an IQ of 64. Judith is presently working in the employee's cafeteria and is being considered for transfer to the commissary. She expressed vocational preference for the following types of work:

First: "I like to be a waitress."
Second: "Factory work; do rubber work like making rubber gloves or balloons."
Third: "Do laundry work."

Figure 3 presents Judith's inventoried

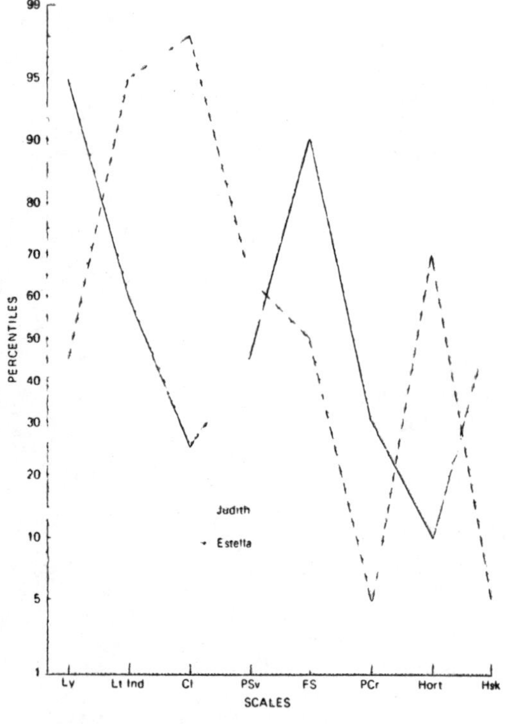

FIGURE 3. Job trainee profiles of female institutional and public day school workers.

profile on the eight vocational interest scales. Inspection of her profile indicates two scales with high measured interest: Laundry Service (Ly, PR 95) in the first position and Judith's third verbal choice, and Food Service (FS, PR 90) in a second position and her first expressed choice. Her verbal preference for "factory work" was only modestly borne out by measurement

on the Light Industrial scale (Lt-Ind, PR 60). Judith's measured interest was also her expressed interest although a difference in the rank order of job preferences did result.

Subject 4. Estella is a 19 year old student enrolled in special classes for the mentally retarded at a public high school. Her recent IQ was 62. She is completing her senior year in the educable mentally retarded program while working full-time in the school office as a clerical trainee. Estella gave as her vocational preferences the following activities:

First: "Be a secretary and work in a office."
Second: "Make things—do reupholstery work, sew, things like that."
Third: "Be a waitress in a cafeteria."

Figure 3 presents Estella's inventoried profile on the eight interest scales. Inspection of this profile demonstrates a wide scattering of values of extremely high and low interests coupled with average to near-average interests. The Clerical scale (Cl, PR 98) as her first measured interest, was also her first expressed interest. Of the 16 pictorial items keyed to the Clerical scale, Estella chose 15 clerical activities in discriminating the wide range of different job tasks. The Light Industrial scale (Lt–Ind, PR 95) as her second measured interest, was also her second verbal interest. Estella's expressed preference to "be a waitress in a cafeteria" was not borne out by measurement. The Food Service scale (FS) obtained a PR of 50, below the third position Horticulture (Hort, PR 70) and fourth position Personal Service scale (PSv, PR 65). Though the expected relationship did not occur, work sampling opportunities in both food service and horticulture would tend to confirm the preference of one job type over the other.

Summary

The present project was undertaken to develop a nonreading method of assessing vocational preference in educable mentally retarded youth enrolled in public secondary day schools and state residential facilities. Areas of commerce and industry in which retarded workers demonstrated proficiency and productivity were analyzed by job tasks and resulted in 11 male and 8 female interest categories. Extensive item analyses and subsequent reliability and validity studies established test-retest reliability of the scores and concurrent validity of the interest scales. Individual inventoried profiles of educable retarded job trainees were analyzed against present job status and expressed interest.

The results showed high agreement among the three variables while identifying emerging inventoried interests for potential job entry.

Future use of the scales will require long term studies on predictive validity to establish some confidence in the predictive quality of the tool in making guidance recommendations to clients. Studies dealing with populations other than the educable mentally retarded, such as the trainable mentally retarded, the disadvantaged, the illiterate, and those with reading problems would determine the feasibility of this type of design in counseling and guidance of verbally handicapped persons.

References

Barnett, G.J., Handelsman, I., Stewart, L.H., & Super, D.E. The occupational level scale as a measure of drive. *Psychological Monographs*, 1952, 342.

Becker, R.L. *Vocational Picture Interest Inventory.* Columbus, Ohio: Columbus State Institute, 1967.

Becker, R.L. *Reading-free Vocational Interst Inventory.* Final Report. US Office of Education, Research Project No. 452227, Grant No. OEG-0-8-080188-4421, 1971. (Mimeo)

Becker, R.L. *Reading-free Vocational Interest Inventory:* Measurement of job preference in the EMR. *Mental Retardation*, 1973, 11, 11-15.

Becker, R.L., & Ferguson, R.E. A *Vocational Picture Interest Inventory* for educable retarded youth. *Exceptional Children*, 1969, 35, 562-63.

Becker, R.L., & Ferguson, R.E. Assessing educable retardates' vocational interest through a non-reading technique. *Mental Retardation*, 1969, 7, 20-25.

Berdie, R.F. Factors related to vocational interests. *Psychological Bulletin*, 1944, 41, 137-157.

Brogden, H.E. The primary values measured by the *Allport-Vernon Tests*, a study of values. *Psychological Monographs*, 1952, 348.

Carter, H.D. Vocational interest and job orientation. *Applied Psychological Monographs*, 1944, 2.

Craven, E.C. *The use of interest inventories in counseling.* Chicago: Science Research Associates, 1961.

Cronbach, L.J. *Essentials of psychological testing.* New York: Harper and Brothers, 1960.

Darley, J.G. Relationships among the *Primary Mental Abilities Tests*, selected achievement measures, personality tests, and tests of vocational interests. *University of Minnesota Studies in Higher Education*, 1941, 192-200.

Darley, J.G., & Hagenah, T. *Vocational interest measurement.* Minneapolis: University of Minnesota Press, 1955.

DiMichael, S.G., and Dabelstein, D.H. Work satisfaction and work efficiency of vocational rehabilitation counselors as related to measured interests. American Psychologist, 1947, 2, 342-343. (Abstract)

Geist, H. *Geist Picture Interest Inventory.* Beverly Hills: Western Psychological Services, 1964.

Guilford, J.P., Christensen, P.R., Bond, N.A., Jr., & Sutton, M.A. A factor analysis of human interests. *Psychological Monographs*, 1954, 375.

Layton, W.L. (Ed.) *The Strong vocational interest blank: Research and uses.* Minneapolis: University of Minnesota Press, 1960

Nunnally, J.C., Jr. *Tests and measurements.* New York: McGraw-Hill, 1959.

Roe, A. Early determinants of vocational choice. *Journal of Counseling Psychology*, 1957, 4, 212-217.

Strong, E.K., Jr. *Vocational interests of men and women.* Stanford: Stanford University Press, 1943.

Strong, E.K., Jr. *Vocational interests 18 years after college.* Minneapolis: University of Minnesota Press, 1955.

Super, D.E. *Avocational interest patterns: A study in the psychology of avocations.* Stanford: Stanford University Press, 1940.

Super, D.E. Strong's vocational interests of men and women: A special review. *Psychological Bulletin*, 1945, 42, 359-370.

Super, D.E. The measurement of interests. *Journal of Counseling Psychology*, 1954, 1, 168-173.

VOCATIONAL BEHAVIORAL CHECKLISTS

Richard T. Walls

Thomas J. Werner

Authors: **RICHARD T. WALLS**, Ph.D., professor of educational psychology and research associate of the Rehabilitation Research and Training Center, West Virginia University, Morgantown, WV 26506; **THOMAS J. WERNER**, M.A., instructor of psychology, and doctoral candidate, West Virginia University.

ABSTRACT. Thirty-nine behavior checklists containing items (behavior descriptions) related to pre-vocational, vocational, occupational, and work behaviors were reviewed, categorized, and evaluated. The items were counted and categorized into eight subclasses of vocational behavior: prevocational skills, job-seeking skills, interview skills, job-related skills, union-financial-security skills, work performance skills, on-the-job social skills, and specific-job skills. Checklists were classified according to objectivity (degree of behavioral specificity), scope (number of items per subclass), observation setting, and prescriptive-descriptive nature. Strategies for selecting and utilizing vocational behavior checklists to facilitate training and assessment are discussed.

In many types of training programs there is a need for frequent assessment of client, student, or trainee skills in vocational or occupational areas.

Apart from casual or anecdotal observation, there have been two major types of formal observation tools: rating scales and behavior checklists. The primary emphasis of this report is direct observation of behaviors as represented by behavior checklists.

In an attempt to determine the number of behavior checklists available and in use, an advertisement was placed in several periodicals requesting, ". . . behavior checklists used in tabulating behaviors or skills" of various populations. The same request was sent to 883 state schools and rehabilitation facilities.

More than 200 checklists were received; they varied greatly in the extent to which they represented carefully specified and observable behaviors and in item formats and scoring requirements. Classes such as the following were represented: eating, toileting, dressing, health, grooming, communication, mobility, dexterity, vocational, recreational, socialization, orientation, motor skills, self-help, daily living, independence, alcohol and drug use, household responsibility, and work habits. Each of these classes included behaviors representative of that class. Details of 157 of them are reviewed in an annotated bibliography (Walls, Werner, Bacon, Zane, 1977).

As part of the continuing analysis of independent living skills and vocational behaviors, the authors reviewed and evaluated all items related to the assessment of vocational behavior. The goal was a comprehensive reference guide to the selection of vocational behavior checklists. While the same class was sometimes labeled "prevocational," "occupational," "job," or "work" behaviors, any items representing behaviors associated with employment are considered herein as "vocational."

Vocational items from each of 39 checklists were counted and sorted into eight subclasses. Descriptions of these subclasses and representative items follow.

Prevocational Skills include verbal behaviors related to job definitions, the client's job interests and job skills, as well as various prework skills. Item examples are (a) names jobs he could hold related to his own skills; (b) matches items by size; (c) names necessary tools required for specific jobs.

Job-Seeking Skills include searching skills leading to a job interview. Item examples are (a) reads newspaper to locate jobs or training; (b) fills out job applications; (c) determines job opportunities in the community.

Interview Skills include behaviors required during initial contacts with a potential employer. Item examples are (a) wears clothing suitable for the occasion; (b) gets to the appointment on time; (c) answers all questions.

Job-Related Skills include essential job behaviors that are not related to production, but rather to transportation to and from the job, work clothes, meals on the job, and orientation to work area. Item examples are (a) travels to and from work; (b) pays for lunches and transportation, making correct change, if required; (c) goes to each area in center when requested without getting lost or retracing his steps or entering 'off limits' areas.

Union-Financial-Security Skills include all behaviors related to job and financial security. Item examples are (a) calculates wages for hours worked minus approximate deductions; (b) works out a simple budget and budgets paycheck; (c) knows the function of union picketing.

Work Performance Skills include the primary production and performance characteristics such as punctuality, tool and work station maintenance, work rate, evaluation of own performance, persistence, work quality, and safety. Item examples are (a) follows instructions when job involves three or more specific tasks; (b) assembles materials needed on which to work; (c) begins work and continues for thirty minutes.

On-the-Job Social Skills include appropriate interpersonal skills with both peers, customers, and supervisors. Item examples are (a) interacts with others during breaks or lunch; (b) offers assistance when someone he is working with needs help; (c) works to improve from criticism.

Specific-Job Skills include information and behaviors related to particular occupations. Item examples based on "sales" behaviors are (a) stocks shelves; (b) cleans stock; (c) wraps packages.

As noted, 39 of the behavior checklists contain vocational items. They vary widely with respect to scope, objectivity, setting, and prescriptive-descriptive nature.

Scope connotes two dimensions, (a) total number of vocational items and (b) number of different subclasses represented. Scope, as represented by number of items in each subclass, may be noted in Table 1. For example, the *Behavioral Characteristics Progression* and the *Eastmont Training Center Checklist* differ greatly with respect to scope. Although they both contain approximately the same total number of items (50 and 56 respectively), the distribution of those items among the eight subclasses is dissimilar. The *Behavioral Characteristics Progression* contains 3 items in Prevocational, 7 items in Job-Seeking, 2 items in Interview, 10 items in Job-Related, 10 items in Union-Financial-Security, 16 items in Work Performance, and 2 items in On-the-Job Social. In contrast, the *Eastmont Training Center Checklist* contains 53 items in Prevocational and 3 items in Work Performance. To illustrate the other connotation of scope, the total number of vocational items for the *Group Home Candidate Checklist* is 254, but for the *Track Profile* only 9 items.

Objectivity is another important variable in the consideration of vocational checklists. The objectivity of these checklists is also represented in Table 1. "Objectivity" refers to how observable (i.e., behavioral) the checklist items are. The checklists were evaluated independently by two trained reviewers. They assigned a value from 1 to 5 based on the following criteria: Rating 5 clearly specifies (a) observable behaviors, (b) standards of performance (rate or accuracy of response), and (c) conditions of performance (situation prior to response). Rating 4 indicates one of the above (a, b, or c) is poorly specified or omitted. Rating 3 indicates two of the above are poorly specified or omitted. Rating 2 indicates behaviors not observable (poorly defined but potentially specifiable), and the standards and conditions are poorly specified or omitted. Rating 1 indicates the items are so vague and general that specification would be difficult or impossible, and the standards and conditions are poorly specified or omitted. When a rating difference of not more than one point on the five point scale was considered agreement, the agreement/agreement + disagreement index of interrater reliability was 0.974.

Objectivity also varies greatly among the vocational checklists. Items from the *Colorado Master Planning Guide for Instructional Objectives* specify (a) observable behaviors and (b) standards of performance. For example one item states, "Begins work at the beginning of the day and continues to work throughout the day, except for scheduled breaks." *North Central Regional Center Skill Evaluation and Assessment* items are behaviorally stated but do not include standards or conditions of performance; such an item is, "reads newspaper". Items that would not be readily specified objectively appear in the other scales. An example reads, "Enthusiasm towards work."

Specification of setting or place of observation is not usually included in a checklist or manual. Since items geared toward on-the-job settings may not be useful in prevocational or classroom training, (and *vice versa*), we have attempted to categorize items according to one of three settings (On-the-Job, Training Class, or Both). Some items illustrate an on-the-job or non-classroom setting. For example, the *Nebraska Client Progress System* contains the following item: "States prescribed policy for receiving paychecks, calling in sick, leaving work station at nonroutine times, etc." An item from the *Mid-Nebraska Competitive Employment Screening Test and Teaching Manual* illustrates a training class setting. It states, "Sees advantages to outside employment." Some items might be observed either on-the-job or in a training class. As an illustration, the *Adaptive Functioning Index #2* lists, "Works through small disruptions, e.g., phone rings, someone walks by." In Table 1, on-the-job settings are coded as OJ; training class settings are denoted by TC. B indicates that behaviors in the subclass may be observed in either setting or that both OJ and TC items are included in that subclass.

The only other descriptor included in Table 1 is an indication of whether the checklist is prescriptive (P), descriptive (D), or marginally prescriptive-descriptive (M). In a descriptive checklist, definition of an individual's current skill repertoire is the central concern. If a client "assembles two-part objects that fit together in a simple but secure way" (as indicated on the *Minnesota Developmental Programming System*), that action is known to exist in the client's vocational repertoire. If the client cannot perform the task, remedial training may be implied, but the training procedures are not specified. A prescriptive checklist goes further by describing the means for training the skill deficit. To illustrate, the *COMPET (Commonwealth Plan for Education and Training of Mentally Retarded Children)* not only describes whether the individual, "names necessary tools required for specific jobs," but then prescribes procedures for training the skill. It suggests that the trainer should "bring tools into classroom and discuss domestic and vocational use of each; provide

TABLE 1

VOCATIONAL BEHAVIOR CHECKLISTS[a] CLASSIFIED BY EIGHT SUBCLASSES, NUMBER OF ITEMS PER SUBCLASS, OBJECTIVITY,[b] SETTING,[c] AND PRESCRIPTIVE-DESCRIPTIVE NATURE[d]

| | | Subclasses | | | | | | | | | | | | | | |
| | | Pre-vocational Skills | | Job-Seeking Skills | | Interview Skills | | Job-Related Skills | | Union, Financial & Sec. Skills | | Work Performance Skills | | On-The-Job Social Skills | | Specific-Job Skills | |
Title	Prescr/Descr/Mar	#	S	#	S	#	S	#	S	#	S	#	S	#	S	#	S
Objectivity Range 4.0 – 5.0																	
Behavioral Char. Pgrsn.	M	3	TC	7	B	2	B	10	OJ	10	OJ	16	OJ	2	OJ	0	
Colorado Mast. Guide	M	0		4	OJ	5	OJ	4	OJ	6	OJ	45	OJ	8	OJ	6	OJ
COMPET	P	61	TC	2	TC	2	TC	8	TC	8	TC	0		0		98	TC
Higginsville Beh Scale	D	0		1	OJ	0		5	OJ	5	B	18	OJ	1	OJ	0	
Job Seeking Skills Ref. Manual	P	0		2	TC	13	TC	0		0		0		0		0	
Minnesota Dev. Pgm Sys.	D	13	TC	0		0		2	B	0		4	B	0		0	
Nebraska Client Pgs.	M	0		0		1	OJ	2	OJ	3	OJ	17	OJ	1	OJ	0	
Washington Assessment & Tr. Scale	D	7	TC	0		0		0		0		17	B	1	TC	0	
Objectivity Range 3.0 – 3.9																	
Adult Sv. Eval. Form	D	14	TC	0		0		0		0		1	OJ	0		0	
Beh. Profile Eval. Booklet	D	11	TC	1	OJ	1	OJ	2	B	15	B	9	B	0		0	
Camelot Beh. Check.	M	15	TC	1	OJ	1	OJ	2	OJ	4	OJ	10	OJ	4	OJ	0	
Eastmont Tr. Ctr. Checklist	D	53	B	0		0		0		0		3	B	0		0	
Household Act. Eval.	D	113	B	0		0		0		0		0		0		0	
W. A. Howe Ctr. Check.	D	16	TC	0		1	B	5	B	1	B	6	B	4	B	0	
Mat. Development Ctr. Beh. Identification	D	4	B	0		0		2	TC	0		26	B	12	B	0	
Mid-Nebraska Compet. Emp.	P	45	TC	3	TC	9	B	4	TC	5	TC	50	TC	10	TC	0	
NYU Voc. Status Indicators (Draft)	D	0		17	OJ	15	OJ	0		24	OJ	45	OJ	18	OJ	0	
North Central Skill Eval.	D	5	TC	7	OJ	7	OJ	7	B	0		5	B	4	B	0	
Roadmap to Eff. Teach.	D	89	TC	0		0		0		0		0		0		0	
Track Profile	D	8	TC	0		0		0		0		1	OJ	0		0	
Vineland Soc. Maturity	D	14	TC	0		0		0		0		2	OJ	0		0	

TABLE 1 (continued)

Title	Prescr/Descr/Mar	Pre-vocational Skills		Job-Seeking Skills		Interview Skills		Job-Related Skills		Union, Financial & Sec. Skills		Work Performance Skills		On-The-Job Social Skills		Specific-Job Skills	
		#	S	#	S	#	S	#	S	#	S	#	S	#	S	#	S
Objectivity Range 2.0–2.9																	
Adaptive Funct. Index#	D	10	TC	0		0		4	B	0		45	B	22	B	0	
Adult Perform. Scale	D	64	TC	0		0		0	OJ	1	OJ	16	B	3	B	0	
Class. Code for House Act.	D	0		2	B	1	B	5	B	3	B	8	B	0		7	B
Craig Ctr. Prog. Rpt.	D	14	TC	0		0		2	TC	1	OJ	6	B	0		0	
Fairview Social	D	13	TC	0		0		4	TC	0		13	B	0		0	
Group Home Candidate Check.	D	96	TC	37	B	14	B	19	B	49	B	21	B	18	B	0	
Life Skills for DD	M	37	TC	0		0		0		0		8	TC	0		0	
Obs. & Client Eval. Guide	D	6	TC	0		0		4	B	0		56	B	56	B	0	
Scale of Employability	D	15	B	5	OJ	7	OJ	7	OJ	1	OJ	45	OJ	18	OJ	0	
Selinsgrove (mild)	D	0		0		0		1	OJ	0		14	OJ	3	OJ	0	
T.M.R. Perform. Profile	D	2	TC	0		0		2	B	1	TC	3	B	2	B	0	
Voc. Behaviors Scale	D	3	TC	1	TC	4	B	2	B	3	B	8	B	5	B	0	
Work Beh. Rating Scale	D	0		0		0		0		0		10	B	3	B	0	
Objectivity Range 1.0–1.9																	
AAMD Adapt. Beh. Scale	D	3	TC	0		0		0		0		9	B	0		0	
Comprehensive Eval. Form	D	32	TC	0		0		6	B	0		36	B	17	B	0	
Porterville Eval. Form	D	0		0		0		3	OJ	0		12	OJ	9	OJ	0	
Tech Counselor's Evaluation	D	82	TC	0		0		4	TC	0		20	TC	14	TC	0	
Vocational Training Evaluation	D	5	TC	0		0		1	OJ	0		8	B	6	OJ	0	

[a] Checklists are listed alphabetically within objectivity ranges. Full names and sources are listed under Reference Notes.

[b] 1.0 Least Objective; 5.0 Most Objective, as described earlier in the present article.

[c] OJ =On-the-Job (non-classroom setting).
TC=Training Class
B =Either setting *or* both OJ and TC items.

[d] P =Prescriptive.
D=Descriptive.
M=Marginally Prescriptive-Descriptive.

practice in actual use." Marginally prescriptive-descriptive refers to checklists that are extensively sequenced and suggest training, but do not specify explicit prescription. Only three were determined to be prescriptive, five were marginally prescriptive-descriptive and the remainder were descriptive (see Table 1).

The vocational checklist characteristics presented (scope, objectivity, setting, and prescriptive-descriptive nature) must be considered in relation to the needs of the checklist user. Different populations, facilities, training programs, and staffing patterns dictate different weightings among the characteristics. By any analysis, objectivity and scope are prime considerations. Ideally, both high objectivity and wide scope would be present in a given checklist. Unfortunately, no vocational behavior checklists reviewed fully meet these requirements.

One strategy might be to select subclasses from the higher objectivity checklists. If a sufficient number of items are not available in those subclasses of that checklist, then the user might broaden scope by selecting items from less objective checklists. For example, if clients in a training program need Job-Seeking Skills, trainers could begin by examining the seven items from the *Behavioral Characteristics Progression* (see Table 1). If a greater variety of Job-seeking behaviors is required, the trainers could then refer to the 37 items of the *Group Home Candidate Checklist*. Although these latter items are less objective, they provide increased scope.

The current state of vocational checklisting demands consideration of a trade-off between scope and objectivity. This trade-off is one of relative merits. Objectivity is crucial if reliable observation of behaviors is to occur. But a subclass with only two items, however objective, may be of little value in a comprehensive training effort.

Vocational behavior checklists are not training programs. The prime reason for use of checklists is careful assessment of individual competencies. They provide direction and may serve as either foundations for new training programs or adjuncts to revision of existing ones. First and foremost, they are behavior description and curriculum planning tools. Their potential usefulness will depend on an interaction of several factors (type of training program, clients' initial vocational behavior repertoire, training setting, scope and objectivity of the checklist used, and the capability of the checklist to provide prescription).

In the final analysis, the best measure of training program effectiveness is client progress in the acquisition of vocationally relevant skills. Careful specification and reliable observation of those relevant skills is central to effective training. Vocational behavior checklists are intended to be tools in that process.

Checklist References

All behavior checklists cited herein are listed in alphabetical order by checklist title to facilitate location. The authors are listed in parentheses following the title. The source from which we obtained the checklist is then noted.

AAMD Adaptive Behavior Scale (1974 revision). American Association on Mental Deficiency, 5201 Connecticut Avenue, N.W., Washington, DC 20015.

Adaptive Functioning Index #2. (Marlett). The Vocational and Rehabilitation Research Institute, 3304 33rd St., N.W., Calgary 44, Alberta, Canada.

Adult Performance Scale. Michael R. Dillon, Superintendent, Connecticut State Dept. of Health, Central Connecticut Regional Center, Box 853, Meriden, CT 06450.

Adult Service Treatment Team Resident Evaluation Form. John Campfield, Syracuse State School, P.O. Box 1035, Syracuse, NY 13201.

Behavior Profile Evaluation Booklet. Anna State Hospital, Developmental Disabilities Division, Anna, IL 62606.

Behavioral Characteristics Progression. VORT Corporation, P.O. Box 11132, Palo Alto, CA 94306.

Camelot Behavioral Checklist. (Foster). Camelot Behavioral Systems, P.O. Box 607, Parsons, KS 67357.

Classification Code for Household Activities. (Chapin). In *Human Activity Patterns in the City* by F. Stuart Chapin, Jr. Wiley-Interscience, John Wiley & Sons, 605 Third Avenue, New York, NY 10016.

Colorado Master Planning Guide for Instructional Objectives. (DD Master Planning Committee). Division of Developmental Disabilities, 4150 South Lowell, Denver, CO 80236

COMPET: Commonwealth Plan for Education and Training of Mentally Retarded Children. (PA Departments of Education and Public Welfare). Department of Education, Box 911, Harrisburg, PA. 17120

Comprehensive Evaluation Form. William R. Phelps, West Virginia Rehabilitation Center, Institute, WV 25112.

Craig Developmental Center Educational Progress Report. Craig Developmental Center, Sonyea, NY 14556.

Eastmont Training Center Checklists. Eastmont Training Center, Little Street, Glendive, MT 59330.

Fairview Social Skills Scale. (Giampiccolo). Research Department, Fairview State Hospital, 2501 Harbor Blvd., Costa Mesa, CA 92626.

Group Home Candidate Checklist. (Turnbull). Ann P. Turnbull, Dept. of Special Education, University of North Carolina, Chapel Hill, NC 27514.

Higginsville State School and Hospital Behavioral Scale. Higginsville State School and Hospital, P.O. Box 522, Higginsville, MO 64037.

Household Activities Performance Evaluation. (Phelps). William R. Phelps, Disabled Homemaker Program, Division of Vocational Rehabilitation, Charleston, WV 25305.

W. A. Howe Development Center Behavioral Checklist. R. J. Van Dyke, W. A. Howe Developmental Center, 7600 W. 183rd Street, Tinley Park, IL 60477.

Job Seeking Skills Reference Manual. (Prazak, Walter). Multi Resource Centers, Inc., 1900 Chicago Avenue, Minneapolis, MN 55404.

Life Skills for the Developmentally Disabled (Vol. III: Manual for Training Clients). Geneva Folsom, The George Washington University, Div. of Rehab. Medicine, 2300 Eye Street, N.W., Washington, DC 20037.

Materials Development Center Behavior Identification Form: MDC. Materials Development Center, Department of Rehabilitation and Manpower Services, University of Wisconsin-Stout, Menomonie, WI 54751.

Mid-Nebraska Competitive Employment Screening Test and Teaching Manual. (Schalock). Robert L. Schalock, Mid-Nebraska Mental Retardation Services, 518 East Side Blvd., Hastings, NE 68901.

Minnesota Developmental Programming System. (Bock, Hawkins, Jeyachandran, Tapper, Weatherman). Warren H. Bock, Outreach Training Program, 301 Health Service Bldg., St. Paul, MN 55108.

Nebraska Client Progress System. Special Education Section, Department of Education, Lincoln, NE 68508.

NYU Vocational Status Indicators (Experimental Draft). Margret Brown, Rehabilitation Indicators Project, N.Y.U. Medical Center, Institute of Rehabilitation Medicine, 400 East 34th Street, New York, NY 10016.

North Central Regional Center Skill Evaluation and Assessment. North Central Regional Center, 73 Rockwell Avenue, Bloomfield, CT 06002.

Observation and Client Evaluation Guide. Research

Utilization Laboratory, Jewish Vocational Service, 1 South Franklin St., Chicago, IL 60606.

Porterville State Hospital Work Evaluation Form. Porterville State Hospital, P.O. Box 2000, Porterville, CA 93257.

Roadmap to Effective Teaching. Monterey County Office of Education, Special Education Department, P.O. Box 851, Salinas, CA 93901.

Scale of Employability. (Original version). Research Utilization Laboratory, Jewish Vocational Service, 1 South Franklin St., Chicago, IL 60606.

Selinsgrove State School and Hospital Resident Rating Scale for Mildly Retarded. Selinsgrove State School and Hospital, Selinsgrove, PA 17870.

T.M.R. Performance Profile for the Severely and Moderately Retarded. (DiNola, Kaminsky, Sternfeld). Educational Performance Associates, 563 Westview Avenue, Ridgefield, NJ 07657.

Technical Counselor's Evaluation Form. William R. Phelps, West Virginia Rehabilitation Center, Institute, WV 25112.

Track Profile. State of Oregon, Mental Health Division, Salem, OR 97310.

Vineland Social Maturity Scale. (Doll). American Guidance Service, Inc., Publishers' Building, Circle Pines, MN 55014.

Vocational Behaviors Scale. (Krantz). Gordon Krantz, Ph.D. Dept. of Educational Administration, 225 Health Services Bldg., University of Minnesota, St. Paul, MN 55108.

Vocational Training Evaluation. Central Connecticut Regional Center, Undercliff Road, Box 853, Meriden, CT 06450.

Washington Assessment and Training Scales: WATS. Dr. Sandra Belcher, Fircrest School, 15230-15th Ave., N.E., Seattle, WA 93155.

Work Behavior Rating Scale. Exceptional Children's Foundation, 2225 West Adams Blvd., Los Angeles, CA 90018.

References

Walls, R. T., Werner, T. J., Bacon, A., & Zane, T. Behavior checklists. In R. P. Hawkins & J. D. Cone (Eds.), *Behavioral assessment: New directions in clinical psychology.* New York: Brunner-Mazel, 1977.

FOCUS...

The U.S. Civil Service Commission reported 5,784 retarded persons employed in sixty-six different federal government job title areas in mid-1969. These jobs consisted of the following (President's Committee on Mental Retardation, 1969):

Animal Caretaker
Bindery Worker
Building Maintenance Worker
Buoy Maintenance Helper
Card Punch Operator
Carpenter
Cartographic Aide
Carpenter Helper
Charman
Clerk
Clerk, File
Clerk (Money Counter)
Clerk (Numbering)
Clerk-Receptionist
Clerk-Typist
Control Clerk
Cook
Currency Examiner
Dishwasher
Elevator Operator
Engineering Aide
Farm Laborer
Food Service Worker
Forest Worker
Furniture Repairman Helper
Garageman
Groceryman
Ground Maintenance Worker
Housekeeping Aide
Janitor
Laboratory Worker
Laborer
Laundry Marker

Laundry Worker
Library Assistant
Mail Clerk
Mail Clerk (Motor Vehicle Operation)
Mail and File Clerk
Mail Handler
Medical Technician
Messenger
Mess Attendant
Nursery Worker
Office Draftsman
Office Machine Operator
Paint Worker
Photocopy Operator
Photographic Processing Aide
Physical Science Aide
Porter
Press Cleaner
Presser (Flatwork)
Printing Plant Worker
Publications Supply Clerk
Radio Repairer Helper
Sales Store Worker
Small Arms Repairer Helper
Stock Clerk
Substitute Mail Handler
Supply Clerk
Telephone Operator
Vehicle Maintenance Worker
Ward Attendant
Warehouseman
Washman
Washman Helper

A Publication, *Preparing for Work,* by the President's Committee on Employment of the Handicapped lists these jobs as feasible for the retarded.

Stock Clerk
Dishwasher
Vegetable Peeler
Landscape Laborer

Apple Picker
Upholsterer
Bus Boy
Bus Girl

Elevator Operator
Concession Attendant
Sewing Machine Operator
Housemaid
Sales Clerk
Mail Handler
Farmhand
Assembly Worker
Supermarket Checkout Clerk
Factory Worker
Seamstress
Kick Press Operator
Truck Loader
Baker's Helper
Playground Attendant
Clerk-Typist
Egg Collector
Freight Handler
Mimeograph Operator
Mother's Helper
Painter's Helper
Laboratory Helper
Bottle Washer
Nurse's Aide
Wallpaperer
Photocopy Machine Operator
Housekeeper
Ward Attendant
Office Cleaner
Mechanic's Helper
Brass Polisher
Waitress
Food Handler
Groundsman
Textile Machine Worker
Fish Cleaner
Bookbinding Worker
Bottle Filler
Parking Lot Attendant
Messenger, Indoor

Office Clerk
Janitor
Sorter
Garbage Collector
Carpenter's Helper
Mail Carrier
Drillpress Operator
Kitchen Helper
Unskilled Laborer
Candy Wrapper
Tile Setter
Wrapper
Tree Pruner
Messenger, Outdoor
Office Boy
Office Girl
Porter
Packer
Truck Helper
Laundry Worker
Gas Station Attendant
Ironer
Saw Machine Operator
Bootblack
Usher
Animal Caretaker
Laborer, Crops
Collator
Railroad Track Worker
Mangle Machine Operator
Maid, Hotel
Car Washer
Ticket Taker

Manicurist
Warehouseman
Building Maintenance Worker
Cannery Worker
Mail Bag Handler
Houseman
Routeman's Helper
Gatekeeper
Office Machine Operator
Bag Filler
Bellhop
Shoe Repairer
Window Washer
Floor Polisher
Newspaper Deliverer
Dairy Hand
Hand Trucker
Locker Room Attendant
Doorman
Stevedore
Watchman

A Vocational Assessment Battery For The Educable Mentally Retarded And Low Literate

Abstract: In developing a vocational assessment battery, attention was given to the special needs of the retarded: reading level, attention and interest span, following directions, time limitations and the need for format variety. Measures of intelligence, achievement, personality, aptitudes, and special abilities were included. Procedural steps are detailed for evaluating a group during a school day using cassette tapes, earphones and three trained evaluators. An immediate interpretation of the 16 Personality Factor Test is made through use of a programmable calculator. The final report, which includes an interview, places emphasis upon specific educational, vocational and behavioral recommendations useful to teachers and counselors.

CHARLES A. ALCORN *is Associate Professor of Education, North Carolina Central University, Durham.*

CHARLES L. NICHOLSON *is Professor of Education, North Carolina Central University, Durham.*

For the psychologist, vocational assessment of the mentally retarded and low literate individuals is particularly difficult because many general aptitude, personality, and other vocational assessment instruments are not applicable to these individuals. Low reading level, short attention and interest span, difficulty in following instruction and time limitations are some of the problems that plague the examiner who attempts to use assessment instruments not specifically designed for this group.

Limitations

Once aware of these limitations, it was the task of the authors to assemble a battery of assessment instruments which would yield data useful for making specific educational, vocational, and behavioral recommendations for the use of counselors and teachers. Individuals to be evaluated would qualify for the services of Vocational Rehabilitation because of some mental, physical, emotional, or other disability. An additional task was to assemble a battery, part of which could be used in a group testing situation. It was also necessary to organize the battery and necessary equipment so that it could be transported from place to place. In order to accomplish this, the authors had to take into account a number of factors related to validity of test results and administration procedures.

Validity and Test Administration

The principal difficulty is that most vocational assessment instruments have a reading level around the sixth grade, or higher, while the mentally retarded and low literate seldom read above the fourth grade level. As an example, a recent edition of the Kuder Vocational Interest Survey, Form E, reports a reading level of approximately fifth grade. The personal experience of one of the authors is that unless the individual has a reading level at the fifth grade, or higher, the results of the Kuder will be invalid, as indicated by the V Score, in about 50% of the cases. In another instance, instructions for the MMPI indicate that persons should have a reading level of at least the sixth grade. The authors examined the questions on the MMPI and, out of the total of 566 questions, found only 212 questions at the third grade level or lower. An additional 108 questions were at the fourth grade level. Even

"A Vocational Assessment Battery for the Educable Mentally Retarded and Low Literate," Charles A. Alcorn, Charles L. Nicholson, *Education and Training of the Mentally Retarded,* Vol. 10, No. 2, April 1975.
©Division on Mental Retardation.

when all 566 questions were presented orally to the client, many of the words were not comprehended.

Another problem involving many testing instruments is the time limitation. For example, the Differential Aptitude Tests have various timed sections. Again, the reading level is approximately the fifth or sixth grade. For the mentally retarded and low literate, the time limitation is just another obstacle that they must overcome in addition to the reading difficulty. Even when the retarded read at the fifth grade level, they frequently read at a slower pace than persons of average intelligence reading at that grade level; depressed scores are the result. The substitution of an oral presentation frequently does not benefit the low literate client, and in many cases the oral presentation is not practical. In addition, many instruments are standardized for timed presentation and with the subject reading his own material. Oral presentation thus violates the standardized procedure by setting a pace for item completion.

It has been the experience of the authors that short attention and interest span can invalidate test results of retarded individuals, as well as those of higher ability. Additionally, many retarded and low literate individuals approach the testing situation with a negative attitude because of past unpleasant experiences and frustrations with verbally-oriented tests. Length of testing session and number of different tests administered are factors to be carefully weighed. Through the use of a variety of tests, verbal and non-verbal, individually-administered and group-administered, paper-and-pencil tests and manipulative-type tests, attention and interest span can be somewhat controlled. Once these individuals learn that they are not required to read or do academic work on most of these instruments, they frequently develop a more positive and receptive attitude. Regardless of the task, it is essential that a trained evaluator work closely with those being evaluated, even in a group testing situation, to insure that directions are understood and consistently followed. Constant surveillance of the testing situation and periodic encouragement is often necessary.

Recommended Battery of Tests

The following battery of tests has been found useful and is presently being used by the authors in working with vocational rehabilitation counselors.

1. Wechsler Intelligence Scale for Children (or Wechsler Adult Intelligence Scale) — Verbal and Performance Scales of intelligence

2. Ravens Progressive Matrices (if time permits) — Nonverbal intelligence

3. Wide Range Achievement Test — Achievement in spelling, reading, and arithmetic

4. Bennett Mechanical Comprehension Test — Mechanical aptitude

5. Slosson Drawing Coordination Test — Visual Motor Perception

6. Differential Aptitude Tests:

   Clerical Speed and Accuracy — Routine clerical aptitude

7. Purdue Pegboard — Fine finger dexterity and assembly skills

8. Stromberg Test of Manual Dexterity — Gross arm dexterity

9. California Picture Interest Inventory — Vocational interest areas

10. 16 Personality Factor Test, Form E — Personality assessment with implications for educational, vocational, and personal adjustment

11. Bender Gestalt — Perceptual dysfunction and personality assessment

12. Minnesota Multiphasic Personality Inventory (to selected clients) — Personality assessment

4. HANDICAPPED

With the exception of the short oral reading test on the Wide Range Achievement Test (WRAT), the ability to read is not required. Directions, timing, and presentation of questions for a number of the tests have been recorded on cassette tapes. Other tests must be administered individually. Many of the instruments can be modified for administration without violation of the standardized procedure. For two tests, the 16 Personality Factor Test (16PF) and the Bennett Mechanical Comprehension Test (BMCT), commercial tapes are available from the test publishers. The spelling section of the WRAT, which is usually administered orally, can easily be taped, along with directions and control of time limits for the WRAT arithmetic section. This is also true for the Differential Aptitude Test: Clerical Speed and Accuracy (DAT: CS & A), which has standardized directions usually given orally, as well as a time limitation. It should be remembered that the tests described above may also be used with individuals of higher ability as well. In some instances, the person being evaluated will want to read the test question for himself without the use of the tape or he will want to follow along in the test booklet as he listens to questions presented on tape. The instruments for which directions and questions are taped do not require a high degree of training to administer and can be supervised by a competent individual with limited training in test administration.

Steps in Administration of Test Battery

In the administration of the tests, the authors have found from experience that eight to ten individuals is a feasible number to be evaluated in a school day. To accomplish this, three evaluators are required: two trained in individual testing (psychological examiner or practicing psychologist) and one trained for group administration of tests. The latter person can be easily trained in the administration of this battery since procedures are standardized.

The organization and administration of the battery of test in a school setting is accomplished through the following steps:

A. Initially, student clients are met as a group at which time the evaluators introduce themselves, and one of the evaluators explains the purpose of the evaluation and answers any questions students may have. A special effort is made to put students at ease with the following explanation: "We are going to do a number of different things today: look at pictures, answer questions, work problems, and put pegs in holes. Except for a short reading word test, the ability to read is not required because we know that some people read well and some people do not read very well. We want to be fair with everyone, so most directions and questions have been recorded on cassette tapes. You can listen to them through earphones, if you like. Everyone has some things he can do better than other people. We want to find out what you can do best. This will help you and your counselor when you talk about getting along better in school and when you talk about what kind of job you can do best when you finish school. Some of the tests will be taken one at a time. Most of the time you will be working in a group. Do the very best you can."

At this time, polaroid pictures are taken; these will later be attached to reports which are sent to the vocational counselor. It is explained to students that this is to help us (the evaluators) remember names and faces. Each student is then furnished with a looseleaf notebook containing test booklets and answer sheets.

B. The group of eight or ten is arbitrarily divided into two subgroups. One group of four or five is seated around a table which is equipped with sets of earphones and a cassette tape recorder. Students listen to directions and mark answers as questions are presented. The 16PF, Form E, a personality test, which for most of the questions students pick statements that fit themselves best. This is followed by the BMCT, a mechanical aptitude test, also presented from a commercial tape. The WRAT spelling is presented next on a tape prepared by the authors. Level I is used because students of low ability typically have more success with this level. Next, the WRAT arithmetic is presented, with directions and timing included on tape. Again, most students of low ability prefer to work Level I, which begins with very simple problems that most can do. The last test on the tape is the DAT: CS & A, a short test of routine clerical speed and accuracy. As students begin each test, the group evaluator checks to make certain that all are following directions and are marking answer sheets properly. The group evaluator also spot checks and offers periodic encouragement.

At a nearby table, the other group of four or five will work with the group examiner on the Bender Gestalt, a test for identifying possible perceptual problems and also some personality characteristics, the WRAT oral reading test, and the PPB, all of which are administered individually. Students usually enjoy the Purdue Pegboard since manipulation of pegs and other parts is involved. Members of this group also take the California Picture Interest Inventory, a test of vocational interest areas, and the Slosson Drawing Coordination Test, a perceptual drawing test. If time permits, students do the Ravens Progressive Matrices, a nonverbal test of intelligence. These three tests are untimed. When necessary, the CPII is administered individually by the group examiner, especially if a client has a great deal of difficulty following directions or is very slow making responses.

C. From this group, students are taken one at a time for an interview and for individual administration of the Wechsler Intelligence Scale, which is a measure of general ability as well as a help in identifying possible perceptual problems. If administered before the Wechsler, the Stromberg Test of Manual Dexterity helps with the establishment of rapport between the examiner and the client. The Wechsler, of course, must be administered by a person especially trained in individual testing.

The tape runs about two hours, which is the time required for both groups to complete their respective tests. The groups are then switched so that by the end of the school day all students have taken both the individual and the group tests. A check sheet is used by the group examiner to make certain that all students have finished all tests. Brief rest periods are periodically given. Often the lunch break occurs near the mid point in the evaluation. The entire evaluation requires approximately four and one-half to five hours and can easily be accomplished within a school day.

Scoring Considerations

Scoring of most of the tests is accomplished through the use of hand scoring keys and manuals. The results of the 16PF are sent to the publisher for a printout interpretation. This is well worth the extra cost, as much information is provided in the area of personality, vocational predictions, behavioral characteristics, and treatment considerations. Form E should be used in conjunction with the tape presentation as the reading level of this form is approximately third grade. Utilizing the tape, the reading problem is further minimized. After one has used the printout of the 16PF over a period of time and has a library of statements from the 16PF, he can recognize values associated with statements and behavior characteristics. Many of the equation necessary for interpretation appear in the Handbook of the 16PF; others must be solved. A calculator which is programmable and which has a minimum of ten memories is needed for

these solutions. The authors use a portable Compucorp 142E calculator to furnish values for the 16PF interpretation. This immediate feedback is useful to counselors, as results may suggest that further behavioral evaluation is advisable. Depending on the client's reading level, the MMPI, or other instrument, may then be used.

Alternative Tests

From the battery which has been described, the psychologist has obtained a level of achievement, intelligence, dexterity, aptitude in two areas, vocational interests, as well as personality and adjustment information. Coupled with the interview and other available information from school records and the vocational counselor, this combined data can form the basis for meaningful recommendations. The above battery, however, is not without its limitations. Some of the instruments are poorly standardized, have somewhat complicated instructions and answer sheets, and other faults. Nor is the above battery complete. Other tests may be added or deleted, and other follow-up tests may be suggested by the results of this battery. In addition, work samples and work experience can be used. Two instruments not included in the present battery should be noted. The Wide Range Interest and Opinion Test, developed for the low literate and retarded consists of 150 pages, three pictures to a page. The client's task is to choose the picture of the work he would like to do and the work he would not like to do. This instrument contains pictures of both men and women, as well as both blacks and whites, in work situations. The scales and fields of interest are more complete than those for the CPII; however scoring this instrument by hand is not practical since a total of 22 keys is used. Machine scoring is available from the publisher. The authors have found that the retarded and low literate have some difficulty in taking this test and need to be very carefully supervised. If this is practical, the extra information is well worth the effort. The Jastak-King Work Sample is another instrument which provides valuable information concerning work aptitudes. The cost of this instrument is below the cost of many other work samples.

Reporting Test Results and Recommendations

Test data is then combined with information and impressions gained during the interview and is used as the basis for a written report. In addition to the basic identification of the client, the report consists of the following di-

4. HANDICAPPED

visions: *Circumstances of Test, Objective Test Results, Summary of Test Results, and Recommendations.*

Under *Circumstances of Test,* the client's appearance, general attitude and manner (rapport, verbalization, assurance, mannerisms), ability to follow directions, and work habits as they apply to the Wechsler and other tests are noted. Information concerning home background, vocational aspirations, work experience, hobbies, school subjects liked and those disliked, as well as other pertinent information such as standardized test results and teacher or counselor comments is included.

On the page of *Objective Test Results* (mimeographed form), test data in the form of scaled scores, grade levels and percentiles is recorded. A *Summary of Test Results* follows. This includes the examiner's opinion of the client's mental ability, an interpretation of the Wechsler subtests, discussion of the possibility of a perceptual problem, as well as a narrative summary of test results. A printout of the 16PF (MMPI, when applicable) also appears in this section.

Recommendations are divided into three parts: Educational, Vocational, and Behavioral. Under Educational Recommendations, the client's achievement level in reading, spelling, and arithmetic is compared with the level expected of a person of his ability level. Depending on the nature and extent of his learning disability (low achievement, for example), remedial instruction, special education, or a basic occupational curriculum is recommended. The 16PF printout gives an indication whether this person can profit from further academic instruction, at his own level of abilities. Perceptual instruction may also be recommended. Vocational Recommendations are based upon the client's stated interests during the interview and upon results of the CPII, various dexterity tests, and aptitude tests. Predictions from the 16PF, which include such factors as accident-proneness, need for interpersonal isolation at work, liklihood of success in interpersonal areas, potential for leadership, dependability, and potential for growth to meet increasing job demands, are included. Behavioral Recommendations are based upon results of the 16PF, the Bender Gestalt, (MMPI or other test, in some cases), and upon school behavior reports furnished by the vocational counselor. Depending on anxiety level, acting out tendencies, behavior control, and self-concept, suggestions from the 16PF include such treatments as needed for a controlled environment, a graded series of success experiences to improve self-confidence, a structured active program to reduce anxiety, emotionally supporting situations, and emphasis upon plans and their execution.

Summary

In summary, the authors would like to emphasize the following points:

A. A carefully chosen battery of tests, administered within a school day, can provide useful data for making specific educational, vocational and behavioral recommendations.

B. Group administration of many of the tests is feasible with the use of cassette tapes and earphones.

C. Eight to ten clients is an ideal number for three evaluators (two trained in individually-administered tests and one trained in group-administered tests). The latter person can easily be trained in a short time since test procedures are standardized.

D. Immediate interpretation of the 16PF is possible through the use of a portable programmable calculator. Results may suggest the need for further behavioral evaluation.

WORK SAMPLES: ANOTHER VIEW

SIMON OLSHANSKY

Introduction

THERE continues to be much interest* in the development and use of work samples as an evaluation tool within workshops. The University of Wisconsin-Stout and the Jewish Employment and Vocational Service of Phila-

Mr. Olshansky is director, Community Workshops, Boston. He was a selective placement director for the U.S. Employment Service and then spent 10 years with the Massachusetts Division of Vocational Rehabilitation as a vocational rehabilitation counselor. Mr. Olshansky served as a research associate for the Joint Commission on Mental Illness and Health (1957-1959). Prior to his current post, he was study director for the Children's Development Clinic, Cambridge, Mass.

delphia are providing much of the impetus to and guidance of this growing interest. It has been estimated that at least 50 percent of the workshops in the United States use some form of work samples. The reliability of this estimate is not known.

Before more workshop professionals in sheeplike fashion adopt work samples, it is time for them to pause to consider another view. While work samples may be an improvement over pencil and paper tests, they still fail to answer the basic question: What can a person learn to do? What a person can do as evidenced by work samples is not the same as what he can learn to do. Where a person *is* does not tell us where he *can go!*

Some Limitations of Work Samples

First, while work samples may be an improvement over traditional psychological tests, they still are viewed by those engaged in performing them as another test, which many disabled and vulnerable persons might find very anxiety-provoking. Often the results may reflect more a measure of anxiety than of work potential.

Second, what a person can do at a given moment of time within a contrived situation under the pressure of time, does not tell us what he can learn to do within a more normal situation. There is no evidence to suggest that a

person "failing" a particular work sample cannot become proficient in its completion, given adequate time and a real interest in performing the task. No matter how much work samples may resemble real job tasks. they have a quality of make-believe and of unreality that are likely to discourage many persons in their responses.

Third, work samples represent a situation controlled by an evaluator, without any planning or participation by the person to be tested. He is a test subject. For many adults this is a childish role, reminiscent of school. Generally, he is given the work samples, without his prior consent, though formally he has the right to refuse. Of course, all this is done for his own good! This latter fact provokes some resentment since adults do not want to be dealt with as objects, however beneficent the intent.

Fourth, evaluation by work samples is another example of reductionism so popular in American psychology, as witnessed by the current commitment to Skinnerian ideology. On the surface, work samples provide professionals a relatively quick, painless, and low-cost solution for evaluating one's work potential. For the clients involved, it may be viewed as another example of professional autocracy, solving a problem in terms of professional ideology, rather than in terms of client needs. Many clients may view this evaluation as another instance of getting less than a fair chance to demonstrate their work capacity.

What is overlooked by many professionals is that a person comes to a workshop with all kinds of mixed feelings and attitudes that are deeply implicated in his responses to authority figures, to fellow workers, and to work tasks. What has to be achieved for many of these clients is better feelings and attitudes toward themselves and others and toward the idea of work as a legitimate goal, i.e., to be preferred to idleness. Concepts of separate work traits and a "work personality" relate to robots better than to real persons. Until one knows a person fairly well and knows that he is reasonably at ease in the new work situation, it is difficult, if not impossible, to know how to evaluate his responses to his work tasks. Are his responses slow because of temperamental reasons or because he is angry at his plight or resentful of his DVR counselor? Is he giving wrong responses to prove publicly that he is a nobody? Is he malingering to strike back at his family for allowing him to be at a workshop rather than at a school? Is he working too rapidly, thinking speed is more important than accuracy, despite advice to the contrary?

The repeated assertion that work samples assess interest,

*It has been reported (May, 1974) that the level of interest in work samples is so great that a Work Sample Clearinghouse has been created at the Materials Development Center at University of Wisconsin-Stout.

behavior, and performance in relation to work capabilities is at best a half truth. The frequent repetition of this half-truth does not change it into a whole truth.

Fifth, work samples represent a deception for many clients, who come to a workshop with the serious intention of becoming workers. Instead of doing real work for money, they are asked in effect to play at being workers, to perform contrived tasks that are likely to provoke anger and resentment, and to measure their anxiety and docility more than their work potential and interest.

Two Inescapable Truths

The first truth is that for many clients coming to a workshop, there is no alternative to a realistic work tryout, interacting in a *natural* way with other workers, over a sufficient span of time with monetary rewards sufficient to stimulate their efforts. For a demoralized and depressed population such as those who are likely to come to a workshop, any *formal* process like work samples is much too threatening. Any formal testing process for many of these clients, whether work samples or pencil and paper tests, provokes too much anxiety to produce an accurate measure or forecast of their work capabilities. This group requires much encouragement and reassurance (a sense of trust) before they become comfortable enough to perform with the effectiveness of which they are most capable.

The second truth is that the majority of clients coming to a workshop lack the stability and stamina to become competitively employed. They require some kind of sheltered employment. At present only five states have begun to meet the needs for such employment.* The undue concern with work samples as a tool of evaluation is deflecting our attention from this second truth, and from the urgency of meeting the needs of those disabled persons who are eager for secure and sheltered employment. Too many clients enter a workshop demoralized and depressed and leave in the same condition, convinced of society's indifference to their problems. Bringing them into a workshop to confirm their incapacity for regular employment is a cruelty which we have practiced and tolerated too long. They need a work opportunity, not a work evaluation!

---

*Massachusetts is one of the five states.

The Remaining Question

It has been contended by some professionals that, despite the obvious limitations of work samples, some assessment is better than none.* But is it? Unless the assessment can provide a more dependable and defensible basis of vocational prediction, what is gained? If it falsifies the picture of what a person can *learn* to do, if it misleads professionals by giving them false clues, if it provides an unhappy experience for many clients entering a workshop, if it wastes time and money, what is the point to the contention?

Why engage in a relatively meaningless charade, especially with a vulnerable population who have been *taken* too many times by too many professionals in too many places? Why should we not spend our time and money to provide much better work opportunities to develop whatever talents the clients may have?

Conclusion

George Boas, American philosopher (Johns Hopkins, Emeritus), wrote that "we can say without fear of contradiction that a man with only one arm will not become a violinist and that a low-grade moron will not become an astronomer. But that is about as far as such predictions can go."

In essence, we just do not know any easy or quick way to predict vocational outcome, and we should confess our inability in this regard. Since work samples cannot form a defensible basis of prediction (or diagnosis), they, therefore, cannot be considered a basis of purposeful evaluation. They, therefore, perpetrate a deception on many clients in much the same way as pencil and paper tests. In large measure, at least for many demoralized and depressed clients seeking a sense of autonomy and a sense of integrity, work samples represent for them another exercise in futility and frustration, another assault against their dreams of a better future, another instance of opportunity denied—a rejection without a fair trial.

---

*For an interesting discussion of vocational testing, see: Peter Koenig. They Just Changed the Rules on How to Get Ahead. *Psychology Today*. June, 1974. 8:1:87-92, 94, 96, 100, 102, 103.

WORK-STUDY: A LIFE SPACE CURRICULUM

PAUL RETISH

PAUL M. RETISH *is Associate Professor, Division of Special Education, College of Education, The University of Iowa, Iowa City, Iowa.*

The traditional system of teaching by subject matter seems ineffective and unrealistic when working with students who are preparing for work when leaving school. Therefore, the curriculum for work-study students should reflect the types of situations they will face once they leave school. This author, based upon his own teaching experience, would suggest that the classroom lose their school-looking atmosphere and take on the characteristics of work, play, and home. The learning taking place in these situations would reflect what the students will actually have to face outside of the schools.

Role Playing

The home is used to illustrate the above design, with the philosophy of integrating the normal academic breakdowns into this proposed situation. In this school-home situation, each student is asked to develop a pattern that would be appropriate for him once he is not in school. Questions raised by the teacher for each student should cover the following topics.

1. Marital status
2. Children, if any
3. Kind of housing (apartment, house of your own, room, at home with parents)
4. Average *take home* pay per week
5. Outstanding debts accumulated as of this point (car, stereo, charge accounts, insurance, etc.)

Tasks

Each student designs a role that he/she deems appropriate. The student is asked to make a realistic assessment of his home life style once he/she is out of school. Each part of their home life will be covered and a realistic appraisal is made. The cooperation of the teacher and student is important in making realistic judgments. This is one of the situations that the entire class must do, therefore, all can learn about what occurs in each of these situations. This role is carried out in the classroom via use of:

1. *Scrapbook.* Each student develops a scrapbook consisting of all the material things they have bought with the price or the loan value of each. Research is done by each student as to cost, shopping, techniques, and appropriate prices. With the advice of the teacher, a decision is made as to what is paid for, what has been bought on time, and what is charged on ones credit card. Therefore, the scrapbook would reflect a ''life-space'' of the student once out of school.
2. *Budget.* Using the above decisions, a budget, based upon costs and the students' agreed upon earning power, is designed. This budget should be comprehensive, realistic, and understood by each student. The budget is organized into the expenses that the student will face once out of school. As the students' pay increases (or decreases) the budget must be reviewed and adapted to newer needs and resources. If the student decided to marry, have children, or change residence, this should be reflected in his expenses. Each change and/or update becomes a mini-lesson for each student based upon an assessment of the individuals' needs.

Activities

Near the end of the pay period the budget should reflect expenses the student has incurred. When the student tries to purchase new products or grocery shops, the money spent should be carefully deducted from what is left in the budget. These crisis periods in the ''life-space'' of each student allows the teacher to introduce the topics of loans, credit purchases, and social service organizations available to help the students once they are out of school. Therefore, the curriculum becomes an integral part of the ''life-space'' of each student.

Each day in the class the students are responsible for updating their scrapbook and budget by purchasing or selling items. This experience is also considered their work time which the students are paid for at the end of the week. Work then becomes a task of developing their "life-space" as well as an investigation of new areas to help in coping with their adult life.

The teacher acts as a banker, salesman, loan agent, and financial consultant. In each of the roles assumed by the teacher, the student gets experience in interviewing, filling out forms, applications, etc., that the teacher evaluates and gives immediate feedback regarding appropriateness and whether the form will accomplish what it is supposed to do. It is important that the teacher gives this feedback immediately in allowing loans, increasing wages, costs, usability of materials handed in, etc., so that the students can understand its ramifications to their "life-space." Furthermore, field trips to business locations where these transactions take place are a necessity. Contact with the businessman, with their input, makes the experience much more realistic. These trips are followed up by in-class work that indicated the value of the trip and how it will affect their "life-space". The teacher then has taught the "academic" subjects through the mechanism of a "life-space" curriculum by altering the classroom to an experimental program.

As a culminating activity, it will be necessary to set aside one-half to one day a week in which each student can determine their pay (gross and net) and to negotiate any large purchases that the students feel are necessary. A time clock, adding machine (simple one), and a cash register are some of the equipment that would add realism to this process. Each student should be required to punch in and out. Coffee breaks should be planned and time for lunch should also be established. (Lunch is without pay so the student must punch out and in during this period.) At the end of the week the students compute their pay at the rate they have picked using his time card. The teacher in this activity coordinates, teaches, and aides each student. Deductions for benefits, taxes, social security, and payments due are determined by the student and teacher. The teacher then pays the student in the tender that has been established for the classroom. The new cycle of purchasing for the coming week is ready to begin, and the curriculum for the next week has its beginning.

Research for costs of food, clothing, etc., are done in the local stores and through advertisements. Letters written to fulfill payments or to order new materials are developed with an eye to costs and needs. Budget skills on a weekly, monthly and yearly basis are developed and a cycle of the students "life-space" has been developed that will enable the student to make an easier transition from school to life.

Generalizations

This program is especially designed for the junior and senior high school level. The added input from those students who are working makes this curriculum that much more rich and realistic. These students can describe how they use their pay and how it is budgeted to their needs (needs student's permission). Secondly, the social and emotional needs of a job and its responsibilities can be shared and then implemented as part of the training program in the class. The part-time worker becomes an additional teacher and a valuable asset to the classroom. The frank discussions as to realistic problems and how they are coped with are welcome additions to the curriculum. Ample opportunity for this sharing should be available to all of the students.

The teachers assume the role of banker, loan agent, salesman, and information coordinator as problems arise on an individual and class basis. An example of this would be the decision as to whether or not a student should buy insurance, change jobs, or find another residence, etc., were all questions that teachers could raise and use as teaching aides. The budget consideration and the benefits from such programs can be seen by the students as it relates to their own budgets.

Curriculum Impact

The realistic designates of the school curriculum rather than reading, writing, and language arts, etc., should put the student more at ease. Transference of this knowledge and the flexibility the teacher can inject into the curriculum are the additives necessary for the student to actively cope with their society. A note of caution throughout the project is that material, design, and appropriate behaviors are geared to the students needs rather than to the teachers or the schools. The dangers of a "life-space" curriculum is for the schools not to comprehend what students really need.

This type of "life-space" curriculum can be implemented in other areas besides the home situation. In a coordinated effort throughout the work-study program each setting can be altered to depict a part of the "life-space" of a person out of school. In the areas of industrial arts, home economics, the translation of the material to functional use for the students is obvious. Other areas that need to be translated into functional "life-space" areas may not be obvious but yet are as important. Realistic contacts before taking a job, interpersonal relationships, and on the job training are vital skills that any student needs. It is the responsibility of the teacher to present the material in a manner that the student can readily understand and "life-space" teaching is a product of this concern.

OCCUPATIONAL EDUCATION: ASSESSMENT AND IMPLEMENTATION

Tim Crowner

Recent thinking regarding occupational programming for the severely handicapped appears to follow two lines of thought. First, if occupational education-special education programs are to be successful, they must become more community based. A second line of thought involves the use of applied behavioral analysis to the occupational needs of the severely handicapped. Unfortunately, community programming advocates of applied behavioral analysis have not collaborated as well as they might have. The Individual Education Program (IEP) may furnish the ground upon which this communication will begin to occur. A systematic application of the available technical concepts underlying both lines of thought may be reflected in IEP's for the severely handicapped. Such plans would include descriptions of the various contexts in which work might be performed in a given community. A delineation of specific skills required to operate within various contexts would follow. Finally, task analysis would be applied to components of these contexts and instructional sequences, leading to the student's acquisition of specific relevant skills.

A useful organization of information on occupational evaluation and instruction will be set forth here. Discussion will be based upon an operating program in Madison, Wisconsin. It is felt that the Madison program exemplifies a marriage between the two schools of thought and occupational education for the severely handicapped. Emphasis will be placed on three key themes: (1) precision, (2) completeness, and (3) cooperation. *Precision* refers to how well an IEP details strategies for goal attainment, measurement, evaluation, and delineation of roles and responsibilities for parent, staff, and related agencies. *Completeness* refers to how thoroughly the IEP deals with those contingencies affecting the environmental context in which the vocational goals must be performed. *Cooperation* refers to evidence that the plan has been well coordinated across all individuals and relevant agencies.

The phrase *severely and profoundly handicapped* is meant as a functional term to encompass a population of students who require extraordinary medical, therapeutic, and educational prescription in order to compensate for, or habilitate, presenting handicaps. It would be unrealistic to assume that one day all severely and profoundly handicapped persons will be competitively employed. It is, therefore, necessary to operationally define what is meant by occupational goals for this population. Writers of IEP's must be able to discriminate the aspects of occupational training which are important across all children of any age or degree of handicap.

Occupational education is used here to convey a broad view of prevocational and vocational education ranging across age and ability. An occupational goal continuum must be established as a conceptual guide in planning for the severely and profoundly handicapped. This continuum is based on the concept of community effort required to sustain the handicapped individual. It is assumed that, for some handicapped individuals, self-maintenance is a reasonable occupational goal. The economic contributions to society gained by a handicapped person's maintenance are only different in degree from those gained through competitive employment. Certainly, the human dignity that a profoundly handicapped individual achieves through self-maintenance is as significant as economic self-support achieved by a mildly handicapped person.

"Occupational Education: Assessment and Implementation", Tim Crowner, *Developing Effective Individualized Education Programs For Severely Handicapped Children and Youth*, Department of Health, Education and Welfare, August, 1977.

4. HANDICAPPED

There are obviously many degrees of economic self-support and self-maintenance. Figure 1 represents a continuum leading from complete reliance on others to complete economic self-support.

Figure 1. *Occupational Continuum*

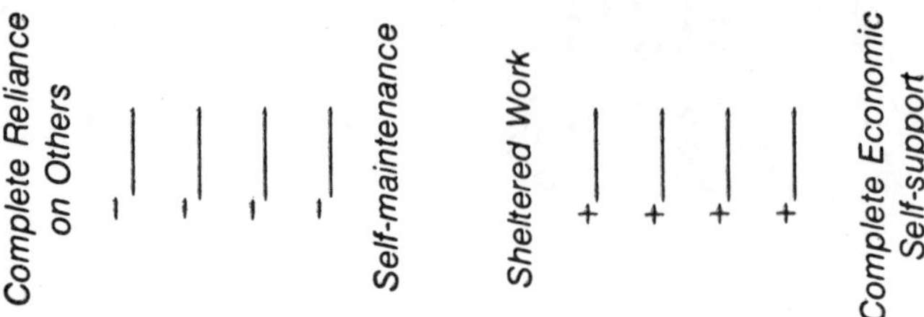

There is no dichotomy in this continuum. Individual educational plans for occupational goals should identify jobs for severely and profoundly handicapped individuals regardless of placement on the occupational continuum. For example, a job may be serving food to oneself. Many skills needed and developed for competitive employment by the handicapped are the same as those necessary for self-maintenance. Following directions, being socially appropriate, and having self-discipline are examples of such common skills. In particular, rate, endurance, and quality of performance are essential to holding down a competitive job. Enhancing these skills, even in a preschooler, has direct connection to occupational success in later life. Each of these skills will be discussed in more detail later. They are brought up at this point to imply that IEP's should address occupational goals even for the most profoundly handicapped.

Writers of IEP's should also bear in mind that existing occupational programs often fail. The U.S. Department of Health, Education, and Welfare commissioned a study of occupational preparation programs for the handicapped in 1972. The report of this study, *Improving Occupational Programs for the Handicapped,* cites three basic ways in which existing programs fail:

> They fail to prepare the environment for the student as well as they prepare the student for the work environment. Secondly, they fail to take advantage of, or solicit assistance from, services or groups outside of the immediate administration of the program. Thirdly, they do not assure the relevance of program content to the job market and environment in which the students will live when they graduate. (HEW, 1972, p. 6)

In addition to the above observations, occupational education is too often treated as an isolated goal. It is seen as task oriented. A narrow view of sheltered workshop tasks prevails for the severely handicapped. However, well-designed IEP's may help the student avoid many of the deficiencies which have been identified in the past with vocational preparation of the handicapped. Especially as IEP writers recognize the advantages of combining applied behavioral analysis to community-based occupational preparation. IEP's can force focus upon long- and short-range goals for each child and provide parents and advocates with a blueprint from which to check progress. Well-written IEP's will, with precision, completeness, and coordination, set forth goals to which professionals will be held accountable.

RECENT RESEARCH

Perhaps the most striking aspect of the literature concerning vocational preparation of the severely handicapped is that it illustrates the range of complex skills which such persons can acquire. Crosson (1969); Schroeder and Yarbrough (1972); Bellamy, Peterson, and Close (1975); and Gold (1976), among others, have demonstrated that the severely handicapped can learn complex assembly skills through the use of task-analysis strategies and chained instructional sequences. Furthermore, Huddle (1967), Brown and Pearce (1970), and Schroeder and Yarbrough (1972) have demonstrated that arrangement of environmental contingencies can enhance the productivity of severely handicapped persons.

Researchers have been successful in proving that severely handicapped individuals can learn rather sophisticated behaviors. However, a number of unresolved issues remain which concern the ability of handicapped individuals to generalize these learned skills. Williams (1975) contends that trainers must determine whether or not these skills can be performed across persons, places, instructional materials, and language cues. In short, are many of the behaviors performed by severely handicapped individuals stimulus bound? If learned behaviors are in fact bound to a specific set of circumstances, then there is a danger that skills being taught later in time will be more difficult to teach because of earlier learning. This phenomenon, proactive inhibition, is discussed by Underwood (1964). Underwood has found that habits learned earlier in time will tend to interfere with newly acquired skills, increasing the probability that these new skills will be forgotten.

Furthermore, retention of a given skill may be affected by the importance of that skill to the student. For years, general educators have been calling for "relevant curriculum" in public schools. Ferrara (1973) observes that behaviors learned earlier in time were not retained by a group of severely and profoundly handicapped students. However, when skills were taught that had immediate application to a student's needs, these skills tended to be retained. For example, if a severely handicapped person is taught to go to a refrigerator and to pour a glass of milk, this behavior has great utility to the individual. Ferrara notes that such behaviors are more readily generalized by severely handicapped students from the classroom to the home setting. Examining educational structures may help explain this phenomenon.

Crowner (1977) suggests that there is a relationship between restriction and structures developed to instruct students. A *structure* is defined as an element constructed in the learner's environment designed to direct, guide, or inhibit the learner's behavior. Structures may be physical or behavioral in nature. Physical structures include room arrangements, degree of isolation from a normalized environment, or some prosthetic device such as a jig used in an assembly task. Behavioral structures encompass all personal interactions such as social reinforcement, language cues, and home-school relationships. The degree to which such structures are available or natural in many different settings is directly related to how easily a behavior being taught in one environment will be generalized and retained across settings. Thus, structures must be constructed that are available in naturalized environments if the trainer wishes the learner to generalize behaviors.

In an extensive review of the literature on sheltered workshops, Pomerantz and Marholin (1977) state:

> In general, sheltered workshops are not now using available instructional technology in ways that lead to job placement of severely handicapped clients. Workshop programs rely on production and adjustment training within the workshop, in the hope that a general upgrading of client skills may lead to future placement (p. 131).

These authors call for more aggressive job placement activities. They suggest a more active involvement with the community. The HEW study of occupational programs for the handicapped (cited earlier) draws this same conclusion.

Wolfensberger (1975) voices dissatisfaction with another aspect of services provided to handicapped individuals—diagnosis. He cites a number of "embarrassments in the diagnostic process" (p. 181–185). His observations that are particularly relevant to this discussion are these:

1. Diagnosis for the family is quite often a dead end, frequently resulting in a frustrating series of cross referrals instead of leading to a meaningful service assignment.
2. Many diagnostic centers do not provide adequate feedback counseling and consider their duty when the diagnostic process is satisfactorily completed.
3. Diagnostic services are often overdeveloped in comparison to other available resources.

In summary, the literature reviewed indicates that the severely handicapped can learn complex and sophisticated behaviors. However, service delivery models that assure generalization of learned behaviors are underdeveloped. Diagnostic services have been characterized as overdeveloped and irrelevant. The solution proposed to alleviate

4. HANDICAPPED

service deficiencies involves more active involvement with the community on the part of service purveyors.

Literature addressing the occupational needs of the profoundly retarded is nonexistent. This may be due to a narrow definition of what constitutes occupational preparation. Yet, many of the efforts designed to lead a severely handicapped person to gainful employment are applicable to the needs of the profoundly handicapped person.

Before discussing the specific aspects of assessment, prescription, and implementation, an overview of an operating program may prove useful. In an article tracing the evolution of a community-based vocational preparation program, Certo, Brown, Belmore, and Crowner (1977) review the facts that led the Madison Metropolitan School District (MMSD) away from the schoolhouse and into the community. Essentially, MMSD found the following to be true:

1. A model which prescribed a single teacher and single class (the traditional elementary school model) had administrative convenience as its greatest advantage. That is, the number of variables needing attention by the service purveyors was smallest in this model. Small groups attached to a single teacher were easy to monitor. However, the structures evolved in such environments tended to be static. Thus, students tended to become stimulus bound to a given teacher and classroom.
2. A departmentalized model—the traditional secondary school model where teachers specialize in a specific subject and students rotate from teacher to teacher—tended to provide for better student generalization. It also allowed for the rapid development of a specialized curriculum because the teacher could attempt to teach the same concepts to a variety of students. This model, however, led to a disjointed program where various skills become isolated.
3. MMSD finally moved to a model which combined the self-contained class with community-based experiences. A brief description of this model will assist the reader in understanding the context from which positions taken in this paper arise. In the community-based training model, students spend about a fifth of their instructional time out of the classroom. Certain teachers operate as community-based instructors, and they have flexible schedules which allow them to operate during the evening hours with days free when appropriate. Community-based instructors have six functions: (1) to identify community environments in which students will ultimately function, (2) to analyze the elements of a given environment to determine criteria for survival in that environment, (3) to work with classroom teachers to evolve instructional strategies leading to survival skills, (4) to aggressively prepare the environment for the eventual presence of the severely and profoundly handicapped individual, (5) to implement an instructional program directly within that environment with targeted students, (6) to follow up into postsecondary placement—transition to the Division of Vocational Rehabilitation (DVR).

Community-based instructors, support staff, and classroom teachers work with parents and outside agencies to identify skills that are immediately meaningful to a given student. Activities are then designed for skill development and are executed in the classroom, home, and community. Skills immediately meaningful to the student are related to skills ultimately needed. In the classroom, for example, the teacher may work with students on simple meal preparation as a desired skill while stressing work-site preparation and clean-up duties. At home, the parents are instructed to work with their child in table setting and cleaning skills. In the community, the trainer stresses proper arrangement of tools before work is begun.

Cognitive, affective, sensory, motor, and language goals are identified for each student, as are ways in which these goals may be achieved through functional activities. For example, language may involve indicating a student's need to use a public bathroom. Cognition for the student may involve learning that soap works better if water is applied to the hands first. Affective learning may involve learning to act unobtrusively, and sensory goals may relate to desired water temperature while washing, while motor goals may relate to the zipping and buttoning of clothing.

One can see the importance of using the precise, complete, and coordinated IEP as a document to guide parents and professionals through the complexity of such interrelated and comprehensive programming. MMSD has observed two great advantages in this community-based approach. There have been rapid skill acquisition and retention by students, and the community is becoming increasingly sensitized to the presence and needs of severely and profoundly handicapped persons. However, a main disadvantage to the community-based model is that it is administratively inconvenient. Scheduling becomes a horrendous problem; monitoring staff time is very difficult; and liability related to safety factors increases. Of course, our moral obligation does not involve the development of administratively convenient models. Yet, any model should produce individual programs that can be clearly understood and held to account. Thus, the significance of IEP's as blueprints or even contracts becomes clear.

INITIAL ASSESSMENT

Initial assessment for occupational skills should occur across the occupational continuum described earlier. Thus, all students should be assessed for functional occupational level. Focus for occupational assessment of a given student will be drawn from information regarding the student's age, ability, and need. Age will dictate the amount of time left in school. The shorter the time in school available, the greater the focus on specific occupational goals will be. Ability will dictate the kinds of environments in which occupational information will be collected. That is, will information on student performance occur in a community-based work site, or would a room in a small group treatment facility be a more appropriate site to observe the student's performance? It may be appropriate, for some students, to observe dressing or feeding in the student's home. Need may dictate both emphasis and choice of work site. For example, a seriously behavior-disordered student may be 20 years old but have such bizarre behavior that self-discipline as a self-care objective may dominate his needs. A multihandicapped/hearing-impaired student may need a work site where very little verbal direction occurs.

Occupational assessment should be an integrated part of a general assessment strategy. This is particularly important because much guiding information on ability arises from a general assessment process. Assessment for severely and profoundly handicapped individuals is a very complex process because of the multiple needs of the child. Occupational assessment is then a component of a transdisciplinary-based evaluation. To clarify, Crowner (1977) makes the following distinction regarding a transdisciplinary model:

> There are three across-discipline service delivery models. Multidisciplinary models join a number of separate disciplines so they are available for evaluation and prescription. Interdisciplinary models enforce interrelationships among each of the disciplines so that there is coordination of effort. Transdisciplinary models not only enforce interdisciplinary cooperation but encourage interchangeability across disciplines. This process can be referred to as "skills swap," where each discipline must inservice all other disciplines so that all disciplines acquire many "traded" skills. (p. 6)

Often a primary professional is designated to carry out the recommendations made by other members of the transdisciplinary team.

Depending on specific circumstances, the community-based trainer may be the most logical choice as primary professional. If not, the community-based trainer often is involved in making program recommendations to the primary professional (generally a classroom teacher). The IEP can act as a transdisciplinary guide for the primary professional and, if well written, can hold supportive disciplines accountable for their specific responsibilities.

General Assessment Strategies

Severely and profoundly handicapped individuals are usually assessed by the classroom teacher, physical therapist, occupational therapist, speech and language therapist, and the psychologist. If the initial assessment calls for observation in the community environment, the community-based trainer becomes involved. This always occurs with students over 14 years of age. A good assessment is the primary basis for a good IEP. Clear, complete, and well-coordinated assessment strategies are essential in individual program development. Four assessment strategies are followed within the context of a transdisciplinary model using applied behavioral analysis designs:

1. When assessing a severely and profoundly handicapped student, it is advised that specific activities for the student be created to provide a standard of observation for each discipline.
2. It should also be made clear, initially, who will collect what information so that duplication of duties does not occur. Each discipline should focus upon specific areas for assessment purposes.
3. It is important to determine how information will be collected. For example, it might be decided that the classroom teacher will engage the student in certain activities while the other professionals observe unobtrusively. Or perhaps the occupational therapist will visit the home during mealtime. Some standardized measures associated with psychology or therapy may be deemed appropriate.
4. There must be interdisciplinary agreement. That is, a behavior, or lack of a behavior, must be considered absent or present by two or more disciplines. Often, the parent fills the role of a reliability checker. This strategy is continued throughout the student's schooling.

Use of these strategies will produce guiding information that may be used in developing the initial IEP. Information should be generated regarding cognitive, affective, motor, language, medical, and physical stamina. This information should be based on functional examples such as rate, endurance, and quality of performance in a given environment and across different environments.

Occupational Assessment Strategies

Once again, depending on age and ability and need of a given student, occupational assessment may be the focus for the general assessment of a student. That is, if age, ability, and need imply it, then the transdisciplinary team may decide to make their assessment in a community-based site. This would be in accordance with the first assessment strategy discussed earlier. For purposes of this discussion, it will be assumed that occupational assessment was chosen as a primary focus.

Applied behavioral analysis comes into play very heavily once the decision on assessment focus has been made. Staff must bring to bear task analysis and observational technique. Measurement will focus on rate, endurance, and quality. Observations must be made under strict baseline conditions. *Baseline conditions* means that precise objectivity is used in assessments. Information gathered at this point must be standardized in a way which will allow it to be compared with information gathered later in time. Precision then is a key because precision implies detail, detail that can communicate clear and concise information about the student. The information must be validated by more than one person and not only verify the presence of a behavior but also specify rate and endurance and quality of the behavior.

Task analysis is essential. It forms the cornerstone of assessment for severely and profoundly handicapped individuals. Task analysis provides information on a task that can be matched against pupil skills. Thus, a pupil's location on a given task at a given level of the occupational continuum can be pinpointed.

Applied behavioral analysis may be overly task oriented, but it provides the tightest information on students one can achieve. Its importance to precise IEP's, and, ultimately, to accountability is obvious. Within the context in which it is being applied here, there is far less need for concern over becoming task oriented. Because of the community-based and transdisciplinary nature of the program, it is important that precision be maintained. Skill transfer, generalization, and reliability of information are enhanced by the community-based transdisciplinary approach.

For example, understanding student motivation is of major concern to the trainer. The trainer is interested in why a student performs well in a given work environment. What is reinforcing the student's behavior, and are the reinforcers natural to a given work environment? For example, some severely handicapped students perform only to please a trainer or because the task is novel and seems fun. These reinforcers are not likely to sustain the learner once the trainer withdraws from the work site. After determining what the natural work site reinforcers are, existing student reinforcers may be paired with natural reinforcers in the environment using basic operant strategies. The probability of a student's sustained performance will then be enhanced. The trainer's understanding of student motivation is essential to other members of the transdisciplinary team. Basically, this information is used to form many of the programs for a child. In the example just used, a natural reinforcer would likely be money. Thus, the classroom teacher, acting on this information, will initiate educational programs related to money and its usage.

Assessment Tools

A primary tool for occupational assessment is the checklist. Checklists are used extensively in assessing the severely handicapped. Unfortunately, few efforts to publish generalizable checklists have been made to date. Often checklists are location specific and would have little meaning across different communities. This is why understanding how to conduct a task analysis is an important competency for professionals working with the severely and profoundly handicapped. Not only is it necessary for professionals to develop their own complete checklists through task analysis but often existing checklists must be broken down considerably in order to be applied to the severely handicapped. Some task analyses are generalizable across settings. The annotated bibliography refers to examples of these.

Understanding the student's potential within a given work site is founded upon a thorough understanding of that work site. In addition, information about community-based sites influences curriculum at all levels. Belmore and Brown (1976) describe an analysis format for work sites. An outline of that format appears below. This detailed analysis provides information on related work skills, transportation, legal considerations as well as simple job site descriptions. It is an excellent format with which to collect precise information for IEP's. Also, it helps delineate where coordination among disciplines and agencies should logically occur. Teachers of even very young or profoundly handicapped persons may use the information gathered by this tool in developing occupational oriented sections of IEP's for their students. Schwartz (1976) has developed a complete job site and skill analysis for a dishwashing work site. Schwartz's study is an excellent example of the use of the job skills inventory developed by Belmore and Brown.

An Outline of the Madison Job Skill Inventory

A. *General Information*
  1. Reasons why severely handicapped students are considered for this job.
  2. A general description of the job.
  3. A general description of the work setting.
  4. A general description of the social environment:
    a. Information related to fellow workers.
    b. Information related to supervision.
    c. Information related to special contingencies.

B. *Specific Skill Requirements of the Job under Analysis*
  1. A list of the basic physical-sensory motor skills required.
  2. A list of the basic interpersonal skills required.
  3. A list of the basic language skills (verbal and nonverbal) required.
  4. A list of the basic functional academic skills required.
  5. A list of the basic machine and tool skills.
  6. A list of the basic hygienic skills required.

C. *Supportive Skills and Other Information Required*
  1. Transportation skills required.
  2. Skills related to work preparation.
  3. Basic money management skills required.
  4. Time-telling and time-judgment skills required.
  5. Health code requirements.
  6. Informed consent and legal requirements.

Rating scales are another method for gaining information on occupational needs of the severely handicapped. Ferrara (1977) has designed a rating scale for community survival screening. This scale rates performance across transportation, general behavior, clothing, direction following, staying in a group, frustration level, toilet needs, waiting, walking, locating destinations, and number of supervisors needed. Sections of the scale dealing with these latter two areas are provided in Figure 2 as examples of a rating scale.

4. HANDICAPPED

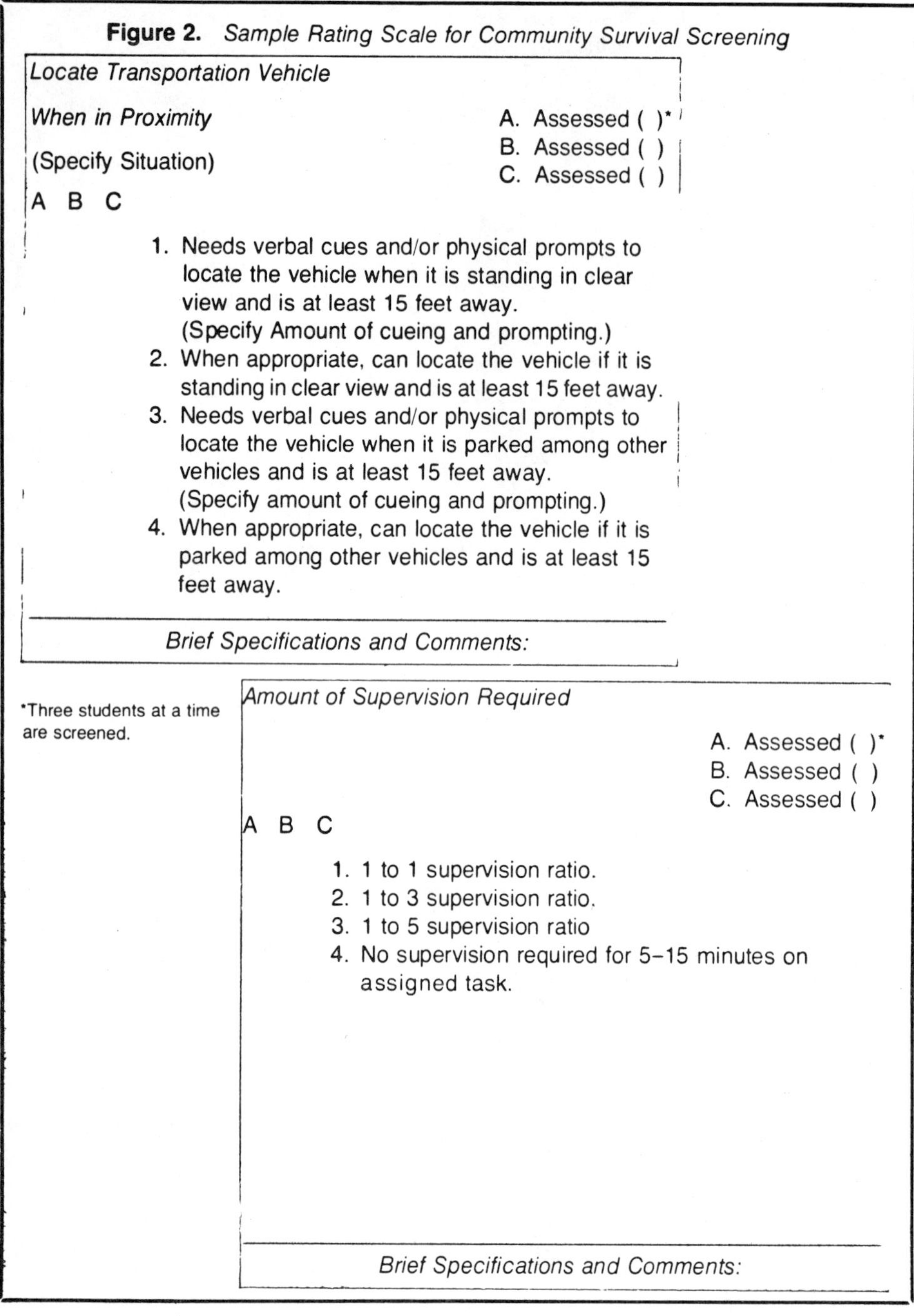

Figure 2. *Sample Rating Scale for Community Survival Screening*

INDIVIDUAL EDUCATIONAL PLANS

Goals and Objectives

Once occupational information is gathered it must be integrated with general information in order to form a complete and coordinated IEP. Long- and short-range goals must be stated in the IEP. Because of the functional nature of occupation, many of the goals relating to it are very pragmatic. To begin, a general goal relating to work site should be established. Goals may be evolved by asking key questions. For this first general goal, one might answer the following two questions:

1. Was performance in the work site used for initial assessment such that the student is ready for placement in that particular environment? If question 1 is answered no, then the primary goals may involve reaching criteria for entrance into some particular environment. If question 1 is answered yes, then goals should be developed which are based on criteria for complete success in the chosen site. Criteria will be set for rate, endurance, and quality of performance as well as affective behavior.

2. How much time does the student have left in school? The answer to this question will relate to emphasis on occupational goals and will dictate the long- or short-range nature of occupational goals. For instance, should emphasis be on specific job training or on surveys across many work sites, and how much instructional time should be spent in occupational preparation as compared to other activies?

In some regards, setting occupational goals is a process of moving from the general (guiding information) to the specific. Once goals related to criteria for rate, endurance, quality, and affective behaviors have been determined, then relationships between occupational activities and other goals need to be examined. Specifically, what are the general goals in language, cognition, motor, medical, and affective areas, and what specific subgoals in each of these areas can be set for occupational preparation? For example, what is the language goal in the work environment?

Writing the IEP

This paper has taken the position that individual educational plans for severely handicapped students should include occupational goals as part of precise, complete, and coordinated statements about pupil needs and programming. Rate, endurance, quality, and affective behavior are seen as relevant occupational goals which may be connected to general educational goals for children. Because of the number and complexity of goals for this population, the IEP becomes an essential blueprint for parents and professionals. The IEP can marry applied behavioral analysis to realistic community-based occupational training. It can provide a format for transdisciplinary and interagency planning and cooperation. Individual Educational Plans appear as formal written documents. The IEP document should be a record of past events and of events which should occur in the future of a student's life. Specifically, the information that must, by law, appear is the student's current level of functioning, expectations (goals) for immediate and long-range future functioning, and "precisely" how and when the student's goals will be achieved. Writing an IEP provides an opportunity for interested parties to organize and verify information about a student.

Information about a student's occupational functioning, both presently and in the future, should be an integrated part of an IEP. A separate IEP dealing with occupational information would encourage discontinuity in a student's program. If there are separate IEP's for general and occupational information, it might be reasoned that the programming implied will occur as distinct and separate. In fact, certain information regarding occupational expectations should be stated in all IEP's. The student's age and time left in school should influence the focus of information and, specifically, of information relating to occupational programming. If, for example, a student is graduating at the end of the school year, then general educational and therapeutic activities would all be designed to support occupational goals. This fact would be reflected in the IEP.

Complete IEP's will contain answers to many occupational-related issues, which are arrived at through the strategies outlined in this paper. Specifically, the complete IEP will address at least these questions:

1. How much time is available before graduation?
2. Where is this student in terms of the occupational continuum?
3. What things may the student be able to do with prosthetic support?
4. What is currently reinforcing this student?
5. Of those behaviors a student has, what are his rates, levels of endurance, and quality of performance?

The well-coordinated IEP will spell out how persons will work together to achieve the occupational goals that have been set. For example, with proper coordination, desirable recreation could become contingent upon work performance. However, if agencies responsible for recreation have not been involved, it is not likely that such a plan could be worked out. In short, the educational services being provided should be supported and reinforced by as many persons and agencies as possible.

The precise IEP will spell out specifically who will do what by when. It will be based on sound behavioral-oriented objective data. It will specify how available instructional sequences will be used to achieve goals. It will delineate measurement strategies, objective criteria, a schedule for examining progress, and dates by which goal achievement might realistically be expected.

EVALUATING THE IEP

It should be obvious by this point that IEP's should be evaluated on the basis of precision, completeness, and coordination. However, there is a final consideration which is crucial to the evaluation of an IEP. That is, does the IEP reflect a realistic plan for the student? What information will help answer this question? First of all, judgments about precision, completeness, and coordination will help the consumer in assessing the relevancy of a plan. The consumer/evaluator of IEP's must look at the structures that are implied by instructional strategies. Are the structures natural or contrived? Have the educators provided for continued progress to a higher level on the occupational continuum once the most immediate next level is reached (good, long-range goals)? Does the plan reflect the skills needed for survival in the local community?

REFERENCES

Bellamy, G. T., Peterson, L., & Close, D. Habilitation of the severely and profoundly retarded: Illustrations of competence. *Education and Training of the Mentally Retarded,* 1975, *10,* 174–186.

Brown, L., & Pearce, L. Increasing the production rates of retarded students in a public school simulated workshop. *Education and Training of the Mentally Retarded,* 1970, *5,* 15–22.

Certo, N., Brown, L., Bellmore, K., & Crowner, T. A review of secondary level service delivery models for severely handicapped students in the Madison Public Schools. In E. Sontag, J. Smith & N. Certo (Eds.), *Educational Programming for the Severely and Profoundly Retarded,* Reston, Va.: Division on Mental Retardation, The Council for Exceptional Children, 1977.

Crosson, J. A. A technique for programming sheltered workshop environment for training severely retarded workers. *American Journal of Mental Deficiency,* 1969, *75,* 814–818.

Crowner, T. T. Environmental restrictions within instructional settings of public schools. In A. Rehmann & T. Riggen (Eds.), *The Least Restrictive Alternatives a Partnership of General and Special Education: Implications for Special Education Leadership* (Vol. 3). Minneapolis: Minneapolis Public Schools, 1977.

Ferrara, P. Evolutionary aspects of public school services for students with severe handicaps. A presentation to the 99th Annual Meeting of The American Association of Mental Deficiency, Portland, Oregon, May 1973.

Ferrara, P. *Community survival screening.* Madison, Wis.: Madison Metropolitan School District, 1977.

Gold, M. W. Task analysis: A statement and example using acquisition and production of a complex assembly task by the retarded blind. *Exceptional Children,* 1976, *43*(2), 78–87.

HEW. Improving occupational programs for the handicapped. Washington, D.C.: U.S. Department of Health, Education, and Welfare, 1972.

Huddle, D. D. Work performance of trainable adults as influenced by competition, cooperation, and monetary reward. *American Journal of Mental Deficiency,* 1967, *72*(2), 198–211.

Pomerantz, D. J., & Marholin, D., II. Vocational habilitation: A time for change. In E. Sontag, J. Smith & N. Certo (Eds.), *Educational Programming for the Severely and Profoundly Handicapped,* Reston, Va.: Division on Mental Retardation, The Council for Exceptional Children, 1977.

Schroeder, S. R., & Yarbrough, C. C. Programming and automated recording in a sheltered workshop. *Mental Retardation,* 1972, *10*(6), 9–11.

Underwood, B. J. Laboratory studies of verbal learning. In E. R. Hilgard (Ed.), *Theories of Learning and Instruction: Part I of the 63rd Yearbook of The National Society for the Study of Education.* Chicago: University of Chicago Press, 1964.

Williams, W. Procedures of task analysis as related to developing instructional programs for the severely handicapped. In L. Brown, T. Crowner, W. Williams, & B. York (Eds.), *Madison's Alternative for Zero Exclusion: A Book of Readings* (Vol. 5). Madison, Wis.: Madison Public Schools, 1975.

Wolfensberger, W. Embarrassments in the diagnostic process. In J. J. Dempsey (Ed.), *Community Services for Retarded Children.* Baltimore: University Park Press, 1975.

CAREER AND VOCATIONAL EDUCATION FOR THE RETARDED

More literature exists on career and vocational education for the mentally retarded than for any other handicapped group.

As mentioned in a previous chapter, low expectations hinder the performance of the handicapped. For the mentally retarded, this is a very evident fact and has always been an unfortunate and debilitating one.

The mildly retarded are much more like the normal population than many people realize. They are expected to reach self sufficiency and full independence.

Competitive employment is a reality for many mildly retarded and given proper preparation and adequate support, the mildly retarded can successfully join the work force of this coutry functioning in the normal range and remaining gainfully employed.

Unfortunately, to date, the work record of the mildly retarded has not been good. The main reason for this lack of success is lack of vocational preparation. Many of our school systems possess curricula that do not meet the vocational needs of the mildly retarded and graduate them without skills to survive. There is too little done in regard to work personality and work attitude for example.

There is an even bleaker picture for the moderately and severely retarded populations.

The moderately retarded, or trainable are usually found in sheltered workshops where they perform tasks for token reimbursement and are supported and guided in their lives. Many of these citizens have not been challenged to reach full potential and have not received meaningful vocational education.

The severely retarded, in many cases, have been ignored vocationally.

With no expectations from any segment of society, the severely retarded have been allowed to merely exist without challenge and without any possible fulfillment of potential.

Public Law 94-142 has supposedly changed the situation. The severely retarded must now be planned for educationally on an individual basis. Potential must be considered and approached for the first time for many of these citizens.

Career education for the mildly retarded and vocational education, training and rehabilitation for the moderately and severely retarded can greatly enhance their chances of occupational success and fulfillmenlt of potential.

The following articles will, hopefully, give some insights as to the retarded and their vocational preparation.

A Vocational Delivery System For The Mildly Retarded

HARRY P. BLUHM
University of Utah

It is estimated that there are 6.1 million retarded persons in the United States. Approximately 2.4 million of these individuals are children and young people under 21 years of age. According to conservative estimates, three-fourths of these individuals could become self-supporting and another 10% to 15% partially self-supporting as adults if appropriate education and training are given to them.

To attain these expectations, delivery systems must be implemented to enable the retarded citizen to become employed either competitively or under sheltered conditions. My purpose is to discuss a vocational delivery system that is aimed primarily at the competitive employment market. This system consists of two phases, a prevocational or educational phase and a vocational or work-oriented phase. The components of each phase are diagrammed in Fig. 1.

THE PREVOCATIONAL PHASE

The prevocational phase is educationally based and incorporates several fundamental aspects of occupational training. This phase generally commences at the junior high school level and is maintained in the initial senior high curriculum. It precedes the vocational phase, which begins in the upper grades of high school and may continue at the postsecondary school level. Curriculum considerations provide for the development of functional academic skills, exploratory experiences pertaining to the world of work, and the attainment of personal-social and home-living skills needed to function in society.

Functional academic skills

The purpose of academics, according to Syden (1962), is to provide retarded individuals with information and experiences that should assist them in meeting daily problems, finding their place in the economic world, and giving them an understanding of their responsibilities as citizens. Basic skills would be taught in reading, language, and number concepts during the elementary years with the emphasis taking a decidedly vocational direction during the junior and senior high school years.

Reading. Baroff (1974) suggests that a secondary reading skills program with the primary focus on protection and information is necessary. The ability to read safety and warning signs are primary examples of the protection emphasis. Reading for information includes the functional use of catalogs, telephone directories, maps, classified ads, magazines, television and movie listings, etc.

Language. The primary focus of language instruction is oral expression or the effective use of expressive language (Martens, 1950). Listening for comprehension, carrying on conversations, talking on the telephone, and being able to ask and answer questions are all critical to the development of basic communication structures. A degree of writing proficiency should also be attained by retarded individuals, permitting them to write legibly and accurately in either print or cursive form. They should develop experience in completing various printed forms and in writing personal and business letters.

Number skills. The basic skills in arithmetic would essentially be delimited to addition and subtraction, although multiplication, short division, and simple fractions are also relevant concepts of the arithmetic curricula for this population. The ability to read time

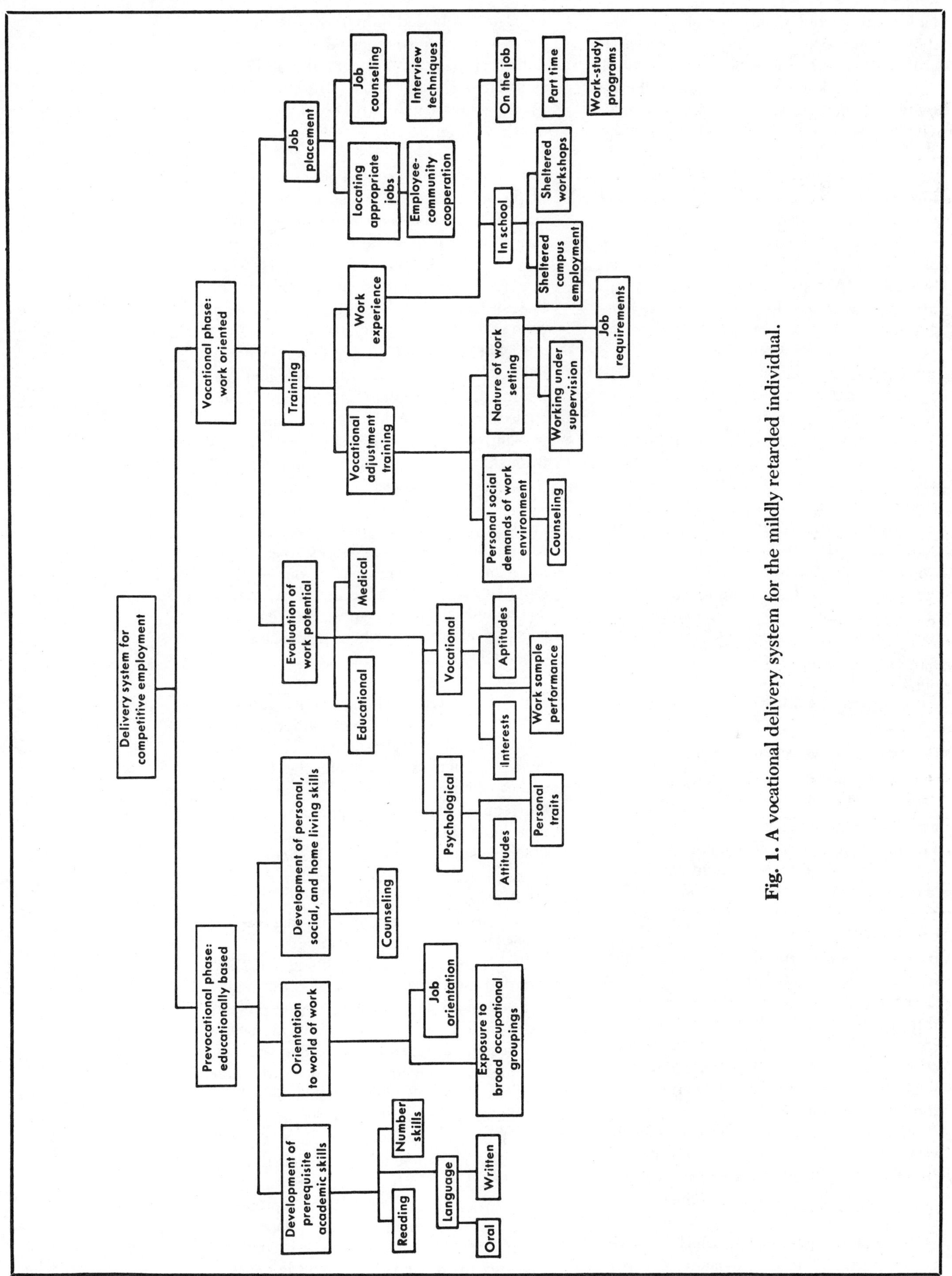

Fig. 1. A vocational delivery system for the mildly retarded individual.

tables and schedules and to employ common units of measures must be emphasized in order to ensure job survival.

The application of number skills to the activities of daily living becomes essential. Thus retarded individuals must develop the skill of using coins and bills of all denominations and must learn about budgeting, banking, credit buying, insurance, taxes, and wage and payroll deductions.

Summary. Although functional academic skills are accented in the retarded individual's educational program, literature in this area has suggested that the absence of functional reading and number skills does not seriously limit the employment of retarded individuals in unskilled work. Dinger (1961) indicates that almost one-half (47%) of the jobs engaged in by employed retarded individuals required no more than counting, and 10% of the jobs required no number skills at all. Approximately 69% of the jobs required no more writing than signing a paycheck or application form. Additionally, 67% of the jobs required only the reading of single words (word recognition), and 33% required no reading at all. These findings suggest that at the junior and senior high school levels the educational experience should not be limited totally to academic training but should also include prevocational and vocational experiences as well (Baroff, 1974).

Orientation to the world of work

Special education teachers and/or school counselors have the responsibility of orienting retarded individuals to the world of work. Vocational guidance deals with the matters of occupational choice, preparation, placement, and adjustment on the job (London, 1973). Typically, vocational guidance regarding career choice is initiated during the latter part of the adolescent years. However, during junior high school retarded individuals are generally introduced to the world of work through simulated and on-the-job exploratory experiences. They learn about various occupations, participate in industrial tours or field trips, and experience certain jobs through in-school work situations.

Specifically, classroom experiences for the retarded individual would involve learning about the opportunities and requirements of service, clerical, agricultural, skilled, semiskilled, and unskilled occupations. These seem to be the job areas in which most retarded persons find employment. The percentage of retarded individuals employed in given job areas is reported to be: service (30%), clerical (12%), agricultural (5.9%), skilled (5.4%), semiskilled (19.3%), unskilled (21.2%), and family worker (6.2%) (President's Committee on Employment of the Handicapped, 1963).

It is also highly recommended that parents of the retarded be involved in this orientation. This permits both parties to obtain information regarding the opportunities available, facts about entry requirements, working conditions, duties performed, health hazards encountered, and the rate of pay for each of the studied occupations.

Field trips. The field trip experience provides the retarded individual with firsthand information regarding alternative career choices. The individual becomes aware of working conditions and worker requirements through this direct observation method (London, 1973). These field trips, organized as part of the orientation process, include visits to laundries, medical centers, hotels, restaurants, large retail stores, meat packing plants, and large farms or dairies. It is important to note that the use of audiovisual media and specialized guest speakers is an effective alternative when personal direct observation is not possible.

Simulated work experiences. The in-school simulated work experience provides another means of orienting retarded individuals to occupational alternatives. These simulated experiences coordinate the interests and capabilities of the retarded individual to the requirements of the work setting. Common junior high experiences include school lunch, custodial, shop, school office, and library clerical jobs. The in-school work placement program at the senior high level provides specific preparatory training experiences prior to on-the-job training.

Personal-social and home-living skills. The retarded individual must possess the requisite personal-social and home-living skills in order to function independently in society and become engaged in productive work experiences. Throughout the junior and senior high school levels, instructional objectives should focus on assisting retarded individuals to: (1) become aware of themselves, their strengths, and their limitations; (2) develop good health and nutritional practices; (3) become aware of and maintain appropriate dress and grooming; (4) get along with others—adults, the opposite sex, and the same sex peers; and (5) develop home economic skills (Baroff, 1974).

Retarded individuals who are experiencing poor peer relationships, feeling of inadequacy, and a tendency toward self-depreciation may need counseling services. When a counseling service is available the counselor should seek to provide a much more friendly, accepting, and supportive learning situation than would be required for nonretarded individuals with these same feelings (Thorne, 1960).

THE VOCATIONAL PHASE

The primary purpose of the vocational phase is preparation of the retarded individual for placement in the world of work. The components of this phase, including the evaluation of work potential, job training, and placement, have their roots in the trait and factor vocational theory (Shertzer and Stone, 1968; Zaccaria, 1970). This theory provides for the following steps:

1. The traits of the retarded individual are to be assessed by psychological tests and other evaluative tools. This permits the retarded individual and those who work with him or her to obtain a clear understanding of the individual's attitudes, abilities, interests, ambitions, resources, and limitations.
2. An assessment is obtained regarding the requirements and conditions for success, advantages, compensation, and the prospects of alternative occupational opportunities as they relate to the retarded individual.
3. The counselor (school and/or rehabilitation), the special education teacher, or the vocational coordinator seeks to match the retarded individual to the job with the greatest opportunity for success.

The relationship between the components of the vocational phase and the steps associated with the trait and factor theory is shown in Fig. 2. Burrow (1964) suggests that the match between the job and the individual is the culmination of the entire job development process. The retarded individual's prospects for job stability are not good if the match is not made on a completely selective basis.

Evaluation of work potential

The purpose of evaluating the work potential of retarded individuals is to determine what type of work they can do or can be trained to do. This requires identifying the specific abilities or assets they may possess. The evaluation should be comprehensive in order to examine the retarded individual's intellectual abilities, academic achievement, manual skills, personality traits, vocational interests, etc. (Patterson, 1964; Katz, 1968; Kolstoe, 1960).

Instruments used to collect these data include standardized tests, attitude scales, vocational adjustment scales, checklists, rating scales, personal-social inventories, performance scales, interest inventories, and work samples. A basic concern regarding the use of these instruments is their reliability and validity. One problem with standardized tests is that they have not been normed on mentally retarded individuals, thus making their reliability and validity questionable with this population (Walthall and Love, 1974; Katz, 1968).

Personality inventories have been of little use with the retarded since it is unclear whether they tap the characteristics important to job success. The utilization of work samples for evaluative purposes has also been questioned because of the lack of a specified criteria and a low correlation with job requirements (Patterson, 1964). However, direct observations by trained personnel are essential. They are useful in providing information on the retarded individual's vocational interests, attitudes, and work habits.

It is essential that only skilled personnel be included in the comprehensive evaluation. The team approach involving psychologists, physicians, social workers, educational specialists, and rehabilitation counselors is highly recommended (Katz, 1968). The evaluation may be conducted by public

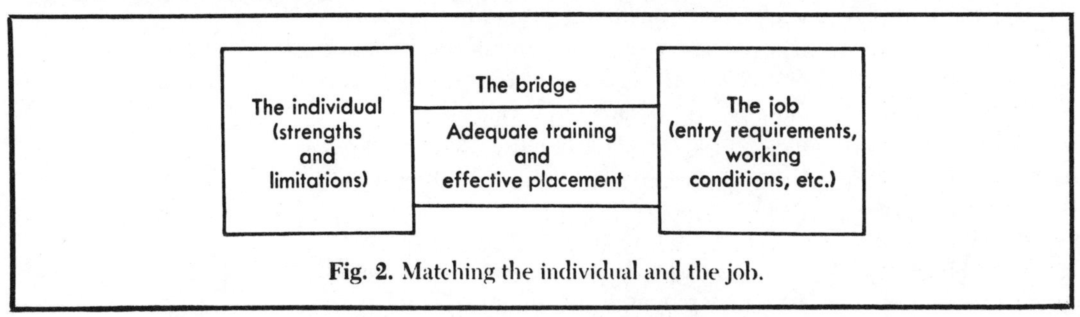

Fig. 2. Matching the individual and the job.

5. VOCATIONAL

schools, sheltered workshops, or rehabilitation agencies. It may last from several weeks to 1 or 2 years, depending upon the problems presented by the retarded individual (Bolanovich, 1972). The evaluation of the retarded individual's work potential should be considered as a process of gathering, interpreting, analyzing, and synthesizing all vocationally significant data (Malikin and Rusalem, 1969).

Training

The employability of the retarded individual is dependent upon the successful development of vocational skills in combination with desired personal-social skills. This goal is attained through vocational adjustment training and work experiences. Personal-social factors have been recognized as the most important determinant of the retarded individual's employability (Syden, 1962; Deno, 1966). Vocational adjustment training serves to assist the individual in becoming dependable and emotionally mature. Additionally, work experiences enable the retarded individual to practice job skills in a protective environment under the supervision of an employer and school official.

Work adjustment training. Work adjustment training is work rather than education oriented (Daniels, 1974). It may be given without any specific job in mind, but generally occurs when the retarded individual is obtaining job training in an on-campus or community job.

The purpose of work adjustment training is for the retarded individual to experience actual work situations under the guidance of a work supervisor and counselor. During such training retarded individuals are oriented to the personal-social demands of the work environment and to the nature of work settings. They are taught courteousness, cleanliness, punctuality, cooperation, tolerance toward pressures of meetings and deadlines, and the need to work harmoniously with other employees, to stick to given work tasks, and to take responsibility for work assigned (Davis, 1959; Stahlecker, 1964; Daniels, 1974; Bolanovich, 1972).

The counselor conducting the training can assist the retarded individual in learning appropriate behaviors and eliminating those that are undesirable. Individual or group counseling may be utilized depending upon the situation or problem that exists. Two techniques, role playing and behavior modification, have been found to be very effective in a variety of these counseling situations. Role playing is effective in providing retarded individuals the opportunity of confronting interpersonal problems in a simulated and sheltered environment. Behavior modification focuses upon specific behaviorally defined problems incorporated within a system of consistent feedback. This facilitates the monitoring of client progress within a designated program structure (Halpern and Berard, 1974).

Counselors and sheltered workshop foremen may monitor or assess the work adjustment behavior by using one of several vocational adjustment scales (Daniels, 1972; Bitter and Bolanovich, 1970). The scales purport to measure job readiness but may be limited by interrater variations and the lack of empirical data correlating measured behavior to rehabilitation needs (Bitter and Bolanovich, 1970).

Work experience. Erickson (1947) defines work experience as

. . . a means and method in the program of the school by which the learner actually produces goods or renders useful service through participation in socially desirable activities in the community under real conditions. [p. 355]

Successful in-school work experiences should precede out-of-school vocational encounters. These in-school work experiences may be obtained through sheltered campus employment and sheltered workshops. Out-of-school experiences result from student participation in work-study programs.

Work experience serves as a valuable testing ground for practicing related job skills under the supervision of school officials. The retarded individuals are in a protective environment where they may learn by trial and error with no fear of losing the job. The practical experience they obtain serves to help them develop work confidence (Stahlecker, 1964; Kokaska, 1964; Burdett, 1963). Additionally, school officials have the advantage of observing the retarded individual's work attitude and response to supervision. Deficits that are noted can be incorporated into the vocational adjustment program. A disadvantage of sheltered on-campus work experiences is that the supervising personnel, including custodians and cafeteria workers, may look at the retarded individual as merely a helper and thus fail to instruct or supervise (Hickman, 1967).

The sheltered workshop program has two basic functions: (1) to train retarded individuals for employment in competitive jobs, and

(2) to provide a terminal employment opportunity for retarded adults who cannot succeed in competitive employment conditions (Wallin, 1960; Bolanovich, 1972). As a rehabilitative facility, the sheltered workshop seeks to prepare mildly retarded individuals for unsheltered employment through the molding of attitudes, vocational training, and achievement of social skills (Zaetz, 1971; Conley, 1973).

On-the-job training of retarded individuals between the ages of 17 and 21 years is facilitated through the establishment of work-study programs. Generally, individuals participating in work-study programs are considered to be emotionally stable and socially mature. Physically, they should be able to perform the job requirements and not represent a danger to themselves or their fellow workers (Shawn, 1964).

The responsibility for work-study programs is shared by the local school district and community agencies. School officials must identify employers within the community that have jobs suited to the needs and limitations of the retarded client. Vocational rehabilitation offices and state employment agencies should assist in this process. Once identified, employers must be willing to assume responsibility for training the retarded individual and orienting current employees to the exceptional needs of the retarded client. Retarded individuals must also accept responsibility. They must be willing to work cooperatively with their fellow employees and supervisory personnel. Retarded individuals who participate in work study programs profit by (1) learning the characteristics of a particular job, (2) knowing what the job requirements are, (3) receiving assistance in job interviewing, (4) understanding the purpose of wage deductions and various fringe benefits, and (5) acquiring an identity as responsible and productive workers (Daniels, 1974).

Job placement. Job placement is the culminating activity of the delivery system for competitive employment. It consists of matching the right person to the right job. Job placement brings the employer, school or rehabilitative counselor, and the retarded client together. Burrow (1964) outlines several steps a counselor should follow in securing employment for the retarded individual in a competitive labor market. First, the counselor seeks to identify employers with jobs available that meet the skill requirements of the retarded client. The counselor then discusses with the employer the needs, capabilities, and limitations of the retarded client. When the employer and counselor are reasonably sure that the client matches the job, the retarded individual is brought in for a formal job interview. Role playing of the job interview should have been previously conducted in order to prepare the retarded individual for this situation. Once the job has been secured the counselor is obligated to conduct follow-up assessment on the retarded individual's job performance. The previously discussed delivery system will be successful if the retarded individual, through continual employment in the labor force, attains the expected goal of self-sufficiency.

REFERENCES

Baroff, G. A.: Mental retardation: nature, cause, and management, New York, 1974, Halsted Press.

Bitter, J. A., and Bolanovich, D. J.: WARF: a scale for measuring job readiness behaviors, Am. J. Ment. Defic. **74:** 616-621, 1970.

Bolanovich, D. J., Drought, N. E., and Stewart, D. A.: Full employment for the mentally retarded, St. Louis, 1972, The Jewish Employment and Vocational Service.

Burdett, A. D.: An examination of selected prevocational techniques utilized in programs for the mentally retarded, Ment. Retard. **1:** 230-237, 1963.

Burrow, W. H.: Job development: a problem in interpersonal dynamics training, Training School Bull. **61:** 12-20, 1964.

Conley, R. W.: The economics of mental retardation, Baltimore, 1973, The Johns Hopkins University Press.

Daniels, L. K.: An experimental edition of a rating scale of vocational adjustment for the mentally retarded, Training School Bull. **69:** 92-98, 1972.

Daniels, L. K., editor: Vocational rehabilitation of the mentally retarded, Springfield, Ill., 1974, Charles C Thomas, Publisher.

Davis, D. A.: Counseling the mentally retarded, Vocational Guidance Quarterly **7:** 184-188, 1959.

Deno, E.: Vocational preparation of the retarded during school years. In Michael, S. G. D., editor: New vocational pathways for the mentally retarded, Washington, D.C., 1966, American Personnel and Guidance Association, pp. 20-29.

Dinger, J. C.: Post-school adjustment of former educable retarded pupils, Except. Child. **27:** 353-356, 1961.

Erickson, C. E.: A basic text for guidance workers, New York, 1947, Prentice-Hall, Inc.

Halpern, A. S., and Berard, W. R.: Counseling the mentally retarded: a review for practice. In Browning, P. L., editor: Mental retardation: rehabilitation and counseling, Springfield, Ill., 1974, Charles C Thomas, Publisher, pp. 269-289.

Hickman, L. H., Jr.: A foundation for the preparation of the educable child for the world of work, Training School Bull. **64:** 39-44, 1967.

Katz, E.: The retarded adult in the community, Springfield, Ill., 1968, Charles C Thomas, Publisher.

CAREERS OF MENTALLY RETARDED YOUNG PERSONS: SERVICE, JOBS, AND INTERPERSONAL RELATIONS

STEPHEN A. RICHARDSON
Albert Einstein College of Medicine of Yeshiva University

Life histories and follow-up data at age 22 were obtained for a total city population of children classified as mentally retarded (index cases). Histories were also obtained at age 22 from matched comparisons who at no time had been classified as retarded. Matching was on age, sex, and social background. Placement at school-leaving age and major occupation at age 22 were reported for the index population. Those 22-year-old index cases not receiving mental retardation services and their matched comparisons were examined on objective and subjective measures of the jobs they held and selected indicators of interpersonal relationships.

This is the initial report of a study designed to describe the life courses from age 10 to 22 of a total population of young people in a city who were administratively defined during childhood as mentally retarded. My purpose in this report is to give a summary of the life courses of the total population and to examine the postschool careers of the subpopulation of young adults who cease to be officially considered as mentally retarded after leaving school.

Since 1910, there have been a number of reports of studies that follow-up into adulthood young people who had been classified as mentally retarded. The earliest and most numerous studies dealt with people who had been in residential institutions for retarded persons and were released or had escaped. The results showed that these persons, in many cases, were able to function in the community, find and hold jobs, and marry and raise families. They did not exhibit the social-pathological behavior ex-

pected of retarded persons and those who had children did not produce large numbers of retarded children (Cobb, 1972; Goldstein, 1964; Tizard, 1965). The studies were valuable in that they challenged the conventional wisdom of the early 20th century that genetic factors were dominant in the etiology of mental retardation. It was a time of segregating mentally retarded persons into large isolated institutions, a time when legislation was passed permitting sterilization of retarded persons, and a time when there seemed little point in social habilitation. Major difficulties in interpreting these studies are the absence of data on the level of functioning of the individuals when they were children and knowledge about whether they were in any way representative of the populations in residential institutions. Placement in institutions occurred for many reasons other than clear evidence of severe mental retardation, including placement of people who were judged to be nuisances or troublemakers by families, courts, or influential members of the community; some were orphans or persons for whom no other placement could be found. Although it might be expected that studies of residents and ex-residents of mental retardation institutions would focus on severely retarded persons for whom placement in residential facilities has some rationale, the focus has been largely on adults with mild degrees of mental retardation, for

This study was supported by the Foundation for Child Development, the Grant Foundation, the National Institute of Child Health and Human Development Grant No. HD 07907, and the Social Science Research Council of the United Kingdom. The author thanks Helene Koller, Janice McLaren, and other members of the project who participated in the study and Raymond Illsley, Gordon Horobin, and Barbara Thompson who provided scientific consultation and administrative support.

whom institutional care was probably in-appropriate.

A second kind of study has been the follow-up into adulthood of young people who were placed in special classes for mentally handicapped individuals (Ferguson & Kerr, 1955, 1958; Tizard, 1974; Kennedy, Note 1; Saenger, Note 2). These researchers have shown that many of these young people were able, as young adults, to live in the community away from their parents' homes, a proportion found employment, and some married, raised families, and were able to function as adults in the society. Others experienced real problems in achieving satisfactory living conditions.

These investigators have focused attention on neglected problems and have challenged dogmatic and limited conceptualizations of mental retardation. There are, however, a number of methodological and substantive limitations that make it difficult to generalize about the studies or apply them to some of the contemporary issues in the field of mental subnormality:

1. The studies are largely retrospective, with limited information on the adults when they were of school age.

2. The criterion for inclusion in the studies has predominantly been placement in special facilities for mentally handicapped persons and sometimes the availability of an IQ score.

3. Often, the study populations in the United States included a heavy representation of individuals from minority groups or recent immigrants.

4. The nature of the selection process for special educational placement is not known.

5. Few of the studies have any comparison group matched on age, sex, and similar social background, so it is not possible to interpret the extent to which the functioning of mentally retarded persons at later ages is a consequence of their intellectual impairment.

6. Because total populations of mentally retarded young persons have not been followed up, it has not been possible to examine the subsequent life histories of people with different subtypes of mental retardation living in the same community.

7. There have been no longitudinal studies of mental retardation in which investigators examined the experiences of young people as they progress from childhood to adulthood. Neither has there been emphasis on the influence of parents, relatives, neighbors, and friends who are significant to the young people, and of the influences of various agencies of the community, e.g., education, health, social work, vocational, and residential services.

Little is known about the life course after leaving school of those who are no longer classified as mentally retarded. The rise in the prevalence of mental retardation to a peak in the late school years, followed by a rapid decline was first reported by Penrose (1963) using data from the Lewis (1929) survey. Gruenberg (1964), in a review of seven epidemiological studies, estimated that the prevalence of mental retardation among young adults is only half as high as the peak rate reached around the age of 14. It is clear from several studies that those persons who disappear from official note are mildly retarded (Innes, 1975; Kushlick & Blunden, 1974; Susser, 1968). These findings pose critical questions for understanding the nature of mental retardation and for decision making in public policy. Gruenberg (1964), e.g., suggested that:

> For this drop in prevalence to occur, a large group of people regarded as retarded at fourteen must improve in their functioning to the point where people no longer regard them as retarded and also must succeed in escaping their history of earlier unsatisfactory performance. (p. 274)

> Either these individuals are continuing to be extremely handicapped in later life and are unknown because the services they need are unavailable to them (in which case society is failing to do its duty toward them and ought to learn how to find and help them), or they have stopped being retarded in any real sense at all and do not need any special protection, help or services, in which case one had better change one's concept of what "real" retardation "really" is. . . . The phenomenon cries out for investigation. (p. 274)

To examine this issue requires identifying all children in a community who at any time during schooling have been administratively classified as mentally retarded and then following them into adulthood to determine who are and are not receiving services related to mental retardation after leaving school. In addition to obvious questions such as whether they are employed, it is important to examine the quality of their lives compared to lives of peers from comparable social backgrounds who went to regular schools. Clearly, a major research challenge is to work out objective indicators of what constitutes quality of life.

Method

A city in the United Kingdom was selected that met the following requirements of the study design: (a) a relatively stable population in order to make possible a follow-up study over a 14-year period; (b) a comprehensive administrative structure for the careful identification of the total population of children in the community who are mentally retarded, based on a clinical judgment taking into account IQ, school performance, social competence, and a medical evaluation; (c) in order to have an adequate number of cases for study, a community that has a minimum of 30 children in each birth year who are administratively defined as mentally retarded when at school; (d) standardized information on the level of functioning and the health and social environments of the young adults when they were children; (e) as a basis for selecting a comparison set of cases who are not mentally retarded, adequate data on children in the community who were not mentally retarded; and (f) a high degree of cooperation from the study population; the authorities responsible for health, education, and welfare services; and other scientists working in the community.

Data used in this report were derived from a standardized interview with the young adults when they were 22 years old. Whenever possible, an interview with parents was used as a cross-check on the basic outlines of the young adult career. The parent interview was the primary source in cases where the young adult had severe communication limitations and cases where we were unable to interview the young adult. Records from a variety of institutions provided further independent data sources. The data necessary for the selection of the mentally retarded subjects and the matched comparisons were obtained in 1962 in a program of research in the same community (Birch, Richardson, Baird, Horobin, & Illsley, 1970).

To examine the level of skill, training, and responsibility of the jobs held, we developed an occupational classification in conjunction with the Director of Youth Employment Services in the city, who has an intimate knowledge of the various jobs held by young adults. This special classification was developed only after finding that the widely used national occupational classification of the Registrar General did not discriminate sufficiently for 22 year olds who came predominately from the lower end of the socioeconomic scale. A 6-point scale was used: professional, highly skilled, skilled, semi-skilled, limited skill, and unskilled. The classification was developed from job descriptions without the classifier knowing whether the job was held by a young person who had or had not been considered mentally retarded as a child.

To obtain some indication of how the young adults felt about their social relationships, they were asked, "On the whole how do you feel you have got along with other people since you left school? Would you say you got along well or not well?" If the response were "well," a follow-up question was asked, "Would you say you got along very well or well?" If the response was "not well," the follow-up was, "Would you say you got along not well or badly?" These questions provided four categories of response, but young adults only had to choose between two alternatives. This procedure was adopted to simplify the task for young adults who had difficulty in thinking in conceptual terms.

The study population for the present report was selected from all persons who were born in the years 1951 and 1952 and resided in the city in 1962. The index cases were children who were administratively classified as mentally retarded and placed in special education facilities or residential care at any time during their school years. For each index case a matched comparison was selected who had at no time during schooling been administratively defined as mentally retarded. The matching variables were age, sex, occupation of head of the household, where the child lived at age 8 to 10, and the type of housing at this time. Comparison children did not include any child who at age 7 and 9 had scored less than 75 and 80, respectively, in group intelligence tests given to all children in the city and might therefore on psychometric grounds alone be considered as borderline retarded, even though they had not been administratively defined as mentally retarded.

Where an index case migrated away from the city before the age of 18, no comparison was selected. This was done because had a comparison been selected, differences found between the index case and matched comparison could be due to differences in the communities (e.g., different employment opportunities or differences in the availability of mental retardation services) rather than differences due to mental impairment.

In presenting results, index cases who moved away from Aberdeen before the age of 18 and for whom no comparisons were selected were omitted from analyses involving index and comparison cases. In addition, where index and comparisons were not both engaged in the activity being examined they were excluded from analysis.

Results

There were 97 cases born in 1951 and 1952 who met the definition of an index case. Two had died, leaving 95 survivors at age 22. Data were obtained on 88 (93 percent) of the survivors (50 males, 38 females). Of the 7 index cases for whom data were not obtained, 6 refused to be interviewed and 1 had migrated away from Aberdeen and has not yet been interviewed.

Seventy-six of the 88 index cases were matched. Twelve comparisons are missing for the following reasons: comparisons were not selected for the 8 index cases who had left Aberdeen before 18 years of age, interviews with 3 comparisons have not yet been completed, and 1 index case could not be properly matched because he had been in various forms of foster and institutional care since birth.

A brief summary of the life careers of all the index cases (their last school placement at the minimum school-leaving age of 15 and their major occupation at age 22) is given in Tables 1 and 2. It is noteworthy that 14 percent of the index cases returned to regular schools after spending a period of time at the school for the educationally subnormal (Table 1). Of those who remained in special facilities for mentally retarded persons until school-leaving age, three-quarters were at the school for the educationally subnormal, with the remaining quarter in a junior training center or in a residential institution for total care.

TABLE 1

PLACEMENT OF INDEX CASES ($N=88$) AT SCHOOL-LEAVING AGE (15 YEARS)

Placement	Male	Female	Total
Regular school following period at ESN[a] school	7 (14)	5 (13)	12 (14)
ESN school	32 (66)	23 (61)	55 (63)
Junior training center[b]	5 (10)	7 (18)	12 (14)
Residential institution for total care	5 (10)	3 (8)	8 (9)
Approved school[c]	1 (2)	0 —	1 (1)

Note. Percentages in parentheses.
[a] Educationally subnormal (educable mentally retarded in U.S. terminology).
[b] For trainable mentally retarded persons in U.S. terminology.
[c] In U.S. classification, residential facility for juvenile delinquents.

At age 22, two-thirds of the index cases were not receiving any special mental retardation services (Table 2). Of this subpopulation, 89 percent of the males were in full-time jobs, with the remaining 11 percent unemployed. With one exception, all the index cases not receiving mental retardation services at age 22 had attended the school for the educationally subnormal. There was a tendency for more males (73 percent) than females (58 percent) to function without mental retardation services at age 22, but the difference was not statistically significant. For those index cases receiving mental retardation services at age 22, there was a tendency for more females (75 percent) than males (38 percent) to be in

day care rather than residential total care facilities (Table 2).

The histories of the index cases between school leaving and age 22 were examined

TABLE 2

MAJOR OCCUPATION OF INDEX CASES AT AGE 22

Occupation	Male[a]	Female
Cases not receiving MR[b] services		
Full-time job	27	10
Full-time plus part-time job	4	0
Full-time job plus further education	1	1
Unemployed	4	1
Housewife	—	7
Housewife plus part-time job	—	3
Total of cases not receiving MR services	36	22
Cases receiving MR services		
In day care at senior occupation centers	5	12
In total care at residential institutions	8	3
Special placement by social services, living with elderly couple and receiving disability pension	0	1
Total of cases receiving MR services	13	16

[a] For one male case information was not obtained on major occupation at age 22.
[b] Mental retardation.

by grouping them into subsets based on their placement at school-leaving age. Of the 12 young people who returned to regular schools after a period at the special school, 11 have received no subsequent mental retardation services. The remaining individual, a female, worked at a senior occupational center. Of the index cases who stayed at the special school until they left school, 80 percent received no subsequent services, and there was no difference in this percentage between males and females (Table 3). Nine percent were in a daytime senior occupational center and living at home, and 9 percent were or had been in residential facilities for mentally retarded persons. The primary reason for institutional placement for all cases was behavioral disturbance or antisocial behavior. The remaining 1 case (2 percent) was placed with an elderly couple. She received social security and helped around the house. Of the remaining index cases who were at the junior training center or in residential care at school-leaving age, all were receiving mental retardation services with the exception of 1 male who presently had a full-time job but who earlier was receiving mental retardation services.

TABLE 3

POST SCHOOL SERVICES RECEIVED BY INDEX CASES WHOSE LAST SCHOOL WAS THE EDUCATIONALLY SUBNORMAL SCHOOL

Services	Males[a]	Females
No mental retardation (MR) services at any time since leaving school	25 (80.5)	18 (78)
No MR services at present but some services between ages 16 and 22		
Stay in MR institution because of behavior problems	2 (6.5)	0 —
Receiving MR services at age 22		
At a senior occupational center	2 (6.5)	3 (14)
At MR institution because of behavioral problems	2 (6.5)	1 (4)
Living with elderly couple, receives social security and does some housework	0 —	1 (4)

Note. Percentages in parentheses.

[a] In addition, there is one male case for whom this information is not known.

There was little interchange between the day-care senior occupation center and residential treatment in an institution. One case from the senior occupation center spent a brief period in the residential facility because of psychiatric problems, and another case from the center received brief respite care to enable her parents to have a holiday.

Careers after Leaving School of Those Index Cases not Receiving Mental Retardation Services at Age 22

To examine the issue discussed by Gruenberg in the introduction to this paper, we investigated the extent to which the careers of the subset of index cases who have not received mental retardation services after leaving school were similar or different from their comparisons. The overall study encompassed many aspects of the young people's lives—their vocational careers; spare-time interests and activities; the institutions of society that impinge on their lives; their social relationships with family, relatives, neighbors, and fellow workers; and their subjective evaluations of their lives and themselves. In this paper we will give results illustrating examples of objective and subjective indicators of the young peoples' job histories and their social relationships.

Table 4 shows the current major occupations of the subset of index cases not currently receiving mental retardation services and their matched comparisons. There were no significant differences between the index cases and their comparisons. There was somewhat higher unemployment and no full-time further education among the index cases.

Three measures were used to examine the kinds of jobs held by the index cases who were in open employment and their comparisons: (a) a classification of the degree of skill, training, and responsibility the job requires; (b) take-home pay; and (c) whether the job deals with objects only or persons as well.

Job classification. The results are shown for the subset of matched pairs where both index and comparisons were working (Table 5). For those unemployed, their most recent jobs were used for purposes of classification. Those in full-time education were excluded. For both males and females, the index cases had a higher fre-

TABLE 4

CURRENT OCCUPATIONS OF INDEX CASES NOT CURRENTLY RECEIVING MENTAL RETARDATION SERVICES AND THEIR MATCHED COMPARISONS

Occupation	Male[a]		Female	
	Index	Comparison	Index	Comparison
Full-time job	21 (73)	22 (76)	9 (43)	7 (33)
Full-time plus part-time job	4 (14)	1 (4)	0 (0)	0 (0)
Full-time job plus further education	1 (4)	0 (0)	1 (5)	0 (0)
Full-time job plus housewife	0 (0)	0 (0)	0 (0)	2 (10)
Part-time job plus housewife	0 (0)	0 (0)	3 (14)	4 (19)
Unemployed	3 (10)	1 (4)	1 (5)	0 (0)
Full-time housewife	0 (0)	0 (0)	7 (33)	7 (33)
Full-time further education (FTE)	0 (0)	4 (14)	0 (0)	0 (0)
FTE plus casual job	0 (0)	1 (4)	0 (0)	0 (0)
FTE plus housewife	0 (0)	0 (0)	0 (0)	1 (5)

Note. Percentages in parentheses.

[a] $n = 29$ in each male group and 21 in each female group.

RICHARDSON

TABLE 5
KINDS OF JOBS HELD AND FEELINGS ABOUT JOBS FOR INDEX AND COMPARISON CASES

Job information	Males		Females	
	Index	Comparison	Index	Comparison
Job classification by level of skill[a]				
Semi-skilled & skilled	5	15	4	10
Limited skill and unskilled	14	4	6	0
Weekly take-home pay[b]				
Greater than 32 pounds	2	9	—	—
23–32 pounds	5	6	—	—
22 pounds & less	9	1	—	—
Proportion of cases whose job requires interpersonal skills[c]				
Skilled	0/1	2/6	0/4	6/6
Semi-skilled	0/4	2/9	0/4	3/4
Limited skill and unskilled	0/14	0/4	2/6	—
Response to Question 1[d]				
Yes	9	12	3	8
No	13	10	8	3
Response to Question 2[e]				
Yes	7	15	3	5
No	15	7	8	6

Note. Data for subset of index cases who were not receiving mental retardation services at age 22.
[a] Full-time students excluded.
[b] For females, too few cases for analysis.
[c] Controlled for level of skill. For the comparison group holding skilled jobs, 33 percent of the males and 100 percent of the females required interpersonal skills; for the semi-skilled comparison group, 22 percent of the males and 75 percent of the females required such skills.
[d] "Is there any other work you would rather have done?"
[e] "Is there anything you would change about your working life?"

quency of less-skilled jobs ($\chi^2 = 8.55, p < .01$ and Fisher's exact test $p = .005$ for males and females, respectively.)

Take-home pay. The amount a person is paid is indicative of community values about the worth of a job. Weekly take-home pay was ascertained. The male index cases received, on the average, two-thirds the income of the comparisons. As can be seen in Table 5, the distribution of the amount of take-home pay shows that the index males received significantly less pay than comparisons ($\chi^2 = 10.95, p < .01$). There was an insufficient number of females for analysis where index and comparison matched pairs both worked.

Person- and object-oriented jobs. Because social competence is a criterion used in the assessment of mental retardation, all the jobs held by the study population were evaluated to determine whether they involved skills related primarily to objects or to persons as well. The evaluation was done without knowing who held the jobs. Because it is reasonable to expect that jobs requiring higher levels of occupational skill will more often require interpersonal skills, level of occupational skills was used as a control variable (Table 5). The results support this expectation. Fewer index males and females held jobs that required personal skills. For both index and comparisons, women had a higher proportion of

jobs requiring interpersonal skills than did men. The number of cases was so small that statistical tests were inappropriate.

In addition to considering objective indicators of the young adults, it is important to learn something about their subjective reactions to their job experiences. Responses to two questions are illustrations. "Is there any other work you would rather have done?" and "Is there anything you would change about your working life?" Although the index cases had jobs requiring less skill and received less take-home pay, they did not more often feel there was other work they would rather have done (Table 5). In fact, the trend was in the opposite direction ($\chi^2 = 2.91, p < .10$ for females). Again, the index cases less often said that there were changes they would like to make in their working lives and for the males the difference was significant ($\chi^2 = 4.45, p < .05$).

Interpersonal Relationships

An important potential source of personal satisfaction is the network of interpersonal relationships that individuals develop and use. Within this network there will be others who will probably be of particular significance, e.g., parents, siblings, spouse, and close friends. In addition to whether these relationships do or do not exist, individuals' feelings about their

TABLE 6
INTERPERSONAL RELATIONS FOR INDEX AND COMPARISON CASES

Interpersonal relations	Male		Female	
	Index	Comparison	Index	Comparison
Cases able to name two best friends	13/21 (62)	18/21 (86)	9/17 (53)	16/17 (94)
Cases who said they had special opposite sex friends[a]	3/16 (19)	10/16 (63)	5/8 (63)	6/8 (75)
Marital status				
Single	22/29 (76)	12/29 (41)	10/21 (48)	6/21 (29)
Cohabiting	0 —	0 —	1/21 (4)	0 —
Married	7/29 (24)	15/29 (52)	10/21 (48)	15/21 (71)
Separated	0 —	1/29 (3)	0 —	0 —
Divorced	0 —	1/29 (3)	0 —	0 —
Answers to relationship question[b]				
Very well	9/26 (35)	21/26 (81)	6/17 (35)	12/17 (71)
Well	12/26 (46)	5/26 (19)	11/17 (65)	5/17 (29)
Not well	4/26 (15)	0 —	0 —	0 —
Badly	1/26 (4)	0 —	0 —	0 —

Note. Data from subset of index cases not receiving mental retardation services at age 22.

[a] Question, "Do you have any special boy/girl friend now?" Only asked of single, separated, and divorced persons.

[b] Question, "How well have you got along with other people since you left school?"

interpersonal relationships also need to be considered. In this study the interpersonal network of each young adult was examined. A few examples appear below.

Young adults were asked to name their two best friends. The index cases were less often able than their comparisons to name as many as two friends (Table 6). For the females, the difference was significant ($\chi^2 = 5.44$, $p < .05$). The male response was in the same direction but was not significant. The young adults who were not married or cohabiting were asked, "Do you have any special (opposite sex) friend now?" The index males answered in the affirmative less often than did the comparison males ($\chi^2 = 4.66$, $p < .05$). Examination of Table 6 shows that, for the males, a higher proportion of index cases were single than were married or cohabiting ($\chi^2 = 4.5$, $p < .05$). The difference was not significant for the females. As might be expected at 22 years of age, more females than males were married. Of the young adults who were married, there was no difference between the male and female index and comparison cases on how many children they had. The numbers of children ranged from one to three.

The answers to the subjective question, "On the whole how do you feel you have got along with other people since you left school?" show that the index males less often than their comparisons responded "very well" ($\chi^2 = 9.53$, $p < .01$). For the females the trend was in the same direction ($\chi^2 = 2.95$, $p < .10$).

Discussion

The summary of the life courses from 10 to 22 years of the total population of chil-

dren who at any time had been placed in special facilities for mentally retarded persons during their school years shows that the classification does not have to be a one-way irrevocable process. Fear has been expressed that once a child is classified or labeled as mentally retarded, declassification will not occur either because educational authorities feel that it will be regarded as an admission of a mistaken earlier judgment or that once classified the initial judgment is never revised. Another fear is that the rate of educational progress is so much slower in the educationally subnormal (special) than in the regular classroom that with increasing length of stay in a special classroom, the more difficult it becomes for a child to return to a regular class. Of the index children who were at the special school, 18 percent returned to regular schools, indicating that at the time and place of this study, placement in special education was not a one-way process.

Lewis (1929) and O'Connor and Tizard (1956) found that approximately 25 percent of the administratively classified cases of mental retardation had IQs below 50. The present investigator found a similar percentage. Twenty-seven percent of those index cases who remained in mental retardation placement until school-leaving age and whose IQs were predominantly below 50 were in a junior training center or in residential care.

Gruenberg (1964) estimated that about one-half of those classified as mentally retarded as children disappear from administrative note after leaving school. At age 22, in the present study, two-thirds were not receiving any mental retardation service and were not administratively considered as mentally retarded. This is a higher proportion than that given by Gruenberg.

Eighty percent of the index cases who finished schooling in special classes received no subsequent mental retardation services. This suggests that the term "educationally subnormal" used in Britain as a description of a current functional level is more appropriate than the American term "educable mentally retarded," which has the connotation of a more permanent state.

Of the index cases not receiving any mental retardation services at age 22, 8 percent were unemployed as opposed to 2 percent of the comparisons. It is important to know that most of those who were considered mildly mentally retarded at school obtained jobs under conditions where there is virtually full employment in their age group.

My second purpose in this paper was to determine to what extent the index cases who disappeared from administrative note after leaving school had careers that were similar or different from the comparisons. The evidence considered in light of the two alternatives suggested by Gruenberg (see p. 350 of this article) is that they are not "continuing to be extremely handicapped" (p. 274). Whether "they have stopped being retarded in any sense at all" (p. 274) depends on the meaning of "retarded" and the point of view that is adopted. From the viewpoint of whether those index cases would stand out as different when encountered by strangers in public places, they are probably indistinguishable. But when their lives are compared with those who are of the same age, sex, and general socioeconomic background in childhood and who were at no time classified as mentally retarded, there are important distinguishable differences. Of jobs held at the age of 22, the index cases, as a group, differed in holding positions requiring lower levels of skill, with less take-home pay, and requiring fewer dealings with people as compared to objects. When, however, subjective reactions to their work were elicited, the index cases appeared to have a lesser degree of discontent. This suggestion should be treated with caution because the index cases may be limited in their ability to envisage other work they would rather have done or ways in which they would have changed their working lives.

The findings about jobs should not be generalized beyond the age of 22. If there is differential advancement in the kinds of jobs held by the index and comparison young people, the differences early in their careers may be far less noticeable than, e.g., at the mid-point of their job careers. While the index cases may not perceive invidious comparisons between their own jobs and other people's at age 22, they may become aware of differences in another 10 to 20 years. Later, as job careers draw to a close and retirement begins and when society's expectations for an individual's work performance diminishes and ends, then the index and comparison cases may again appear more alike.

The discrepancy found between the objective and subjective measures related to jobs does not occur in the results related to interpersonal relations. The objective indicators suggest that the index young adults have a more restricted set of interpersonal relations than do the comparisons. But here the index cases assess how they get along with other people less favorably than do the comparisons. It should be noted, however, that the subjective questions related to interpersonal relations probably require less conceptual ability than the subjective questions about jobs.

Further analysis will broaden the picture of ways in which the index cases who disappear from administrative note after leaving school do and do not differ from comparisons in their past and present daily lives. It will also show the variation that exists in this subset of index cases and how these variations are related to their social and biological histories.

The present report is restricted to two birth cohorts while the overall study will include five birth cohorts. The research design requires the young adults to be interviewed at age 22. Data-gathering must therefore span 5 years. The total number of cases will provide larger numbers and, consequently, opportunities for more wide-ranging analysis. We felt it important, however, not to delay the presentation of any results until data gathering was complete.

Department of Pediatrics
Albert Einstein College of Medicine
 of Yeshiva University
1300 Morris Park Ave.
Bronx, NY 10461

Reference Notes

1. Kennedy, R. J. *A Connecticut community revisited: A study of the social adjustment of a group of mentally deficient adults in 1948 and 1960.* Hartford: Connecticut State Department of Health, Office of Mental Retardation, 1966.
2. Saenger, G. *The adjustment of severely retarded adults in the community* (Report). Albany: NY State Interdepartmental Health Resources Board, 1957.

References

Birch, H. G., Richardson, S. A., Baird, D., Horobin, G., & Illsley, R. *Mental subnormality in the community: A clinical and epidemiologic study.* Baltimore:

5. VOCATIONAL

Williams & Wilkins, 1970.

Cobb, H. V. *The forecast of fulfillment: A review of research on predictive assessment of the adult retarded for social and vocational adjustment.* New York: Teachers College Press, 1972.

Ferguson, T., & Kerr, A. W. After-histories of girls educated in special schools for mentally handicapped children. *Glasgow Medical Journal,* 1955, 36, 50–56.

Ferguson, T., & Kerr, A. W. After-histories of boys educated in special schools for mentally handicapped children. *Scottish Medical Journal,* 1958, 3, 31–38.

Goldstein, H. Social and occupational adjustment. In H. A. Stevens & R. Heber (Eds.), *Mental retardation: A review of research.* Chicago: University of Chicago Press, 1964.

Gruenberg, E. M. Epidemiology. In H. A. Stevens & R. Heber (Eds.), *Mental retardation: A review of research.* Chicago: University of Chicago Press, 1964.

Innes, G. A multi-disciplinary study of mental subnormality in North-East Scotland. In D. A. A. Primrose (Ed.), *Proceedings of the Third Congress of the International Association for the Scientific Study of Mental Deficiency.* Warsaw: Polish Medical Publishers, 1975.

Kushlick, A., & Blunden, R. The epidemiology of mental subnormality. In A. M. Clarke & A. D. B. Clarke (Eds.), *Mental deficiency: The changing outlook* (3rd ed.). London: Methuen, 1974.

Lewis, E. O. Report on an investigation of mental deficiency in six areas. In *Report of the mental deficiency committee, 1925–1927.* London: Her Majesty's Stationery Office, 1929.

O'Connor, N., & Tizard, J. *The social problem of mental deficiency.* London: Pergamon Press, 1956.

Penrose, L. S. *The biology of mental defect* (3rd ed.). London: Sidgwick & Jackson, 1963.

Richardson, S. A. Growing up as a mentally subnormal young person. In P. Mittler (Ed.), *Proceedings of the Fourth International Congress of the International Association for the Scientific Study of Mental Deficiency.* In Press.

Susser, M. *Community psychiatry: Epidemiologic and social themes.* New York: Random House, 1968.

Tizard, J. Longitudinal studies: Problems and findings. In A. M. Clarke & A. D. B. Clarke (Eds.), *Mental deficiency: The changing outlook* (3rd ed.). London: Methuen, 1974.

Tizard, J. Longitudinal and follow-up studies. In A. M. Clarke & A. D. B. Clarke (Eds.), *Mental deficiency: The changing outlook* (2nd ed.). London: Methuen, 1965.

Toward A Social Skills Curriculum For Developmentally Disabled Clients In Vocational Settings

PAUL H. WEHMAN

A MAJOR FACTOR in habilitating mentally retarded adults into community living is effective vocational training. For successful community transition and toward a goal of normalization, mentally retarded persons must develop some marketable occupational skill and be able to

---

Mr. Wehman is currently a doctoral student and research assistant in the Department of Studies in Behavioral Disabilities, University of Wisconsin-Madison. He is studying under Dr. William I. Gardner. From 1972 to 1974 he was a psychologist at Lincoln State School, Lincoln, Ill. Prior to this he obtained an M.S. in psychology at Illinois State University. Mr. Wehman is a member of the Council for Exceptional Children and the American Association on Mental Deficiency. Requests for reprints of this article should be sent to: Paul Wehman, Department of Studies in Behavioral Disabilities, Waisman Center, University of Wisconsin, Madison, Wis. 53706.

---

perform this skill adequately. Mentally handicapped clients must also display appropriate social behavior in the presence of coworkers who may not be handicapped. Examples of appropriate social behavior required in a job setting include shaking hands when introduced to someone, greeting a peer by saying "hello," having a neat personal appearance, knowing how to work a vending machine, and developing a knowledge of whom to trust, and whom not to trust.

Hence two integrants can be identified in the process of effective vocational training: *1)* developing a marketable skill (acquisition) and performing it consistently on the job (production) and *2)* displaying the appropriate adaptive behavior or social skills necessary for acceptance of the client by coworkers.

Research evidence indicates that the majority of mentally retarded clients are capable of developing marketable job skills.[9] Gold[10, 11] has demonstrated the acquisition, transfer, and retention of complex motor tasks, such as assemblying a bicycle brake, in moderately to severely retarded persons. Increasing production levels and maintenance has also been consistently demonstrated through utilization of reinforcement contingencies.[24, 30] Yet it continues to be difficult to help developmentally disabled clients become integrated into a wide number of job settings that require more complex skills. Gold[9] notes:

Whatever the reasons for the present status of the retarded, a wide discrepancy exists between what the retarded do, vocationally, and what they are potentially capable of doing both qualitatively and quantitatively. *(p. 41)*

A major reason for this wide discrepancy may be a critical deficit that many mentally handicapped clients have in their social skill repertory. There are a number of skills that make up appropriate social behavior on the job and that pave the way for successful vocational adjustment. Acquisition and maintenance of social skills are necessary to keep a job. Time has shown, unfortunately, that those persons in society who behave "differently" may be stigmatized, excluded, and even feared. The developmentally disabled client who is a steady worker but who displays improper oral hygiene habits, fails to return friendly greetings, or cannot perform simple survival skills, i.e., using the telephone, may very well be excluded by coworkers, and eventually lose his job.

Rehabilitation counselors, workshop supervisors, and educators face an increasing responsibility for training clients in social skills as well as establishing consistent task performance. The current report represents an effort to identify and delineate systematically social skills required for successful vocational adjustment, to arrange these skills into a hierarchical curriculum for training and evaluation, and to suggest viable methods of implementing the curriculum. Relevant and supportive empirical research is collated and synthesized as the underlying basis of the social skills curriculum. The curriculum is not intended to be wholly comprehensive. It should be viewed as representative of the adaptive behavior necessary for occupational success of mentally handicapped clients.

Previous Curriculums with Mentally Retarded Persons

An educational curriculum should fulfill three basic functions: *1)* provide behavioral objectives as training goals; *2)* provide an approximate sequence or direction

5. VOCATIONAL

in which skills should be trained; and *3)* provide a basis for periodic evaluation and accountability.

There have been several efforts to establish curriculums of different skills for mentally retarded persons. Resnick,

About the Article ...

A CURRICULUM of social skills necessary for successful vocational adjustment is proposed for developmentally disabled clients. The curriculum is presented in a concise format of four hierarchically sequenced levels of increasing complexity. The four levels are: Personal Care Level, Primary Interaction Level, Job and Community Survival Level, and Advanced Interaction Level. Relevant supportive research is reviewed as the underlying basis of a valid social skills curriculum. A functional analysis approach is suggested as a strategy for rehabilitation professionals to utilize in implementing the curriculum in vocational training centers.

Wang, and Kaplan[20] developed a flow-charting pattern of introductory mathematical operations. Winkelstein, Shapiro, and Shapiro[29] established a curriculum for training art skills in mentally retarded children. Language skills have been arranged in a developmental sequence for severely retarded children.[12] Brierton[2] has provided a comprehensive survey of self-help skills sequenced on an easy-to-hard basis. Hamre and Williams[13] have developed a home-living skills curriculum that is unique in that it provides specific teaching procedures. The majority of the curriculums that have been advanced have a supportive empirical research base. Well-developed curriculums should draw empirical research studies or programs in related areas into a cohesive and interrelated network for instructional direction. Research studies alone are of only limited value; for optimal utility they should be integrated into a valid training model or curriculum.

A Social Skills Curriculum for Vocational Adjustment

The primary target population that the proposed social skills curriculum serves are mildly through severely retarded clients. It is these persons to whom the greatest opportunities for vocational employment will be presented in the next decade.

The basic organizational structure of the social skills curriculum is delineated in four levels (*see* Figure 1). Level I is the Personal Care Level, which is made up of selected self-help skills. Level II is the Primary Interaction

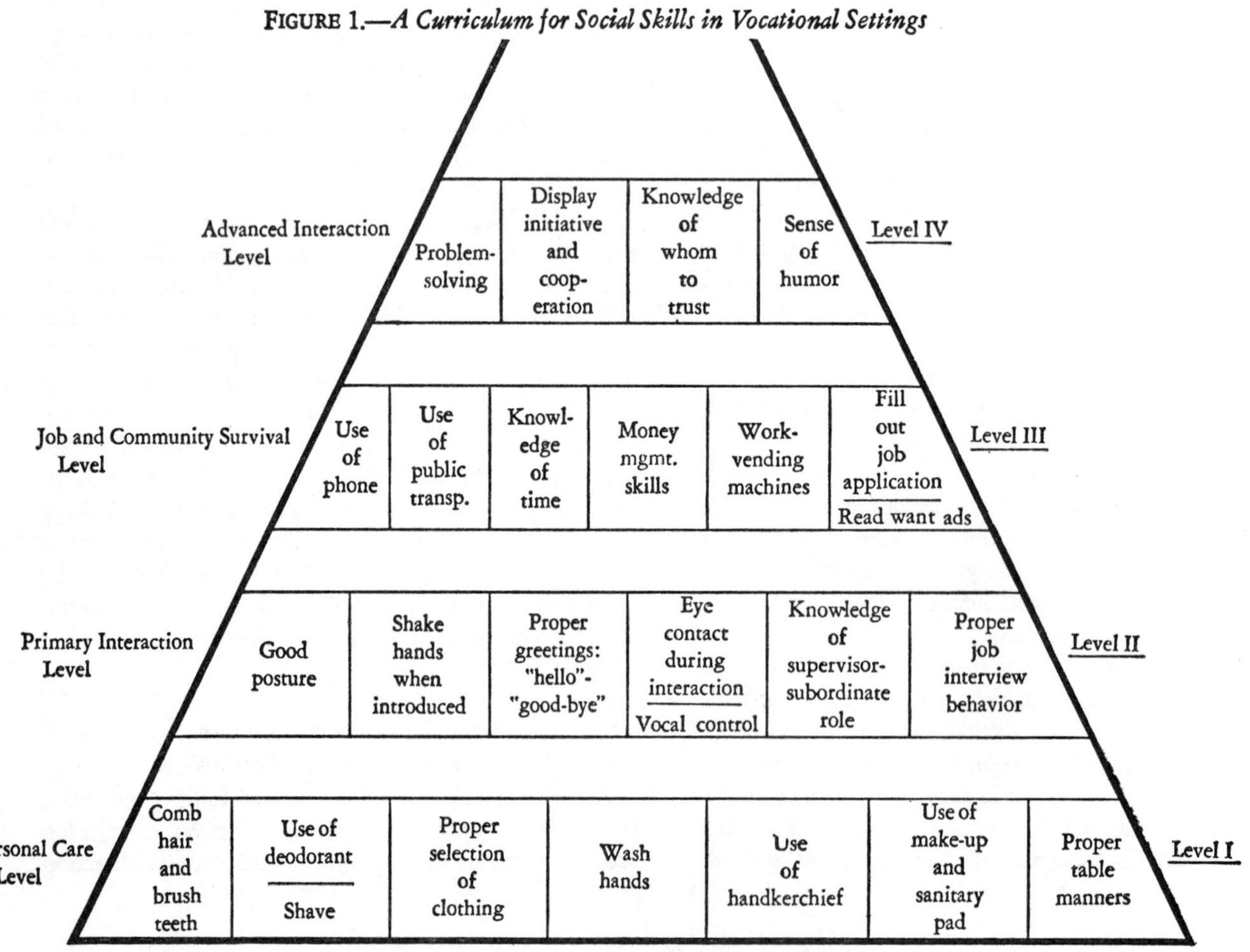

FIGURE 1.—*A Curriculum for Social Skills in Vocational Settings*

Level, a level encompassing certain remedial communication skills. Level III is made up of critical survival skills necessary to exist on the job. Level IV, the Advanced Interaction Level, deals with the more subtle and sophisticated forms of human interaction, i.e., trust, cooperation. Several remarks should be directed toward interpreting the rationale behind the curriculum:

1. Skills are viewed as prerequisites to total vocational habilitation.

2. Skills are described behaviorally rather than as constructs, i.e., self-esteem, whenever possible.

3. An easy-to-hard learning sequence is established; that is, it is presumed that learning takes place more readily at the lower stages of the model.

4. Where appropriate, skills in the curriculum are broken into subcomponents and discussed.

5. The emphasis is not on the level of retardation of the client; rather, the emphasis is on the level of skill complexity that should be initially fitted to the client for training needs.

Personal Care—Level I

Personal care skills form the foundation of the social skills curriculum. The emphasis is on the finer self-help skills that directly affect how people will look at the client. Toileting, simple dressing, and eating behaviors are presumed to be already in a person's repertoire. Proper table manners, one of the suggested personal care skills, can be subdivided into: eating with mouth closed; not spilling food; not talking with mouth full; proper use of utensils and napkin; and correct amount or portion put on utensils.

Azrin and Armstrong[1] have demonstrated that profoundly retarded adults can learn neat eating habits within several days when utilizing the "mini-meal" method of training. The "mini-meal" training method allows the person more chances to learn and practice correct eating habits. This is done through the presentation of several meals during the day instead of only three meals. The amount of food is the same as for three meals except it is given in smaller portions over several meals during the day. The importance of neat eating habits cannot be minimized. During coffee breaks and lunch periods, the client will be eating with coworkers daily. Poor eating habits can cast a negative reflection on the client.

Dedrick[5] has presented a program for teaching severely retarded adolescent females how to care for themselves during menstrual periods. She used a method of simulation during the training period. In training oral hygiene skills, Nietupski[16] has demonstrated a program to teach trainable-level adolescents how to use mouthwash. Successful acquisition and maintenance of grooming skills

have also been demonstrated by Treffry, Martin, Samels, and Watson[26] and by Wehman.[28] Cleanliness, through proper oral hygiene, is a vital social prerequisite to the vocational success that many retarded people are capable of but frequently fail to attain consistently. Prevocational training instructors must train clients in the need for daily hygiene maintenance.

Proper selection of clothing is another personal care skill that may have to be trained. The ability to dress oneself capably does not itself meet the stringent requirements of social acceptability. Some understanding of what clothing is appropriate for the job is required. Proper selection of clothing can be subdivided into several related clothing areas, and assessed in the following way: shoes on correct feet; fine motor dressing skills completed, i.e., zipping; shirt tucked in pants; clothes appropriate for work setting, i.e., factory; jacket hung up properly every day; and clothes pressed and not wrinkled. The care and selection of clothing is important in job success, particularly in the initial stages when the client must develop credibility.

It should be evident that the Personal Care Level aims directly at external appearance and the way a person looks. It may appear that the client is being asked to conform too much, that he is losing his identity. This need not be the case. However, it must be recognized that society has set standards of social acceptance and success. For the developmentally disabled client to succeed, he must conform to a certain level to establish credibility. Staff personnel in sheltered workshops, halfway houses, and institutional workshops must take an active role in teaching and maintaining these skills. It would seem that most clients would be able to perform personal care skills with some degree of competency. The focus must come on maintenance and generalization of skills in different work settings. Some ways in which generalization can occur is through letting the client practice new behaviors in other work settings, having the client work under different supervisors, and teaching the client self-control procedures.[25]

Primary Interaction—Level II

The Primary Interaction Level also encompasses a range of behaviors that; if absent, immediately cues coworkers that there is something "wrong" with the client. Eye contact during interaction and knowing when to interject into a conversation, i.e., at coffee break, are extremely important subtleties largely taken for granted. It is usually natural to look at the person with whom one is talking. Unfortunately, many retarded clients do not display this behavior and may mumble or not speak clearly due to articulation difficulties. Some clients may speak too loudly and not have an acceptable voice intensity. These are social skills that have been trained in other retarded persons; behavior modification has been a successful teaching method. Voice intensity has been modified and generalized to other settings through the use of token reinforcement.[14] Attending behavior has been trained frequently in retarded persons and emotionally disturbed children.[27] The general procedure followed is reinforcement of each period of eye contact with the experimenter. In the situation mentioned above, the workshop supervisor would reinforce the client contingent on eye contact during interaction. Initially, verbal prompting might be required but could be faded as interactions became the discriminative stimuli for looking at the person being talked to.

Proper greetings of "hello" and "good-bye" are also social skills necessary for vocational development in clients. Waving one's hand is an accepted practice of nonverbal greeting. In a recent study, Stokes, Baer, and Jackson[23] trained severely retarded children to use hand-waving as a greeting response. Generalization of hand-waving was programed across three different environments and four different experimenters. Sitting up straight and walking with one's head up is another subtle social skill that reflects on a person. Clients should be encouraged to develop good posture at all times. O'Brien and Azrin[17] demonstrated that posture can be taught and maintained in institution ward employees. It would appear that the same method of positive reinforcement procedures could be successfully used with mentally handicapped clients.

Another social skill that, in effect, may subsume much of the Primary Interaction Level, is proper job interview behavior. Many employers have varied stereotypes in mind about what to expect when meeting a mentally retarded client initially. The client must be thoroughly trained by rehabilitation and education personnel in the mechanics necessary to a job interview. This means shaking hands, giving some form of greeting, maintaining eye contact, and being responsive to communication directed at the client. The client should also have some familiarity with the supervisor-subordinate relationship and understand who gives orders. He must understand that only certain workers can tell him what to do and that he must sometimes accept constructive criticism.

The skills present at the Primary Interaction Level are not complex and are within the capabilities of most retarded people. Essentially they are those requiring somewhat more subtle discriminative cues. For example, the client who is trained in a rote fashion to shake hands may do so only with those he is familiar with, or, alternatively, will offer his hand to people without an introduction. Similarly, a person who is taught to increase eye contact with peers may stare too much. Therefore, it is important that the basic behavioral training principles of fading, reinforcement schedule attenuation, and generalization are used carefully. Training methods and curriculum implementation will be discussed at greater length in a later section of the paper.

Job and Community Survival—Level III

It is felt that the community and the job are interrelated and cannot be separated. Relevant social skills, however, are emphasized and interpreted in regard to how they relate to vocational adjustment. Many prerequisite behaviors and programs under each social skill must be developed before full acquisition of the Job and Community Survival Level is attained.

Use of the telephone is definitely a survival skill for the retarded adult. He must be able to communicate to his supervisor if he is ill or cannot come to work. He must be able to ask for help if he must leave work and has no transportation. Being able to use a telephone effectively has been taught with use of colors and numbers to trainable level students.[15] Teaching use of the telephone is made up of at least three different subcomponents: read numbers 0 to 9; dial numbers correctly; and make change correctly if at pay phone. Each of these subcomponents may have to be further divided into smaller learning steps depending on the behavioral level of the client.

The developmentally disabled client may have to take public transportation, such as bus, train, or taxicab, to get to work. Certo and Schwartz[4] have taught trainable-level adolescents to ride a bus in a medium-size midwestern city. Prerequisite skills included making change, knowing at which stop to get off, learning simple sight words, and telling time. Students were taught initially through a videotaped simulation of various community bus routes. Gradually, students began taking real bus trips in the community without supervision.

Knowledge of time is an important survival skill for vocational success. The client must be able to tell time for promptness. If his work shift changes, he must know the days of the week he is to work. Knowledge of time represents a number of skills depending on the dimension being taught. Learning calendar time involves: reading the 7 days of the week; reading the 12 months of the year; and learning the sequence or cycle in which time occurs. Learning clock time involves: reading numbers 1 to 12 and discriminating the hour hand from the minute hand. Pierce[19] has demonstrated teaching time-telling to trainable retarded students through use of a task analysis teaching method.

Money management is another class of social skills necessary for success on the job. Money management includes behaviors such as counting and making change, cashing and depositing a paycheck into a bank account, working vending machines for food and drinks, and using the pay telephone. Money management skills require a series of prerequisite behaviors that at the minimum include sight word reading and simple arithmetic operations.

The Job and Community Survival Level encompasses a range of skills that require increasingly complex behaviors. Discriminative cues or signals for responding are even more subtle, and reinforcement is delayed. It is not expected that workshop professionals would spend long portions of the work period establishing social skills. Rather, it might be appropriate to pick one section of the Job and Community Survival Level and, in cooperation with the sponsoring social agency of the client, begin to gradually develop that skill in the client.

Advanced Interaction—Level IV

The Advanced Interaction Level includes cognitive-oriented skills, like problem-solving, planning, trust, initiative, cooperation, and humor. These skills, also termed competence skills by Edmondson,[6, 7] are high-level thought behaviors that are ultimately the link to "normalcy" or achieving personal independence. The influence of this skill group on vocational success and vocational opportunities should be obvious, particularly in the area of problem-solving. The ability to think and to solve problems largely distinguishes intellect at all levels of normalcy and of retardation. Taking the initiative is frequently a function of how rapidly one is able to foresee where help is needed, and then having the confidence to intervene.

Unfortunately, many retarded clients seriously lack problem-solving and planning skills that are needed for greater vocational responsibility and self-direction, as well as social skill competence. According to Ross and Ross,[21] who have worked with educable mentally retarded children:

... retarded children lack skill in everyday problem solving and planning and tend toward passive avoidance when confronted with situational problems and tasks that require ordering of responses. . . . Frequently, they are rewarded for their passivity in problem solving and planning situations, with increased adult attention, but unfortunately the attention generally takes the form of overprotection rather than an attempt to transmit the requisite skills. Yet the ability to solve problems and to plan effectively could contribute to the psychological well being of the mentally retarded child by increasing his feeling of independence, level of activity, and expectancy concerning his ability to successfully control his own environment. *(p. 20)*

Ross and Ross[21] conducted two experiments that trained problem-solving and planning skills in EMR children through simulated real-life situations practiced by the children. The aim of the training program is to have the clients listen and understand a statement of the problem, acquire the habit of identifying the elements in a problem that would be of use in solving it, and perceive that many problems have multiple solutions. (A preschool and primary curriculum for training cognitive skills is available from the same authors, Ross and Ross.[22]) The Ross and Ross report is valuable in that it identifies the necessary components of training in problem-solving and planning skills and then demonstrates an effective training program for behavioral change.

Knowing whom to trust and whom not to trust is a social skill many retarded people are deficient in. The writer was unable to locate any published reports of training an understanding of trust in mentally handicapped clients. Perske and Marquiss[18] acknowledge trust as being a difficult concept for retarded adults who are being habilitated into the community to understand:

Live-in friends have provided specific training discussions on the proper use of the telephone, thermostat, medicine cabinet, garbage disposal, light switch, and so on. They must also teach their roommates how to deal with salesmen, taxicab drivers, and other community members. Learning whom to trust in the community is not an easy concept to grasp. *(p. 18)*

Demonstrating a sense of humor is a social behavior requiring more than random laughing. Ellis[8] discusses humor as defined by Berlyne:

A cognitive process whereby a sequence of stimuli or ideas are strung together in such a way to generate an expectation which is shattered or a conflict which is suddenly resolved surprisingly. *(p. 100)*

The retarded person must know when to laugh and what is accepted as funny or not funny. Mentally handicapped people unquestionably have a sense of humor. The problem is that it may be socially misplaced or not occur at the appropriate times.

The Advanced Interaction Level is a Level where little supportive data-based research is available. Cognitive skills are more difficult to train and to generalize than are concrete behaviors found at the Personal Care Level. The developmentally disabled client must eventually attain these skills for complete vocational success and independence.

Methods of Implementing and Utilizing the Social Skills Curriculum

In implementing the social skills curriculum in vocational centers, workshops, and institution training centers, it would be helpful for rehabilitation counselors and workshop supervisors to take an active role in teaching social skills as well as work skills. A client who is functioning at a superior production level on the job, but who cannot "get along" with other workers, doesn't want to be "bothered," and so on, should be targeted for social skill training. Vocational training centers should hire additional personnel or convert positions to add social skill specialists who may monitor and train clients in social behaviors. It is granted that the purpose of a workshop is to attain production goals and to develop occupational expertise in clients. However, of what value is a skill if the client cannot function socially with coworkers who may not be handicapped? Brown, Bellamy, and Sontag,[3] in a general discussion of development of appropriate social behavior

FIGURE 2.—*A Functional Analysis Approach to Implementing the Social Skills Curriculum*

Step 1

> Assess all clients on curriculum.
> Find appropriate level for each client on curriculum.
> Record initial level of client.

↓

Step 2

> Establish objective on curriculum for each client. Include clients in objective-setting.

↓

Step 3

> Choose appropriate training methods or combination of methods. Selection may come from: behavior modification, role-play, counseling, etc.

↓

Step 4

> Spend small portion of each workday in training target skill. Training area should be removed from work area.

↓

Step 5

> Continue monitoring and recording data. Make necessary modifications if data indicate.

in work settings, state:

There are those who state that social behaviors are incompatible with appropriate vocational behaviors. That is, if a person is working efficiently, and if the incentives for work are sufficiently powerful, he does not have time to aggress or otherwise act in a socially inappropriate way.(*p. 336*)

This viewpoint is perhaps naive, as it presumes the client rarely would have an opportunity to interact with other workers. Also it does not take into account that coworkers will be observing the client and evaluating him according to the social behavior he displays.

There are a number of possible administrative and clinical strategies for adapting the curriculum in a vocational setting. However, one suggested rehabilitation strategy that might be utilized is the behavioral approach. Figure 2 depicts the following five steps:

1. Initially assess all clients in workshop on social skills curriculum. Use data and/or videotape for recording purposes for pretreatment evaluation; find level where individual cannot function consistently.
2. Establish objective for each client. Choose one skill at the designated level of the curriculum, in conjunction with the client, for training.
3. Select appropriate training method. This may depend on the level of social skills at which the client is functioning. At the lower levels, a behavior modification approach would be used. Levels III and IV might require other teaching methods, most likely in combination. Such methods might be viewing a videotape, role-playing, behavioral counseling, practice in decision-making, and self-control procedures. Research evidence from Ross and Ross[21] indicates, however, that EMR individuals:

   . . . perform better under training procedures that combine active participation with opportunities to observe peer models performing in similar task sequences than under intentional training conditions alone. (*p. 22*)

4. Every workday spend a small portion of time in the general vocational setting, but removed from the work area, for training in the target social skill.
5. Continue monitoring and recording data during training sessions. Make modifications in program according to data results.

This is one strategy, based on a functional analysis of behavior, that could be most successful in a rehabilitation setting. Extent and intensity of social skill programing in vocational training centers would be contingent on budget limitations and professional staff training.

Conclusion

Developmentally disabled clients have a strong need for social skill development in vocational settings. Social behavior is not the only factor that effects successful vocational experiences, but it is largely instrumental in helping clients adjust to work expectations of employers. Rehabilitation professionals must play an increasingly active role in providing social skill training services. More research and programs need to be directed at skills delineated in the curriculum, particularly in Levels III and IV. The curriculum presented in this paper represents an effort to develop a training package for teaching social behavior. It is expected that this tool can and should be modified for different settings. Only data-based programs can eventually verify the reliability and validity of the proposed curriculum.

List of References

1. Azrin, N. H., and Armstrong, P. M. The "Mini-Meal"— A Method for Teaching Eating Skills to the Profoundly Retarded. *Mental Retardation.* Jan., 1973. 11:1:9-13.
2. Brierton, G. Self-Help Continuum. Lincoln State School, Lincoln, Ill., 1973, *unpublished.*

3. Brown, L.; Bellamy, T.; and Sontag, E. *The Development and Implementation of a Public School Prevocational Training Program for Trainable Retarded and Severely Emotionally Disturbed Children.* Madison, Wis.: Madison Public Schools, 1971.

4. Certo, N., and Schwartz, R. Teaching Trainable Retarded Students to Ride a Community Bus. Dept. of Studies in Behavioral Disabilities, Univ. of Wisconsin, Madison, 1973, *unpublished.*

5. Dedrick, P. Premenstrual Training. In: Brown, L.; Williams, W.; and Crowner, T., *eds. A Collection of Papers and Programs Related to Public School Services for Severely Handicapped Students.* Madison, Wis.: Madison Public Schools, 1974.

6. Edmondson, B. Arguing for a Concept of Competence. *Mental Retardation.* Dec., 1974. 12:6:14-15.

7. Edmondson, B., and others. *The Test of Social Inference.* Freeport, N.Y.: Educational Activities, 1974.

8. Ellis, M. J. *Why People Play.* Englewood Cliffs, N.J.: Prentice-Hall, 1973.

9. Gold, Marc W. Factors Affecting Production by the Retarded: Base Rate. *Mental Retardation.* Dec., 1973. 11:6:41-45.

10. Gold, Marc W. Stimulus Factors in Skill Training of Retarded Adolescents on a Complex Assembly Task: Acquisition, Transfer, and Retention. *Am. J. Mental Deficiency.* Mar., 1972. 76:5:517-526.

11. Gold, Marc W. Research on the Vocational Habilitation of the Retarded: The Present, the Future. In: Ellis, Norman R., *ed. International Review of Research in Mental Retardation. Vol. 6.* New York: Academic Pr., 1973.

12. Hallet, Patricia; Sype, M. Susan; and Gates, Jane K. A Language-Based Curriculum for the Mentally Retarded. *Mental Retardation.* Dec., 1971. 9:6:9-12.

13. Hamre, S., and Williams, W. Family-Life Curriculum. In: Brown, L.; Williams, W.; and Crowner, T., *eds. A Collection of Papers and Programs Related to Public School Services for Severely Handicapped Students.* Madison, Wis.: Madison Public Schools, 1974.

14. Jackson, Donald A., and Wallace, R. Frank. The Modification and Generalization of Voice Loudness in a Fifteen-Year-Old Girl. *J. Applied Behavior Analysis.* Fall, 1974. 7:3:461-472.

15. Leff, Ruth B. Training the TMR to Dial the Telephone. *Mental Retardation.* Apr., 1974. 12:2:12-13.

16. Nietupski, R. Use of Mouthwash. In: Brown, L.; Williams, W.; and Crowner, T., *eds. A Collection of Papers and Programs Related to Public School Services for Severely Handicapped Students.* Madison, Wis.: Madison Public Schools, 1974.

17. O'Brien, F., and Azrin, N. H. Behavioral Engineering: Control of Posture by Informational Feedback. *J. Applied Behavior Analysis.* Winter, 1970. 3:4:235-240.

18. Perske, Robert, and Marquiss, Jim. Learning to Live in an Apartment: Retarded Adults from Institutions and Dedicated Citizens. *Mental Retardation.* Oct., 1973. 11:5:18-19.

19. Pierce, L. Teaching Time-Telling. In: Brown, L., and Sontag, E., *eds. Toward the Development and Implementation of an Empirically Based Public School Program for Trainable Mentally Retarded and Severely Emotionally Disturbed Students.* Madison, Wis.: Madison Public Schools, 1972.

20. Resnick, Lauren; Wang, Margaret C.; and Kaplan, Jerome. Task Analysis in Curriculum Design: A Hierarchically Sequenced Introductory Mathematics Curriculum. *J. Applied Behavior Analysis.* Winter, 1973. 6:4:679-709.

21. Ross, Dorothea M.; and Ross, Sheila A. Cognitive Training for the EMR Child: Situational Problem Solving and Planning. *Am. J. Mental Deficiency.* July, 1973. 78:1:20-25.

22. Ross, Dorothea, and Ross, Sheila A. *The Pacemaker Primary Curriculum.* Belmont, Calif.: Fearon, 1974.

23. Stokes, Trevor F.; Baer, Donald M.; and Jackson, Robert L. Programming the Generalization of a Greeting Response in Four Retarded Children. *J. Applied Behavior Analysis.* Winter, 1974. 7:4:599-610.

24. Tate, Bobby G., and Baroff, George S. Training the Mentally Retarded in the Production of a Complex Product: A Demonstration of Work Potential. *Exceptional Children.* Feb., 1967. 33:6:405-408.

25. Thoresen, Carl E., and Mahoney, Michael J. *Behavioral Self-Control.* New York: Holt, Rinehart, & Winston, 1974.

26. Treffry, Doug, and others. Operant Conditioning of Grooming Behavior of Severely Retarded Girls. *Mental Retardation.* Aug., 1970. 8:4:29-33.

27. Walker, Hill M., and Buckley, Nancy K. The Use of Positive Reinforcement in Conditioning Attending Behavior. *J. Applied Behavior Analysis.* Fall, 1968. 1:3:245-250.

28. Wehman, Paul. Maintaining Oral Hygiene Skills in Geriatric Retarded Women. *Mental Retardation.* Aug., 1974. 12:4:20.

29. Winkelstein, Ellen; Shapiro, Bernard J.; and Shapiro, Phyllis P. Art Curricula and MR Preschoolers. *Mental Retardation.* June, 1973. 11:3:6-9.

30. Zimmerman, Joseph, and others. Operant Conditioning in a Sheltered Workshop. *Rehab. Lit.* Nov., 1969. 30:11:326-334.

TIME AND MONEY FOR VOCATIONAL REHABILITATION OF CLIENTS WITH MILD, MODERATE AND SEVERE MENTAL RETARDATION

RICHARD T. WALLS, M. S. TSENG, AND HAROLD N. ZARIN
West Virginia University

Mildly, moderately, and severely mentally retarded vocational rehabilitation clients comprised a random national sample of 600 clients. One-half of the sample had been closed (services completed) "rehabilitated," and half had been closed "nonrehabilitated." Variables selected for analyses were time in referral, training, and rehabilitation process; dollars in evaluation, facilities, all services, and earnings. Rehabilitated clients tended to require more time in referral, less moneys for extended evaluation and rehabilitation facilities, and earned more per week than the nonrehabilitated clients. Severely mentally retarded clients required more time in training and higher costs for extended evaluation, rehabilitation facilities, and all services than the moderately or mildly retarded groups. A consistent interaction across five variables indicated that the greatest amounts of service in time and money went to the nonrehabilitated severely retarded group.

In the 1973 Rehabilitation Act (Public Law 93-112, 93rd Congress, H.R. 8070, September 26, 1973), services were specifically mandated to severely handicapped individuals, ". . . provid[ing] such [vocational rehabilitation] services for the benefit of such [handicapped] individuals, serving first those with the most severe handicaps, so that they may prepare for and engage in gainful employment" (p. 2). Further, Section 401, Title IV, concerning program evaluation includes reference to the severely handicapped client, requiring ". . . [a] reassess[ment of] priorities to which such activities [research, demonstration, etc.] should be directed; and review [of] present research, demonstration, and related activities to determine . . . whether and on what basis such activities should be continued, revised, or terminated" (p. 31).

One of the primary target groups for vocational rehabilitation thus becomes the clients whose disability is classed "mental retardation, severe." Although the vocational rehabilitation system has always dealt with such clients, their number has been disproportionately low. Many more clients assessed as "moderately" or "mildly" retarded have traditionally been accepted for and provided with vocational rehabilitation services.

Cobb (1972) noted similarly that the overwhelming majority of studies of community adaptation have involved individuals classified as mildly retarded. Recent emphasis toward decentralization of residential services has prompted increased interest in the rehabilitation potential associated with moderate and severe mental disability. Deinstitutionalization has become a watchword, and predictive characteristics in union with innovative effective intervention curricula are widely sought.

From a noninstitutional setting, Saenger (Note 1) reported a high frequency of moderately retarded adults who were former special-education students in New York City achieving stable social and occupational adaptation on a semi-independent basis. Katz (1968) emphasized the importance of social, educational, and occupational community services. While several investigators have reported that mildly retarded pupils can function in adult society with little or no postschool intervention (e.g., Cobb, 1972; Deno, Note 2), those with moderately and severely retarded intellec-

This investigation was supported in part by the Rehabilitation Services Administration (U.S. Department of Health, Education, and Welfare) through the West Virginia Regional Rehabilitation Research and Training Center (West Virginia University and West Virginia Division of Vocational Rehabilitation).

tual capacity often require much more in the way of rehabilitative aid.

Researchers continue to extend and document the inadequacy of simple demographic or unidimensional predictors of vocational "success." Students' IQ and cognitive behavior are integrally related to maturational and cultural factors and provide poor prognostication of adult adaptation (Baller, Charles, & Miller, 1966; Charles, 1966). Such factors have proven to be substantially malleable via skillful programs of rehabilitation or changes in environmental constraints. Brolin (1972) found retarded clients, judged to have received "adequate services" in accordance with the diagnostic evaluation, were more likely to attain a favorable vocational outcome than those receiving "inadequate services."

Elo and Hendel (1972) compared mildly retarded, moderately–severely retarded, and nonretarded clients on a number of outcome dimensions. These vocational rehabilitation clients were from a single state. The moderate and severe disability classifications were combined with no report of the respective numbers of clients composing that group. As might be expected, when the retarded clients (mild and moderate–severe) were compared with nonretarded clients, the retarded clients had greater cost of rehabilitation, lower earnings at closure, more time in referral and applicant statuses, and were more likely to be placed in a sheltered workshop or service occupation. When the mildly retarded group and moderately–severely retarded group were compared, few salient differences were identified. The only major finding Elo and Hendel reported was, "Moderately–severely retarded clients earned less than the mildly retarded clients in professional and clerical, farming, and blue collar occupations but earned slightly more in service occupations".

The present investigation was directed toward possible differentiation by monetary and duration variables of clients classified as mildly, moderately, and severely retarded within the framework of the intake, process, and outcomes system of vocational rehabilitation. In the present comparisons of these three groups of retarded clients via a rehabilitated–not rehabilitated criterion, the subjects were from all 50 states representing a national sample of vocational rehabilitation clients with mental retardation.

Method

Subjects

The subjects were 600 vocational rehabilitation clients closed in fiscal year 1971. From the national records of approximately 750,000 clients whose services were completed or terminated in that year, the 600 clients were randomly sampled to meet the following requirements of mental retardation and outcome. One-half of the sample (300 clients) had been closed "rehabilitated" (vocational rehabilitation status 26) and half (300 clients) "nonrehabilitated" (vocational rehabilitation status 28 or 30). The Rehabilitation Services Administration definition in the former case required the client to have completed several steps in the rehabilitation process and to "be suitably employed *for a minimum of 30 days* [our italics]." Nonrehabilitated clients did not successfully achieve this criterion.

These two groups were further subdivided into three groups: (a) mild, (b) moderate, and (c) severe, as defined in the *Rehabilitation Service Administration Service Manual* based on recommendations by the American Association on Mental Deficiency. The primary design was thus a 2 (rehabilitated, nonrehabilitated) × 3 (mild, moderate, severe) format with 100 clients in each cell.

Procedure

Time and money variables were selected to represent evaluative and pragmatic concerns. Finite time and resources constitute major rehabilitation process variables of historic significance in the selection of clients for services. Many false-negatives relative to accepting clients for services have undoubtedly been created within the moderate and to an even greater extent within the severe retardation classification because of such cost/benefit concerns in the system. Specifically, the variables selected for analyses were:

1. Time in the referral status—the number of months (rounded to the nearest month) from the first referral to completion of the referral process
2. Time in training—the number of months (rounded) in occupational training
3. Time in the vocational rehabilitation process—the number of months (rounded) from acceptance to closure
4. Money in extended evaluation—the dollars spent by vocational rehabilitation for extended evaluation of the client
5. Money in facilities—the dollars spent by vocational rehabilitation for services within a center, workshop, or other facility
6. Money for all services—the dollars spent by vocational rehabilitation for all services combined
7. Money earned at closure—the weekly earnings by the client in dollars

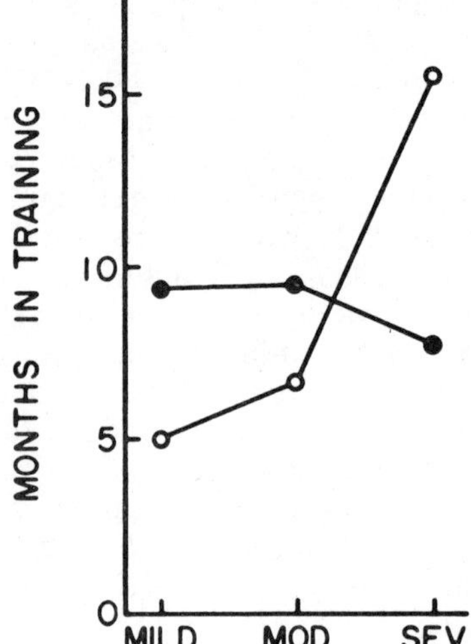

FIGURE 2.   Number of months in training.

Results

Separate 2 (rehabilitated, nonrehabilitated) × 3 (mild, moderate, severe) factorial analyses of variance were computed for each of the variables listed above. Missing data were excluded from the analyses. Results of these analyses are summarized below. Figures 1 through 7 depict these findings:

1. Months in referral did not differ among the three retardation classifications, but the main effect for outcome was significant with rehabilitated clients spending more months in referral than nonrehabilitated clients ($F = 10.8$, $1/587\ df$, $p < .01$). The interaction of these factors was nonsignificant.

2. A significant main effect for retardation and multiple comparisons by the Duncan procedure revealed more months in training for severely than either moderately or mildly retarded clients ($F = 4.9$, $2/536\ df$, $p < .01$). Moderately and mildly retarded clients did not differ. The main effect for

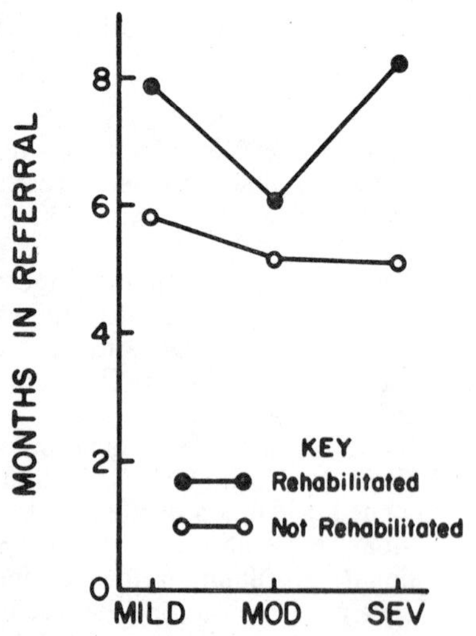

FIGURE 1.   Number of months in referral status.

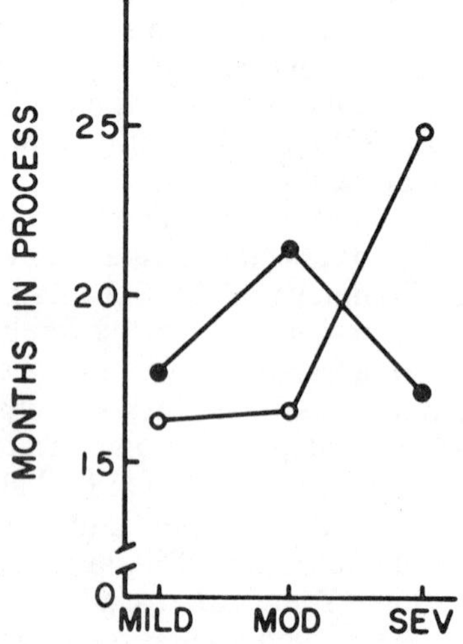

FIGURE 3.   Number of months from acceptance to closure.

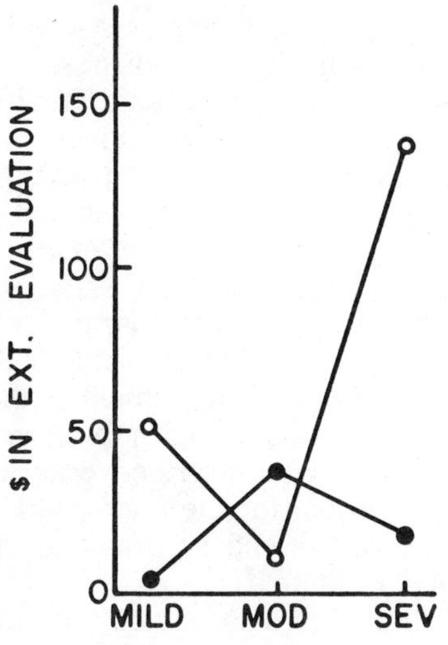

FIGURE 4. Dollars spent for extended evaluation.

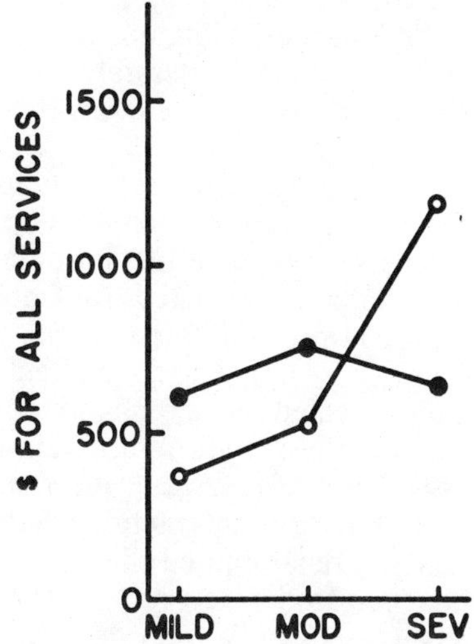

FIGURE 6. Dollars spent for all services.

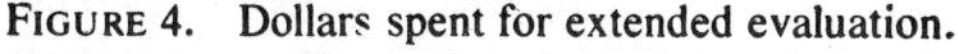

outcome was nonsignificant; however, the interaction yielded a significant effect ($F = 10.4$, 2/536 *df*, $p < .01$). Multiple comparisons to interpret this interaction revealed a marked increment in training time for severely retarded clients who were not rehabilitated as compared to nonrehabilitated moderately retarded or rehabilitated severely retarded clients.

3. The main effects of retardation and outcome did not yield differences in total time from acceptance to closure. However, the same pattern of interaction was disclosed ($F = 5.7$, 2/480 *df*, $p < .01$). That is, severely retarded nonrehabilitated clients spent more time in the process than moderately retarded nonrehabilitated clients or severely retarded rehabilitated clients.

4. Analysis of funds expended for extended evaluation yielded a significant main effect for outcome ($F = 5.3$, 1/519 *df*, $p < .01$), with less expended for rehabilitated than for nonrehabilitated clients. The retardation main effect was significant, with more spent in extended evaluation for severely than for mildly or moderately re-

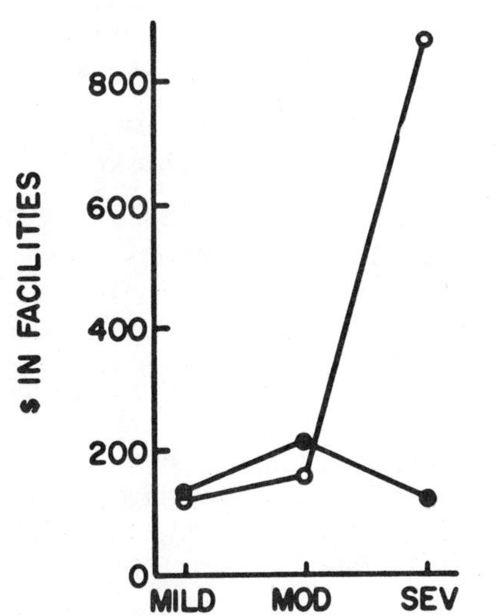

FIGURE 5. Dollars spent for services in facilities.

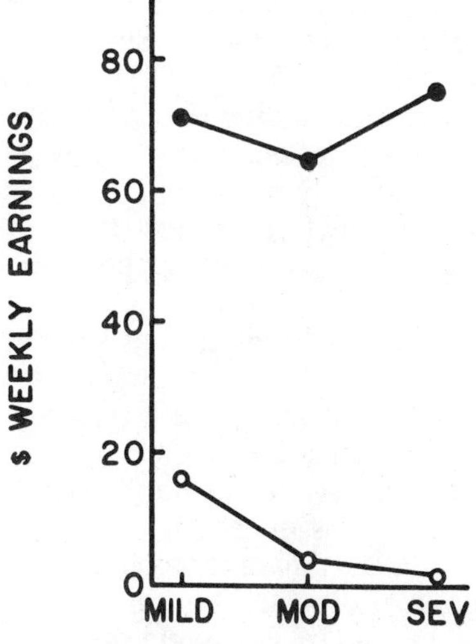

FIGURE 7. Dollars earned per week by client at closure.

tarded clients ($F = 3.3$, 2/519 *df*, $p < .05$). Again, the interaction produced a similar picture ($F = 4.0$, 2/519 *df*, $p < .01$). Severely retarded nonrehabilitated clients required more funds than moderately retarded non-rehabilitated or the severely retarded rehabilitated group.

5. The analysis of variance for money spent by vocational rehabilitation facilities yielded a significant effect for outcome with fewer dollars expended for rehabilitated than for nonrehabilitated clients ($F = 9.4$, 1/539 *df*, $p < .01$). The main effect for retardation revealed more funds for severe than for moderate or mild retardation ($F = 9.4$, 2/539 *df*, $p < .01$). Again, the same pattern emerged in the interaction. Severely retarded nonrehabilitated clients utilized more funds than moderately retarded nonrehabilitated or severely retarded rehabilitated clients. Other salient findings within that interaction were more facility funds for rehabilitated moderately retarded than rehabilitated mildly, rehabilitated severely, or nonrehabilitated moderately retarded clients. Finally, more funds were spent for the nonrehabilitated moderately retarded than nonrehabilitated mildly retarded group.

6. Cost of all services yielded a significant main effect for retardation ($F = 6.3$, 2/590 *df*, $p < .01$). Cost was greater for severely retarded than moderately or mildly retarded clients. Once again, the same relationship emerged, noted in 2, 3, 4, and 5 above for the significant interaction ($F = 6.9$, 2/590 *df*, $p < .01$). Severely retarded clients who were not rehabilitated had greater total service cost than the moderately retarded nonrehabilitated or the severely retarded rehabilitated group.

7. As would be expected, those clients who were rehabilitated earned much more per week than nonrehabilitated clients ($F = 100.4$, 1/512 *df*, $p < .01$). Perhaps a more interesting finding here was that there was no difference among the mildly, moderately, and severely retarded rehabilitated groups with respect to earnings at closure. This relationship is readily apparent in Figure 7.

Could the finding that severely retarded rehabilitated clients earn as much as the mildly and moderately retarded clients be accounted for by some unique pattern of occupations in which they were placed? To answer this question, we further analyzed the data set relative to the three rehabilitated groups, especially in reference to (a) work status and (b) occupation at closure. Results are summarized in Table 1. As can be seen, there were no appreciable differences among the frequency distributions for the three client groups (mildly, moderately, severely retarded) in terms of their work statuses as characterized by competitive, sheltered workshop, self-employed, state-agency-managed business enterprises, homemaker, and unpaid family worker. In addition, there were no distinctive differences in the frequency distribution of occupational fields as represented by the first digit of the DOT (*Dictionary of Occupational Titles*) code (see Table 1). We should point out, however, that the criterion of rehabilitation used here is that of 30 days gainful employment as defined by the vocational rehabilitation agencies for case closure and that this circumscribed criterion could be responsible for the findings. Therefore, inferences should be drawn within this particular context.

It should also be noted that the severely retarded group represented only 8 percent of the mentally retarded persons who were accepted for vocational rehabilitation services. The mildly and moderately retarded group constituted 62 and 30 percent, respectively. Further, of these clients who were accepted for services, this vastly under-represented severely retarded group achieved the rehabilitation criterion slightly less frequently than the other two groups (mildly retarded, 81 percent; moderately retarded, 78 percent; and severely retarded, 74 percent). Thus, the equal cell sizes chosen for analysis in this investigation must not be misinterpreted as representing the actual frequencies in the vocational rehabilitation system.

It should be noted in the above discussion of interactions relative to Variables 2, 3, 4, 5, and 6 that of the 15 possible multiple comparisons, only a selected number of significant mean differences were presented to reflect the more important aspects of the relationship. Figures 2 through 6 are further explications of these interactions.[1]

Discussion

Using a national sample of mentally retarded clients, we investigated three time variables (months in referral, months in training, and months from acceptance to closure) and four money variables (dollars for extended evaluation, facilities, all services, and weekly earnings) in the vocational rehabilitation process. It was assumed that such variables might reflect significant main effects of mental retardation (mild vs. moderate vs. severe) and rehabilitation out-

---

[1] A complete summary is available upon request from the authors.

TABLE 1
NUMBER OF CLIENTS FROM EACH GROUP ACCORDING TO WORK STATUS AND OCCUPATION

| | Group | | |
Variable	Mildly retarded	Moderately retarded	Severely retarded
Work status at closure			
Competitive	76	74	74
Sheltered workshop	3	7	4
Self-employed	4	6	3
BEP[a]	0	0	0
Homemaker	8	5	14
Unpaid family worker	3	1	3
Dot code (first digit)			
0 Professional, technical, and managerial	8	9	7
1 Professional, technical, and managerial	3	6	5
2 Clerical & Sales	13	14	13
3 Service occupations	26	26	23
4 Farming & related	4	4	8
5 Processing occupations	11	8	18
6 Machine trades	15	2	9
7 Bench work occupations	12	8	6
8 Structural work	4	7	7
9 Miscellaneous	4	12	4

[a] State-agency-managed small business enterprises.

come (rehabilitated vs. nonrehabilitated) and the Retardation × Outcome interaction effect.

When clients were classified on the basis of rehabilitation outcomes (as defined by vocational rehabilitation agencies) and compared, rehabilitated clients (those who were closed on the criterion of 30 days gainful employment) tended to require more time in the referral status, less moneys for extended evaluation and rehabilitation facilities, and to earn more per week at closure than nonrehabilitated clients. It is of interest to note that, on the average, about the same amounts of rehabilitation services were rendered to both the rehabilitated and nonrehabilitated groups in terms of months in training, months from acceptance to closure, and dollars for all services.

Multiple comparisons among the combinations or rehabilitation outcomes and disabling conditions revealed that the largest amounts of service time (months in training and months from acceptance to closure) and money (costs for extended evaluation, rehabilitation facilities, and all services) went to the nonrehabilitated severely retarded group. The amounts of service rendered to this group were significantly greater than those given to the rehabilitated severely and nonrehabilitated moderately retarded groups. This, together with the finding that on the whole the rehabilitated severely retarded group did not require more rehabilita-

tion time or cost as compared to the rehabilitated moderately, rehabilitated mildly, nonrehabilitated moderately, or nonrehabilitated mildly retarded groups, would suggest the following. Given the existing intervention, placement practices, and closure criteria in vocational rehabilitation, an appreciably large investment is being made by the rehabilitation agency (in terms of time and money) for assisting the severely retarded clients until they are closed as nonrehabilitated cases. Post hoc examination of demographic characteristics revealed no apparent differences between the severely retarded clients achieving successful rehabilitation and their nonrehabilitated counterparts.

In light of the growing emphasis that is being placed on serving severely handicapped individuals as mandated by the 1973 Rehabilitation Act, the findings of this study concerning time and money for serving severely retarded clients (both rehabilitated and nonrehabilitated) can be used as baseline data. Any refined and/or new intervention strategies, job development and placement schemes, and rehabilitation outcome criteria contemplated and implemented in the future may eventually yield the kind of data which can be systematically related to the baseline. Thus, effectiveness of such services may be assessed in a data-based fashion.

Reference Notes

1. Saenger, G. *The adjustment of severely retarded adults in the community. A report.* A report to the New York State Interdepartmental Health Resources Board, Albany, 1957.

2. Deno, E. *Retarded youth: Their school-rehabilitation needs* (Technical report VRA-RD-681). Minneapolis: Minneapolis Public Schools, 1965.

References

Baller, W. R., Charles, D. C., & Miller, E. L. *Mid-life attainment of the mentally retarded, a longitudinal study.* Lincoln: University of Nebraska Press, 1966.

Brolin, D. Value of rehabilitation services and correlates of vocational success with mentally retarded adults. *American Journal of Mental Deficiency,* 1972, 76, 644-651.

Charles, D. C. Longitudinal follow-up studies of community adjustment. In S. G. DiMichael (Ed.), *New vocational pathways for the mentally retarded.* Washington, DC: American Personnel and Guidance Association, 1966.

Cobb, H. V. *The forecast of fulfillment: A review of research on predictive assessment of the adult retarded for social and vocational adjustment.* New York: Teachers College Press, 1972.

Elo, M. R., & Hendel, D. D. Classification as "mentally retarded": A determinant of vocational rehabilitation outcomes? *American Journal of Mental Deficiency,* 1972, 77, 190-198.

Katz, E. *The retarded adult in the community.* Springfield, IL: Charles C Thomas, 1968.

Vocational Training of the Severely Retarded: Expectations and Potential

PAUL WEHMAN, Ph.D.

Dr. Wehman is assistant professor, Department of Special Education, Virginia Commonwealth University, Richmond. He was recently awarded his Ph.D. degree in behavioral disabilities from the University of Wisconsin—Madison. From 1972 to 1974 he was a psychologist at Lincoln State School, Lincoln, Ill.

Requests for reprints should be addressed to: Paul Wehman, Assistant Professor, Department of Special Education, Virginia Commonwealth University, Richmond, Va. 23284.

CURRENTLY, there is a growing emphasis on vocational training programs for severely retarded adolescents and adults. State and federal agencies are allocating large sums of money for vocational rehabilitation programs that serve the severely impaired. This is, to a large extent, a result of recent legislation providing for increased efforts at vocational rehabilitation of the severely retarded *(Rehabilitation Act of 1973—P.L. 93-112)*. With the push to rehabilitate many clients once thought beyond the scope of most rehabilitation agencies has come the dilemma of what to expect from these clients. It is difficult to evaluate programs and establish accountability with the lack of awareness of what severely retarded clients can do and what potential they have for habilitation into society.

It is a common belief of professionals in many rehabilitation settings that severely retarded people are able to perform only the simplest of tasks. In recent years, however, significant progress has been made in the behavior technology of vocational training for the severely and profoundly retarded. The purpose of the present article is to familiarize rehabilitation administrators, counselors, and workshop supervisors with the behavioral expectations and vocational potential associated with severely retarded persons. A secondary purpose is to discuss briefly implications for preparing rehabilitation counselors to cope effectively with severely retarded clients needing vocational rehabilitation.

Behavioral Characteristics of the Severely Retarded

There is considerable variability between individual learning and behavioral characteristics of severely retarded persons (IQ 21-35). Most severely retarded people have behavior deficits or insufficient self-management skills to function without supervision. However, some severely handicapped persons also display behavior excesses such as extreme episodes of aggression or self-abusive behavior. Frequently, a combination of behavior deficits and excesses may be present as well.

While it is difficult to draw a reliable behavioral profile of the severely retarded, certain statements are indicative of their adaptive behavior. Severely retarded clients usually have basic self-help skills but may not have developed fine motor skills such as buttoning or zipping. Also, there are usually deficits in attending skills and in imitation learning. Language is generally restricted to simple receptive communication with few expressive verbalizations that are understandable. Cognitive skills such as problem-solving, concept formation, and dealing with abstracts are usually minimal. Cooperative social interaction between peers is rarely present. Also, severely retarded persons do not make generalizations as easily or rapidly as do intellectually average individuals.

Severely retarded clients may exhibit behavior excesses in the form of self-stimulatory body-rocking, head-weaving, or self-abusive head-banging. They frequently display bizarre verbal behavior through strange sounds or grunts. Excessive outbursts of physical aggression may develop in response to frustrating social situations or demanding work task requirements.

In short, severely retarded persons represent different and challenging cases for rehabilitation agencies and workshops. Traditional psychotherapeutic counseling and training methods that require verbal counseling are usually not effective with these clients and must give way to a behavioral approach.

Work Skill Expectations

Increasing research evidence is available to suggest that severely retarded clients can be effective workers on complex manual tasks.[6, 13] Several researchers have investigated the viability of presenting severely retarded workers with complex tasks such as putting together a drill machine[3] or bicycle brakes.[7] In the Crosson[3] report, a 16-step task analysis was utilized to teach severely retarded adolescents how to put together a drill machine. In a task analysis approach, a behavior is divided into smaller increments and presented in a logical sequential chain. Difficult learning discriminations are made easier as positive reinforcement is delivered for successful responses. Brown and his associates[1,2] have also used a task analysis approach successfully in studying the effects that different reinforcement contingencies have on rate of production with moderately and severely retarded adolescents.

Gold provides a series of research studies demonstrating the effectiveness of moderately to severely retarded clients on complex work tasks.[6] Through the use of errorless learning, or easy-to-hard discriminations, moderately to severely retarded adults were trained to put together a 15-piece bicycle brake.[5] In the same report, subjects demonstrated successful transfer of training by putting together a 24-piece bicycle brake. A one-year follow-up study indicated significant retention effects by clients.

Through use of an easy-to-hard method of errorless learning, it was also shown that moderately to severely retarded clients were able to make discriminations between different bolt lengths as fine as one-eighth of an inch.[8] Gold[5] also reports the successful performance of 20 moderate to severely retarded clients in putting together a 14-piece coaster brake. An important finding of this study was the nonsignificant statistical relationship between IQ and production rates of clients participating in the program. This is in direct conflict with earlier reports that supported the notion of higher IQs being related to greater production rates in severely retarded clients.[15]

Tate and Baroff[14] describe a demonstration workshop project in which severely retarded persons put together a 20-piece assembly design of a relay panel. Clients were expected to make wire connections and solder them. After one year in operation, the shop was operated 6 hours a day, Monday through Friday, with 26 clients employed. Several reports demonstrate the use of token reinforcement systems to increase production rates of severely retarded clients.[10,12]

Social Behavior in Vocational Settings

The issue of work skill expectations has been discussed through a brief review of relevant research literature. However, efficient work production is only part of successful vocational adjustment. Appropriate social behavior is required to integrate the client into the mainstream of the labor force. Few published reports have been directed at the adaptive social behavior of severely retarded individuals in vocational settings.

Edmonson, Leland, and Leach[4] have developed a Test of Social Inference for educable mentally retarded adolescents. Pictures of different social situations are used to assess inferences and comprehension of clients. Social-perceptual training materials are also available to assist clients in social cue recognition and interpretation. Film-strips and tape recorders are used to present materials to clients. The basic content includes pictorial representations of persons engaging in different adaptive behavior necessary for successful vocational and community adjustment. Classroom curricula of various topical areas in social skills development are utilized as a supplement to the audio-visual aids.

There are several drawbacks to the Social Inference Curriculum presented by Edmonson and her colleagues. First, methods of measuring change are not behavioral, but rather computed on paper-and-pencil tests through teacher ratings on such scales as those of Social Range, Social Invisibility, and Social Relationship. Secondly, the curriculum, which purports to be for prevocational training, is extremely broad in scope and lacks the specificity required for programing. Thirdly, the curriculum does not appear to be sensitive to the unique needs of a severely retarded population.

Goldstein[9] presents an extensive social learning curriculum for the mentally retarded, also. The broadly defined objectives of this curriculum are to help mentally retarded people develop social skills necessary for successful adjustment in the community. This curriculum also fails to provide specific behaviors for training, and the logic of sequencing is suspect. It appears to be more theoretical in orientation and tends to rely on hypothetical constructs such as self-concept and self-awareness.

Recently, a social skills curriculum was proposed specifically for developmentally disabled clients in vocational settings by the writer.[17] The curriculum is divided into four levels: Personal Care Level, Primary Interaction Level, Job and Community Survival Level, and Advanced Interaction Level. A major strength of this curriculum is the sensitivity to all functioning levels of mentally retarded persons. Furthermore, goals within the curriculum are stated behaviorally and are directly related to requisite social behaviors required in most work settings. Most of the behavioral goals at the different curriculum levels are empirically supported through previous research. Examples of some of the specific behavioral goals across different levels of the curriculum include: proper selection of clothing, proper table manners, good posture, eye contact during interaction, proper social greetings, knowledge of time, use of phone, knowledge of whom to trust, and demonstration of cooperative behavior.

Components of an Effective Vocational Training Program for the Severely Retarded

An analysis of the existing vocational and social skill research with severely retarded clients indicates that there are several integral components present in successful training programs. These elements are briefly outlined and discussed as an aid to workers in rehabilitation settings faced with the vocational training of a severely retarded population.

A task analysis method of presentation is instrumental in making the job easier for the client, thus increasing the probability of success. Breaking a social skill or work task into smaller, logically sequenced increments allows the severely retarded person to absorb the information easier. The smaller increments of behavior are gradually chained together through reinforcement, thus developing the whole skill. It would appear in vocational programing with low-functioning retarded persons that work tasks should be task-analyzed by rehabilitation workers previous to beginning training sessions. Eventually, a program notebook of task analyses can be completed and prescribed for each client.

A high degree of structure in the vocational setting and consistency in approach by trainers in the initial stages of training is required for optimal performance. Instructions used during training must be consistent and there should be little variability in the methods of presentation and the criterion for reinforcement. Initially, the physical environment should be a setting with few distractions.

Reinforcers must be individualized for each client and demonstrate that they are instrumental in increasing behavior. Often it is difficult to discern what reinforcers will influence the behavior of severely retarded persons. The rehabilitation worker must test out different reinforcers and evaluate the effect of each on work performance. Severely retarded workers demonstrate a wide variability in reinforcer preference. Presenting a variety of functional reinforcers initially on a continuous schedule of reinforcement and gradually on a more intermittent schedule will result in acquisition of the desired vocational behaviors.

Vocational programs utilizing carefully gathered data of a client's work performance are most effective in making program modifications and decisions. The severely retarded make behavioral gains slowly, and evaluation of program methods is usually subjective without careful documentation. Previously, the writer has presented a list of several points that are advantageous in using a data-based approach to programing.[17] These are:

1. Gain an accurate pretreatment index of the degree (frequency) of behavior.
2. The behavior must be defined clearly and be discrete and observable.
3. Gradual improvements can be charted and graphed, and thus provide positive feedback to staff and parents.
4. Length of treatment time can be identified precisely, as well as the effects that treatment has on behavior.
5. An objective index of accountability is gained with parents and administration.

Methods to facilitate transfer of training and response maintenance must be planned and developed within the overall program. It cannot be expected to occur spontaneously. As mentioned earlier, severely retarded persons frequently lack imitation and incidental learning skills

and do not generalize across settings or tasks readily. A number of methods for enhancing generalization are available and are discussed in depth by the writer elsewhere.[18] Briefly, however, they include: *1)* varying the stimulus conditions of training, *2)* including parents and peers in training, *3)* gradually fading reinforcement contingencies and substituting naturally occurring reinforcers, *4)* training skills that have a high probability of being performed daily by the client and that are meaningful in content, *5)* altering reinforcement schedules, and *6)* developing self-control techniques.

Toward a Behaviorally Oriented Rehabilitation Counselor

For rehabilitation counselors to continue to be a formidable force in the vocational rehabilitation of severely retarded clients, several changes in preparatory, as well as inservice, training are necessary. Presently, most rehabilitation counselors are not prepared for the unique behavior deficits and excesses exhibited by many markedly retarded individuals. Previous research strongly indicates that competent work and social skill performance are within the grasp of this population. However, rehabilitation counselors will need to serve more as behavioral engineers and change agents of the environment.

The following suggestions are advanced for development of a behaviorally oriented, rather than psychometric test-oriented, rehabilitation counselor:

1. *Complete understanding and working knowledge of fundamentals and principles of behavior management.* This can be achieved through part-time course work or independent reading. Several good elementary texts are available for beginning reading.[11, 19] Knowledge of basic principles is helpful because it gives the counselor familiarity with the educational technology that has been proven effective with a severely retarded population. Further, it helps the professional disallow incorrect allegations as to the moral and ethical "wrong" of behavior management methods.

2. *A commitment to a data-based system of training and programing.* This requires understanding by the counselor in the formulation of behavior objectives, behavior observation methods, and data presentation techniques. Through a data-based system, research information is generated, thus facilitating greater knowledge about the rehabilitative process with the severely retarded.

3. *Rehabilitation counselor education programs should include an opportunity for practicum experience with severely retarded populations.* Many graduate students working toward an advanced degree in vocational rehabilitation have never encountered severely retarded persons. It should be helpful to sensitize students to

the particular rehabilitative and training difficulties presented by this population.

Vocational Outlook for the
Severely Retarded: Conclusions

The following conclusions about the vocational training potential of the severely retarded seem warranted:

1. Under appropriately arranged learning conditions, the severely retarded worker has the potential to perform reasonably complex (manual) work tasks.

2. Supervision and training are maximal in the initial training stages, which may be at least three months depending on task complexity, but as the task is acquired supervision can be substantially reduced.

3. A significant problem in programing for the severely retarded in vocational settings is the critical lack of appropriate social behavior. Inability to cope with frustrating events, the presence of bizarre verbal or motor behaviors, and basic social skill deficits all may contribute to rejection of the severely retarded individual as a successful employee.

4. Few programs are available that demonstrate that the severely retarded are capable of competitive employment level production rates; this is an area requiring investigation and one in which the writer and his colleagues are presently involved.

Although the work skill research reported in this article serves as a demonstration of vocational behavior potential in severely retarded individuals, there are several issues, aside from social skill deficits, that may well prohibit their entry into community work forces. An initial problem is the probable reluctance of employers to take on severely retarded workers. There have been immense job placement problems with the mildly handicapped; certainly, acceptance of the severely retarded, a population with unique behavior characteristics, will be no easier.

Two potential avenues are open for overcoming this difficulty. Use of discrimination lawsuits or related litigation may alter employer behavior, if not attitudes. Secondly, the possibility exists that government subsidies might temporarily be directed to employers who are sympathetic to giving severely handicapped workers a chance to prove themselves.

Another issue that must be addressed by rehabilitation counselors is the preparation of appropriate transitioning experiences from the original training site to the least restrictive work environment, that is, a job placement in which the clients can perform at his or her optimal level of independence. Most vocational rehabilitation failures of developmentally disabled persons revolve around placement without proper preparation for the job. Role-playing, similar work environments, behavior rehearsal, and gradual on-the-job training are ways of overcoming such failures. Volunteers and university practicum students might be used to assist busy rehabilitation counselors in this transition phase.

A final consideration in the eventual job placement of the severely retarded is the type of task or skill that they can perform. The complex assembly skill research reported herein, although most impressive, is not all that practical. Many communities do not have any industry or need for performance of complex tasks. It may be wisest to train clients to meet the vocational needs of the community. Perusal of local newspaper job openings is one possible method of determining viable skills to train.

THE long-range outlook for severely retarded clients is presently at a pivotal point in time. Rehabilitation professionals, with their broad-based training and service with many disabled populations, are in a position to help severely retarded persons adjust to vocational settings. However, vocational rehabilitation counselors must gain familiarity with behavior management techniques and give acceptance to this training technology. With these added skills, counselors can become even more effective in delivering vocational training and services.

PREVOCATIONAL TRAINING OF THE SEVERELY RETARDED USING TASK ANALYSIS[1]

William P. Friedenberg
Andrew S. Martin

Authors: WILLIAM P. FRIEDENBERG, M.S. (Syracuse University), currently completing work for his Ph.D. in clinical psychology at Texas Tech University, Lubbock and is also a research assistant at the Research and Training Center in Mental Retardation, Texas Tech University; ANDREW S. MARTIN, Ph.D. (University of Connecticut), a research scientist at the Research and Training Center in Mental Retardation, P.O. Box 4510, Texas Tech University, Lubbock, Texas 79409.

ABSTRACT. Two severely retarded students were trained on a task requiring multiple, multidimensional discrimination. Two procedures for accomplishing the task were subjected to task analysis and training procedures for each devised. Each student was trained on both a hand and machine procedure for stapling labels on plastic bags. Subsequent production tests suggested that tangible reinforcement may be a necessary ingredient in maintaining low-error performance with an inherently non-reinforcing task. Recommendations are made for in-depth analysis of tasks prior to setting up training programs.

Prevocational programs for the mentally retarded are designed to evaluate and train potential workers in basic skills. Gold (1973b) shows that intelligence tests, manual dexterity tests, and work sample tasks are of limited usefulness in predicting work performance. An actual work assignment is preferred because it can develop valuable skills in the client while it is being used for evaluation.

Crosson (1969) set the standard for extending behavioral techniques to sheltered workshop settings through his use of task analysis and intensification of cues by the trainer. In this training procedure, "the trainer demonstrates each of the component behaviors in the proper sequence and prompts the trainee to immediately model the behavior. This can be accomplished by verbal or gestured command although it is occasionally necessary to mold the response by physically guiding the trainee through an appropriate topography" (p. 815). Other researchers have since added evidence that laboratory techniques can be used with success in the real life setting of the workshop (Zimmerman, Stuckey, Garlick, & Miller, 1969; Gold, 1972; Gold, 1973a; Brown, Bellamy, & Sontag, 1971).

The current study applied task analysis procedures to train students in the prevocational area of a sheltered workshop. Gold's thesis (1973a) that pay or praise in some form are not the only reinforcers available for work was tested using a task with different reinforcing properties from that used by Gold. The assumption that retarded students would require more training time and have lower subsequent production rates using a "complicated" piece of equipment than they would with standard techniques was also investigated.

Participants. Patrick, a 21-year-old severely retarded male (IQ = 30) and Tommy, a 30-year-old male with a measured IQ of 36 were assigned to the prevocational area of the workshop since neither was judged to be ready for work in the sheltered workshop.

Setting. The state school where the study took place is a residential facility for the mentally retarded. The school has a sheltered workshop of the extended care type and a newly instituted pre-vocational training area.

Training Task. The workshop presently has several contracts involving production of goods for local businesses. One such contract consists of the bagging, labeling, and displaying of spices for sale in grocery stores. Stapling labels onto plastic bags filled with garlic bulbs was chosen as a training task since the skills involved were applicable to other workshop jobs.

Task Analysis. The task of putting a label on a plastic bag filled with two garlic bulbs was analyzed for economy and ease of physical movement using task analysis procedures adapted from Gold (1975). The task was first method-analyzed to establish the method or methods which would be easiest to learn or teach. Two alternatives were designated—stapling by hand and stapling using a foot-operated machine (See Figure 1). This machine required coordinated use of eyes, hands, and feet in a sequence unfamiliar to the trainees. Based on the fact that the machine required more effort from the student and more input from the instructor, it would not appear at first glance to be the method of choice. Content analysis was used to break the two tasks into teachable units. The steps for hand and machine stapling are pre-

5. VOCATIONAL

sented in Table 1. Finally, process analysis determined the format and type of feedback used in training. Following a procedure developed for use with housekeeping tasks (Brown, Bellamy & Sontag, 1971), four levels of instruction were used: nonpunitive indication of error, verbal direction, modeling, and priming.

FIGURE 1

Foot-operated stapling machine

TABLE 1

Steps in Machine and Hand Stapling
from Task Analysis

LABEL STAPLING – MACHINE

1. Pick up one label with one hand.
2. Place the label in front of you (face down with the open end of the flap facing you).
3. Retrieve a bag of garlic from the tray, with both hands, holding only the corners of the open end.
4. Insert the mouth of the garlic bag into the "v" shaped space made by the raised flap of the label.
5. Hold the bag in place with the thumbs.
6. Now press the flap down (over the mouth of the bag) with the forefingers.
7. Carefully put your thumb on the flap also and press down.
8. Now remove your forefingers and carefully pick up the bag without moving your thumb.
9. Insert under the stapler and staple by depressing the pedal.
10. Place the labeled bag in a tray.

LABEL STAPLING – HAND

1. Pick up one label with one hand.
2. Place the label in front of you (face down with the open end of the flap facing you).
3. Retrieve a bag of garlic from the tray, with both hands, holding only the corners of the open end.
4. Insert the mouth of the garlic bag into the "v" shaped space made by the elevated bag.
5. Hold the bag in place with the thumbs.
6. Now press the flap down (over the mouth of the bag) with the forefingers.
7. Carefully put your thumb on the flap also and press down.
8. Now remove your forefingers and carefully pick up the bag without moving your thumb.
9. Insert under the stapler, carefully letting go of assembly on side of label to be stapled first.
10. Using free hand, hit or push down on stapler.
11. Push label over, keeping assembly under stapler.
12. Grasp with free hand, letting go with other hand.
13. Position and staple other side of label.
14. Place labeled bag in a tray.

General Procedure. Each student was trained to staple labels onto bags using one of the two methods, machine or hand, for approximately 20 minutes each day. This period was lengthened to allow a block of 10 trials in progress to be completed. After the student met the criterion of 20 consecutive trials without error, he was tested for production in three 20-minute sessions. During these test sessions, the student was told to work as fast as he could and staple as many labels as possible for 20 minutes. When the production test was completed, each student was trained using the alternate production method. Three production test sessions followed to test speed and accuracy using the second stapling method. A production test session using the hand method was given between the 1st and 2nd machine production sessions for Patrick, and a machine session was given between the 2nd and 3rd sessions for Tommy. These interpolated trials were used to test for practice effects.

Training. The trainer began by physically modeling the steps necessary to obtain a completed product while stating verbally the operations he was performing according to the task analysis. He then told the student to try the task. An inability to complete a step correctly was dealt with first by a non-punitive indication of error ("Try it another way"). If this had no effect, a verbal direction was given such as "hold the bag tightly." If the verbal instruction did not result in the performer correcting his error, a physical cue was given in the form of the step being modeled by the trainer with accompanying verbal instructions. The fourth level of correction (priming) consisted of manipulating the boy's hands to help him complete the step correctly. No tangible reinforcement was given. The experimentor tried as much as possible not to make eye contact or provide other social reinforcement since the student's constant checking with the trainer to see if he is correct can easily disrupt learning (Gold, 1973c).

Production Test. When criterion was reached, three production test sessions of 20 minutes each were given. In these sessions, the student was encouraged to complete as many units as he could with no corrections made by the trainer. Earlier experience had indicated that production rates were not easily maintained without any reinforcement so non-contingent verbal reward was included in this stage. This consisted of dramatic exhortations to try hard and work quickly, and praise of current performance. The verbal reinforcement was not tied to specific performance of the student at that moment.

Results

Figures 2 and 3 show the number of errors and the number of completely correct products made for each block of 10 trials during training for both procedures. Patrick took only two sessions or approximately 40 minutes to meet the criterion of 20 consecutively correct responses using the hand stapling procedure. He quickly went from 10 step

FIGURE 2

Number of substep errors and completely correct products produced per block of ten trials during training.

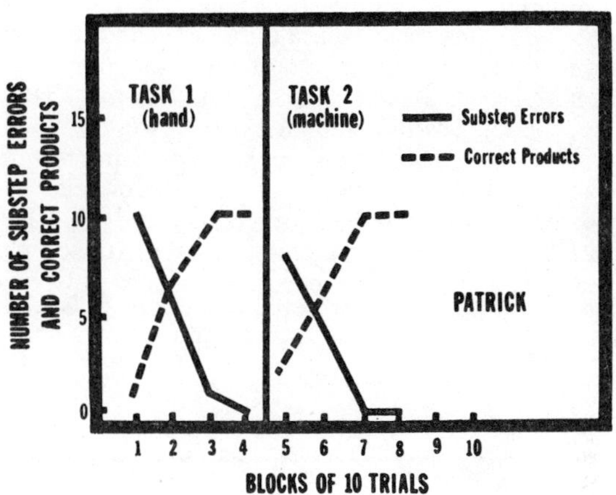

FIGURE 3

Number of substep errors and completely correct products produced per block of ten trials during training.

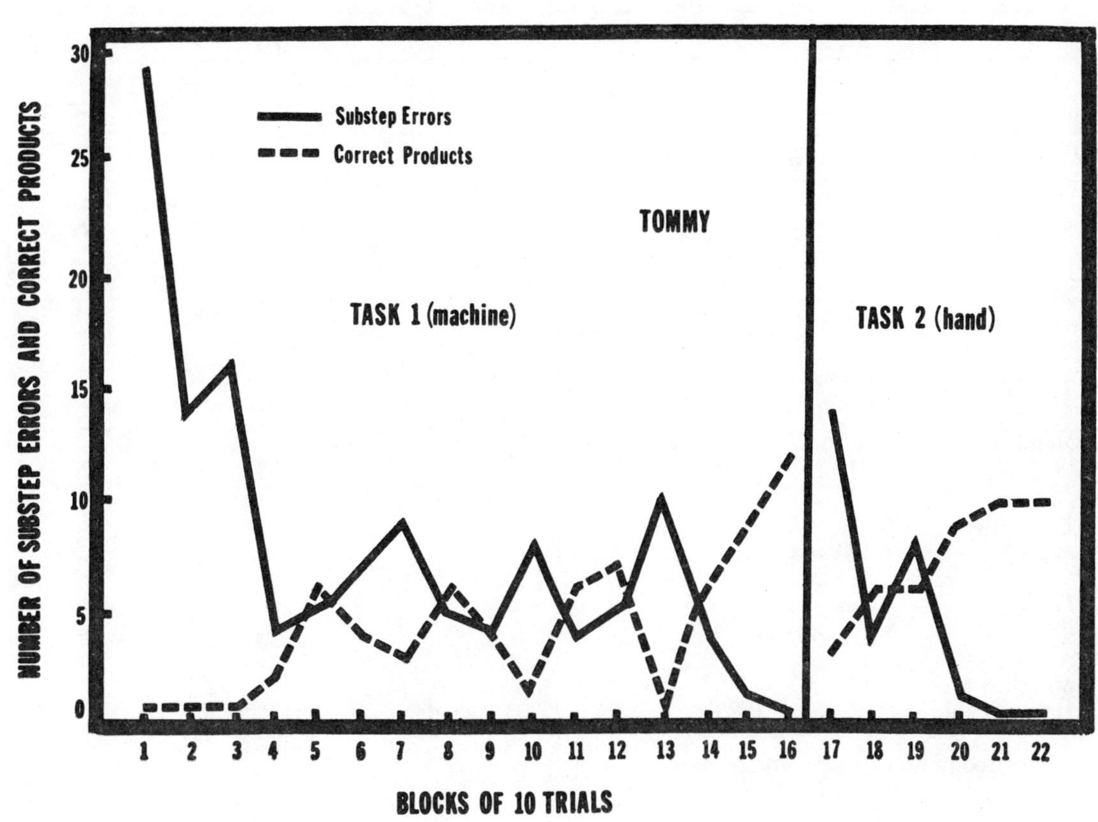

errors per 10 products to zero errors. The transfer of training to the second method can be seen in lower initial step errors, higher initial number of completely correct products, and shorter training time (approximately 20 minutes for the machine training). Tommy took longer to learn the machine procedure than Patrick took to learn the hand procedure. His total training time over 6 days was, however, less than 2 hours (107 minutes). He started with lower overall performance characteristics than did Patrick, reached a plateau for several sessions, then quickly reached criterion within one day's session. This fast rise to criterion after a period of plateau performance has been described by Zeaman and House (1963) for visual discrimination learning in retardates. Transfer was accomplished (lower step errors and more correct products), with complete training taking place in 2 days (60 trials) on hand stapling.

Table 2 shows the relative numbers of completely correct products and unacceptable products for each test session, and the mean performance on these two measures for both students.

Patrick produced an average of 21 correct products by hand with an average of 9.5 unacceptable. This represents an average unacceptable rate of 31%. When tested after being trained on machine stapling, he produced an average 20 correct with an average 7.34 unacceptable. This yields an unacceptable product rate of 27% —an improvement of 4% for machine over hand stapling. Tommy produced 31.75 correct and 6.5 unacceptable by machine with an unacceptable product rate of 17%. His performance after being trained to staple by hand shows 29 correct and an average 6.0 unacceptable for an error rate of 17%—the same as for machine stapling. No apparent differences are seen between interpolated and original test session production rates, thus indicating that the second stapling technique results were not enhanced by practice effects.

In test sessions the average number correct produced by both students was 26.7 by machine and 24.4 by hand. For both the average number of unacceptable products was 6.85 by machine and 8.0 by hand, representing an unacceptable product rate of 20% and 25% respectively.

TABLE 2

Mean Production in Test Sessions on
Machine and Hand Stapling

| | MACHINE | | | | | | HAND | | | | |
| | Sessions | | | | | | Sessions | | | | |
	1	2	3	4	$\bar{X}$		1	2	3	4	$\bar{X}$
TOMMY											
Number Correct	31	30	33	33*	31.74		30	20	37		29.0
Unacceptable	6	7	8	5	6.5		6	8	4		6.0
PATRICK											
Number Correct	23	10	27		20.0		22	28	8	26*	21.0
Unacceptable	10	10	2		7.34		6	6	13	13	9.5
Machine Correct		$\bar{X}$ = 26.7				Hand Correct		$\bar{X}$ = 24.4			
Machine Unacceptable		$\bar{X}$ = 6.85				Hand Unacceptable		$\bar{X}$ = 8.0			

*Interpolated trials — using alternate method

Discussion

In addition to showing that training was successfully completed for both students within a very short period of time, the results tend to favor machine stapling slightly over hand stapling in number produced, unacceptable products, and error rate. One of the aims of this study was to see if possible increased training time on machine stapling would be offset by improved performance. Although no conclusions can be drawn from such a small sample, the results at least indicate that one should consider possible gains in the long run production obtainable by investing in a longer initial training period, and the fact that quality may deteriorate less over time due to the standardization provided by the machine. In addition, the trainer should not be overly apprehensive about the use of work aids that seem complicated but which are contributory to increased production. A careful study of potential work aids and training methods to teach use of these aids should be made before assuming a simpler method is preferable.

Concerning the high unacceptable rate seen in production after errorless performance had previously been reached in training, the possibility that the criterion was too low for assurance of complete learning or that over-learning should have been instituted to insure retention is discounted. The criterion for acquisition used in the present study (20 consecutive correct trials) is considerably higher than that used in other studies. In addition, Gold (1972) found no positive effect of over-learning on retention rates. A more likely explanation is that the inherent interest in the task (Gold, 1972; Gold, 1973a) and social reinforcement was not strong enough in the present study to maintain performance at a high level. The present task is a fairly difficult one, and unlike the bicycle brake used by Gold, the discriminations necessary for successful completion of this task are multiple and multidimensional rather than simple 2-choice discriminations. The fine motor coordination necessary for holding a thin plastic bag and stapling a label is substantial. There are many possible errors in such fine work and any lack of precision would result in an unacceptable product. Once the task had been learned, the inherent reinforcement value of the task may have been low compared to that of longer-cycle assembly tasks with an impressive "mechanical" look. Lack of interest may have caused attention lapses, resulting in small errors. Thus, either tangible rewards (Logan, Kinsinger, Shelton, & Brown, 1971), tokens (Zimmerman, Stuckey, Garlick, & Miller, 1969), competition (Huddle, 1967), or more explicit social reinforcement (Logan, Kinsinger, Shelton, & Brown, 1971) are probably necessary to maintain performance. Both students were aware that workers in the sheltered workshop were paid for their work. One finished his first performance trial by asking the trainer for payment. Although Gold's (1973a) students received no response-contingent reinforcement, they still received their regular workshop pay.

References

Brown, L., Bellamy, T., & Sontag, L. (Eds.) The development and implementation of a public school prevocational training program for trainable retarded and severely emotionally disturbed children: Progress report part I. Unpublished manuscript, Madison Public Schools, Madison, Wisconsin, 1971.

Crosson, J. E. A technique for programming sheltered workshop environments for training severely retarded workers. *American Journal of Mental Deficiency*, 1969, 73(5), 814-818.

Gold, M. W. Factors affecting production by the retarded: Base rate. *Mental Retardation*, 1973, 11(6), 41-45(a).

Gold, M. W. Research on the vocational habilitation of the retarded: The present, the future. In N. R. Ellis (Ed.), *International review of research in mental retardation*, (Vol. 6). New York: Academic Press, 1973 (b).

Gold, M. W. Stimulus factors in skill training of retarded adolescents on a complex assembly task: Acquisition, transfer and retention. *American Journal of Mental Deficiency*, 1972, 76(4), 517-526.

Gold, M. W. Utilization of task analysis and task complexity in training. Paper presented at Training Techniques and Approaches for the Mentally Retarded, Research and Training Center in Mental Retardation, Texas Tech University, Lubbock, Texas, May, 1975.

Huddle, D. D. Work performance of trainable adults as influenced by competition, cooperation, and monetary reward. *American Journal of Mental Deficiency*, 1967, 72(2), 198-211.

Logan, D. L., Kinsinger, J., Shelton, G., & Brown, J. The use of multiple reinforcers in a rehabilitation setting. *Mental Retardation*, 1971, 9(3), 3-6.

Zeaman, D. & House, B. J. The role of attention in retardate discrimination learning. In N. R. Ellis (Ed.), *Handbook of mental deficiency*. New York: McGraw-Hill, 1963.

Zimmerman, J., Stuckey, T., Garlick, R., & Miller, M. Effects of token reinforcement on productivity in multiply handicapped clients in a sheltered workshop. *Rehabilitation Literature*, 1969, 30, 34-41.

Acknowledgments

The authors wish to express their appreciation to Mr. Jerry L. Morris for his assistance in designing and building the stapling apparatus, Dr. Carol K. Sigelman and Dr. Robert W. Flexer for their editorial assistance, and Ms. Jan Chapman for her help in preparing the manuscript.

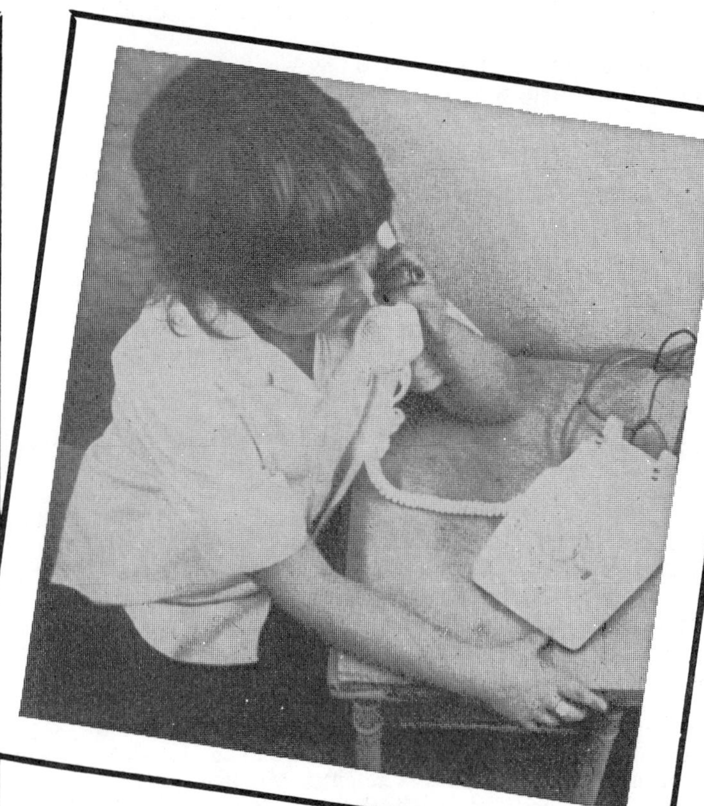

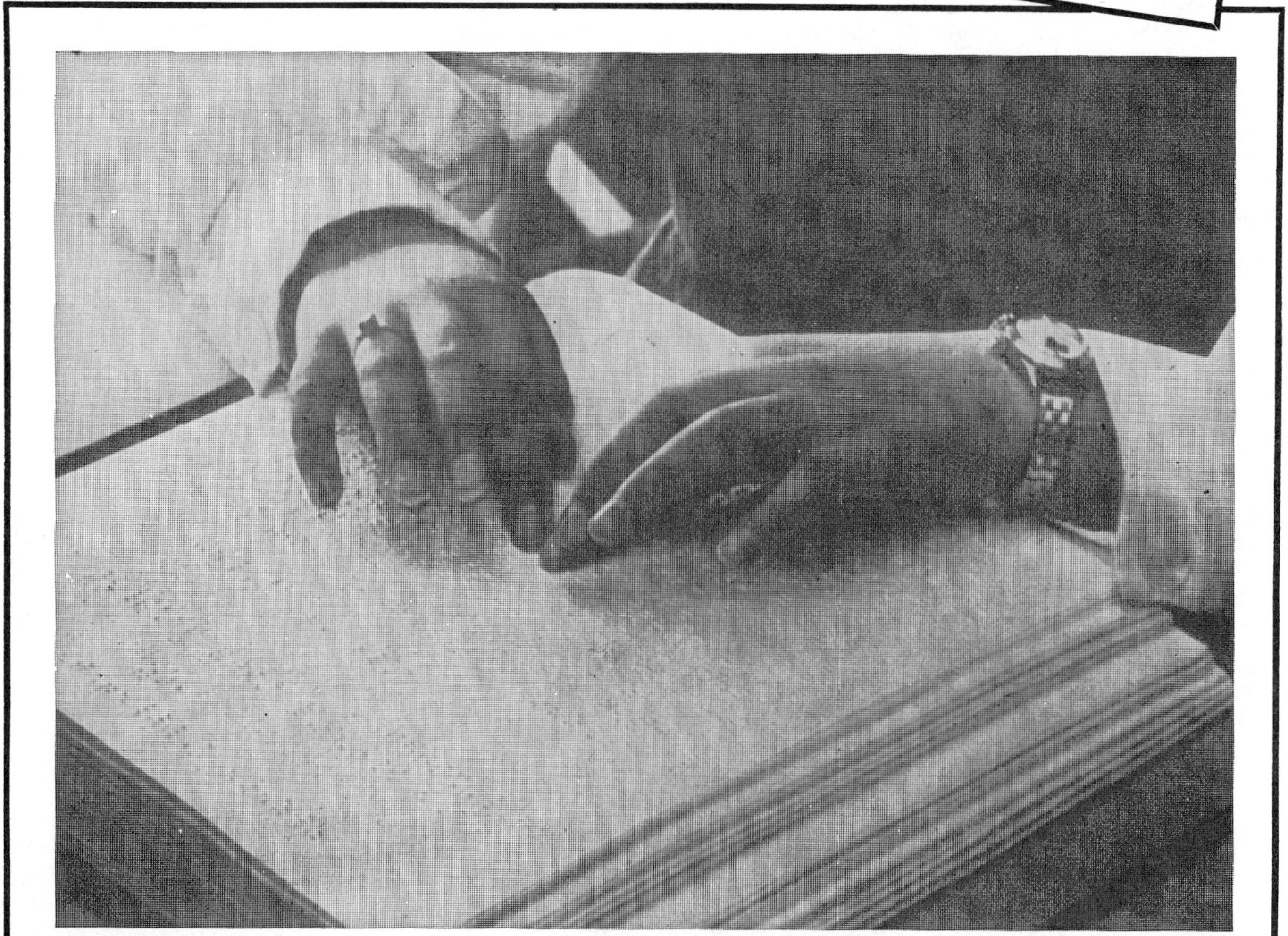

VOCATIONAL AND CAREER EDUCATION FOR SPECIFIC HANDICAPS

(Multiply Handicapped, Learning Disabled Physically Handicapped, Deaf and Blind)

All of the handicaps presented in this chapter are specific in nature with identifiable characteristics. Vocationally, definite measures must be taken to allow these populations to perform adequately.

The multiply handicapped can perform up to potential only if they are allowed to prepare themselves in a meaningful vocational program with realistic goals and objectives and if they are given the opportunity to perform by an employer.

The physically handicapped are in much the same situation. For both of these populations, measures must be taken to allow these citizens to be ambulatory on the job. Ramps, elevators and floor plans may be very important and reflect on job success.

The deaf and blind with their specific handicaps must also be prepared vocationally, and must be given the oppor-tunity to reach highest potential in order to compete for employment. Employers must be able to accept the talents and expertises of these populations to even allow the possibility of success.

The learning disabled depending on the severity of the problem, must be vocationally prepared in a meaningful program of assessment, prescription, remediation and vocational preparation.

Because a child has problems academically does not mean that he cannot perform vocationally. If he improves his academic skills as much as possible, vocational opportunities exist and successful employment is possible.

An effective career and vocational education program can benefit all of the handicapped. Adequate preparation in regard to work skills, work attitude and self help has been lacking in the past. Perhaps the new legislation and new curricula will change the situation.

Occupational Help for The Severely Disabled

A Public School Model

BRUCE S. COOPER, Ph.D.

Dr. Cooper received his Ph.D. degree from the University of Chicago, specializing in school management and educational policy. He is currently an assistant professor of education at Dartmouth College and is special consultant to the Taconic Foundation, New York, on special programs for adolescents.

Introduction

AS PUBLIC SCHOOLS have expanded their educational programs for children with severe handicaps, there is an increasing need to improve the occupational counseling and support for these young adults.[5] It is, in effect, a bitter pill to guide students through school and then to drop them at the crucial juncture: the crossing from school life to occupational life.[3] It is not that public schools cease caring once students reach age 18 or so; rather most school counseling programs are neither staffed nor structured to help those with severe and multiple handicaps.[6] Currently, few good models exist.[1]

It is, then, the purpose of this study *1)* to describe one such counseling program, the Handicapped Employability Learning Program, called H.E.L.P., located in Atlantic County, New Jersey; *2)* to explain the new counseling model that the school counselors used; and *3)* to analyze initially the results of the project. As a form of social and programmatic research, this study is descriptive enough to provide advice to the practitioner and analytical enough to allow us to examine the counseling and placement process with some perspective.[2]

No set hypotheses were to be tested. Rather the very development of the H.E.L.P. project was designed as a pilot and therefore a form of social research.[4] Data were gathered on its development and impact through observation of participants, interviewing, and the generation of case studies of particular students. Results were reached on a tentative basis, awaiting the full career development of the young adults involved and the continuation of the project itself, once federal funds are used up.

History and Purpose of the Project

Atlantic County has a number of facilities for people with handicaps, operated by the Longport School District: Children's Seashore House, an inpa-

"Occupational Help for the Severely Disabled," Bruce S. Cooper, Ph.D. *Rehabilitation Literature*, Vol. 38, No. 3, March 1977, Pgs. 66-74, ©1976 by the National Easter Seal Society for Crippled Children and Adults, 2023 W. Ogden Avenue, Chicago, Ill., 60612

About the Article . . .

IT APPEARS that a small, personalized, and well-structured occupational training program for the severely handicapped has great potential. Project H.E.L.P. (Handicapped Employability Learning Program) was designed to provide occupational training for young adults who are severely and multiply handicapped in the public schools. The project tested a new model of counseling and training the handicapped, one based on a six-step procedure: *Conferring*, in order to locate eligible students and potential job placements; *Assessing*, wherein students are screened as to their abilities and needs; *Placement* in jobs supported by government, private agency, and employer sources; *Training* on the job by employer and H.E.L.P. counselors; *Evaluating*, wherein the progress of students is recorded and monitored; and *Referring-Releasing* when students are deemed ready. These C.A.P.T.E.R. procedures provided a format for working with the 38 students as well as the rationale for presenting this report.

H.E.L.P. was founded by Title VI, ESEA, for 18 months for a total of 75 students, though only 38 are reported to time of writing. Located within the public schools of Atlantic County, New Jersey, it hired 2 full-time vocational counselors, who conferred with some 60 people to locate students and jobs. The 38 students were then assessed: almost 80 percent had sufficient prior testing; the remaining were given the TOWER and Singer tests and a more general physical to determine their capabilities. Currently, 33 students with disabilities ranging from mental retardation, epilepsy, and blindness to cerebral palsy and emotional difficulties have been placed on various public and private sector jobs. They received wage-stipend packages from a variety of state, federal, and local fund sources, as means of support while on-job training was initiated. Of the 35 students completing training, 23 (61%) are employed or deemed employable and are job hunting. The remaining 26 percent, having been evaluated, were then referred to other agencies for additional training or sheltered workshop experiences.

But claims for the success of this Project should be cautious. Data are not yet collected on the long-term effects of H.E.L.P. Perhaps Atlantic County is unique, with its long history of programs and institutions devoted to the handicapped. Perhaps New Jersey's model legislation for the assistance of the handicapped gave the Project a special edge. Or perhaps the particular dedication of the counseling staff and the administrative team of the Longport district makes H.E.L.P. a special phenomenon. Only a longitudinal study of the 38 students will allow us to learn of the utility of programs like H.E.L.P.; only the transfer of similar projects to other school districts (more urban, less urban, perhaps) will indicate the generalizability of these findings and the applicability of the model.

The cost of the project was high, budgeted at $63,257 for 34 clients, or $1,860.50 per student. But at the current rate of 38 students per 9 months, H.E.L.P. should easily reach 75 students by the end of the 18-month funding period, cutting per pupil costs to $843.43, a difference of over $1,000 per student. (One might also assume that the second 75 students might be yet less costly as the advisors became more expert.)

tient pediatric facility with a full educational and recreational program, and the Winchell Orthopedic School, a nonresidential educational and rehabilitative program. Staff and administrators of the Longport System, able to provide advanced and sophisticated help in case of severe handicap, realized that many students seemed to "drop out of sight" or, as one administrator explained, "fall through the cracks" as they outgrew the public school system but were unable to find work or further training.

In 1975, the school system received a grant of some $63,000 from Title VI, Elementary and Secondary Education Act (ESEA), to pilot a new approach to vocational counseling and placement for the handicapped. Project H.E.L.P. was the effort of public school officials, the County Supervisor of Child Study Teams, and representatives of special interest groups such as the Association for Retarded Citizens, and Youth and Family Services. All knew young adults in the county who needed special attention and realized that existing programs were inadequate.

6. EDUCATION

The underlying philosophy of the program was based on what these professionals and lay people knew about persons who are severely handicapped. First, the effort had to be a limited one: the counseling and placing of students with special physical and neurological difficulties require *personal, individual attention*. H.E.L.P. contracted to work with only 34 students over an 18-month period, though they may eventually be able to nearly double that number. Second, staff had to be *experienced with vocational counseling, with those with handicaps, and with the Atlantic County business community*. Most traditional school guidance counselors have little training or experience in these areas. Hence, the Project looked outside the school system and employed a counselor with long counseling experience and active membership in the Lion's Club, city council (as president), and youth activities. Additionally, this counselor was president of his own company and exhibited a businessman's background and perspective, an essential outlook in the employment phase of the H.E.L.P. project.

The second staff member, a speech therapist and disabled veteran, was hired because of his training and his ability to demonstrate the capabilities of those with disability. A paraplegic, he manages a wheelchair and his car, is married, owns a home, and is deeply involved with his community.

Third, the H.E.L.P. effort had to *extend beyond the walls of the school*, well into the community. Counselors had to make personal contact with possible employers, had to transport the students to the work site, and often had to work right alongside the students. These efforts were attempts to relieve the pressure on the employer and to meet the work needs of the handicapped young adult. And fourth, H.E.L.P. had to be a *joint effort*, using, for example, resources of the New Jersey Rehabilitation Department, the Atlantic County Opportunity Center for the Handicapped, Inc., the school district, and various special interest groups. Hence, H.E.L.P. was seen as a coordinated effort of other interested agencies that could not provide the special services for these students.

Thus, H.E.L.P. was born out of the shared concern of various public school and rehabilitation officials. All agreed on the need for occupational counseling and believed that the public schools were in the best position to help. An application secured ESEA funds and allowed the district to hire two full-time counselors and to utilize office space in the Winchell School and transportation for the physically disabled. The purpose of the grant was to assist the Longport school program to develop and test a new model of counseling and placement.

The H.E.L.P. approach involves six interrelated steps in assisting those with severe handicap: *1) Conferring* with potential student-clients, employers, support staff, and others to determine whether students would benefit from Project H.E.L.P.; *2) Assessing* these students' problems and prior training, based either on available test data from organizations like the New Jersey Rehabilitation Department, the Atlantic County Opportunity Center for the Handicapped, Inc., and, perhaps, the public school system or upon data gathered by the H.E.L.P. staff after the student is accepted into the Project; *3) Placing* students in an available work situation, assisted personally by H.E.L.P. vocational counselors and supervised by representatives of both the employer and H.E.L.P.; *4) Training* on the job by employer personnel and H.E.L.P. staff (It is important to note that often the student is placed and then trained, to avoid the frustration of nonspecific training and the chance of no placement at all); *5) Evaluating* the student's performance based on job and social adjustment and employer satisfaction; and *6) Referring-Releasing* students once a determination is made that they are ready to work on their own, to receive additional help, or to be transferred to other agencies. See Table 1 for a schematic of the process.

The C.A.P.T.E.R. model (Conferring, Assessing, Placing, Training, Evaluating, and Referring-Releasing) provides not only a rationale and process for working with the multiply handicapped but also a structure for this analysis. As the data on the 38 H.E.L.P. students will show, however, the model is only a basic framework and can be adapted. For example, students can go through the process of Conferring through Evaluating and need more assistance. The counselor may advise additional assessment and training. Or if, in the case of some students, they are successfully fulfilling a job when the job itself is eliminated, only Placement and some monitoring is called for. So while all clients were put through the six-step process, many received part or all of a second cycle of help.

Hence, the model allowed the researcher to follow the progress of students throughout the process and to present the findings of this study in a logical order.

Results

The results of the data on model application are reported below. Statistical information on students is provided where useful. Besides an analysis of the model, information will be given on the cost effectiveness of personalized counseling and placement for students with severe handicap. Analysis of the six phases of the C.A.P.T.E.R. process is as follows.

TABLE 1.—*Structure, Purpose, and Activities of Counseling Process: C.A.P.T.E.R.*

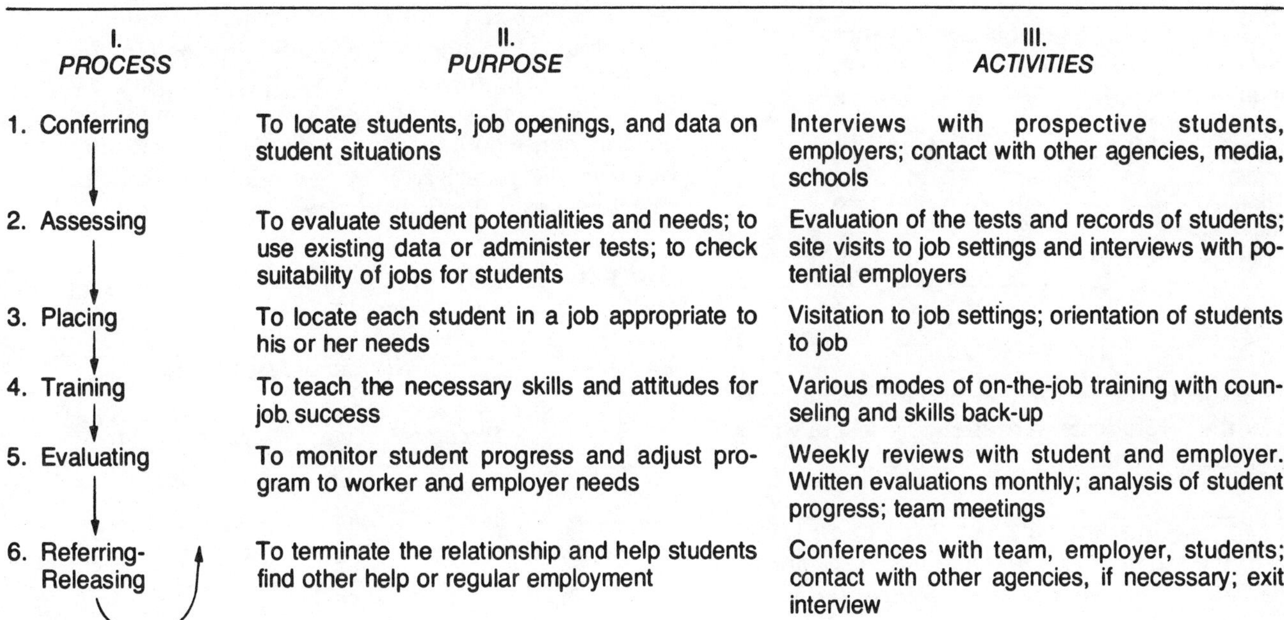

I. PROCESS	II. PURPOSE	III. ACTIVITIES
1. Conferring	To locate students, job openings, and data on student situations	Interviews with prospective students, employers; contact with other agencies, media, schools
2. Assessing	To evaluate student potentialities and needs; to use existing data or administer tests; to check suitability of jobs for students	Evaluation of the tests and records of students; site visits to job settings and interviews with potential employers
3. Placing	To locate each student in a job appropriate to his or her needs	Visitation to job settings; orientation of students to job
4. Training	To teach the necessary skills and attitudes for job success	Various modes of on-the-job training with counseling and skills back-up
5. Evaluating	To monitor student progress and adjust program to worker and employer needs	Weekly reviews with student and employer. Written evaluations monthly; analysis of student progress; team meetings
6. Referring-Releasing	To terminate the relationship and help students find other help or regular employment	Conferences with team, employer, students; contact with other agencies, if necessary; exit interview

1. Conferring. The first phase of attending to the occupational needs of the severely handicapped consists of locating students and job openings. This phase requires "talking it up," spreading the word about the program, and attracting both clients and jobs. At Project H.E.L.P., the long history of programs for the handicapped in Atlantic County and the favorable legislation in New Jersey made the conferring stage relatively painless. With little work, the counselors located (by December, 1975) 38 eligible students. Hence, with a minimum of "conferring," the quota of 34 students (plus) in the project was filled.

In fact, Project H.E.L.P. was conceived and funded with several clients in mind. As the principal of Children's Seashore House, Dr. John Glassey, explained, "We had all known certain students who needed occupational help but we lacked a program to do it. Once Project H.E.L.P. came along, we just gave the counselors a list of names."

The H.E.L.P. counseling staff in fact conferred with representatives from five categories in search of students and training sites and job slots: the county Child Study Team, parents and pupils themselves, officials and counselors of the public schools (including the H.E.L.P. staff itself), special agencies like New Jersey Rehabilitation Department, and civic groups like the Jaycees and Lions. Of the 22 young men and 16 young women (ages 15 to 35), only one was referred by the Child Study Team and one by a civic group; the rest came to H.E.L.P. through parent-student decisions (10), from within the system (12), and from special agencies (14). *See* Table 2.

The criteria for selection were based on two dimensions of human exceptionality: severity and multiplicity. In each case, the students had either problems to such extremes that they could not easily function at work (for example, four students had severe emotional disabilities) or they had both primary

TABLE 2.—*Sources of Client Referral and Placement*

SOURCES	STUDENTS	PLACEMENT
Child Study Team	1	0
Parent and self-referral	10	5
H.E.L.P. staff and other school personnel	12	21
Special agencies	14	7
Civic groups	1	0
Total	38	33

handicaps and secondary difficulties. (*See* Table 3.) For example, of the four students with cerebral palsy, three also had severe speech and movement problems. Virtually all the 38 students, furthermore, showed signs of emotional strain because of their impediments.

The Project accepted 38 students, 22 men and 16 women, most between the ages of 18 and 22, the critical years to find a job and receive the necessary work experience. The vast majority of H.E.L.P. students had completed formal schooling when accepted for placement and on-the-job training. The goals of the Project—to assist young adults with severe handicap who had slipped through the system and were with-

6. EDUCATION

TABLE 3.—*Disabilities and Ages of H.E.L.P. Students (N=38)*

Disability	Sex		Ages		
	M	F	13-17	18-22	23+
Mental retardation	8	4	0	8	4
Neurologic disorder (epilepsy, cerebral palsy)	6	3	0	5	4
Orthopedic	4	3	1	4	2
Blind/impaired	0	2	0	0	2
Learning disability	2	0	0	2	0
Emotional	2	4	0	5	1
Total	22	16	1	24	13

out work—seem relevant in the recruitment process: only 3 of the 38 students were attending school when H.E.L.P. found them.

2. Assessing. Once students have been located and accepted, the staff has to determine their capabilities and the appropriate work setting.[7] Hence, the process of candidate assessment begins. Since the Atlantic County area has strong public and private programs for the handicapped and has had for a long time, the chances of students reaching the age of young adulthood without extensive testing are slim. In fact, our data show 79 percent (30 out of 38) had sufficient assessment prior to recruitment. (This, by New Jersey law, involves a full report by a Child Study Team comprised of a psychologist, physician, social worker, and a learning disabilities specialist—teacher with special training; furthermore, H.E.L.P. counselors assembled the reports of former schools and agencies like the New Jersey Rehabilitation Department.) For those without adequate records, the Project referred the client to the Atlantic County Opportunity Center for the Handicapped, Inc., where a battery of performance and achievement tests was administered, the TOWER and Singer tests being but one example.

The usefulness of assessment in the screening, placing, and training process cannot be minimized. It provides guidance to staff, employers, parents, and students alike. It may be done formally, as in the interpretation of test data, but also it is often a matter of instinct, as the counselor and student seek together to place the client in the appropriate job. Assessment, after all, is only the first approximation of what a student-employee can do; only trial and error can really tell whether a student can handle a new job and whether the job will remain available to the student.

3. Placing. The placement phases should be seen as a protected and supportive opportunity for students to receive training and to grow. Students are carefully supervised by a H.E.L.P. counselor, often working alongside them for as long as two weeks. Through a "matching" process, client and job are brought together. As shown in Table 4, the Project tapped both the private (17 students) and public sector (16 students), lining up jobs as kitchen helper, secretary, engineer with industry and positions with municipal government, school systems, and county prosecutor's office in the public area. A few others worked for themselves as painters, baby sitters, and typists.

TABLE 4.—*Location and Number of Placements of H.E.L.P. Clients*

Location	Number of Placements				
	Awaiting Placement	One	Two	Three or More	Total
Private industry	2	13	2	0	17
Public sector/ nonprofit	2	11	2	1	16
Self-employed	1	1	0	3	5
Total	5	25	4	4	38

Not all these placements worked out: students were placed a second and even, in a few cases (4), a third time. The counselors were concerned, of course, to see that students could cope with the demands of the tasks; thus, transfers were a sign of the sensitivity of the staff and not a failure for the clients.

Besides finding an employer willing to hire the students, the counselors were called upon to negotiate salary and stipends for 33 students. The philosophy relevant here was that of first finding the job and then bargaining with the employer. If he could not afford to pay but could offer training opportunities, then the counselors could "package" financial support from local, state, and federal sources. If the employer could pay for work done, then a portion of the wages was paid for work and the remainder was made up from other sources. Minimum wages were not necessarily paid, since handicapped people often worked below the capacity of the average worker. The state employment office could determine the amount of work performed and the level of pay required. Or, in a few cases, the clients did full work for full pay and received no stipends.

As shown in Table 5, only five students earned full wages from the employers *while training*. For students placed in the nonprofit or public sector (in schools, city offices, county maintenance departments), federal funds from the Comprehensive Education and Training Act (C.E.T.A.) and some Social Security monies were secured. The New Jersey Rehabilitation Department provided support for 17 students out of 33, while other agencies like the Association for Retarded Citizens supported a few students

TABLE 5.—*Distribution of H.E.L.P. Students by Job Sector and Source of Funding (N=33)*

EMPLOYMENT SECTOR	Employer Wages	C.E.T.A. & Soc. Sec.	N.J. Rehab	Other (Assoc. for Retard. Citz.)	Total
Private Industry	2	0	12	1	15
Public/nonprofit Sector	2	8	3	1	14
Self-Employed	1	0	2	1	4
Total	5	8	17	3	33

during their on-job training (O.J.T.). All students received some financial assistance during Project H.E.L.P., in amounts ranging from $1,112 for O.J.T. from the New Jersey Rehabilitation Department to $7,000 from employer and Social Security.

The counseling staff were skilled at putting together wage-stipend packages, taking into consideration the needs of the student, the willingness of employers to pay wages, and the availability of public and private funds for job training and support.

The placement phase, in sum, was characterized by flexibility, as staff sought the right match. Sources of job training sites included private business, public institutions, self-employment, and, for a number of students, a sheltered workshop operated by the Atlantic County Center for the Handicapped, Inc., where work was contracted for and done by the handicapped. Of the 38 students, all but 5 have been placed and have moved on to the next phase of the counseling process. The remaining students are awaiting assessment and job openings.

4. Training. The on-job education of handicapped students consists of two components. First, trainees are required to learn certain skills, both mental and physical. Second, students must adjust emotionally to the independence, the regimen of work, other workers, and the public with whom they have contact. In some cases, training is a painstaking process of close interaction with counselors and employers, later leading to self-regulation and intermittent monitoring by staff. In other situations, the students, once they obtained a job, seemed to train on their own.

Project H.E.L.P. would not be classified as an advanced training program, like a college or trade school. Rather the training in most cases, but not all, involved relatively simple job tasks requiring diligence, an even temperament, punctuality, and some dexterity. These job abilities could be provided in a few weeks by staff and employer, once the student was ready. In a few cases, clients responded to more advanced training such as silk-screen design and

newspaper writing. The more physically and intellectually able the student, the more lengthy and involved the training phase.

Since the students, in a sense, already had a job before training began, the training and working phases were not artificially separated as in some occupational training programs. Thus, the following two phases of the C.A.P.T.E.R. model, Evaluating and Releasing-Referring, were directly linked with ongoing training, as the case materials will reveal.

5. Evaluating. Appraisal of training and work quality was done in a most hard-headed and direct manner: If the student held a job, brought in money, and stuck, the evaluation was positive. If the job dried up but the student was capable of doing similar work elsewhere, the evaluation of training was also positive. If the student could do even more advanced work, an optimistic prognosis was made and the student was ready for the next phase. Or, if the client had proved unable to sustain further work in the particular setting, the evaluation was done and the appropriate referral, step 6, completed. In every case, few elaborate assessments were made: The statistics of 23 out of 38 students employed, as a result of Project H.E.L.P., is evaluation enough.

6. Referring-Releasing. Once the final assessment is made of the client's progress, the decision must be made to *release with only minor follow-up*, to *recycle through phases of the C.A.P.T.E.R. process*, such as further Conferring, new Placement, and later Evaluation, or to *refer to another agency with minor follow-up*. None of the 38 students was dropped, though the degree of later involvement depended upon the client need.

As shown in Table 6, five students are currently being processed and have not reached the final stage (Referring-Releasing) as yet. Of the remaining 33 students, 17 and 6 (*columns II and III*) were evaluated as successfully trained—by nature of the jobs they held and statements of employers—as the result of

TABLE 6.—*Levels and Percentages of H.E.L.P. Students Referral-Released, Based on Final Evaluation (N=38)*

Students:	I. Currently Being Processed	II. Employed: Released w/Minor Follow-up	III. Trained: Job-Hunting w/Minor Follow-up	IV. Recycling: Further H.E.L.P. Training	V. Referred: No Further Process in H.E.L.P.	VI. Referred: Advanced Training Elsewhere
Number	5	17	6	6	2	2
Percentage of 38	13%	61%		16%	5%	5%

the H.E.L.P. effort. When taken as a percentage of 33, the 23 students comprise about 70 percent of the clients; when considered as part of the total pool of 38 students, the percentage still remains high at 60 percent and may be higher when all 38 are trained.

The remaining students are being given additional assistance: 16 percent through more participation in the Project (Assessing, Placing, and Training—an abbreviated C.A.P.T.E.R. process); 5 percent are believed beyond the resources of the Project and are referred with follow-up; another 5 percent were found capable of more intensive training in a school or program, also with follow-up.

Case Materials

To illustrate how the C.A.P.T.E.R. model functions and what the outcomes were, the following brief cases are presented.

In Case 1, the student is successfully completing the program and hopes to hold a full-time job at the same site as O.J.T.

Case 1.

An employment opportunity was established in the maintenance department of a local town for *Harold*, a 21-year-old severely epileptic and mentally retarded man, contacts being made by the H.E.L.P. staff. Conferring with the client, the job supervisor from the State Rehabilitation Commission, and the town manager, an assessment having been made, an on-job training program was established over nine months with wages totaling $2,100. After training had begun, the city's insurance broker raised questions about the municipality's liability and expense should the handicapped trainee be injured. Once the broker learned that the existing policy covered workers of all abilities, the counselor started to work closely with the young man: for two weeks they mopped, dusted, vacuumed, and scrubbed together until the trainee showed the basic skill and orientation to continue training independently. Evaluations periodically are carried out to see that work progresses. Currently, the student is finishing his training period and expects to remain on the job permanently.

In Case 2, the client received a full cycle of the C.A.P.T.E.R. process and is holding a full-time job; prior to employment, however, the H.E.L.P. staff were called upon to counsel the student on personal matters that had little to do with job training. But until these "family" problems were solved, other concerns were secondary.

Case 2.

Carol is a 20-year-old woman with cerebral palsy. She is ambulatory with the help of crutches, has a high school diploma, and lives with her unemployed mother and young sister. On June 25, 1975, the H.E.L.P. staff held interviews with Carol and her mother, learning that the mother planned to remarry shortly and that it would be difficult for Carol to remain in the home. Hence, she needed both a job and a place to live. Assessment had not previously been completed; hence, TOWER and Singer tests were administered. It was learned that Carol had no strong manual skills and only limited verbal ones. But before placement could be attempted, she needed housing. One of the H.E.L.P. staff knew of a family with a disabled wife who needed someone to live in. Carol agreed and helped the wife for three weeks until Carol's father and grandfather interceded and insisted that she receive additional job training, a decision with which the counseling staff agreed. A job at a bank was located, though it was doubtful that Carol could handle it without an extended orientation period. The Division of Vocational Rehabilitation provided funds for the on-job training phase, which began in the Atlantic County Work Opportunity Center, where the work conditions were constructed, and moved to the bank site once the requisite skills were obtained. After three months, the bank began picking up the salary and Rehabilitation phased out support. Currently, Carol is working as a file clerk in the bank, is supporting herself, and is living in an apartment.

Not all H.E.L.P. cases ended so successfully; in at least two, the students were either *unwilling* to receive counseling and placement or were *incapable* of extensive training. The Project continues to assist these clients, though little more can be done.

Case 3.

Robert is a 21-year-old man from a poor family. Besides being evaluated as mentally retarded, he has been arrested for drug use. He lives at home with his mother (his parents are separated) but lives a normally independent social life. He was referred to Project H.E.L.P. by the state Division of Mental Retardation. An initial conference with Robert was held on April 24, 1975. The counselors' general impression was that he was capable of various types of employment with sufficient training. As a first step in assessment, the counseling staff requested that Robert register himself with the state Division of Vocational Rehabilitation, so that records could be made available to the H.E.L.P. staff. The applicant was skeptical, however, and did not generally trust state agencies; as a result, he did not register with the state. Other offers of assistance from the Project were also turned down, even help in filing for a drivers license. Though the Project staff made occasional visits to Robert's house, in order to overcome distrust, he still did not seek help from the counselors. Robert was discontinued from the program before the assessment phase was under way.

Case 4.
Bonnie is 20 years old, an emotionally disturbed, trainable retarded, and is Black. She lives with foster parents who work as baby sitters and foster parents for the community. She was referred to Project H.E.L.P. by her foster mother, who heard through local welfare agencies of the occupational assistance available. Conferring began on May 6, 1975; assessment was immediately begun. It was learned that Bonnie was still in special education classes in the public school, grade 12, but that her mental abilities were so limited that she was unable to take advantage of most classroom experiences. Her school day consisted of a sewing class; she did not read, write, or communicate verbally. More assessing was called for. The counselors checked with the Division of Vocational Rehabilitation, requesting data on her case. Within a week, the information was received, indicating that she had a low IQ and only limited physical-motor skills. Furthermore, she had emotional problems. The H.E.L.P. staff decided that Bonnie posed too great a problem to community-based jobs and that she required a closely supervised work situation. Checking for support with the Youth and Family Services agency of New Jersey, the counselors learned that Bonnie was eligible for support in a sheltered workshop. She was then referred to the Atlantic County Work Opportunity Center's sheltered workshop, funds provided through Youth and Family Services. The Project counselors checked monthly with the student and the foster mother to see that Bonnie was continuing.

Conclusions and Recommendations

It appears that a small, personalized, and well-structured occupational training program for the severely handicapped has great potential. Project H.E.L.P. was able to place and train a number of young adults, ages 15 to 35, who had a variety of handicaps: cerebral palsy, emotional disturbances, mental retardation, and orthopedic limitations. The use of a logical and sequential—yet flexible—process of Conferring, Assessing, Placing, Training, Evaluating, and, finally, Releasing/Referring (C.A.P.T.E.R.) proved appropriate for the 38 clients admitted to Project H.E.L.P. in 1975. As a public school program, the Handicapped Employability Learning Program was able to draw clients from the rolls of various programs and agencies including the New Jersey Rehabilitation Commission, the area Guidance Center, the Opportunity Center for the Handicapped, and the Association for Retarded Citizens.

Claims for the success of this Project should, however, be cautious. Data are not yet collected on the long-term effects of H.E.L.P. Perhaps Atlantic County is unique, with its long history of programs and institutions devoted to the handicapped. Perhaps New Jersey's model legislation for the assistance of the handicapped gave the Project a special edge. Or perhaps the particular dedication of the counseling staff and the administrative team of the Longport district makes H.E.L.P. a special phenomenon. Only a longitudinal study of the 38 students will allow us to learn of the utility of programs like H.E.L.P.; only the transfer of similar projects to other school districts (more urban, less urban, perhaps) will indicate the generalizability of these findings and the applicability of the model.

The results from the project show that 38 students were placed and trained, after a screening and assessment effort. Thirty-three have completed one cycle and five are being processed. Data show that 61 percent of the 38 students are deemed employable or are employed, 26 percent need further work, and 13 percent are just starting. The cost of the project was high: budgeted at $63,257 for 34 clients, or $1,860.50 per student. But at the current rate of 38 students per 9 months, H.E.L.P. should easily reach 75 students by the end of the 18-month funding period, cutting per pupil costs to $843.43, a difference of over a thousand dollars per student. (One might also assume that the second 75 students might be yet less costly, as the advisors become more expert.)

Some recommendations seem appropriate from the H.E.L.P. experience:

1. State goals clearly, in terms of client group, hoped for results, and process. Project H.E.L.P. knew from the onset who its constituency was and what it wanted to do.

2. Work closely with other agencies. Since other organizations have worked with many handicapped young adults before they are ready for job placement and training, programs like H.E.L.P. should draw upon their expertise and support. Furthermore, handicapped people are entitled to financial assistance from the federal (e.g., C.E.T.A.), state (e.g., New Jersey Rehabilitation Department), local (e.g., public school programs), and philanthropic (e.g., Association for Retarded Citizens) agencies. H.E.L.P. grew out of a mutual concern of public schools and other agencies and continued to work closely with them.

3. Utilize a sequential and efficient process for training students. The quality of the counseling and training will depend on the ability of the program to handle a number of students effectively. A process such as C.A.P.T.E.R. (Conferring, Assessing, Placing, Training, Evaluating, and Referring-Releasing) allows each student to receive an appropriate treatment. Counseling the severely handicapped cannot be a casual operation; it should be done thoughtfully and logically.

4. Work small and over an extended period of time. The severely handicapped require special attention and extended support. If the budget allows, projects like H.E.L.P. should be established in the public schools or elsewhere to work with a few who are multiply/severely impaired over a long time: in this case, 38 students for 18 months and longer.

5. Select counselors who understand the handicapped and know the business and public sectors. H.E.L.P. hired a businessman and a handicapped speech therapist, a veteran of Vietnam. Traditional credentials in school counseling do not necessarily qualify personnel to do this kind of work.

6. Utilize all existing and any new data on students in deciding on placement. Assessing the competency of students is vital in a successful training experience. If existing data are inadequate, sophisticated new testing systems like TOWER or Singer are available and should be used. Subjective evaluations by counselors of the emotional and physical states of students should also be useful. Sometimes these gut reactions and displays of confidence can help students work up to their potential. (Don't put over-faith in standardized tests!)

7. Place and supervise students personally and carefully. Students may require that counselors work with them, once the employer has agreed to take a trainee. Counselors should remain on the site until the student is able to work alone.

8. Do not make wage support from employers a precondition for placement. Often an employer is willing and able to provide a training site but has no funds for salary. Since on-job training monies are available for the handicapped and training is more important than salary initially, counselors should negotiate with the supervisor and should "package" wages and stipends for the clients from existing local, state, and federal sources.

9. Be flexible, recycling students through placements and training until a secure situation is found. Severely handicapped people need long-term support in finding jobs, based on past training and the current job market. Counselors should be willing to move students to new sites and to act as a job clearinghouse. The role of counselor to the handicapped should be a permanent one in school systems and rehabilitation agencies.

10. Work to influence school policy; local, state and federal laws; and public attitudes toward the handicapped. All professionals and lay people who work for the rights of the handicapped are part of a national movement. The passage in December, 1975, of P.L. 94-142, the *magna carta* for the handicapped, now requiring equal rights for the impaired, is a keystone in this effort. Certainly leaders in programs like H.E.L.P. have a responsibility to lobby for new programs and use moral persuasion to bring about changes in the opportunities for the handicapped.

ACKNOWLEDGMENTS

Special thanks to H.E.L.P. staff and administration, including counselors Joe Williams, Paul Glenn, Jr., and Ms. Marie Natale and principals Dr. John Glassey and Mr. Tom Caffrey.

List of References

1. Australian Council for Rehabilitation of Disabled. *Educational Equality for the Handicapped: Report of the 5th International Seminar on Special Education.* Surrey Hills, New South Wales, Austral: The Council, 1974.

2. Berkowitz, Monroe, and Anderson, Merilee, *PADEC: An Evaluation of an Experimental Rehabilitation Project.* Brunswick, N.J.: Rutgers Univ., Bur. of Economic Research, 1974.

3. Coleman, James S., and others. *Youth: Transition into Adulthood—Report on Youth of the President's Science Advisory Committee.* Chicago: Univ. of Chicago Pr., 1974.

4. Granger, Ben P. Developing Community-Based, Small-Group Living Programs in Rehabilitation Services. *Rehab. Lit.* June, 1975. 36:6:170-174, 177.

5. Nagy, Karoly. Special Human Services Are a Part of Our Human Concept. *Rehab. Lit.* June, 1975. 36:6:175-177.

6. Payne, James S.; Mercer, Cecil D.; and Epstein, Michael H. *Education and Rehabilitation Techniques.* New York: Behavioral Publications, 1974.

7. Wisland, Milton V. *Psychoeducational Diagnosis of Exceptional Children.* Springfield, Ill. Charles C Thomas, 1974.

Career Attitudes among Boys with and without Specific Learning Disabilities

GRACE BINGHAM

Current conceptualizations of career education for exceptional children emphasize affective experiences and activities in regard to occupational choice, as well as preparation in specific job related skills. Children with specific learning disabilities are among the groups included in career education programs. Typically, such children have had less success with school related tasks than have those without specific learning disabilities. If achievement in school is viewed as the logical precursor of achievement in the broader society, then it might be questioned whether children with specific learning disabilities have incorporated attitudes about themselves and their eventual work behaviors that are reflective of their unsuccessful experiences with school.

Career attitudes refer to the affective rather than intellectual reactions of individuals toward career choice. Incorporated in the concept are the person's feelings related to involvement in the career choice process, orientation toward work, independence in decision making, preference for career choice factors, and conceptions of the career choice process. Crites' (1971) research using the Attitude Scale of the *Career Maturity Index* has shown that attitudes mature with age and grade and that they relate closely to the educational process.

This study examined the extent to which boys with specific learning disabilities differed from those without specific learning disabilities on career attitudes. The null hypothesis of no difference was formulated.

Method

A cross sectional design was used to compare two groups, those with and those without specific learning disabilities at two stages of development, preadolescent (grade 6) and adolescent (grades 9 and 10). Subjects were selected from suburban public school districts in one New Jersey county. The sample consisted of 120 boys: 30 with and 30 without specific learning disabilities at each of the two developmental levels.

The specific learning disabilities group was selected from those youngsters who were classified by the district's child study team as perceptually impaired (the classification used in the state of New Jersey to identify children with specific learning disabilities) and who were in regular class placement.

For both groups, boys were selected who fell within the average intelligence range (one standard deviation above or below the mean on standardized tests of intellectual ability).

All subjects were administered the Attitude Scale of the *Career Maturity Index* (Crites, 1973) to assess career attitudes. Differences in mean career attitude scores were analyzed by the t statistic; the significance level was set at .05.

Results and Discussion

There were significant differences in mean scores between the groups with and without specific learning disabilities at both the preadolescent and adolescent levels. The mean score for preadolescent specific learning disability boys was 25.20 ($sd = 5.03$) as compared to 32.00 ($sd = 5.19$) for preadolescent boys without specific learning disability, yielding a t value of 5.15 ($p < .01$). The mean score for adolescent specific learning disability boys was 31.60 ($sd = 5.00$) as compared to 35.43 ($sd = 4.32$) for adolescent boys without specific learning disabilities, yielding a t value of 3.17 ($p < .01$). On this basis, the null hypothesis was rejected.

Although it is difficult to substantiate which specific attitudinal behaviors are affected by the presence of a learning disability, it is likely that orientation toward work and conceptions of the career choice process may show such influence. Behaviors that have often been observed in children with specific learning disabilities is their difficulty with planning and organization of sequences. Since planning has consistently been shown to be an important correlate of vocational maturity (Super, 1974; Super & Overstreet, 1960), their independence in decision making related to careers is also likely to reflect immaturity.

The significant differences noted in the affective variable of career attitudes between specific learning disability boys and their grade peers at both the preadolescent and adolescent levels would imply that boys with specific learning disabilities are less mature in their responses to demands associated with career choice and would, therefore, need to be provided with carefully planned experiences and activities that accommodate the developmental differences noted in this dimension of vocational maturity.

References

Crites, J. O. *Career maturity inventory: Attitude scale.* Monterey CA: CTB/McGraw-Hill, 1973.

Crites, J. O. *The maturity of vocational attitudes in adolescence.* (American Personnel & Guidance Association Inquiry Series No. 2). Washington DC: American Personnel & Guidance Association, 1971.

Super, D. E. *Measuring vocational maturity for counseling and evaluation.* (National Vocational Guidance Association monograph.) Washington DC: American Personnel & Guidance Association, 1974.

Super, D. E., & Overstreet, P. *The vocational maturity of ninth-grade boys.* New York: Bureau of Publications, Teachers College, Columbia University, 1960.

WHERE DO I GO FROM HERE?

The Involvement of Vocational Rehabilitation and Occupational Education with the Learning Disabled In North Carolina

TOBY JOANNE BLACK, O.T.R.

THE TRENDS of working with learning disabilities are now focused on early identification. Catch the problem before the frustrations of academic work set in. Provide the child with early intervention to minimize his learning problems.

That's fine! Great! I am all for early intervention. But, while our time and money are turned toward the younger

---

Mrs. Black is an occupational therapist at the Child Development Institute, Biological Sciences Research Center, Division for Disorders of Development and Learning, University of North Carolina at Chapel Hill. She graduated from Washington University (1971).

---

set, the children who have already been identified as learning disabled are growing up. Take a look around at your school systems. How many schools provide special programs for the learning disabled on the junior and senior high school level? If you are a professional working in some capacity with the learning disabled, how many adolescents do you see?

I found myself shuddering when I had to evaluate anyone over 11 years old. If the child has perceptual-motor disorders—so what! He's too old to start the "miracle" programs we attempt with younger children. If he continues to demonstrate the same learning problems noted five years ago, we aren't helping him by saying, "You're doing just fine, keep up the good work." Underneath we're actually saying, "Good luck kid. The world is tough but for you it's tougher."

I had almost decided to avoid evaluating or talking to children over 11 because I felt so inadequate with them. This attitude would have continued if I had not taken the time to look at the other professionals around me. We were all in the same boat. No one really knew what to do with these kids who had made it to junior high and senior high school and all the extra help they had received in the lower grades was dropped.

Realistically, we cannot ask six different teachers to present their classwork a special way for one child. The

working world will not adjust its pace for someone who learns "differently" than others. A college professor isn't going to stop his lecture to ask the student if he got the important points. We cannot keep these students under our protective wings forever. But we should not forget that the learning problems do not disappear when someone reaches adolescence.

These children need help and guidance but they do not need us following them around from teacher to teacher, explaining the problems and all the special techniques teachers should use to teach a child with learning problems. They need the services of state facilities that can guide them toward meaningful vocational choices.

I attempted to do a literature scan on facilities, organizations, and methods available to work with the learning-disabled adolescent. There are many studies concerned with reading, visual, and auditory problems of children with learning disabilities. But, there has been little written on how to guide a student who can't make it in the world of $2 + 2$ or A, B, C.

I had the following two cases in mind when I decided to investigate possible resources for these adolescents:

1. Jerry

Jerry is a 16-year-old eighth grader. Jerry is reading at a fourth-grade level; his writing needs a translator; his math ability is grade appropriate or above; and his recent IQ score was 105. He has been called "lazy," "stupid," and "dumb" by his peers.

The teachers describe Jerry as unmotivated and constituting a classroom behavior problem. His parents view him as a bright boy who is bored with school and has stopped trying. Jerry views himself as a failure at everything he tries.

The local school system developed a program to help identify children with learning problems. Jerry was among several in his grade referred for further educational and psychological testing. The test results showed a scattering of skills from a 9-year age level to an 18-year age level.

Jerry and his parents were called in for an interpretation of the test. Because he is unable to express his

"Where Do I Go From Here? The Involvement of Vocational Rehabilitation an Occupational Education with the Learning Disabled in North Carolina," Toby Joanne Black, O.T.R., *Rehabilitation Literature*, Vol. 37, No. 6, June 1976, Pg. 168-171, ©1976 by the National Easter Seal Society for Crippled Children and Adults, 2023 W. Ogden Avenue, Chcago, Ill, 60612 thoughts in writing and because he is reading at a lower grade level than are his peers, he can be classified as learning disabled.

This official label will enable Jerry to receive special help with some of his problem academic areas. But, is this going to change the eight years of frustrations he has already experienced in school? Can Jerry now act "normal" because he has finally been given an "excuse" for his failures?

The success rate for remedial help at Jerry's age is very low. When Jerry was told that the extra tutoring might help him catch up, his comment was, "If I can't make it in school, where do I go from here?"

2. *Linda*

Linda is an 18-year-old college freshman. She lived in a small town that had one elementary school and one junior-senior high school. She had difficulty learning to read and she writes from right to left if she does not watch her work. Her spelling rarely agrees with Webster's.

No one working with Linda expressed concern over her difficulties. She is aware of reversals and the backward writing that she tends to do and will correct them from time to time.

She came to the University to major in biology. Most of her freshman courses were subjects familiar to her, with the exception of chemistry. Linda found that she was reversing formulas in her notes or on a test and finally had to drop the course.

Linda's advisor referred her for some further evaluation of her problems. It was verified that Linda has visual and written reversals. So what? She has gone through 12 years of school and is seeking further education. Where does she go from here?

Services Currently Available Through Vocational Rehabilitation and Occupational Education

The cases that were briefly discussed are very typical in the identification of learning problems. Evaluation of a student may not occur before high school. Diagnostic testing may usually be done to evaluate a behavior problem. A difficult problem arises if the behavior problem is *secondary* to a learning disability. This complicates what may have been an "easy" placement for the student. He is too smart to be held back in school, he is not performing at the current grade level so as to benefit from school, and he is still a behavior problem.

Alternatives could include attending technical school, a continued struggling through the current school situation, quitting school, or being referred to Vocational Rehabilitation. Vocational Rehabilitation may be the best alternative for the student to pursue.

There are 34 cooperative Educational/Rehabilitation Units in North Carolina. These Units were established in secondary schools to allow Vocational Rehabilitation to identify the physically and mentally handicapped at an early age. The eligible student would have training, job placement, and follow-up available to him through Vocational Rehabilitation.

A Vocational Rehabilitation program in the school system helps provide cooperative services to the student while he is in school, during specific training, and through to job placement. This provides for continuous training without a gap of delinquency or unemployment.

Students can become part-time clients of Vocational Rehabilitation, starting at age 14. When school services are terminated, they become full-time clients.

A program was established as a result of the Vocational Education Amendment of 1968 to help fill in the gap between identification of problems and acceptance into a Vocational Rehabilitation program. This program is called Occupational Education for the Disadvantaged. (Persons who have academic or other handicaps resulting from socioeconomic or cultural impoverishment that prevent them from succeeding in regular vocational education programs designed for persons without such handicaps come under the definition of *disadvantaged*.)

This program may take place after regular school hours or on weekends or it may supplement the regular program in which the student is enrolled. It can include over-aged persons in grades below high school or in early high school. The programs can be prevocational, preexploratory, or related "academic" (but directly related to vocational training).

In April and May of 1974, a survey was taken among teachers and local administrators in North Carolina to evaluate the attitudes, ideas, and needs of person charged with the responsibility for special programs. The following statement summarizes the general feeling for these programs:

I feel that too much time is lost in workshops identifying the disadvantaged. This is a simple task. The real problem is developing learning packages that will reach the needs of these students. The masses of our teachers are not equipped educationally or emotionally to deal with this problem. You have to have experience of dealing with twelve or fifteen of these students each day to really know how frustrating it can be to deal with these students as compared to a normal group. We need less "what to do" and more "how to do" when it comes to planning and developing programs for the disadvantaged and handicapped.[8]

The teachers in this program are to have met minimum requirements for certification in special education, vocational guidance, or general education (relating to basic skills and knowledges necessary to succeed in occupational programs). They must also receive 6 units of credit or meet minimum requirements for certification in one of the following occupational subjects areas: agriculture education, home economics education, health occupation education, distributive business and office education, trade and industrial education, or introduction to vocations and middle grades occupational exploration.

The Occupational Education programs have to be acknowledged by the State Board of Education as having a general application to average students.

Some characteristics or conditions that apply to a disadvantaged student are: Lacks money for school expenses; lacks proper clothing, food, and housing; comes from an impoverished cultural background; failing in two or more subjects; is a potential dropout; is functioning below the state achievement norms; defies rules and regulations; is hostile; has poor self-image; or is consistently truant from school or absent from home.

Even if a student demonstrates more than one of these characteristics, he cannot qualify for this program unless he has not been able to succeed in a regular program of occupational education.

The teachers are supposed to help modify a regular occupational educational program so it will meet the needs of the disadvantaged students more adequately. This could entail smaller classes for more individualized teaching, after school or week-end work with students, or specific demonstrations. The teachers also work with the family to help them obtain the fullest benefits available from programs and services provided by educational and noneducational agencies.

The teachers are very interested in their work, but they are required to handle all aspects in planning with and for the disadvantaged student. They are not adequately prepared to handle the many problems that occur with this group.

The work done in Occupational Education can have a direct effect on how Vocational Rehabilitation picks up the client.

Federal law mandates that all states provide services including, but not limited to, a comprehensive list of specific medical, therapeutic, training, and related services. They must also offer other goods and services that may benefit a handicapped person in terms of employment. There is no upper or lower age limit although the requirement for potential employment tends to limit the age of persons served.

Resources vary a great deal from state to state. Local legislatures make their own decisions on the amount of money budgeted for these services and this has an impact on the extent of services.

Limited funds result in a "screening-out" of the population who are neglected or inadequately served. Few high schools offer more than minimal opportunities for prevocational and vocational education.

The Rehabilitation Act of 1973 requires that top priority be given to those with "severe handicaps." This law places a heavy burden on State Vocational Rehabilitation Services to serve severely handicapped persons first.

Vocational Rehabilitation can provide the following services to the learning disabled:

Prevocational evaluation of the vocational potential of the client.
Prevocational training involving activities necessary for specific vocational evaluation and training.
Vocational evaluation accumulating all available information necessary to identify the individual with a specific vocational objective.
Vocational training for the development of personal attributes and specific skills necessary for success in a specific job.

Personnel should meet with the parents and teachers for program planning, which may include curriculum changes to meet unmet needs. Vocational Rehabilitation should provide guidance and counseling, job placement, and follow-up for their clients.

Students like Jerry and Linda could benefit from guidance and counseling by qualified Vocational Rehabilitation Counselors. They need to be directed toward beneficial programs that provide training to meet their *intellectual* goals as well as their performance abilities.

What Is Actually Being Done and What Can Be Done?

In North Carolina, Vocational Rehabilitation has given thought to the learning disabled population in high school. The Educational/Rehabilitation Unit in the secondary schools is a good example of the efforts that have been made. But, because of the many factors involved with a learning-disabled student, secondary school may be too late. The emotional aspects and the loss of interest in school that can occur by age 14 will cost Vocational Rehabilitation a lot of money in time and counseling expended.

In the fall of 1974, all students in special education classes were mainstreamed into the regular classrooms. The main load of Vocational Rehabilitation clients in the high school setting are students classified as mentally retarded. Because these students have been identified and will qualify for Vocational Rehabilitation services, they are of main concern to the counselors. They do not have time or funds to seek out the learning disabled who can also benefit from these services.

People working in the State Office of the Division for Exceptional Children have approached state officials in the Department of Vocational Rehabilitation on the topic of services for the learning disabled. These students do qualify for Vocational Rehabilitation services if their disabilities are properly diagnosed. The problem is that no one has gone out of his way to let people know how services are available or even to identify this group.

There is poor communication between Occupational

Education, Vocational Rehabilitation, and the Division for Exceptional Children in North Carolina. State representatives in these areas have commented on this problem and feel that, if the services can pull themselves together on this topic, these students could receive services as early as 10 years of age.

A realistic proposal is for these students to be screened in elementary school by service through the Division for Exceptional Children, to be given vocational experiences by Occupational Education, and to be counseled and/or trained by Vocational Rehabilitation in high school.

Currently, not much is being done in North Carolina (or the rest of the country) with this group. There are no studies or articles concerning any aspect of working with learning-disabled students in elementary school to prepare them for vocational rehabilitation.

These students can usually perform tasks with their hands if given enough time and experience. They do not fit well in sheltered workshops because their intellectual abilities are higher than those of the clients placed for repetitive training or task analysis. They perform well in a structured setting where the routine is familiar but offers some variety. Many of these students can do well in college if they are carefully counseled in a vocational choice and they can avoid areas that present learning difficulties for them.

Jerry is a student who could have benefited from Occupational Education in junior high school. Although he could be picked up by Vocational Rehabilitation, he will need several years of counseling to help prepare him for an appropriate vocational choice.

Linda needs close supervision to help her stay in college by choosing an area for her major in which she can expand her interests and be successful. When in elementary school, she would have benefited from a screening project that would have helped her cope with her learning problems. She would be more aware of the vocational opportunities she can seek in a university setting.

There are many students who become behavior problems or drop-outs or who just "hang in there." Such students may be identified as learning disabled while in elementary school, but no vocational services are provided them until high school or, in some areas, not until after high school. Unless the parents can seek help from a mental health clinic, church organizations, or youth groups, these students have nothing going for them except a label.

If Occupational Education can help provide experiences in elementary school so that these children have an opportunity to develop vocational skills and successful experiences, they can be picked up by Vocational Rehabilitation in high school and be better prepared to make decisions for their future.

Vocational Rehabilitation definitely has a place in working with the learning disabled but personnel need to work closely with those in other state services to spread out the cost and time for these students. They need to let the public know that they work with persons other than the mentally or physically handicapped and that counseling is an available and valuable service.

Although this information is focused on the state of North Carolina, it is very applicable to the rest of the country. No one had the answers I was looking for but I found that sitting back waiting is a slow process.

What is the situation in your state?

Bibliography and List of References

1. *Cooperative School Programs.* Services Available Through the Department of Public Instruction. Raleigh, N.C.: Div. of Vocational Rehabilitation.

2. *Guidelines for Endorsement of Teachers in Disadvantaged/Handicapped Programs.* Raleigh, N.C.: Div. of Occupational Education.

3. Hellmuth, Jerome, *ed. Learning Disorders. Vol. I.* Seattle, Wash.: Special Child Publications, 1965.

4. Into the Mainstream. *Closer Look.* Summer, 1974.

5. North Carolina State Department of Public Instruction. *Occupational Education for the Disadvantaged Through Utilization of Man-Months.* Raleigh, N.C.: Div. of Occupational Education, Jan., 1974.

6. North Carolina State Department of Public Instruction. *Plan of Action: Occupational Education Programs for the Disadvantaged/Handicapped.* Raleigh, N.C.: Div. of Occupational Education, Nov., 1974.

7. North Carolina State Department of Public Instruction. *Programs for the Disadvantaged and Handicapped.* Raleigh, N.C.: Div. of Occupational Education, Feb., 1974.

8. North Carolina Department of Public Instruction. *Report on Attitudinal Survey and Needs Assessment Relative to Programs for the Disadvantaged/Handicapped.* Raleigh, N.C.: Div. of Occupational Education, Aug., 1974.

9. Towne, Douglas C., and Wallace, Sydney. *Vocational Instructional Materials for Students with Special Needs.* Portland, Ore.: Northwest Regional Educational Laboratory, 1972.

CAREER EDUCATIONAL MATERIALS FOR THE LEARNING DISABLED

Edited by: Carlene Van Etten, EdS, and Bill Watson, EdD

High school counselors expend much effort assisting students in planning for their futures. Teachers present career and vocational units, take students on field trips, bring in guest speakers, and provide reading material about various occupations. When the pupil who is considering career planning also has a learning disability, the teacher and counselor must even more carefully plot exploration of possible jobs — in the elementary school curriculum as well as at the secondary level.

Part of our efforts should also be directed toward earlier introduction of vocational information into the school curriculum. The last few years have, in fact, seen a move toward earlier introduction of career awareness activities and exploration of the world of work. This development seems a positive step in the direction of lessening the "I graduate in May, what am I going to do now?" problem.

This column does not attempt to address itself to the current issue of whether the major emphasis in secondary programming should be on basic skills, with career education as a subunit, or on a career education as the primary teaching goal. We do feel, however, that career awareness must be at least a part of the total curriculum for the learning disabled student. Further, many varied, and careful opportunities for exploring career possibilities will more likely result in job selections which will minimize the effect of various learning disabilities in individual students.

We have included examples of career awareness, career exploration, and planning materials. Materials for young children are reviewed here, as well as materials suitable for secondary programming. We have also included materials in a variety of formats. — C.V.E., B.W.

Occupations (Deluxe Inlay Puzzles). *Judy Co., 310 N. Second St., Minneapolis, Minn. 55401. Price: $3.10.*
Judy Company offers a set of Occupations puzzles (wood inlay) recommended for ages 4 through 6. Users of these puzzles have the choice of puzzles with either black or white characters. Each puzzle illustrates specific activities which make up the job illustrated, offering children the opportunity to become aware of a variety of career possibilities at an early age. Occupation titles are printed on the puzzles so children who are learning to read can become familiar with job names.

In this set of puzzles, the expanding role of women in the occupations and professions has been recognized. For example, the Lawyer and Judge puzzles picture a female judge and both female and male lawyers. The Pilot Puzzle also shows both male and female pilots. Another puzzle pictures a telephone line*person*.

Stated objectives for these puzzles are (1) to introduce various occupations to children, (2) to sort and classify occupations in several ways, (3) to stimulate creative role-playing, and (4) to develop hand-eye coordination.

6. EDUCATION

Accompanying every Judy puzzle is a guide which provides ideas for extending use of the puzzle beyond usually expected activity. Ideas for field trips, interviews, and other activities appear in this section. Ideas for games of creative dramatic and occupations further extend the usual puzzle activity. A teacher of young children with a selection of these puzzles and the accompanying teaching suggestions would have excellent career awareness materials at his fingertips.

Similar to the Occupation Puzzles are the Judy Floor Puzzles from Judy Company ($9.75). Two of these five puzzles show the doctor and the firefighter and are also useful in discussing occupations with the young child.

Life Career. *Western Publ., 850 Third Ave. New York, N.Y. 10022. Price. $35.*
Life Career provides a simulated setting in which participants may learn how the labor market, educational opportunities, marriage, and leisure patterns operate in American society. Although the primary audience is high school and college students, the manual suggests other groups may find the material useful.

This material is developed on the premise that there are four basic requirements necessary for making intelligent decisions about future careers. First, there is the need for students to imagine what the future will be like. This material provides a simulated environment in which students may meaningfully learn how decisions and actions they will make in a few years will affect their future. Second, it is imperative that students have accurate information about the types of opportunities and alternatives available. This requirement recognizes the enormous amount of information about jobs and schools which confronts young people as well as their counselors and teachers.

Providing students with a sense of how a life-cycle is patterned recognizes a third requirement necessary for selecting a job. To assist students in understanding how the selection of a career affects all aspects of life, this game requires the student to allocate time between school, studying, job, family, leisure, and other personal demands. The fourth requirement recognizes that practice in making decisions is important. The entire process of the Life Career game is designed to meet this need.

Students move through an 8-year time span as the decision-makers for a fictitious person presented to them in a profile or case history. The same profile is given to teams of decision-makers who compete with each other. Students are required to plan how their person will spend a typical week during each of the 8 years (rounds).

The manual notes the students ideally should work through each of the four profiles included. If time is limited, it is suggested that the profile which most closely resembles the participants be selected. Profiles of low ability are more difficult in terms of planning for the future. Therefore, students have the opportunity to see firsthand what a difference grades and further schooling may make in terms of the future.

A separate Spinner and Scoring Booklet contains the rationale for various scores as well as instructions for scoring. Scoring is based on common sense and actual data about American society. For example, good grades earn higher scores than poor ones. Likewise, high-paying, prestigious jobs earn more points than low-paying, less secure jobs. Events such as the loss of a job or a divorce result in loss of points. The scoring model is developed so that higher total scores are obtained for a combination of appropriate activities that suit the profile. This careful attention to scoring helps assure a more realistic simulated experience.

In the back of the Scoring Booklet is a spinner which is used at various points in the simulation process to increase the elements of chance. For example, the team may decide that it wants the profile person to marry or go back to school. The actual choice is dependent on the selection as indicated by the spinner.

When the team has worked through the step-by-step instructions, it takes the record sheet to the scorer's table. After the record sheet is scored, then one team member draws an Unplanned Event Card. These cards may indicate that the profile person has had a child, has been drafted, divorced, or a number of other unexpected occurrences. The unplanned events must be considered as players begin the next round with their profile person. Both the spinners and cards are included because it is important to understand that luck does play a part in every person's life.

The time required to play the game is dependent on what is to be accomplished. Though playing time varies with age and ability, 6 hours is necesssary to complete the game with one or two discussions. However, the game can be stopped at any point then begun again at the next class session.

A particularly beneficial section of the manual includes specific ideas for adapting the game profiles to meet more nearly the realities of local situations. There is also a section which provides the instructor with ideas for enriching and extending the game beyond its original form. The appendix includes a number of questions which students may ask, along with the possible answers.

In any simulation, the process is a critical factor. Content may be relevant, appropriate, and important, but be overwhelmed by the process. The Player's Rules and the Instructor's Manual of Life Career are designed to insure a reasonable balance between process and content important to the learning disabled student. Also the total game can be easily adapted to local situations and to a wide variety of levels of student ability.

Job Experience Kits. *Science Research Associates, 259 E. Erie St., Chicago, Ill. 60611. Price: $176.55.*
The Job Experience Kits are designed to provide sample work experience for eight, ninth, and tenth graders. The primary purpose is to stimulate students' interest in exploring various careers, rather than to provide the information necessary for making a career choice. The kits may be used for group guidance classes, for part of a career unit in the classroom, or for individual counseling.

The 20 simulated work experiences which make up this program, cover a wide range of abilities, interest, and levels of preparation. Representative examples include beautician, truck driver, secretary, police officer, lawyer, and veterinarian. Eight of the Job Experience Kits cover occupations which can be learned through high school courses or on-the-job training. Eight others require some formal post-high school training. Only four of the job kits describe an occupation requiring a college degree.

Each kit contains a booklet on the career topic and a pad of 30 answer sheets. The booklets have a modified programmed format with questions and answers interspersed with narrative and illustrative text.

Some kits have supplementary items. For example, the truck driver kit has maps. The appliance servicemen kit contains three circuit boards, one circuit tester, and a battery. The draftsman kit contains a T-square, compass, some special drawing paper, as well as a few other occupationally related items. The fact that actual tools of the trade have been included should appeal to many students.

There has been an attempt to design the kits to assure that students can answer the first problems successfully. Initial questions are easily answered by referring to the preceding page. Though the student is never required to memorize facts, he must draw on what he has learned as he progresses through the booklet.

The student is responsible for keeping his own score and record. If he answers correctly, he places a plus on the answer sheet. Each booklet has a numbered rating, based on field test data, which is used as a definition of success.

The guide to the use of the Job Experience Kits provides some background on the development of the program. It also contains some specific suggestions for how the kits might be used. Also there is a report on the field test data, a somewhat unusual, but most welcome addition to a manual.

Exploring Careers, Group I. *Society for Visual Education, 1345 Diversey Pkwy, Chicago, Ill. 60614. Price: 6 filmstrips and 3 records, guide $54.50; 6 filmstrips and 3 cassettes, guide $60.50.*
Exploring Careers, Group I, presented on a sound filmstrip, is designed to present a realistic view of six occupations. The six occupations presented are telephone installer, broadcast technician, newspaper reporter, automotive mechanic, airline cabin attendant, and long-haul truck driver. As indicated in the teacher's instruction, it is suited for upper intermediate, junior and senior high, as well as community college.

We express some reservations about the use at the community college level unless students were unsophisticated and relatively unschooled. Likewise, the careful attention to many specifics of the jobs might make it inappropriate for some students of intermediate age who would neither want nor need such highly specific information about jobs. Both content and manner of presentation make them seem much more appropriate to the junior and senior high level student.

Each filmstrip, with accompanying narration on record or cassette, describes the nature of the job and presents information about the education, training, special skills, and experience required for the job. Also included is information about job availability and future potential for employment. The pay, possible advancement, and some advantages and disadvantages of the job are also described.

Presentation time varies from 16 to 18 minutes. The particular use made of the follow-up will determine the total time.

An individual Teacher's Guide with each filmstrip lists the objectives and contains a complete script. The records and cassettes are prepared with both an audible and inaudible advance signal.

The series would make a valuable addition to a school audiovisual library since it provides a resource for both small groups and individuals who are interested in choosing a job. The series could also be used to develop separate units on careers in the transportation and communications industry. The filmstrips are interesting and the narration, though not particularly exciting, is well done. Generally speaking, it is a good audiovisual presentation.

Pacemaker Vocational Readers: *L. Glasner and M. Thypin. Fearon Publ., 6 Davis Dr., Belmont, Calif. 49002. Price: 5 copies of 10 books plus 2 teacher's guides, boxed — list $128, school $96; 5 cassettes plus 2 books on each cassette in binder — list $56, school $42.*

Pacemaker Vocational Readers, a series of 10 paperback books on a wide range of vocational topics, are designed for the secondary student with reading disabilities. Designed to be taught as a unit, each reader is accompanied by a teacher's guide.

Books contain general source material for the teacher and student and a list of recommended films, and guides for individual books have sections both for those words not in the Pacemaker Core Vocabulary and on background information, discussion, suggestions, activities, and teaching resources.

The editors of the column asked a second-grade teacher to have children in her class read the books and record their errors. The teacher reported that pupils in her top reading group read the material without error. Average readers were able to read and comprehend the material although there was occasional difficulty with specific occupational terms.

Pupils in the lowest reading groups in the second-grade class had more difficulty with the books; however, the major problem was vocabulary specific to the occupation. Comprehension appeared to be adequate. Granted the limitations of such sampling, students at the secondary level would probably have little difficulty either reading or comprehending the content of the Vocational Readers.

The books are illustrated with black and white photographs by Bernard Vidal. The photographs are very well done and provide excellent context clues to the reader. In fact, they are so well done the poor reader may choose to study the pictures carefully rather than read the text. In the back of each text is a Picture Dictionary. In a few instances, only a label appears because a complete definition would involve words at a higher reading level.

The 10 jobs described in the books require almost no entry-level skills and, according the teacher's guide, "are ones that special need students have demonstrated they can succeed in." The first three of the 10 books describe jobs; the last seven stories deal with full-time vocations.

Care has been taken to avoid negative ethnic and sexual implications. Four books feature girls as the main character and six feature boys. In books such as "Power On and Start Print" on the job of duplicating room worker, both boys and girls are shown on the job. The main character in "Until Joe Comes Back" is David Martinez; in "I'll Try Tomorrow" (gardener) the main character is Jerry, an Anglo; and in "Give the Kid a Chance" (baker's helper) James is a black.

This series gets high marks in almost every category. Whether the major emphasis is on reading or career education, the Pacemaker Vocational Series would be a useful tool in most special education classrooms serving pupils in elementary and secondary classes.

Occupation Word Hunts I & II. *Developmental Learning Materials, 7440 Natchez Ave. Niles, Ill. 60648. Price: $30.*

Occupation Word Hunts I and II are designed "to provide career awareness for the older student as well as provide visual-perceptual practice skill." Ten spirit masters comprise each set.

The child is presented with a matrix of letters within which are the correct spellings of occupational titles. The occupations are grouped into various categories. In Occupational Word Hunt I, there are 39 job titles under the following 10 categories: community service, transportation, military, stores, arts, sports, school, services, law and farming and natural resources.

In Word Hunt II, 105 occupation titles are listed in the following 10 categories: office workers, communications, doctor of medicine, health careers, financial careers, political careers, tradesman, life science careers, entertainment and crafts or trades.

The level of difficulty between Word Hunts I and II and between lessons 1 to 10 is considerable. Occupational Word Hunt II appears to meet the publisher's aim of providing career awareness and visual discrimination practice for the older student better than Word Hunt I. Word Hunt II, with the exception of the tradesmen and crafts or trades categories, definitely focuses on professional careers. Many of these careers may not be within the realistic aspirations of older students with serious learning disabilities. However, most of the occupations are open to youngsters with less severe learning difficulties, especially those listed in Word Hunt I. The value of these lessons for visual perceptual practice is questionable unless this means improved spelling by means of practice on visual memory tasks.

Career Card File. *Developmental Learning Materials, 7440 Natchez Ave., Niles, Ill. 60648. Price: $25.*
Career Card File provides a large number of classroom-tested ideas for the development of reading and arithmetic skills as a by-product of studying nine career areas plus a group of general career awareness activities. The career areas include auto mechanic, carpenter, food service, hair styling, law enforcement, plumber, postal service, telephone worker, and truck driver.

Although these appear to be excellent materials, the statement that the materials foster "the development of reading and arithmetic skills" is misleading. Reading and, to a lesser extent, arithmetic tasks are involved, but only for the purpose of practicing skills already learned. Further, when the statement is made that the materials have been "classroom-tested," teachers would have more confidence in the statement if a brief description of that testing were given.

The activities are described on 225 color-coded 5- by 8-inch cards. Eighteen black and white Occupational Photographs and two illustrations complement the Career Card File. In this file is a list of Career Information Sources and a Key to Objectives. The latter is an alphabetic index of subject area and skills purportedly taught by the suggested activities. For example, under Categorizing is a reference to the suggestion on card 1 in the Career Awareness Activities.

Called From Product to Source, one card asks the students to think of how many people, by job title, are involved in serving and supplying the ingredients for a hamburger. After the lists are prepared, the students are asked to classify the workers according to the 15-cluster approach of the U.S. Office of Education which is given. Another suggestion is to have the class prepare its own Dictionary of Occupational Titles.

Also included in the file under each occupational title is a bibliography of other materials

available. The Key to Objectives greatly increases the usefulness of these materials.

Career Association Cards. *Developmental Learning Materials, 7440 Natchez Ave., Niles, Ill. 60648. Price: $5.50.*
Career Association Cards show four pictures of people engaged in various occupational tasks. Three of the occupations are related and the fourth is not. The set consists of 30 cards picturing 120 occupations. A major advantage of this material is the large number of ways it can be used and the wide range of task difficulty. At the simplest level, the pictures can be labeled in terms of the occupation portrayed. The cards can be used to stimulate a discussion of occupations and the equipment associated with them. At a higher level, the student may be asked to identify the occupation not related to the other three.

For a still more abstract task, he may also be asked to tell how the three occupations are related. The latter task can be quite difficult. In one picture which shows people in a football stadium, a baseball field, a hockey rink, and a gymnasium, the similarity is that the person shown in the dominant position is a referee or umpire in three pictures; in one picture the only person shown is the player. The stimulation of such high level cognitive tasks as seeing similarities and identifying categories in a nonreading format makes this material useful for handicapped pupils.

Career Environment Cards. *Developmental Learning Materials, 7440 Natchez Ave., Niles, Ill. 60648. Price: $2.25.*
Career Environment Cards are made up of 15 colored drawings of career-associated people and 15 drawings of matching career environments. The career-associated people shown are a scuba diver, photographer, pressman, dancer, football player, baker, minister, TV cameraman, airplane mechanic, judge, logger, life guard, jockey, librarian, and horticulturist. On the instruction sheet, four uses are described: (1) to stimulate motor and visual image, (2) to encourage verbalization of ideas suggested by the pictures, (3) to formulate statements relating the two pictures, and (4) to provide an interest in career alternatives. The cards appear to be most useful in stimulating verbal and written expression. Their use in career awareness appears only to be secondary.

A good deal is also made in the instruction sheet of their usefulness in stimulating visual, motor, and kinesthetic imagination. There is perhaps some face validity in these statements;

however, no data are offered and other attempts as specification of these terms has not been generally successful.

Career Identity Cards. *Developmental Learning Materials, 7440 Natchez Ave., Niles, Ill. 60648. Price: $2.75.*
Career Identity Cards consist of 15 cards showing career-associated people and 15 cards depicting matching, career-related objects. Careers identified are Air Force pilot, astronaut, butcher, construction worker, disc jockey, fashion illustrator, florist, keypunch operator, musician, painter, policewoman, sanitation worker, telephone serviceman, upholsterer, and X-ray technician. The stated purpose for these cards is the same as for the Career Environment Cards. The instruction sheets indicate that the Career Identity Cards are appropriate for older students. Since the drawings are somewhat more complex than the Environment Cards, this is probably true.

In order to facilitate checking of independent work, "the short red lines will connect to make one longer line when the cards are paired correctly." This is true. However, since the career-associated people cards all have a short red line in the lower right-hand corner, and the career-related object cards all have the short red line in the lower left-hand corner, the student can make a long line when matching a telephone serviceman and a police car as well as when matching a telephone serviceman and a telephone. Consequently, it would seem that the red lines might confuse rather than help. Further, using these materials in independent work would probably take away any usefulness to stimulate verbal expression.

and waitress. Not all the instructions indicate the most appropriate age for use, and some of the objects associated with the occupations would be unfamiliar to many elementary school children. For example, the four small pictures associated with the architect are a drawing board, blueprints, architectural drawing equipment, and a transit.

The instructions state that "the order of difficulty is left to the discretion of the teacher, since the child's familiarity with an occupation will vary depending on his cultural and social background." The role of social and cultural factors is often overlooked. These variables are especially important in career education. Children in urban areas may not know anyone who is a farmer and may have never even briefly experienced rural life. Architect and physical therapy may be unknown occupations to children from a low socioeconomic background.

Teachers must be also cautious not place higher value on occupations which fit their cultural and social history. The role of materials such as these is to expand the awareness and knowledge of a wide range of occupations. This information is extremely important if a child's handicapping condition places limitations on his choices of career. For example, a learning disabled child of professional parents may never have considered auto mechanic or carpentry as possible choices. To the child's detriment, his parents may not have considered these jobs as possible choices either.

Although the instructions do not emphasize the fact, these materials would be useful to increase vocabulary specific to an occupation and verbal and written expression. With a little forethought and inventiveness, the teacher can weave these materials into a reading program for older students.

Occupations Match-Ups. *Developmental Learning Materials, 7440 Natchez Ave., Niles, Ill. 60648. Price: $2.25.*
Occupations Match-Ups is very similar in its task to Career Identity Cards and the Career Environment Cards, except that it uses a game format. The set consists of 12 master cards with an occupationally specific picture at the top. Forty-eight smaller cards, four for each occupation, show objects related to the various careers. The 12 Master Cards illustrate the work of an architect, artist, astronaut, auto mechanic, beautician, carpenter, cook, deep-sea fisherman, farmer, physical therapist, secretary

Written Language Cards-Careers. *Developmental Language Materials, 7440 Natchez Ave., Niles, Ill. 60648. Price. $6.75.*
Written Language Cards-Careers consists of eight large (11 $\frac{7}{8}$ - by 18 $\frac{3}{8}$ - inches) laminated colored drawings depicting different occupational settings such as a veterinarian's examining room and a heavy construction site. Some of the individuals in the pictures have cartoon-like ballons which are blank. The number of balloons ranges from one to four and they are large enough to allow for several words.

Many of the illustrations require the student to think about the situation from more than one perspective, a task many learning disabled children find difficult. For example, in a fire scene, the child is to fill in a balloon for the fire chief, a television reporter, and a television cameraman.

The set provides "a multisensory experience for all age groups" and are useful for "role-playing storytelling, sequential learning, vocabulary building and affective relationship under-standing." To these uses taken from the instruction sheet, I would add the obvious: written expression.

Wax pencils and erasing cloths are provided. Since the pictures appear handy for a wide age range and are reuseable, the material is economical. Overall, Written Language Cards-Careers appears to be very useful.

The Relationship of Types of Post-High School Education to Occupation and Economic Independence Of Physically Handicapped Adults

JANET ROSENBERG, Ph.D.

Dr. Rosenberg is assistant professor of sociology, Widener College, Chester, Pa. She received the Ph.D. degree in sociology from the University of Pennsylvania in 1972. Her major research interest is in the relationship of role orientations to individual and situational factors. Dr. Rosenberg's professional memberships include: American Sociological Association, American Academy of Arts and Sciences, and Society for the Study of Social Problems.

AMERICANS have traditionally considered higher education intrinsically valuable and instrumental to the attainment of high occupational status and economic security. As opportunity for higher education has increased so has the proportion of high school students enrolling in college programs. As of 1972, 59 percent of all persons between the ages of 18 and 21 were enrolled in college, compared to 38 percent only a decade before.[4] No doubt the motivation for continued education is enhanced by the well-demonstrated relationship between educational attainment and income among normal populations. White men who have graduated from college earn approximately 58 percent more per year than high school graduates. Though differences are attenuated for women and minorities, the positive relationship exists for them as well. Not only does occupational status and income increase with increments in college education, but persons with more education earn more than those with less when performing within the same occupational categories.[1]

In this paper we will examine the occupational and economic effects of educational choices made by a small group of handicapped high school graduates whose educational experience and ability approximate that of normal graduates. Theoretically their employment opportunities and earnings should be limited only by variations in individual skill and competency, and by constraints on mobility and other aspects of physical performance associated with a specific handicap. We could, therefore, expect that college education will provide the same relative advantages to this population as it does to other high school graduates.

The Study Population

The participants consisted of 79 graduates of a public school for orthopedically handicapped students. The original listing of potential respondents included 147 persons. One hundred four of these were located and the response rate from this group was 76 percent.

The respondents matched the full alumni position on all major characteristics, including the proportional distributions of race, sex, physical diagnosis, date of onset of disability, and degree of impairment. All had graduated from the school during the period 1962 to 1973 after at least five years of attendance. The dates of graduation were equally distributed during that period, and their ages ranged from 19 to 30. Seventy-one percent of the population was white; 29 percent was black; women constituted 46 percent and men 54 percent of the population. Sixty-one percent of all subjects had been handicapped since birth, 26 percent prior to the fifth birthday and 13 percent thereafter. Thirty-eight percent, the largest percent-

About the Article . . .

THE RELATIONSHIP of levels and types of education to employment and financial independence was examined on the basis of the experience of 79 graduates of a public school for orthopedically handicapped children. The data suggest that the positive relationship of college education and occupation established for normal adults is ambiguous for this population. Those with the best chance for full-

time employment and an adequate level of income were the graduates with vocational education after high school.

It is suggested that further clarification of the relationship of types of education to economic functioning is needed to provide an information base for planning educational and counseling programs for handicapped students.

age in any single diagnostic category, had cerebral palsy, 23 percent had residual handicaps resulting from poliomyelitis, and 39 percent were impaired as a consequence of a variety of congenital disorders, illnesses suffered during childhood, and accidents.

Estimates of degree of handicap for the respondents were based on therapy and diagnostic records maintained at the school for all students. Ratings were made on three dimensions including physical mobility, ability to grasp, and competency for self-care. All of these factors affect the likelihood of employment.[2] Though the evaluations were originally made on the basis of four degrees of impairment, the small size of the study population required collapsing them into only two categories: mild-moderate and serious-severe.

TABLE 1.—Degrees of Handicap of Respondents

	Mild-Moderate	Serious-Severe	Total
Physical Mobility	82%(65)	18%(14)	100%(79)
Grasp	91%(72)	9%(7)	100%(79)
Daily Care	87%(69)	13%(10)	100%(79)

Table 1 indicates that the vast majority of respondents were mildly or moderately impaired on all of the measured dimensions. This does not mean that their conditions did not present strategic problems for the individual or that they did not have painful consequences or were not visible. The classification, mild-moderate, indicates that the respondents were able, with the requisite training, to negotiate their environments. Those mildly or moderately handicapped, with reference to mobility, could travel alone unhindered by a major appliance and, with reference to grasping ability, could use a variety of equipment essential to work and person activity. In terms of daily care, they required little or no assistance. Those with serious or severe handicaps suffered impaired mobility and limited function.

Educational Choice, Employment and Economic Independence*

During interviews with 41 percent (32) of our original respondents subsequent to the collection of the survey data presented here, they were found to be a

---

*In a pretest of the questionnaire, respondents demonstrated a resistance to revealing amount of earned income. It was decided to request information on degrees of financial independence resulting from earnings in order to obtain the cooperation of the subjects. This type of information, though admittedly less precise than amounts of earned income, was acceptable, particularly since it was used in later phases of the study to examine the relationship of economic independence to social and psychological adaptations.

TABLE 2.—Degree of Physical Handicap and the Continuing Education of Graduates

Physical Mobility and Continued Education

Degree of Handicap	Vocational Ed.	College	None	Total
Mild-Mod	20%(13)	65%(42)	15%(10)	100%(65)
Serious-Severe	7%(1)	64%(9)	29%(4)	100%(14)

Ability to Grasp and Continued Education

Degree of Handicap	Vocational Ed.	College	None	Total
Mild-Mod	19%(14)	62%(45)	18%(13)	100%(72)
Serious-Severe		86%(6)	14%(1)	100%(7)

Competence—Daily Care and Continued Education

Degree of Handicap	Vocational Ed.	College	None	Total
Mild-Mod	20%(14)	62%(43)	18%(12)	100%(69)
Serious-Severe		80%(8)	20%(2)	100%(10)

highly motivated group of adults who had been encouraged by both parents and school counselors to continue their education. This is objectively evidenced by the high rates of postsecondary school enrollment. Of the original 79 students surveyed, 65 percent (51) entered college, 18 percent (14) enrolled in vocational training programs, and only 18 percent (14) sought immediate employment. The degree of handicap on any of the measured dimensions did not affect the type of education selected. (*Table 2*) A large majority preferred to enter college. The seriously handicapped demonstrated this preference more often than the moderately impaired; about equal numbers of both groups (approximately ⅓) dropped out prior to receiving a degree.

The same proportion of men and women sought further educational experience after graduation, but the choice of program differed by sex. Fifty percent of the women compared to 77 percent of the men entered college and a higher proportion of the women, 31 percent, as compared to only 7 percent of the men, went into vocational programs.

Though the majority of these young adults vigorously pursued a college education as a route to enriched experience and economic success, the observed effects are ambiguous.

When the survey was conducted, 18 of the respondents were still full-time students and one was a housewife. Of the 60 available for employment, 63 percent (38) had full-time jobs, 15 percent (9) had part-time employment, and 22 percent (13) were unemployed.

The relationship of college education to higher status employment holds for this group only to the extent that a few of the college-educated alumni are the only respondents to achieve professional status. Five others list themselves as self-employed, an occupational category conventionally associated with proprietary interest in a business or professional practice. The category had a markedly different meaning for our respondents. Of the five who listed themselves as self-employed, only one operated a small business; the others all listed themselves as free-lance writers, none of whom earned more than 50 percent of their required income. The generally high status attributed to this category of employment is clearly not applicable here.

The respondents with vocational training were heavily concentrated in white-collar jobs and those with no education after high school were more equally distributed among white- and blue-collar or

TABLE 4.—*Relationship of Types of Post-High School Education and Employment**

| | Adequate | Impaired | | |
	Full Time	Part Time	Unemp.	Total
College	53%(17)	22%(7)	25%(8)	100%(32)
Voc. Ed.	71%(10)		29%(4)	100%(14)
None	79%(11)	14%(2)	7%(1)	100%(14)

*Students and housewife not included.

uates (55%) as compared to those who had dropped out before completing their degrees (47%).

The lack of a significant relationship between college education and employment is partially accounted for by the fact that the seriously handicapped alumni, for whom full-time employment is extremely problematic, clearly preferred college to vocational education. Nevertheless, if we examine the employment

TABLE 3.—*Education and Occupational Status of Graduates**

Education	Prof.	Self-Emp.	White Collar	Skilled	Blue Collar	Total
College	22%(5)	22%(5)	44%(10)		13%(3)	100%(23)
Vocational			82%(9)	9%(1)	9%(1)	100%(11)
None		8%(1)	46%(6)	15%(2)	31%(4)	100%(13)**

*Graduates working full (38) and part time (9) are included in this table.
**Five of the graduates with no post-high school education worked in protected settings.

service positions. The most that can be said about the relationship of type of higher education and occupational distribution is that there is a slight tendency for the college-educated to occupy higher statuses than those with vocational education and for the latter to be in a better position than those with no further education subsequent to high school graduation.

Though the data suggest that type of post-high school education may have a slight effect on the occupational status of handicapped adults in a manner roughly approximating the effects for normal populations, this is not the case with the relationship of types of education to the likelihood of being employed full time or the achievement of financial independence. An examination of Table 4 indicates that, when degree of handicap is not taken into account, the college-educated alumni have a significantly ($\chi^2 = .001$) lower rate of full-time employment (53%) than do the alumni who either have a vocational education (71%) or have no further post-high school education (79%). An examination of the data also indicated that the incidence of full-time employment did not significantly increase for college grad-

rates of only the moderately handicapped, we find that the vocationally educated still have a higher percentage of persons fully employed than have the college-educated group, though the positive relationship of vocational education to full-time employment is no longer statistically significant.

TABLE 5.—*Relationship of Type of Post-High School Education and Employment of Moderately Handicapped*

	Full Time	Part Time or Unemployed	Total
College	59%(16)	41%(11)	100%(27)
Voc. Ed.	69%(9)	31%(4)	100%(13)
None	100%(10)		100%(10)

Since the likelihood of full-time employment was not increased by college preparation, neither was the degree of financial independence. Of all of those who had attended college, only 41 percent were fully self-sufficient, in comparison to 61 percent of the voca-

TABLE 6.—*Relationship of Education to Degrees of Dependence of the Graduates**

| | | Proportion of Income From Sources Other Than Earnings | | | |
Education	Financially Independent	Up to 50%	50% to 95%	Fully Dependent	Total
College	41%(13)	9%(3)	25%(8)	25%(8)	100%(32)
Vocational	61%(8)	31%(4)		8%(1)	100%(13)**
None	43%(6)	21%(3)	29%(4)	7%(1)	100%(14)

*Students and housewife not included.
**Financial data not available for one subject.

tionally educated (*Table* 6). Even when examining the economic status of only the moderately handicapped, we find that only 50 percent of the college group are fully independent in comparison with 61 percent of the vocationally educated alumni. Whereas a college education gives the physically normal adult a definite status and economic advantage, it has no clear impact on occupational status and no positive effect at all on the financial security of these handicapped adults in comparison to their peers with a vocational education; in fact, the vocationally educated adult in this population seems to enjoy a slight advantage in terms of full-time employment and rates of financial independence.

Discussion

Several observations are in order. It is apparent that, though we are examining the occupational and financial status of an exceptionally well-educated and highly motivated group of adults, the majority of whom are only moderately handicapped, as a group they suffer from economic disability relative to comparable normal populations. Overall, only 63 percent have full-time jobs and only 46 percent were economically self-sufficient despite the fact that all but 2 respondents were living with parents or other relatives, thus reducing the amount of earnings necessary to achieve full economic self-sufficiency.

Although percentages of alumni with post-high school educations having full-time employment were lower than those of alumni without further educational experience, the latter did not benefit greatly from that employment. Although the moderately handicapped without education all reported that they had full-time jobs, the work tended to be menial and unremunerative, and almost 50 percent were employed in sheltered workshops, so that only 55 percent earned enough to meet their needs in comparison to 81 percent of the college-educated with full-time employment and 89 percent of those with vocational backgrounds.

It is interesting to note that, though women are oc-

cupationally disadvantaged relative to men in the normal working population, our female respondents had a slightly higher rate of full-time employment (68%) than did the males (59%). This may reflect the advantage of vocational education relative to employment and may also be due to the fact that 70 percent of full-time employed women were in white-collar positions in large private firms or government agencies where legal guarantees of equal employment opportunities affect the competitive positions of the handicapped. Only 37 percent of the employed males had comparable positions.

Conclusion

There is no question that degree of handicap is the overriding determinant of the degree of economic disability for this small population. Of the small group of seriously handicapped (14), 10 were in the job market. Though all but one had had postsecondary educational experience, only 3 had full-time jobs and none were earning more than 50 percent of the amount needed to meet their minimum financial needs.

Our data suggest that a strong motivation to achieve and intense efforts to acquire skills, though very important factors in overcoming the serious impediments to the employment of handicapped adults, do not fully guarantee economic security. The alumnus with the best chance for full economic functioning is the moderately handicapped graduate with vocational training or a college education leading to a position in areas of the occupational structure where opportunities are protected by law.

In view of the fact that the ability and the opportunity to perform economic roles and to maintain financial self-sufficiency are at the core of positive adult identity,[3] it is important that further research be done with larger handicapped populations in order to clarify the relationship of educational and career choices to employment and earnings. It should not be expected that educational choices and their related outcomes, open to nonhandicapped populations, obtain for the handicapped. It is clear that the world of work is often indifferent or inhospitable to their needs and aspirations so that no matter how educated or capable, their placement is effectively blocked.

Government and private organizations are working to alter the obvious inequities that exist in the occupational system.

It is the responsibility of educators and counselors to promote and support their efforts and to make certain that information concerning opportunities, education, and career lines is accurately collected and is considered in the decision-making processes that ultimately affect the quality of life of their students.

List of References

1. Miller, Herman P. *Rich Man, Poor Man.* New York: Thomas Y. Crowell, 1971.

2. Moed, Martin, and Litwin, Dorothy. The Employability of the Cerebral Palsied: A Summary of Two Related Studies. *Rehab. Lit.* Sept., 1963. 24:9:266-271, 276.

3. Rosenberg, Janet. Alumni Study, Part 2: The Social and Psychological Adaptations of Handicapped Adults. Institutional Report to the Widener Foundation, Lafayette Hills, Pa., 1975.

4. U.S. Department of Commerce, Bureau of the Census. *Current Population Reports, Population Estimates and Projections. Series P-25*, No. 473, Jan., 1972.

THE PHYSICALLY DISABLED WORKER: MYTHS AND REALITY

Lawrence D. Haber, Ph.D.
Acting Division Director
Division of Survey Operations
HEW National Center for Education Statistics
Washington, D.C.

In my work as a policy analyst and social scientist with the Social Security Administration, I am really several steps removed from direct dealings with the disabled and with the process of disability. We are concerned primarily with the consequences of disability, rather than the process of becoming incapacitated.

The income maintenance system that Social Security is responsible for represents the last of a series of filters that the disabled worker goes through in the process of the recognition of disability, starting with difficulty on the job and the recognition of a pathological health condition. Incapacity, for many workers, represents a failure of the system, of employers, of job placement, rehabilitation and the other social services which are designed to assist them in finding work, using their functional capacities in a way which permits them to remain economically independent and socially productive.

For other workers, the income maintenance system, as represented by private and public pensions, is a safety net on which they can fall back after it becomes apparent that a severe handicap has limited their ability to meet normal work expectations.

To the extent that industrial hiring practices limit or reduce opportunities because of rigid medical criteria or unrealistic work requirements, we contribute to the failure of the system in not providing workers with a chance to use their residual capacities. Practices which deprive workers of opportunity for productive work and the social benefits or work need to be seriously re-examined.

In my talk today, I intend to deal more with the facts than the myths of disability and working ability. One of the key facts that we should recognize is that about 17% of the working age population in this country, people aged 18-64, are disabled to some extent, in that they have a limitation to the kind or amount of work they can do.

Most, however, are workers. Of the disabled men, for example, 75% are in the labor force, working or seeking work; 66% are employed and close to 60% are working full-time. Only about 40% of the disabled men in this country receive any form of public income maintenance and less than 17% are primarily dependent on social insurance or public assistance for their basic income.

It is obvious from these facts that the disabled have substantial capacity for productive employment.

Before looking at the composition of the disabled population, I would like to review very briefly some of the definitions and distinctions we use in defining disability as a pattern of behavior.

First, we can identify the existence of active disease or trauma. To the extent that the pathology has permanent or irreversible effects, they may lead to residual impairments, as more or less permanent abnormalities of physiological and anatomical structure. These impairments may have an impact on normal activities, such as walking and the performance of daily tasks, and thus may be considered functional limitations. In the case of a stroke, for example, the atrophy of muscle tissue would constitute a residual impairment -- the limitation of the ability to walk would be a functional limitation. The disability that may emerge from these functional limitations and impairments is essentially a social condition, defined in terms of a loss or reduction of ability to meet the normal role expectations of an individual.

For most of us, the basic criteria or the basic area of expectation with which we are concerned is work, but there are many other areas in which people can become disabled or defined as disabled. Sometimes the term "handicapped: is used interchangeably with or as an alternative for "disability." It is useful, however, to distinguish a handicap from a disability as essentially representing a form of competitive disadvantage which does not necessarily impact on required work and social activities or expectations.

In answer to the question, "Who are the disabled," the Social Security Administration has conducted a number of studies. The following data are based on these surveys of the disabled adult population.

We estimate that around 17,000,000 people are limited in their ability to work because of a health condition. The disabled as a group can be characterized as older, less educated, less skilled than the general non-disabled population of the same age. A very high proportion are poor and a higher proportion than among the non-disabled population are members of minority groups.

The median age of the disabled is about 49 years, roughly 10 years older than that for the non-disabled population. About 44% have incomes below the minimal level of adequacy considered "poor."

On the average, the disabled have two years' less education than the non-disabled population, although a substantial proportion have completed high school or beyond (36% compared to 58% among the non-disabled population).

In terms of their personal lives and family responsibilities, the disabled look very much like the rest of the population. Close to 75% of them are married, 85% are the head or spouse of the head of a household and about 33% have children.

The most common disabling conditions are arthritis, heart trouble, spine and back impairments, high blood pressure and loss or impairment of limbs. The most prevalent disabling conditions, therefore, are those defined as the chronic degenerative disorders of aging; only secondarily are accidents and injuries a cause of disability. Cardiovascular disorders, musculo-skeletal disorders and respiratory disorders account for

66% of all major disabling conditions. Work accidents account for only 6% of the major disabling conditions, and among men employed at the onset of disability , only 15% attribute the start of their disabling condition to a work accident.

The onset of disability occurs most often around the 30s and 40s, with a median age of 37. However, about 17% of the disabled adults have a limitation going back to childhood and about 33% have a limitation starting in the later years, that is, after 45.

At onset of disability, about 80% of the disabled men were employed; about half that proportion of women were employed. Disabled men, however, were much less likely than non-disabled men to have been employed in white collar jobs and more likely to have worked at farming or laboring jobs. A high proportion of disabled women were employed at domestic work and service industries. A much lower proportion had worked at clerical, sales, professional and managerial jobs. Most of these workers, however, had had relatively long periods of stable employment, with one employer, immediately prior to disability; 55% of the men, for example, had worked for the same employer for six years or longer at the onset of disability.

In terms of current employment, 75% of the disabled men were in the labor force, compared to 94% of the non-disabled. Of these, 66% were employed and close to 60% worked full-time.

The best predictor of work experience on current labor force participation was the extent of functional limitation. Among disabled men, for example, 41% had worked full-time all year, but of those with no functional loss, as measured in our study, 57% were employed full-time all year round. Of those with severe limitations on activities, only 19% were employed on a full-time basis. The more severe the functional limitation, the more direct an impact it had on both the nature and the extent of work activity.

I would like to be able to describe the major work problems which the disabled have, but, unfortunately, there are relatively little data available on the characteristics of work or the work place. We are now developing some of this information in two studies in which we will be able to compare the characteristics of activity limitations with the nature and requirements of the available work.

There are, however, some preliminary data on job requirements which interfere with work after the onset of disability. Of those employed at onset, about 66% had some problems with work requirements. Activity limitations in walking, standing, and lifting heavy weights were the requirements most frequently mentioned as causing difficulty in doing the job. Other job requirements which caused problems were "keeping up with the work schedule" and "working under pressure." Although the proportion having difficulty with the work environment was considerably smaller, problems such as simple noise, heat and cold did create problems for a significant proportion of workers.

Of those currently working, most of them still worked in the same environment with little of no change. The vast majority, however, had made some change in their work requirements. The changed work conditions most frequently mentioned were a reduction in heavy work, less moving around, and taking it easy on the job.

Most disabled men stayed at or returned to the job they had had before. About 17% found another job, and about 17% did not return to work. Relatively few of those who returned to work reduced the hours worked, changed occupation or changed employers. The older men and unskilled workers had most difficulty and less success in returning to work.

These findings echo the findings of a number of studies on plant closing and plant relocation. There is little evidence that occupational change assists many workers in returning to or remaining at work. It would seem that the best chance a disabled or handicapped worker has for returning to work is to negotiate some form of job adjustment or restructuring with his old employer.

The fundamental approach in job adjustment is an emphasis on adapting environments, rather than adapting workers. The history of human intervention shows relatively little success with adjusting people, but amazing things have been accomplished in adapting environments to fit people.

Research on rehabilitation and job placement should look much more intensively at the environment in which people work and how work can be restructured, as well as using the traditional approach of focusing on adapting the individual to the environment.

A number of studies provide examples of the kinds of things that can be done in restructuring work; some are relatively simple, some fairly complex.

In an industrial engineering example, postural training was used to overcome the physical limitations or difficulties of a typist's job. The basic alterations were in the posture of the typist and the distance from the machine. The impairments and limitations involved arthritic conditions, causing difficulty with neck movements and farsightedness. Through biomechanical analysis of the task and repositioning of the work, work strain was reduced and efficiency improved by simplifying eye and head movements.

Using the analog of the crane to the body, recommendations for different lift postures for men as against short women reduced work strain in a particular work situation where the standard lifting posture placed unnecessary strain on tall workers.

Through the biomechanical study of work motions, it is sometimes possible to simplify tasks and reduce work strain while maintaining or improving efficiency. In one case, shortening the work bench by about three or four inches, so that the worker sitting at the packaging bench would be closer to the work, helped to keep a worker with low back injury on the job. Work surfaces can be lowered to assist a cardiac or recovered cardiac in continuing to work, while improving the output per unit of work motion.

Alternatives developed in consultation between the industrial engineer and the plant physician can be used to fit the environment to worker limitations and capacities without loss of efficiency or production. Industrial engineering and biomechanical rehabilitation may also benefit from physical aid tooling. For example, modifications of an electronics assembly board, to simplify location of small parts and special sorting devices, enabled blind workers to maintain and in some cases exceed the productivity of other workers.

The recent vocational rehabilitation program, Projects For Industry, focused on more traditional kinds of training, but in addition to teaching work skills, job seeking skills were developed, to expand the job opportunities for handicapped workers. An important aspect of the success of this program was the emphasis on employer participation.

Companies which the project organizers wanted to interest in hiring the disabled and handicapped workers were first contacted by leading businessmen and company executives, who were themselves involved in job placement programs for handicapped and disabled people. In general, employers were found to be more receptive to new programs when they were introduced by fellow businessmen.

Other Projects For Industry programs have obtained advance commitments from the cooperating industries to hire disabled clients. This commitment, in advance of training, assured the trainees of a real work opportunity and added to their incentive for success, both in training and on the job.

A few years ago, the Bureau of Labor Statistics conducted a series of case studies on job redesign. Ten plants were selected, to examine the kinds of job placement and job adaptation activities that were taking place. They found a variety of simple work adaptation methods being practiced in these plants. These were primarily informal ways of redesigning jobs among workers or between workers and foremen to improve operating efficiency by accommodating to the declining physical capacity of workers, both for older workers and because of worker illness or impairment. Some of the adaptations took the form of task reallocation, shifting tasks among a group of workers, for example, from older workers to younger workers, the younger workers taking on more of the lifting, pushing and carrying, and the older workers taking over other parts of the task.

In one example of mechanization of work, a skilled crane operator was kept on the job by adding hydraulic controls, at a relatively small cost. Not only was the work pressure stemming from his arthritic condition reduced with the new controls, but he could also sit at the job, thus reducing work fatigue.

Other examples, such as the use of fork lift trucks to replace manual lifting, are fairly conventional adaptations, but when applied to the special circumstance of workers with impairments and activity limitations they can make the difference between continuing to work routinely at a productive job where the worker is known and accepted and no longer being able to work.

Many other examples of job adaptation could be cited, but these illustrate the main ideas of job restructuring and redesign. It is important to recognize that many of the work changes were not formal arrangements, initiated by management, and that many cost little or no money. Informal worker-to-worker job shifts and task shifts take place continually. Worker and foreman arrangements are frequent. Some arrangements may involve industrial engineers or the labor relations staff and occasionally plant managers. Job modification can operate at all levels and essentially is going on all the time. Most of us see it around us on the job, sometimes among our own colleagues and in our own offices. Unfortunately, we know very little, in any systematic way, about how these informal compacts and negotiations are arrived at. There is little or no information available on how job restructuring on an informal basis works, how it is stimulated, what effect it has, and how it can be improved and controlled.

The most extensive work on job redesign has been done by the Organization for Economic Cooperation and Development (OECD) and the International Labor Office (ILO), which have sponsored a number of studies on workers' attitudes, handicaps, and capacities, and the methods for matching these capacities and limitations with jobs. Most of their interest has been directed towards the middle-aged and older worker, largely because of the earlier labor scarcity in the European market. These studies, however, tend to focus more on the formal engineering approach towards job modification than on informal adaptations of work.

Job modification, especially informal modification, is useful for the worker who is already on the job. Hiring practices for new employees, however, pose another set of problems.

Several studies have indicated that the physical requirements established for some jobs are not realistic and specify far more physical capacity than the worker is required to put into job performance. Better work evaluation, and, more basically, changes in employer attitudes towards the disabled are needed to bring hiring and job performance requirements into better alignment.

One study of hiring practices found wide variations in employer attitudes towards hiring workers with orthopedic limitations. Some of the factors affecting attitudes were the size and purpose of the firm and the firm's experience with disabled employees. The larger the firm, the more likely it was to hire the orthopedically disabled. Manufacturing firms were more concerned with physical limitations; service companies with environmental and personality factors.

Other studies of job screening methods show that frequently there is little necessary connection between the job performance requirements and the actual abilities required on the job. In contrast to the study of employer attitudes, however, one study of hiring practices found that small firms were more flexible than large firms in their screening criteria and more selective in the kinds of restrictions and ineligibilities they created.

These questions and problems of job modification and hiring practices impact directly on the role of industries and the personnel executive in dealing with the hiring of the handicapped. There is a

clear need for reevaluation of hiring practices, medical standards and
job requirements, reevaluation of job standards and better understanding
of task formation and allocation in terms of the employment of the
physically disabled.

The whole process of job structuring within a plant needs much more
intensive study, both in terms of the formal and informal initiatives
and alternatives, the organizational levels involved, the nature of task
allocation and modification, the structuring of tasks and the effect of
these kinds of changes on productivity.

Some of these findings suggest another function for the personnel
executives -- as missionaries or representatives of big business to small
and middle-size business. You are the people with the experience and
resources and the ones who have worked with job modification and restructuring in your own plants, companies and shops. Small plants and companies
have relatively few opportunities to see the wide diversity of adaptations that can take place, and they have few resources in the form of
industrial engineers, safety engineers, occupational physicians, and plant
nurses that many large plants have to assist in these adaptations. There
is a useful role to be played in assisting small businesses to understand
the problems of the disabled, and to learn more about the principles of
job adaptation, thus developing a better understanding of how job modification can be used productively.

I have been asked to comment on the "myths" about hiring the handicapped. These myths are basically rationalizations for not hiring the
disabled worker. Some of them may also represent coverups for deeper
fears or concerns on the part of employers.

Accident rates, for example, are not higher for disabled workers.
There is no insurance opposition to hiring the handicapped. Insurance
companies have been among the leading exponents of hiring the handicapped,
and hiring handicapped workers does not affect insurance rates. Absentee
rates are not higher for disabled workers. Turnover is about the same.
Productivity, when the worker is properly placed in a job within his
capacity, is as good as that of non-disabled workers in similar jobs.

There is a problem suggesting you hire the handicapped at a time
when unemployment rates for all workers are in excess of eight percent.
The problems of hiring the handicapped and disabled, however, are no
greater than and no different from those of hiring any workers. We still
have an economy with more than 80,000,000 jobs and 20,000,000 job changes
each year. The disabled worker has the same drive, the same needs, and
can be as productive as any other worker. If you are hiring, why not hire
the handicapped? The act of being hired in itself makes them that much
less handicapped. Disability does not exist in a biological vacuum. It
is largely a problem of consequences and of how we treat and respond to
performance needs and limitations.

You are probably all aware of the changing climate for affirmative
action, and the new requirements in rehabilitation and EEO regulations
which bring new pressures on companies and employers to adapt to the
problems of the disabled. In many cases, it may be a case of, do you
jump, or do you get pushed? When you review your hiring practices and
job standards, it may be worth keeping in mind that the chances of landing
on your feet are considerably better when you jump.

6. EDUCATION

Participant: Can you tell us something about second injury funds?

Dr. Haber: Most states have some provision for a second injury fund to provide protection to employers in the case of workers who, for example, have received Workmen's Compensation awards, and, then, have been hired by a different organization. The Workmen's Compensation people should be able to supply more information.

Participant: We have a young woman who has been awarded a total disability benefit from the Social Security Administration. She is working for us part-time, and, therefore, doesn't earn enough to support herself and her family but she has to stop working in order to collect her Social Security which pays more than she is getting. It doesn't seem fair.

Dr. Haber: You can look at it a number of different ways depending on the facts. I don't think there is any one approach which represents simple justice because it is a very complex situation. The Social Security program is essentially a wage replacement program like the retirement program, in which the idea is that if you are earning at or above a certain level, you are not retired, and you lose benefits. In the same way, the concept is that if you are earning at and above a certain level, you are not disabled. That doesn't mean that you do not have an impairment, a serious condition or even a serious functional limitation, but you are not disabled in the sense that you are unable to meet your work expectations. The fact that you are getting paid a substantial wage reflects that you are meeting these work expectations. There is some question about the extent to which the earnings level reflects this.

The Social Security program disallows as ineligible many people who are receiving wage benefits from their private disability insurance program on the basis that the level of disability which applies in the national economy is a different one and stricter than the one a company can apply in negotiating private insurance agreements.

An individual can earn about $200 a month before he loses this income from Social Security, but it is not a rigid rule. It is possible for a person earning more than that to continue to earn it if it can be shown that he is not in competitive employment, and that it is a level of earnings that would not be possible or available to him except for special sheltered circumstances. Most work in a sheltered workshop, for example, would be exempt from that kind of limitation; however, wages paid in sheltered workshops generally don't exceed that amount.

Participant: If a disabled worker returns to work, what is the length
of the trial period?

Dr. Haber: The worker who returns to substantial gainful employment
has a nine-month trial period to show he can sustain this
activity before his benefits are cut off. If, during that
time, or after he has used up the nine months, he finds he
is unable to sustain his work, he can return on to the
disability benefit rolls, but he is no longer entitled to
a new trial work period.

Integrating Deaf Students for Career Education

RICHARD G. HEHIR

Abstract: This article describes an experimental approach undertaken by New York State whereby deaf students from state supported schools for the deaf were integrated for occupational education on a half day basis in a regional public school agency called the Board of Cooperative Educational Services. The problems faced and the results obtained during 2 years of experience with two different schools for the deaf are reported. The success of the integrated program has been demonstrated with additional schools for the deaf being included subsequently.

In New York State there are a variety of educational settings in which deaf children may receive an educational program. The state operates the New York State School for the Deaf at Rome, New York, and supports eight private schools for the deaf located geographically across New York State under provisions established by law and regulated by the commissioner of education. These schools exist along with a number of public school programs located mainly in the large urban centers of the state. In the 1970-71 school year, 2,111 deaf students were enrolled in nursery school (at a minimum age of 3 years) through high school (at a maximum age of 21) in the nine state affiliated schools for the deaf. Six of these schools have high school departments enrolling

Richard G. Hehir is Chief, Bureau for Physically Handicapped Children, New York State Education Department, Albany.

410 students between the ages of 16 and 21 years.

Traditionally, the secondary students attending a school for the deaf have been provided an academic program and a vocational orientation and training experience. The vocational curricula generally offered to deaf students included such areas as home economics, printing, woodworking, business training, advanced business machines, shoemaking, baking, and industrial arts. The vocational training offered depended upon the school the child attended and the vocational teachers employed on the staff of that school. Only one school for the deaf in New York State sent its older deaf students for occupational education to an outside facility. This school used the public vocational high school in the city on an after school basis with the instruction being provided by public school vocational education teachers. The vocational training included welding, auto collision, machine shop, and printing. In the other five schools for the deaf offering secondary school programs, vocational offerings to the students occurred within the schools themselves. Therefore, with the exception of one school and approximately 50 secondary students, the 410 deaf students at the secondary level were receiving occupational education in segregated settings from vocational education teachers teaching deaf children only.

Previous Studies

Recent studies (Boatner, Stuckless, & Moores, 1964; Parks & Bowe, 1970) have shown that the vocational training facilities and offerings in the schools for the deaf are inadequate to meet the needs of the young deaf graduates seeking employment in the occupations needed by the modern world of work. The Babbidge report (1964) indicated dissatisfaction with the status and quality of vocational programs at that time and the problem has been exacerbated since then with continued technological advancement. Reports from six schools for the deaf having secondary programs in New York State and the information reported from counselors in the state's Office of Vocational Rehabilitation indicate that it is becoming increasingly more difficult to place graduates from schools for the deaf in gainful occupations without additional training of a specialized nature. This has resulted in deaf adults being underemployed or unemployed.

A recent national survey by Lacey (1970) reported that 83 percent of the superintendents of schools for the deaf strongly supported the development of vocational education programs in their residential schools. An expanded vocational instruction program would include such activities as a continuing educational program and a work-study program. Further, the superintendents reported a need for more contact with employers and more monitoring of local manpower trends. In recognition of these needs, the superintendents indicated they planned to add more vocational teachers and vocational counselors to their professional staffs.

These problems and considerations exist in New York State as they do elsewhere in this nation. A new campus facility under construction at the New York State School for the Deaf at Rome, like its private and state supported counterparts, faced the problem of meeting the needs of an expanded secondary school age population for whom additional vocational facilities are needed. Some of the questions to be answered were:

1. Should these schools expand their facilities, purchase new kinds of equipment, and hire additional specially trained staff to provide an expanded occupational education program?
2. Can the school for the deaf provide sufficient in-depth training in any one occupational area?
3. Is it feasible to initiate certain kinds of occupational programs for the number of students commuting to the school from various parts of the state?

Consideration of the above and similar questions led to the decision that it was not economically feasible to expand the occupational education program in six separate high school programs for the deaf in New York State.

A regional approach to occupational education for the deaf is contained in the Parks and Bowe (1970) report, which concluded that the small number of deaf students per state makes it infeasible for state residential schools to support quality occupational education programs. The wider range of offerings could be better managed through a regional vocational school for the deaf. This alternative was also rejected as an approach for New York State because of the many administrative, financial, and legal complications involved. A regional approach already exists in New York State wherein occupational education is adequately provided to regular public high school students.

An Integrated Approach

Every public school district in New York State has access to the services provided on an area basis (usually multi-county) by an intermediate type of school district called the Board of Cooperative Educational Services (BOCES). The BOCES provides certain shared services which many districts individually are unable to provide because of the nature of the services or the expense involved. These shared services can be effectively and efficiently provided on a regional basis. Public school districts become component members of the BOCES serving their area of the state and then purchase the services which they need from the BOCES. A recent study (Hehir, 1971) reported that local school district administrators purchase such shared services because of the broad spectrum of programs which BOCES can offer, the specialized personnel which it can provide, and the facilities and equipment it possesses under a favorable state funding formula. Because of these factors BOCES has been successful in offering both special education and occupational education programs to the public school districts of the state.

The state plan for occupational education provides for the development of programs on an area basis through the BOCES and large city school districts. There are 47 BOCES districts in New York State enrolling 50,000 secondary students in a broad choice of programs. Every BOCES has available to its students 12 to 40 occupational choices, including such selections as architectural drafting, medical laboratory assistant, trade electricity, data processing, auto transmission, offset printing, and commercial photography. The BOCES uses both local funding and state funding, as well as Federal monies available under the Vocational Education Act, to financially support occupational education.

Since the BOCES does offer such a comprehensive and varied program of services in occupational education to secondary age students, the use of BOCES by deaf students attending the state operated and the state supported schools for the deaf in New York State was proposed. The answer to this suggestion first depended upon the resolution of a number of other problems. These problem areas included administrative questions such as the legal contractual relationship possible between public and private agencies. Other questions concerned social matters such as the possible success of integrating secondary students from schools for the deaf with hearing students from regular public high schools. The important question, of course, was how such secondary deaf students could be financially supported in a BOCES program since the state funding provisions for the education of deaf students were restricted by law to the support of the education provided in special schools for the deaf.

Once these questions were resolved, deaf students could benefit substantially from participation in a BOCES program. They could take advantage of a comprehensive occupational education program and still remain for their academic and specialized education in their home school for the deaf. This would be possible since occupational education programs are provided on a half day basis to regular public school students who remain in their home school districts for the other half day session. If deaf students could be admitted to such area programs near their school for the deaf, many could continue to be day students living at home while attending the school for the deaf and the BOCES occupational education program. Additionally, the occupational training would be conducted in a "more normal" work situation with hearing people as coworkers and supervisors. Integration of the deaf into the world of work could be initiated through participation in a nonsegregated training environment.

Based on the above a decision was reached that, although limited vocational orientation and training would be maintained at the state operated school at Rome, the advanced occupational education for older deaf students would be obtained through the local Board of Cooperative Educational Services, which offered a comprehensive program. The superintendent of the state school, together with the Education Department's Bureau for Physically Handicapped Children, were instructed to approach the district superintendent of the Oneida-Madison-Herkimer BOCES to determine the feasibility of such a program. The contact was made and the district superintendent agreed to initiate on a limited basis an experimental integrated occupational education program for selected state school deaf students. Subsequently, the superintendent at the school for the deaf reviewed with his staff the students who should participate in such a program.

Criteria for BOCES Admissions

The general criteria mutually agreed upon by the superintendent of the school for the deaf and the State Education Department to be used in selecting the students included the following: (a) the deaf pupils were to be state appointed boys or girls attending the school for the deaf; (b) the deaf pupils were to be in their terminal years of school and therefore above 16 years of age and probably in their junior or senior years of high school; (c) the deaf pupils were to comprise that group of students for whom job placement was probable upon graduation (neither the lowest level students nor the college bound were to be priority candidates for placement in BOCES); (d) the deaf students should hold promise for success in an occupational training program; (e) the deaf students' ability to function in an integrated setting should be considered; and (f) oral fluency, although highly desirable, was *not* to be a critical factor in considering placement in the BOCES program. Using these criteria 12 deaf students were selected to begin their occupational education in BOCES in February of 1971 with the Education Department using P.L. 89-313 funds to pay the tuition charge of BOCES. The occupational education courses in which the students were enrolled included automobile mechanics, maintenance mechanics, clothing occupations, agricultural mechanics, and conservation.

During the summer of 1970 the Rochester School for the Deaf and the staff of the Bureau for Physically Handicapped Children of the State Education Department entered into discussions along similar lines which would allow deaf students from that school to attend the Monroe County No. 1 BOCES occupational education center for training. The Rochester School, however, is a private state supported school, and a public school district (including BOCES) is not permitted by law to contract with a private school to provide instructional services to students enrolled in that private school. Such an opinion was provided by the Education Department's legal counsel after being contacted on this matter. Nevertheless, it was determined that the state should not provide additional funds to the Rochester School to expand a limited vocational program which could not adequately meet the needs of older deaf students. Another approach had to be found.

Since the state supported the Rochester School for the tuition and maintenance of its students, legal counsel determined that the state could support occupational education for the deaf students by contracting directly with BOCES for the occupational instruction of the state appointed pupils attending the Rochester School. Thus, in September of 1970, 10 secondary deaf students from the Rochester School were admitted to a BOCES program.

These students were selected using the same criteria indicated above for the state operated school. A per capita cost determined by BOCES and the Education Department, and provided under contract between them, allowed for occupational education for the state appointed pupils attending the Rochester School for the Deaf. The students were enrolled in occupational courses in data processing, electricity, computer programing, automotive services, food services, and automobile collision.

These integrated programs involving the state school at Rome and the Rochester School are different from the occupational education program provided to deaf students attending St. Mary's School for the Deaf in Buffalo, New York. That school for the deaf, within its state approved budget, has for a number of years sent its older deaf students to two city vocational high schools after the regular school hours for occupational education. These deaf students, however, are taught as a group of deaf students by the occupational education teachers of the city school system. No integration with hearing children is provided. In all three situations, however, the occupational education teachers of the public school district (both BOCES and the city) are regular public school teachers of hearing children and not trained teachers of the deaf. The courses of instruction are the same as those provided to regular hearing students of the public school and the oral approach with extensive demonstration is used.

Problems and Solutions

As indicated previously, a contract was negotiated between the State Education Department and the two BOCES programs providing occupational education to state appointed pupils from two schools for the deaf. The use of the contract overcame legal problems involved in relating public with private schools. The contract also enabled the Department to use Federal funds separate and apart from the regular state budgets to support both the state operated and the state supported schools. New York State was faced with a serious financial crisis during the 1970-71 school year and the use of state funds for the support of all educational programs was seriously curtailed. Therefore, the Federal funds available under P.L. 89-313, the amendment to Title I of the Elementary and Secondary Education Act, was used as the funding source for the contracts. These P.L. 89-313 Federal funds are to be used to support educational services to students attending state operated and state supported schools in educational programs beyond the regular curriculum of the schools.

The BOCES programs receive students from component districts into the occupational education programs available, based on the public school district's evaluation and counseling of its students. This same procedure was generally followed by the BOCES in relation to deaf students from the two schools for the deaf in school year 1970-71. After a short period of time during the fall semester, it was found that the deaf students needed more orientation to occupational education than the school for the deaf was able to offer.

It was soon determined that the deaf students should be allowed to experience various occupational education courses for short periods of time in order to more adequately understand the nature and demands of each occupational education area. This short term involvement in three or four occupational education courses enabled the deaf students to gain a better insight into the courses than the mere visitation of the facility and observation of workshops at the beginning of the school year. It also enabled the deaf students to have hands-on experiences under the supervision of the teachers who could then make recommendations regarding the aptitude of the students and probability for success in certain areas. The deaf students' interests and motivation were heightened by such exposures in several areas. The lack of knowledge by the deaf students of occupational opportunities and their own capabilities and limitations pointed up the need for career development in the schools for the deaf.

When occupational education teachers were first confronted with the prospect of having students with limited communication skills in their classes, they were concerned about their ability to interact and effectively teach such students. Added to this was the generally low expectation level which some occupational education teachers had regarding the achievement possible by handicapped students. This negative attitude may have stemmed from the teachers' feelings of incompetence in working with the handicapped because of their lack of knowledge about the deaf as well as their difficulty in communication. The teachers were also concerned about the safety of deaf students having hands-on experience in occupational courses where large machines and other automated equipment had to be used by the students. The occupational education teachers were also concerned that deaf students finishing their programs would not be employable in industries where such skills are needed.

The deaf students, upon initially entering the BOCES programs, were also unsure of their own ability to succeed in an integrated setting. Faced with the prospect of selecting areas for training, it was evident that the students were naive regarding the content of the courses and the skills necessary for success. The deaf students tended to be reserved and to want to participate in courses with one or two other deaf students.

As the deaf students proceeded through the fall semester it was evident they were having difficulty learning from the group sessions held for students in the occupational education classes. The textbooks and manuals presented language and reading problems to them. The students faced technical language which was totally unfamiliar to them. Tools and the use of other kinds of industrial equipment which relied on a knowledge of certain basic skills such as in measurement also presented problems.

Need for a Coordinator

It soon became apparent that the deaf students could not merely be placed in BOCES without having serious difficulties in many areas. Although a liaison person from the schools for the deaf was available in each BOCES situation, the need for a full time or near full time coordinator was recognized. This resource person from the staff of each school for the deaf was charged with a number of responsibilities to insure the success of the deaf students in the integrated program. The coordinator was expected to handle any discipline problems which might arise as well as to oversee the transportation and scheduling arrangements. He was expected to counsel the students regarding the selection of occupational education courses and to guide such students during their courses and sessions at the BOCES. The coordinator was used for interpretation and was available to meet specific needs of occupational education teachers teaching deaf students.

The coordinator was also responsible for the communication of all needs between the school for the deaf and the BOCES personnel. Reinforcement of new learning in BOCES was to be carried out back at the school for the deaf. Sometimes the occupational education teachers would provide notes to be used in a group lecture session so that these notes might be taught at the school for the deaf prior to the deaf students attending the group lecture session at BOCES. The coordinator was responsible for arranging cross-visitations between the school for the deaf and the BOCES personnel. He also was to participate in conferences on individual students with the BOCES administrators and teachers. He was to provide inservice education to the occupational education teachers on communication skills and the psychology of the deaf.

The coordinator in both BOCES situations, after one year's placement on the job, was viewed as a critical element in the success of the deaf students' integration. His job responsibilities were gradually defined and expanded during the school year as the experience and need indicated. The time involvement also gradually expanded from periodic visits to scheduled times and dates.

In both BOCES situations involving deaf students from the special schools for the deaf there were no reported social or behavioral problems of any significance. Minor misunderstandings did occur but these were easily resolved through the intervention of the coordinator. The hearing students accepted the deaf students as peers in the occupational education program. Several hearing students became good friends with deaf students and invited them to their homes on the weekends when school was not in session. Some hearing students visited the school for the deaf to learn more about their deaf friends' educational program. Some hearing students even learned manual communication in order to be able to "speak" better with their deaf friends. It was noted that gradually the deaf students who preferred to be in classes with other deaf students began to request placement in training settings because they were interested in the training and not because deaf friends were in the class. In some circumstances a deaf and a hearing student worked as partners in the occupational education courses on specific projects.

Evaluation

In any such innovative program, evaluation must play an integral part in determining the success of the program. State Education Department personnel supervised and visited the programs together with the school for the deaf coordinator. Reports on student progress both from the school for the deaf and from the BOCES were requested and evaluated on a periodic basis to determine areas needing change and improvement. It was in this way that the coordinator was appointed on a regular basis, transportation schedules were revised, and inservice activities arranged.

The BOCES were requested to use the same standard measures of achievement with the deaf students as were used with the hearing students in the BOCES program. BOCES used as part of their evaluation system the subjective appraisal of the occupational education teachers and a performance evaluation based on task completion. Some written tests were also used in evaluating student progress. The coordinator in one BOCES situation interpreted the test questions to the deaf students as an aid to the occupational education teacher. Demonstration of the hands-on operation in certain occupational education areas also constituted part of the evaluation of student achievement.

Results After One Year

In the Oneida BOCES program, where 12 deaf students were initially enrolled, at the end of one semester of training 5 deaf students made the honor roll with grades between 85 percent and 92 percent; 2 received honorable mention with grades averaging between 80 percent and 84 percent; 4 students achieved passing grades comparable to the average hearing student in the BOCES programs; and 1 deaf student was dropped from the BOCES program due to poor attendance. The eight occupational education teachers teaching the deaf in this BOCES were favorable impressed with the deaf students and recommended continuation of the students in their classes. The teachers rated 3 of the deaf students as very high achievers, 2 others as above average, and 3 deaf students as average.

Of the 11 deaf students who remained in the BOCES program; 7 graudated from the school for the deaf. One of these students entered a community college for continued training beyond the BOCES course in building maintenance; 5 entered jobs related to the training received in the BOCES (groundsman landscaper on a college campus, maintenance mechanic in a workshop, power machine operator in a dress factory, farm owner, and operator); and 2 went to work in occupations not related to their BOCES training.

In the Monroe BOCES situation, where 10 deaf students were enrolled for occupational education, a grading system using a 5 point scale covered 14 categories. Six deaf students achieved the honor roll under this rating system, scoring above average on all 14 categories. The other 4 students performed satisfactorily in most, if not all, 14 categories. The five occupational education teachers teaching the deaf reported favorably on all deaf students whom they instructed. They reported that the deaf students achieved at the same level as the hearing students in their classes. Two of the 10 students in this BOCES program entered Gallaudet College; 1 entered the National Technical Institute for the Deaf in a course related to his BOCES training in data processing; 4 obtained jobs related to the occupational education training received in BOCES (food service worker in a community college, key punch operator in a bank, automotive repair, groundskeeper on a college, auto collision worker in an auto body shop); and 3 entered jobs not related to the training received in BOCES.

Benefits

Although there were certain legal, administrative, and financial problems which had to be overcome, the occupational education programs in BOCES have provided significant benefits to the state appointed deaf students attending the state operated school for the deaf and a state supported school for the deaf during the 1970-71 school year. A majority of the deaf students who received BOCES training have been placed in jobs related to the training they received, and a number of others have entered specialized programs of higher education which were not envisioned as possibilities for these students. This outcome may have been caused by their renewed interest because of their BOCES experience. The schools for the deaf also reported an increased desire on the part of deaf students in lower grades to remain in school to participate in the BOCES affiliated programs.

Program Expansion

During the 1971-72 school year the cooperative BOCES and school for the deaf occupational education program was continued both at Rome and Rochester. The state operated school continued to send 12 students to BOCES while the Rochester school increased its sending population to 16. Both deaf boys and girls were included in each occupational education setting. Although final progress reports are not in for 1971-72, preliminary reports indicate that all 28 deaf students achieved success in completing their integrated program as BOCES. BOCES staff welcome continuation of the programs and are actively seeking deaf students in their classes. Administrative support is also strong for the programs.

A third state supported school for the deaf was added and provided occupational education for students placed in BOCES. During school year 1971-72 the Mill Neck School for the Deaf sent 12 state appointed deaf students to the Nassau County BOCES for occupational education. With the exception of 1 student whose severe physical problems necessitated his removal, 11 students are reported to have achieved successfully in this initial year of the BOCES program. They have been receiving advanced training during the 1972-73 school year as part of their 2 year instruction in BOCES and have been joined by 5 additional students.

Recognizing that the deaf students were not being adequately prepared for vocational training, it was determined that the students should learn something about the world of work in relation to their own assets and liabilities, likes and dislikes, goals and motivations. The superintendents of the schools for the deaf agreed to cooperate in a 3 year research project on career development for deaf students. This cooperative project funded with Federal monies available under P.L. 89-313 from the Bureau for Physically Handicapped Children, was sponsored by the Rochester School for the Deaf and the University of Rochester. During the 1971-72 school year the project concentrated on inservice education of teachers, the development of "guidance games" for deaf students, and the development of supervisory and in-service materials for teachers. The plan is to extend the project to the other two upstate schools for the deaf in the second year and to all other schools for the deaf in New York State in the third year. This project is a component of the BOCES occupational education program for deaf students.

Another step taken during 1971-72 school year was the planning for an inservice workshop for teachers. This workshop involved occupational education teachers teaching deaf students in the several BOCES and teachers of the deaf teaching academic subjects in schools for the deaf. The focus was on establishing communication between the two groups of teachers and on developing processes by which curriculum and other problem areas could be discussed and resolved. The workshop was funded jointly by the Bureau for Physically Handicapped Children and the Office of Occupational Education of the State Education Department. It was held in the fall of 1972, involved 40 teachers from both disciplines, and was offered by an area manpower institute team.

In September of 1972 the New York School for the Deaf at White Plains sent six of its state appointed deaf students for occupational edu-cation to the Westchester BOCES No. 2. At the same time the St. Mary's School for the Deaf in Buffalo expanded its cooperative arrangement with the city of Buffalo so that state appointed pupils attending that school would be able to participate during the regular school day in a number of occupational areas in three voca-tional high schools operated by the city. Thus, five state affiliated schools for the deaf having secondary programs are providing occupational education to state appointed pupils in settings where adequate training is available. Qualified, technically trained teachers instruct the deaf in a public school agency wherein deaf students are integrated with their hearing peers. Based upon 2 years of experience it is our conclusion that the deaf student in New York State can receive adequate occupational training in inte-grated BOCES centers with essential supportive services being provided by the specialized schools for the deaf.

References

Babbidge, H. D. *Education of the deaf: A report to the Secretary of Health, Education, and Welfare by his Advisory Committee on the Education of the Deaf.*

Vocational Needs in Educational Programs For Deaf Youth

McCay Vernon *and* **Thomas Fishler**

TECHNOLOGICAL DEVELOPMENTS in recent years have brought about radical changes in the world of work which directly and significantly affect the future of deaf youth. These changes have caused crucial questions to be raised with regard to existing vocational programs for deaf students in residential and day schools and day classes.

This issue of vocational education is of greater significance to the realistic deaf student and the parent and teacher involved in helping him prepare for his future than it is to hearing youth and those who educate and guide him. This is because, as data clearly indicate, the overwhelming majority of deaf people who find eventual employment do so in vocational rather than professional areas. For example, the Survey of Occupational Conditions Among the Deaf (Lunde & Bigman, 1959) shows that 75 percent of deaf men and 60 percent of deaf women are employed in skilled and semiskilled occupations. Furthermore, the percent of deaf students who are able to attain college entrance is only one-tenth the percent of those with normal hearing who get into programs of higher education (Schein & Bushnaq, 1962) and the actual incidence of the deaf in the professions is disproportionately low (Connor & Rosenstein, 1963; Crammatte, 1962; Lunde & Bigman, 1959).

Thus, two conditions exist: namely, that automation is changing vocational employment drastically, and that it is to this area of work that the overwhelming majority of deaf youngsters must look for their adult careers, which makes it important that an objective examination be made of the vocational aspects of existing educational programs for the deaf. The basic issues involved are:

1. Should educational programs for deaf school-age students be vocational or prevocational?
2. What concrete steps can be taken to upgrade vocational preparation in existing day and residential programs for deaf youth?
3. How do the occupational trends for the future relate to deaf youth today?

A VOCATIONAL VERSUS A PREVOCATIONAL OR EXPLORATORY PROGRAM

Vocational and technical education for high-school-age students, both deaf and hearing, is presently involved in a controversy over whether or not it should offer a vocational or technical program, an exploratory industrial arts curriculum, or a combination of these. Briefly, in the exploratory industrial arts plan the student is exposed to a number of broad manual arts areas such as woodworking and metal work in which he acquires a cursory knowledge of each without obtaining the training needed to be proficient at even an early apprentice level in any specific vocational subject. The purpose of this plan is to acquaint the student with the use of tools and with various areas of the world of work, leaving his actual vocational preparation for the post high school age years.

In a vocational program, by contrast, the student initially goes through a one- and two-year survey type of industrial arts program. Then, at the age of around 16 or 17 he enters a bona fide vocational curriculum where he is given education in depth in one given trade or technology. The selection of the specific craft which he will study is based on the skills and interests reflected in his work during the survey period and results of aptitude testing and counseling. There are advantages to both the vocational and the exploratory-industrial arts program. The controversy over which is best involves many issues, few of which have been related realistically to the unique factors of occupational planning for deaf students.

In the education of the deaf this debate is most keenly felt in residential schools where vocational or industrial arts courses comprise a significant part of the total curriculum. At present, few day schools or day class programs have obtained enough personnel qualified both vocationally and as educators of the deaf to provide more than a rudimentary industrial arts curriculum (except for those few students who are able to participate realistically in advanced level shop courses in integration with hearing students). For this minority of successfully integrated students, whether or not they get an exploratory or a vocational program depends primarily on which happens to be available in the public school they are attending unless special arrangements are made for work-study plans, on-the-job training, or attendance at local trade schools.

It is the premise of this paper that schools which purport adequately to provide for the educational needs of deaf students of high school age must be prepared to offer a combination vocational and prevocational (exploratory) program based on the type of deaf student they serve.

For students who have the interest and ability for college work or for advanced technical education the emphasis at the secondary level should obviously be on academic work and a limited industrial arts course is usually sufficient and appropriate. This group represents approximately three to nine percent of deaf high school age students (Schein & Bushnaq, 1962).

At the opposite end of the continuum are roughly 10 to 20 percent of deaf high school age students in the 90 or below IQ range. Granted a few exceptions, the overwhelming majority of these students (as well as many with IQ's over 90) will not achieve more than fourth grade level on educational achievement tests and many will be well below this (Kent, 1962). Though it would appear that greater emphasis on formal academic work might be the solution for these youngsters, evidence suggests this may not be the case. Limited research data, the author's experience in teaching and evaluating youngsters from residential and day settings in many states over a period of years, and the experience of others who have taught deaf youngsters is that a third or fourth grade achievement is generally the best that can be accomplished under present methods (Kent, 1962). Studies of achievement test findings on these students generally show a flattening of the learning curve at this level. Though this description of achievement may appear harsh and pessimistic, it is understandable when, by analogy, we consider what we might expect in terms of educational achievement in hearing children of 90 IQ and below if they were required to master a foreign language without benefit of sound and were then expected to get their formal education in this language —which is essentially what is being expected of deaf students.

The point of this discussion of the deaf student of 90 IQ or below is that an appropriate curriculum for this rather large segment of the deaf high-school-age population should consist of strong vocational offerings. Granted that in most cases it may be unrealistic to expect to prepare these youngsters for skilled crafts or technological positions, they need and can benefit from education in semiskilled trades such as power sewing, electronic assembly, body and fender work, welding, painting and other similar occupations. For a number of reasons this kind of vocational education should be an integral part of their schooling when they are of high school age. If such a vocational program were properly planned, it would be related to academic work (especially arithmetic and English) in such a way as to give meaning to these formal courses by relating them to one of their basic purposes which is that of earning a living. A vocational type program related to academic work in this way would result in a graduate who had specific job skills when he was graduated from school. Under present circumstances many deaf youngsters are spending their high school years doing arithmetic computation which they do not know how to apply, trying in social studies to memorize the state capitols, or taking hours of typing and ceramics, all of which have little practical or academic value. Yet, these courses are often integral parts of school curricula which frustrate the youngsters, driving them from school and/or leaving them with bad work habits. To turn these youth out at the age of 18 or 19 with far less than a full elementary education and no adequate vocational preparation is a tragedy. Unfortunately, this is rather common practice in many programs, the rationalization being that the deaf youngster can learn a skill for earning a living after he leaves school. Many cannot because of their low educational achievement and communication problems. Educational programs that are producing this kind of product know that their deaf graduates are ill-equipped to earn a living.

The remaining 70 to 80 percent of deaf students are not below average in intelligence but neither are they bright or interested enough for a college or advanced technical education. Some of these students need a curriculum providing vocational courses leading directly to employable level skills in trades and crafts. Others could benefit from a strong emphasis on academic work supplemented with prevocational exploratory courses if, and only if, adequate provision is made for them to get their vocational education after they leave high school or whatever type of secondary school they were attending. The findings of the New England Survey of the Young Adult Deaf (Boatner, 1964) demonstrate rather conclusively that few of these deaf youth are able to enter and successfully complete vocational and trade courses with the normally hearing unless they are provided assistance in communication and tutoring analogous to that provided in the Riverside City College Vocational Program and the vocational phase of the Idaho State University program. Hopefully, the future will bring more programs of this type and/or vocational-technical schools exclusively for the deaf. However, until this seemingly distant goal is fully achieved, secondary schools for deaf youth that do not provide a strong vocational curriculum leading to employable skills will be neglecting the basic educational needs of most deaf students of average or better ability who are not capable of college or advanced technical education. Granted that in spite of a lack of such courses many of these deaf students will still find work, the sad part is that they will generally be underemployed and, as the world of work changes, many will be unable to find work (Williams, 1964).

STEPS FOR IMPROVING VOCATIONAL PREPARATION IN EXISTING DAY AND RESIDENTIAL FACILITIES FOR DEAF YOUTH

Many parents of deaf and hard-of-hearing children feel that there are certain advantages inherent in day school and day class programs, but they are also often concerned about the lack of more complete vocational education for older youngsters in many of these non-residential schools, and Department of Vocational Rehabilitation counselors express similar awareness of this problem (Rogers & Quigley, 1960; U. S. Office of Voc. Rehab., 1959). Residential schools, on the other hand, have historically given greater emphasis on vocational preparation with marked success in certain fields such as printing (Boatner, 1964; Schein & Bushnaq, 1962). However, in recent years changes in industry have outmoded many of the skills traditionally taught in these residential programs. In addition, other problems such as costs of updating shops, small enrollments, difficulty in obtaining capable teachers, and (in some cases) administrative lethargy towards vocational preparation has resulted in a situation in which only certain state residential facilities such as the New Jersey School provide top level vocational education. Many others have one or two well-taught, up-to-date trades available plus industrial arts. A few residential schools offer primarily outdated and relatively useless courses euphemistically referred to as prevocational.

Suggested ways in which day and residential programs could improve their vocational preparation of deaf youth are:

1. *An on-the-job training or work-study type curriculum:* This is needed as part of almost every secondary school program serving deaf students (Vernon, 1962). It would involve students who had already mastered the basic skills offered in a junior high school industrial arts course, and ideally some vocational courses, and who were of high school age and ready to go into regular vocational training. A student with this background would be placed in a job in the business or industrial world under the supervision of a work-study coordinator and be employed part-time in a vocational area for which he had demonstrated aptitude and interest. The part of the school day not spent in job training would be devoted to related academic studies with emphasis on English and mathematics pertinent to the type of on-the-job training in which the youngster was engaged. The work-study coordinator would function as liaison between the academic teacher and the employer to assure that the English, mathematics, and other courses taught in the classroom would be appropriate to the job the student was learning. A work-study program of this kind would offer all schools a chance to provide deaf youth with up-to-date vocational training which these youngsters are often unable to obtain under present circumstances. It would offer the deaf student a greater probability of getting a job, as he would have estab-

listed himself with an employer before his graduation from school, and at the same time attained at least the basics of a specific vocational skill. It would enable this student to learn many of the work standards in business and industry and it would offer an opportunity for meaningful interaction with hearing people. All of these advantages would be major steps toward counteracting the social immaturity and naïveté about the world of work frequently found among deaf students who are leaving school today (Boatner, 1964; U. S. Office of Voc. Rehab., 1959). The establishment of such a program would require a far greater unity of effort than now exists between schools, labor, vocational rehabilitation, and management. Recent Federal legislation pertaining to reimbursement of local school systems for work-study programs makes this kind of close cooperation feasible, realistic, and mutually beneficial to all concerned, including employers.

2. *Provision of counselor-tutors, who would be trained teachers of the deaf, to assist these young people as they enter local trade schools or other vocational-technical programs:* The communication and educational problems of deafness are such that a large number of bright, capable deaf girls and boys are unable satisfactorily to compete in the numerous technical and craft schools for the normally hearing (Boatner, 1964; Vernon, 1962). However, with the help of counselor-tutors aware of the problems and able to assist in their resolution, many deaf students would be able to realize their full potential, complete the programs of these schools, and become successful craftsmen and technicians. The junior college program established three years ago in Riverside, California, and the vocational, technical, and academic center for the deaf at Idaho State University are examples of how well this can work. In Riverside, twelve deaf students are selected each September from California day or residential schools. They are assigned a counselor who also is a trained teacher of the deaf. These deaf students then take classes with their hearing college classmates but receive special tutoring in English and, where situations warrant, note-taking, and interpreting in finger-spelling and language of signs is provided. As a consequence, deaf students are able to take advantage of the extensive vocational offerings of Riverside City College and Idaho State University and are able to complete a college program leading to either vocational technical skills or academic degrees. Other programs in connection with schools for the deaf have involved similar uses of counselor-tutors in conjunction with business colleges, training facilities for cosmetology, and other vocational schools.

Perhaps the most urgent need relative to greater utilization of existing vocational and technical educational facilities by deaf youngsters is to involve the Department of Vocational Rehabilitation in the vocational education of the child at an earlier age than is generally the case at present. As a rule, it is not until a student has completed high school, or is at the age when he would normally have completed high school, that Vocational Rehabilitation steps in. This delay is often unfortunate. Most deaf students need to begin a vocational education long before completion of formal schooling. Without such an opportunity many become dropouts or nonachievers because of disillusionment and frustration growing out of academic programs inadequately and inappropriately adapted from those designed to meet the educational needs of normally hearing students.

3. *Use of the summer for intensive vocational training:* This plan would make it possible to utilize the vocational plants of residential schools which normally lie idle all summer by making them available to students from both residential and day programs on a full day basis during the vacation months. Although unorthodox, this proposed plan would greatly upgrade the opportunities now available to many deaf girls and boys, and do so at a minimal financial outlay and organizational effort. The fact that these residential school vocational plants generally lie idle all summer while there are deaf young people and adults in need of and capable of vocational training is an unfortunate paradox. Still another possibility for using the summer period to improve deaf students vocationally is to place these pupils in local trade schools that accept qualified applicants only on an all-day basis and could, therefore, not be used during the regular school year.

4. *A split program:* An alternative for helping to improve the vocational opportunities for deaf day school and day class students is one already partially operative in many states. It involves a situation in which the deaf youngster attends nonresidential educational facilities until he is of roughly high school age, at which time he transfers to a state residential school which has a more extensive vocational program. The advantages and disadvantages of such a plan are inherent in the relative merits of day or residential schools and the vocational programs they offer.

The essential point is that ideally both kinds of educational facilities, day and residential, should offer a strong vocational program in order that the child and his parents can be assured that no matter which kind of school is attended, the deaf child will be well prepared for employment (U. S. Office of Voc. Rehab., 1959). Until this is the case it may be necessary to use the best of both the day and residential facility in the education of the deaf child, depending on where the child lives and his age and educational level.

In trying to meet the educational needs of deaf and hard-of-hearing children, it is apparent that action is required to upgrade the present opportunities for developing vocational skills (Rogers & Quigley, 1960; U. S. Office of Voc. Rehab., 1959). The four alternatives listed here, or combinations of these, are suggested as possible ways to do this. Hopefully, in terms of recent legislation, some action will be taken at a Federal level to implement these proposals. Local efforts to do this in the past have often failed because no one has had the jurisdiction and financial backing to coordinate the necessary agencies, schools, individuals, and industries. Consequently, these efforts toward helping deaf people have suffered due to duplications, omissions, and occasional power struggles among vested interests.

THE FUTURE

Opportunities for unskilled workers are sharply declining and the fastest growing occupations are those calling for the most specialized training (U. S. Dept. of Labor, 1963–1964). Though the number of jobs is expected to increase by 30 percent from 1963 to 1968, the important factor for vocational programs for the deaf is where the jobs will be.

The areas expected to expand the most are those involving service workers, construction, finance, government, and positions in the wholesale and retail trades (U. S. Dept. of Labor, 1963–1964; USDL, 1960–1961). Within these broad categories the more specific fields that might be readily open to many deaf people are certain clerical and business machine phases of banking, the building trades, many kinds of civil service, computer operation, data processing, repair work, bookkeeping, automobile maintenance, barbering, and various phases of litho-offset printing (Dobson, 1959; U. S. Dept. of Labor, 1963–1964; USDL, 1959–1960a; USDL, 1959–1960b; USDL, 1959–1960c; USDL, 1959–1960d). The graphic arts industry predicts a 100 percent rise in production volume by 1980, with a 40 percent rise in the number of craftsmen, nearly all of whom will be in the offset field (Dobson, 1959; U. S. Dept. of Labor, 1963–1964). At a professional level, accounting, teaching, mathematics, vocational counseling for the deaf, science, computer programming, medical technology and certain areas of research offer excellent prospects (U. S. Dept. of Labor, 1963–1964).

In view of the fact that over half of employed deaf are now in manufacturing industries (Lunde & Bigman, 1959), it is cause for concern that jobs here will increase at a slower rate than is the case with the overall total (Sutherland, 1960; U. S. Dept. of Labor, 1963–1964). Agricultural workers are another group in which a sharp decline is expected (U. S. Dept. of Labor, 1963–1964). Specific jobs within the graphic arts, such as hot-metal typesetting, photoengraving, and composition where deaf people have excelled, represent especially poor prospects for the future (Dobson, 1959; U. S. Dept. of Labor, 1963–1964).

It must be emphasized that any consideration of sensible future vocational planning for deaf youngsters must begin with a clear realization that the calibre of academic instruction provided these students must be upgraded if the requirements of tomorrow's industrial society are to be met (Connor & Rosenstein, 1963; Rogers & Quigley, 1960; U. S. Office of Voc. Rehab., 1959; Vernon, 1962). A mastery of the crafts and the technology of the future demands that the student be competent in basic reading, writing, and mathematical skills. The prognosis for an advanced vocational training program built upon an inadequate academic foundation is poor, but the addition of a strong vocational curriculum, properly coordinated with academic teaching, improves the latter and gives meaning to the total educational program.

VOCATIONAL COUNSELING AND PLACEMENT OF BLIND YOUTH

Lyle Thume

IT IS NATURAL to be final in the succession on a panel when one's subject deals with vocational guidance and placement of youth. In spite of this, I will dwell only briefly on the historical aspects of guidance as it has been in the past. At present we are undergoing extreme change, and much that has been said about the past may not be relevant to the future. Most references to guidance, as it involves blind persons, tends to emphasize some of the more unusual or atypical occupations that blind persons have entered into. The examples often given are such as is contained in the title of a book, *From Homer to Helen Keller*. Such a reference is always connected with the blind person who became an author, a poet, or some of the other more unusual things that these persons may have done and been. My thinking more often goes back to Robert Louis Stevenson and Blind Pew. I am not certain what the occupational reference handbook would say about the job description of a buccaneer, and it also may not be significant that he was eventually trampled to death by horses, as this is the type of violent end that those who enter this occupation often expect to encounter. The significance of this association is that there are no doubt many jobs, occupations, and professions that various blind people have or can enter into. Too specific a description of any one of these is in great danger of limiting both the flexibility and the horizons of any blind youth who may be seeking vocational guidance or counseling.

Not too recently, in 1955, research work sponsored by the American Foundation for the Blind under the authorship of Raskins surveyed some of the needs as they were being met for guidance of blind students in residential schools for the blind. One might expect that within the purview of the residential school the greatest emphasis would be given to the guidance needs of these blind students. His survey would contend, as well as does the limited support given the guidance workshop in the American Association of Instructors for the Blind, that there are still very many young blind persons who are not receiving the counseling and guidance that would be appropriate for the meeting of their needs.

Important considerations that need to be given are the type of guidance that will be provided and, most importantly, the individual's readiness to receive the type of guidance that is presented at a given time. Concepts that may deal with various jobs or occupations are sometimes found in quite concrete form; at other times they may be very abstract. The environment and the endowment of the individual himself not only may indicate the readiness and timeliness of the guidance that should be given but also may determine the kind of guidance that the individual may ever be able to deal with and to handle. There is no overall panacean solution to this problem except that at the present time it is incumbent on those in guidance work to recognize that there is a difference in this type of material and to exercise their responsibility concerning the type of material that is appropriate and the time at which a given type of material can be presented. It is also important for them to consider the manner in which material will be presented, in terms of the kinds of concepts that the individual will be able to handle.

In a prevocational training situation, we are often dealing with many blind persons who have lost their sight after the time that most of their formal education has been completed or accomplished. There are also, of course, many blind persons who have gone through instructional experiences within the public school situation as well as some of those who have gone through their educational experiences in residential schools for the blind. As a result of this, the need of these young blind people will many times not be the needs that we typically ascribe to those persons who have received their formal educational experiences as blind persons. Today the pressures for change that have already been mentioned are resulting from the fact that demand for unskilled labor in all fields is becoming less. The Department of Labor contends that there is likely to be a 5 to 8 percent core of unemployment at any given time. This can make the competitive placement of blind persons more difficult as well as increase the demand for better job training and the types of job training that will need to take place over a longer duration. This places us under pressure to begin planning and vocational guidance much earlier. It has been said that at early ages fantasy largely determines the young person's choices of vocation. This is the time when a young person aspires to being an actor or actress, a nurse, doctor, policeman, fireman, or what have you. These are the choices that are common to most children, whether they be blind or sighted. Later on more realistic choices are considered. A parallel may be drawn here from dentistry, concerning the time at which the more realistic choices can be moved into. Dentists use a pulp test to determine whether the nerve in a tooth is dead or not. If the nerve is dead, the individual may be advised to have the tooth removed, as decay, infection, and perhaps abscess might occur later. On the other hand, he may wait, as there may be many, many years of good chewing left in that tooth before extraction becomes absolutely necessary. Some of this same form of indecision may pertain to some of the planning that should be entered into in a guidance situation.

Recently there have been some very specific progressive steps taken toward the meeting of the needs of blind persons. One of the most notable is the study by Bauman and Yoder, *Placing the Blind in Professional Occupations*. This publication, again, is not a specific enumeration of jobs that have been done by blind people but a very excellent beginning of the development of a source of information that can be obtained concerning some of the techniques, methods, and experiences that have been undergone by blind persons performing in some of the professional fields. Last year at the Southwest Rehabilitation Center, operated by Arkansas Enterprises for the Blind, we inaugurated a college preparation course, which will be significantly expanded this year. With this group we particularly attempt to meet certain needs of blind individuals who are all ready to matriculate on the college campus. Last summer this group's activity resulted in the operation of an evaluation factor, which was not initially anticipated. Five of the approximately thirteen full-term enrollees are not now, and probably will not be, in college in the near future. Original planning was not deliberately designed to include this evaluation factor but will probably receive continued important consideration in the future. The college prep course is a supplement to the ongoing prevocational training program of a center. The student in this course is considered as one of the trainees of the center, and the group in which he functions is mixed in terms of heterogeneous factors of age, sex, and background. There are only one or two periods a day that are particularly set aside for college preparation. In these groups such problems are dealt with separately. He is scheduled with the other trainees in needed areas such as mobility, communicative skills, daily activities of living, etc. The set-aside daily perods contain one period a week which is almost totally unstructured. During this time, with a leader, the students ventilate and exchange their ideas concerning problems that they feel may relate to college living. These included a variety of matters such as "drinking," "cheating on exams," "matters of one student's relationships to another"; the problem of "student-owned cars" is about the only one that did not appear last summer.

The other sessions during the week contained more directively oriented instruction. Problems involving note taking, the taking of exams, the inter-relationship between student and professor, the responsibility of the student to make advance arrangements for taking his tests so that the problem will not be encountered as a fresh obstacle on the date that the examination is scheduled, as well as the amount of concession he will demand or refuse concerning such problems as taking lab courses, physical education, and such matters are prime considerations in these other sessions. College note-taking techniques developed as a particularly important problem, and guest speakers as well as center staff members were brought in to deliver sample lectures. Following these, rather difficult tests were given on the material. This was found necessary because many of the students had accepted the ancient stereotype that blind people have very "excellent memories." As many of them had been representative of a "bright group" in the schools from which they came, they had been able to do quite well academically and had not always been impressed with the necessity for note taking. Some of them were never impressed by this in the course either, and the rather severe lecture and exam pattern was necessary to convince those that were amenable of the value of note utilization as well as the practical experience of handling this process independently.

This college prep course and Bauman and Yoder's research are constructive steps forward in meeting the needs of blind youth. Primarily they represent blind people in college or entering into professional areas. An area of some neglect remains for the blind person who plans to enter business college or a trade or technical school or to engage in on-the-job training. In most cases these persons are not offered special prep courses. One major contribution in this area is the Visceli course in placement counselor training at the University of Southern Illinois. This deals directly with training counselors who will be working in the field of making industrial placements. It is not dealing directly with the blind individual who may have guidance needs, but it does represent a constructive step in the direction of offering more specialized services. An ideal overview of these developments resulted from the recent St. Louis Conference sponsored by

VRA, AAIB, and the Hadley School. The minimum result of this conference will certainly be the selection of occupational text material and the adaption or authorship of counselor and teacher guides. Eventually these may be used by teachers and counselors or by blind youths in self-study.

Personnel of residential schools, those dealing with blind children and classes in public schools, those in rehabilitation centers, and those in state rehabilitation agencies are probably to some extent unaware of each other's functions. There seems to be a need for exchange of information concerning each other's problems and resources. It is highly important for the school counselor to know something of the follow-up that a student will receive from a rehabilitation counselor after he leaves school. It is necessary to determine whether a transfer at this point is indicated, possible, or unwise. The rehabilitation counselor has a like need to know something of the experiences that the client received as a student prior to reaching him. These experiences are important, as they have contributed to both his educational experiences and his counseling needs. On June 24 we are having an institute of this type in Little Rock. The institute will be composed of personnel both from residential schools for the blind and from special resource people working with blind children in other school systems in the southwest region. In this instance the program content will be presented by the Rehabilitation Center staff and by persons connected with the State Rehabilitation Agencies who will come in. It would seem to me that other institutes or workshops would be important where school personnel would bring in rehabilitation center staffs and rehabilitation agency personnel to learn more of the contribution that each is making and of the potential opportunity for the use that each would have for the resources that the other can offer. This spring we have also had an exchange evening meeting between the Rehabilitation Center and the Arkansas State School for the Blind. These, as more or less informal occasions, are the kind of things that will make staffs and faculties on a one-to-one individual basis much more aware of the job that is already being done.

In work for the blind, as in other fields, there has always been a problem of the stereotyping of the occupation that many blind persons happen to be engaged in as that which perhaps should involve all blind persons. Historically, we may refer to the musician, to the piano tuner, to the broom maker, and probably now perhaps to the vending-stand operator. While vending-stand operations have tended to "mushroom" in recent years, it continues to be very important that development also needs to be encouraged in business, professional, industrial, and other areas. Many times after the administration of the psychological tests that are available—Wechsler, Occupational Preference Records, Personality Inventories, or Dexterity Measures— it is found that even after an individual may have gained insight into the competencies he most easily might develop and would enjoy most, he may be inclined to accept the secure offer of a "sure thing" in an occupation where he believes his earnings might be $50 or so a month more than he thinks they could otherwise have been. This tends to set aside the importance of counseling and evaluation that may have been done and, incidentally, contributes to the reinforcement of these already existing stereotypes. Oftentimes a blind person who functions successfully as a vending-stand operator probably possesses greater security and greater adequacy than many other blind persons who may not be dealing as directly with those elements of the public. On the other hand, it is not taking away from the respectability and dignity of these individuals to suggest that there are many blind persons who probably enter vending-stand or other programs because of the above-mentioned needs for apparent security and not because of the development of any particular insight. A discussion of the development of some of these problems that still contribute to job stereotyping probably relates back to our initial references in this paper to consider the vocational preferences of a number of blind persons. This, then, offers us an ideal suggestion to end our remarks at this point in the hope that further discussion will have an opportunity to occur.

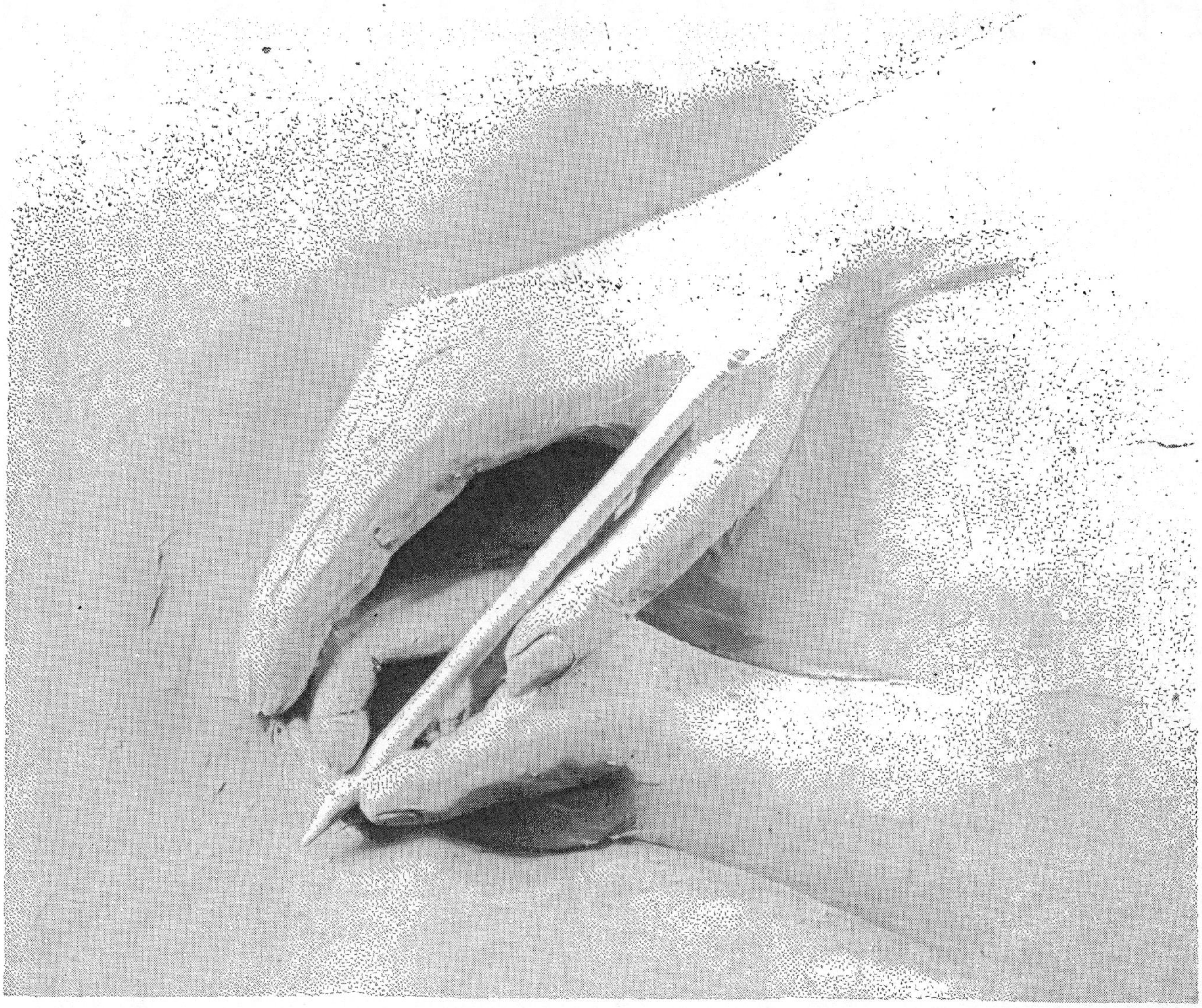

STAFF

Publilsher	John Quirk
Editor	Dona Chiappe
Editorial Ass't.	Carol Carr
Permissions Editor	Audrey Weber
Director of Production	Richard Pawlikowski
Director of Design	Donald Burns
Customer Service	Cindy Finocchio
Sales Service	Diane Hubbard
Administration	Linda Calano

Cover Design	Donald Burns
Cover Photo	Richard Pawlikowski

SPECIAL EDUCATION SERIES

- Autism
- * Behavior Modification
- Biological Bases of Learning Disabilities
- Brain Impairments
- Career and Vocational Education for the Handicapped
- Child Abuse
- Child Development
- Child Psychology
- Cognitive and Communication Skills
- * Counseling Parents of Exceptional Children
- Creative Arts
- Curriculum and Materials
- * Deaf Education
- Developmental Disabilities
- * Diagnosis and Placement
- Down's Syndrome
- Dyslexia
- Early Learning
- Educational Technology
- * Emotional and Behavioral Disorders
- Exceptional Parents
- * Gifted and Talented Education
- * Human Growth and Development of the Exceptional Individual
- Hyperactivity

- * Individualized Educational Programs
- Language & Writing Disorders
- * Learning Disabilities
- Learning Theory
- * Mainstreaming
- * Mental Retardation
- Motor Disorders
- Multiple Handicapped Education
- Occupational Therapy
- Perception and Memory Disorders
- * Physically Handicapped Education
- * Pre-School Education for the Handicapped
- * Psychology of Exceptional Children
- Reading Disorders
- Reading Skill Development
- Research and Development
- * Severely and Profoundly Handicapped
- Slow Learner Education
- Social Learning
- * Special Education
- * Speech and Hearing
- Testing and Diagnosis
- Three Models of Learning Disabilities
- * Visually Handicapped Education
- * Vocational Training for the Mentally Retarded

● Published Titles   * Major Course Areas

Exceptional Children: A Reference Book

An updated and welcome resource for educators and librarians.

COMMENTS PLEASE:

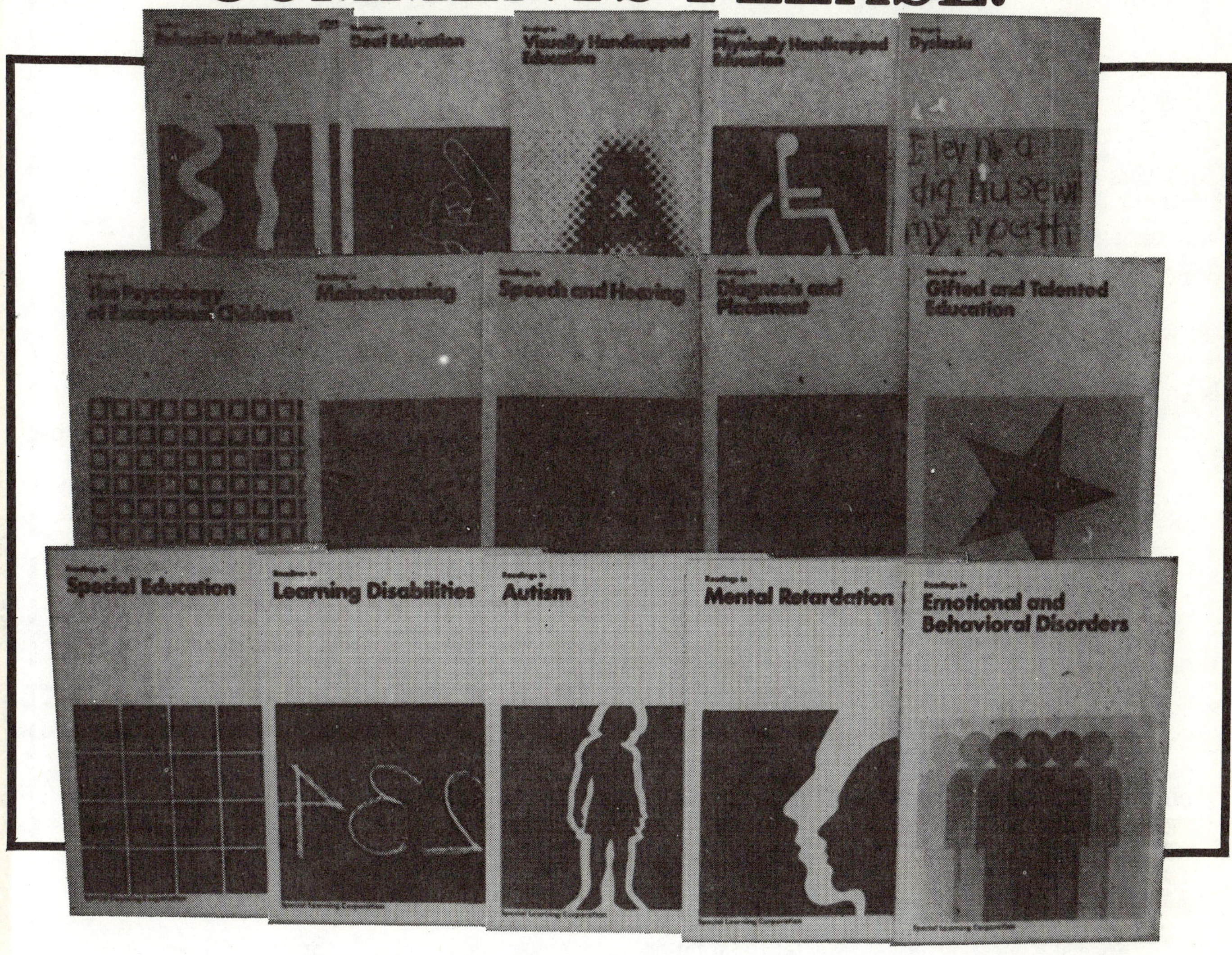

SPECIAL LEARNING CORPORATION

42 Boston Post Rd.

Guilford, Conn.   06437

SPECIAL LEARNING CORPORATION
COMMENTS PLEASE:

Does this book fit your course of study?

Why?   (Why not?)

Is this book useable for other courses of study? Please list.

What other areas would you like us to publish in using this format?

What type of exceptional child are you interested in learning more about?

Would you use this as a basic text?

How many students are enrolled in these course areas?

_____ Special Education _____ Mental Retardation _____ Psychology _____ Emotional Disorders

_____ Exceptional Children _____ Learning Disabilities   Other _____________

Do you want to be sent a copy of our elementary student materials catalog?

Do you want a copy of our college catalog?

Would you like a copy of our next edition?   ☐ yes ☐ no

Are you a ☐ student or an ☐ instructor?

Your name _________________________ school _____________

Term used _________________________ Date _____________

address _________________________

city _________________________ state _____________ zip _____

telephone number _________________________

C/V